Designing the Computational Image
Imagining Computational Design

APPLIED RESEARCH +DESIGN PUBLISHING

Novato, CA

Daniel Cardoso Llach
Theodora Vardouli

Miller Institute for Contemporary Art at Carnegie Mellon University, Pittsburgh, United States
Centre de design de l'Université du Québec à Montréal (UQÀM), Canada

Designing the Computational Image

Imagining Computational Design

Designing the Computational Image, Imagining Computational Design is an exhibition examining the twentieth-century emergence of new methods for representation, simulation, and manufacturing linked to computers, and reflecting on their contemporary repercussions across creative fields. It originated at the Miller Institute for Contemporary Art at Carnegie Mellon University, United States, in 2017, developed by Daniel Cardoso Llach, Associate Professor of Architecture, Carnegie Mellon University. In 2021, an expanded version of the exhibition at the Centre de design de l'Université du Québec à Montréal (UQÀM), Canada, included materials from the history of computational design in Canada newly researched by Theodora Vardouli, Assistant Professor, Peter Guo-hua Fu School of Architecture, McGill University, as well as a selection of contemporary works by Canadian computational designers, architects, and artists collaboratively curated by both authors. This book documents this ongoing curatorial and research project, which also includes a series of essays by guest contributors, and a series of conversations and interviews with historical figures and contemporary practitioners.

Authors and Editors
Daniel Cardoso Llach and Theodora Vardouli

Guest Essays
Gabriela Aceves Sepúlveda, Matthew Allen, Andrés Burbano, Moa Carlsson, Mario Carpo, Emek Erdolu, Jacob Gaboury, Sean Keller, Anna-Maria Meister, Ranjodh Singh Dhaliwal, Akshita Sivakumar, David Theodore, Olga Touloumi

Conversations
Kristy Balliet, Nathalie Bredella, Joseph Choma, Dana Cupkova, Felecia Davis, Jacob Gaboury, Madeline Gannon, Andrew Heumann, Jonah Marrs, Sean Keller, Carl Lostritto, Golan Levin, Leslie Mezei, Frieder Nake, Paul Pangaro, Molly Wright Steenson, George Stiny, Rachel Strickland, Theodora Vardouli, Elizabeth Vander Zaag

Captions
United States, United Kingdom, and Germany items: Daniel Cardoso Llach with the exception of items in p. 134 and 261-2 by Theodora Vardouli; Canadian historical items: Theodora Vardouli; Canadian contemporary materials: Theodora Vardouli and Daniel Cardoso Llach. Captions for items in the following pages are based on artists' texts: 56, 66, 67, 134-135, 137, 142, 144, 155, 159, 161 (bottom), 286, 292, 295, and 296-297.

Editorial assistance
Emek Erdolu, Maxime Leblanc, Eliza Pertigkiozoglou

Graphic design
Operative Space, Berlin, Germany

Graphic integration and image editing
Makenzie O'Connor, Point Line Projects, Pittsburgh, United States

This book is typeset in MAD Sans and Spectral

An excerpt of the essay "Images to think with" appeared in Daniel Cardoso Llach "Architecture and the Structured Image: Software Simulations as Infrastructures for Building Production." In *The Active Image: Architecture and Engineering in the Age of Modeling*, edited by Sabine Ammon, Remei Capdevila-Werning. Springer, 2017. Interview quote in page 48 from: Daniel Cardoso Llach and Robin Forrest. "Of Algorithms, Buildings and Fighter Jets: A Conversation with Robin Forrest." *Arq: Architectural Research Quarterly* 21, no. 1 (March 2017): 53-64. https://doi.org/10.1017/S1359135517000173.

A *lattice space* book
http://www.lattice.space

Published in 2023 by Applied Research + Design

APPLIED
RESEARCH
+DESIGN
PUBLISHING

Generous support for this publication was made available by:

Furthermore: a program of the J. M. Kaplan Fund
Social Sciences and Humanities Research Council of Canada
College of Fine Arts Fund for Research and Creativity at Carnegie Mellon University
Research Group on Democracy, Space, and Technology, Yan P. Lin Centre, McGill University
Peter Guo-hua Fu School of Architecture, McGill University
Hexagram: Réseau de recherche-création en arts, cultures et technologies
The Frank Ratchye STUDIO for Creative Inquiry, Carnegie Mellon University
The Center for the Arts in Society, Carnegie Mellon University

Furthermore: a program of the J.M. Kaplan Fund

Social Sciences and Humanities Research Council of Canada
Conseil de recherches en sciences humaines du Canada
Canada

Carnegie Mellon University
College of Fine Arts

Yan P. Lin Centre for the Study of Freedom and Global Orders in the Ancient and Modern Worlds

McGill | School of Architecture

hexagram

CAS
Center for the Arts in Society
Carnegie Mellon University
www.cmu.edu/cas

The Frank-Ratchye STUDIO for Creative Inquiry

Materialities

Archive

Works

Visualities

Agencies

Materialities

Essays

Conversations

Visualities

Agencies

Images to Think With

Daniel Cardoso Llach

16

Seventy years or so after their appearance on radar screens and oscilloscopes in the wake of World War II, computational images seem about ready to fade into the background of our collective consciousness. They have come to undergird not only vast swathes of the contemporary visual culture – for example through film, software interfaces, games, and mobile media – but also accompanied disciplinary transformations and realignments in fields as varied as art, design, engineering, and architecture, where they have become the sites of new forms of technical work, as well as the prompt for new theorizations of their practice. Glimmering on screens small and large, lurking in the background of algorithmic machineries, and shaping the intellectual life and embodied labors of practitioners across multiple domains, they appear as ubiquitous brokers of the present. And yet, while their allure has made them inescapable, their omnipresence has made them almost invisible.

Computational images are ambivalent, and resist essentialist definitions or reductive analog-digital divides. They are symbolic as well as physical; constituted both by numerical abstractions and the electro-mechanical contraptions required for their display. They are social as well as technical; their histories and politics closely intertwined with the militarism and economic anxieties that shaped the second half of the twentieth century – and with the more recent softwarization of everyday life. They are formal as well as informational; at times devices for creative expression, at times stalwarts for functional or financial rationality. They are conduits for a widespread aesthetics of personalized entertainment and consumption, but also the locus of critical redefinitions of human agency in artistic and humanistic registers.

Artists and scholars have worked to make computational images visible, so to speak, pointing at the attributes and capacities resulting from their technical production. Images, for example, are *operational* when they exist primarily as elements of an automated process such as the operation of a self-guided missile, rather than as objects of human perception or communication.[1] Or *active* when they give structure to, and actively support, social practices – especially but not exclusively those involving computer-aided modeling and simulations.[2] Casting them as *systemic* has helped reveal their roles within cybernetic milieus such as those linked to interactive simulations, and their

1 Harun Farocki. "Phantom Images." *Public*, January 1, 2004. https://public.journals.yorku.ca/index.php/public/article/view/30354. See also: Trevor Paglen, "Operational Images," *E-Flux Journal*, no. 59 (November 2014), https://www.e-flux.com/journal/59/61130/operational-images/.https://www.e-flux.com/journal/59/61130/operational-images/Paglen.; Anthony Downey. "The Algorithmic Apparatus of Neo-Colonialism: Or, Can We Hold 'Operational Images' to Account?" *The Nordic Journal of Aesthetics* 30, no. 61–62 (July 2, 2021): 78–82. https://doi.org/10.7146/nja.v30i61-62.127862. And Nathan W. Saucier. "Operational Images and the Interpretive Turn." Thesis, Massachusetts Institute of Technology, 2017. https://dspace.mit.edu/handle/1721.1/113459.

2 Sabine Ammon and Remei Capdevila-Werning, eds., *The Active Image: Architecture and Engineering in the Age of Modeling*, 1st ed. 2017 edition (New York, NY: Springer, 2017). vii.

3 Inge Hinterwaldner. *The Systemic Image: A New Theory of Interactive Real-Time Simulations*, 2017. https://doi.org/10.7551/mitpress/9989.001.0001.

distinctive regimes of iconicity.[3] Underscoring their *structured* nature has shed light on their symbolic underpinnings.[4] Observing their presence across multiple platforms and spheres of sociality, we may see them as *networked*.[5] They are *objects* whose visual allure can obscure their historicity as well as their material and ideological substrates.[6] These formulations have served distinct (albeit at times overlapping) analytical and descriptive purposes. Instead of adding to this profusion of categories, the term computational image as used here simply aims to contribute a measure of technical and historical specificity.

First experienced on the screens of radar systems displaying battle lines and enemy threats, computational images are specifically linked to the computing technologies for data storage, manipulation, and display that emerged from government-funded technology research projects during the Cold War years.[7] Some of their earliest disclosures were produced by a computer's processing of numerical information describing geometric point coordinates of line segments. Encoded in punched cards, these numerical definitions were converted into electrical signals controlling streams of electrons falling onto a phosphorous layer inside cathode ray tube displays, thus rendering the contours of distant battlefields. Emblematic of this era, the SAGE (Semi-Automated Ground Environment) defense system, launched in 1951 in the United States, used radio waves to track enemy airplanes and displayed their positions relative to a map on a CRT screen. At a rate of several dozen translations per second between the numerical definitions inscribed in software and the images presented to radar operators, they catered to the defensive need for technologically extended lines of sight.[8]

Aside from the phosphorescent glow of these early displays, what distinguished the computational image from its ink and paper or photographic relatives was a fundamental separation between the image, as experienced visually on the screen, and its symbolic definition, as inscribed in storage media such as punched cards. Indeed, in contrast with images produced using analog methods, computational images result from translations across numerical definitions inscribed in a storage medium, software, and a display system, hardware. Regardless of the material substrates of these definitions — e.g. punched cards, rules, solid-state hard drives, or distant servers — or rendering equipment — e.g. cathode ray tube or liquid crystal display

4 Daniel Cardoso Llach. "Architecture and the Structured Image Software Simulations as Infrastructures for Building Production." In *The Active Image: Architecture and Engineering in the Age of Modeling*, Sabine Ammon, Remei Capdevila-Werning. Springer, 2017. See also: Ivan Edward Sutherland. "Structure in Drawing and the Hidden-Surface Problem." In *Reflections on Computer Aids to Design and Architecture*, edited by Nicholas Negroponte, 73-77. New York, 1975.

5 Jacob Lund. "Questionnaire on the Changing Ontology of the Image." *The Nordic Journal of Aesthetics*, no. 61–62 (2021): 6–7.

6 Jacob Gaboury. *Image Objects: An Archaeology of Computer Graphics*. Cambridge, MA: MIT Press, 2021.

The Semi-Automated Ground Environment (SAGE) was an air defense system launched in 1951 in the United States. It was capable of displaying maps on cathode ray tube monitors along with the position of planes obtained using radar technologies. Image credit: MITRE Corporation.

screens — this separation between an image and its computable, numerical, and non-pictorial structure remains computational images' fundamental feature, and an elemental building block of a lucid understanding of contemporary visual media.

Computational images quickly moved outside the battlefield as computers were deployed with comparable vigor towards the reconfiguration of other domains and activities beyond warfare. During the three decades following the Second World War, government investment in university research in North America and the UK funded multidisciplinary projects to investigate the use of computers for manufacturing and design. In their transit from military technologies into professional tools and consumer products, these images — alongside the many technologists, sponsors, academics, and entrepreneurs who developed and disseminated them — helped delineate conceptions of design and creativity that continue to evolve to this day.[9] Practitioners of architecture, engineering, industrial design, and the visual arts were lured by computational images' visual and operative plasticity, and by the promises of creative liberation and managerial efficiency articulated by their promoters. These movements fostered industries, unsettled disciplinary boundaries, and sketched the contours of new fields of creative practice. Computational design is the — at times pliant, at times disobedient — debris of military industrialism. Visually articulating its conceptual and technical trajectories is the aim of the ongoing curatorial and research project documented in this book.

The goal, it must be said, is neither to offer a universal history, nor an exhaustive atlas, of this rapidly expanding set of practices. Instead, it is to sketch the contours of a new, multidisciplinary history that has so far escaped the analyses local to specific disciplines. By examining the confluence of technical developments in graphics and software with the emergence of new theoretical and aesthetic sensibilities across different creative fields, *Designing the Computational Image, Imagining Computational Design* redefines computational design practices in multidisciplinary terms: not as a discipline-specific development but as an "interdiscipline" emerging (timidly at first) in the interstices of mathematics, engineering, and the arts. This approach necessarily entails some trade-offs, and also some departures from the canon.

7 Related developments included, for example, UK engineers Freddie Williams and Tom Kilburn' invention of a proto pixel-based display in the late 1940s to illustrate their pioneering development of stored memory. See Alvy Ray Smith. *A Biography of the Pixel*. Cambridge, MA: MIT Press, 2021 pp. 133-134. For discussions of other early developments outside of North America and the UK see, for example: Stephen Jones. "The First Electronic Digital Computers in Australia." *Dearq*, July 10, 2020. https://doi.org/10.18389/dearq27.2020.10. And Andrés Burbano's essay entitled "Binary Image, Visual Latency" in this book.

8 As media historian Bernard D. Geoghegan shows in his history of the computer screen, this defensive need precedes digital computers, and in the early twentieth century had already led to the development of analog devices able to plot the trajectory of enemy ships. See Bernard Dionysius Geoghegan. "An Ecology of Operations: Vigilance, Radar, and the Birth of the Computer Screen." *Representations* 147, no. 1 (August 1, 2019): 59-95. https://doi.org/10.1525/rep.2019.147.1.59. 67-68.

9 Daniel Cardoso Llach. *Builders of the Vision: Software and the Imagination of Design*. London, New York: Routledge, 2015.

Designing the Computational Image, Imagining Computational Design is an exhibition exploring the twentieth-century emergence of new methods for representation, simulation, and manufacturing linked to computers, and reflecting on their repercussions across contemporary architecture, art, and design. It combines a selection of previously unseen or lesser-known drawings, films, and high-quality reproductions, as well as interactive software reconstructions, illuminating the formative period of numerical control and computer graphics technologies between 1949 and 1980 – primarily at government-funded research laboratories in North America and the UK. The exhibition places these historical materials in conversation with the work of contemporary artists, designers, and architects employing computation as a vehicle of material, visual, and conceptual experimentation. The exhibition thus highlights cross-disciplinary and cross-generational alignments as well as tensions. These juxtapositions – of disciplines, themes, and temporal frames – visually trace the roots of a broader transformation. One revealing of the impact of large technological projects on other domains of cultural production.

The exhibition originated at the Miller Institute of Contemporary Art at Carnegie Mellon University, Pittsburgh, in 2017. Its historical materials were collected during a decade of visits to institutional archives and personal collections in the US and UK, and were selected because of their historical significance or visual potency. The contemporary artworks were curated or commissioned with the aim of drawing a multidisciplinary landscape across architecture, art, and design fostering tensions between technical traditions and present-day experiments. Also on display were interactive software reconstructions of historical computer-aided design systems exploring visual and sensual aspects of these technologies, as well as their operative logic.[10] A significantly expanded version of the show, developed jointly with Professor Theodora Vardouli, was presented at the Centre de design de l'Université de Québec à Montréal (UQAM) in 2021 with the French title *Vers un imaginaire numérique*. This version adapted the show to the Canadian context by including a selection of historical materials from Canadian archives newly researched by Prof. Vardouli, which is contextualized in her introductory essay. In addition, the show included a selection of contemporary works by Canadian computational designers, architects, and artists collaboratively curated by both authors.

10 Daniel Cardoso Llach and Scott Donaldson. "An Experimental Archaeology of CAD: Using Software Reconstructions to Explore the Past and Future of Computer-Aided Design." In *Computer-Aided Architectural Design*, edited by Ji-Hyun Lee, 105–19. Communications in Computer and Information Science. Springer, 2019.

Designing the Computational Image, Imagining Computational Design exhibition at Miller ICA, 2017. Photo by Hugh 'Smokey' Dyar.

Both versions of the exhibition were accompanied by events that fostered an interdisciplinary conversation — as well as a community — around its themes. In conjunction with the Miller ICA exhibition, a two-day event entitled *Computational Design: Practices, Histories, Infrastructures* hosted by the School of Architecture at Carnegie Mellon University invited architecture, media, and science and technology scholars to converse with the artists featured in the exhibition, and to reflect on a specific image of their choice. Contributors were invited to do a "close reading" of the image, using its visual traits as an entry point into the image's historical and socio-technical contexts.

The Centre de design exhibition was accompanied by a virtual event entitled *Digital.Visual.Material*, hosted by the Peter Guo-hua Fu School of Architecture at McGill University and chaired by Prof. Vardouli. Alongside presentations by an equally diverse cohort of scholars and researchers, this event invited some of the exhibition's historical protagonists as panel participants and interlocutors. After a virtual peer review workshop and several rounds of editorial revision, the "close readings" produced during the two events evolved into the essays included in this book. Also included are edited transcriptions of the panels and conversations held during both events.

In the book, archival materials, software reconstructions, contemporary artworks, essays, and conversations are laid out according to the exhibition's thematic triad. The first section, *Materialities*, shows how applications of computer graphics to design research were foreshadowed by new understandings of materials and geometry as computable entities that emerged in conjunction with sponsored university research into numerical control during the war's immediate aftermath. Drawing chiefly from the archives of the numerical control project at MIT, from the Cambridge CAD Group in the UK, and from pioneering efforts to launch a fully computerized numerical control system in Canada, this section shows how early software projects inscribed an impulse to conceptualize design in relation to both material and symbolic economies. In their attempts to codify and automate the operation of machine tools for manufacturing, these materials show, engineers and mathematicians uncovered questions about data processing, storage, and display that prompted the development of new computational abstractions. Shaped by the constraints of available storage media — punched cards and paper tape — these early software experiments began to bridge the messy worlds of materials and machines and the "cleaner" worlds of geometric and mathematical definitions. In dialogue with these historical materials, a selection of contemporary artworks shows how architects, designers, and artists in Canada and the US have sought to challenge numerical control's aesthetic and ideological commitment to manufacturing efficiency. For example, by defining new forms of material articulation, and reconciling computational methods with long-standing design traditions and craft practices.

Computational images are enlivened (and constrained) by their numerical definition, and by the architecture of their data structures — both of which are ciphered in the non-pictorial language of computers: *code*. The book's second section, *Visualities*, showcases materials that examine the formal and conceptual affordances of this condition. Showcasing documents and diagrams from the US Air Force-funded MIT CAD Project, the SRC-funded CAD Project at the University of Cambridge, as well as documents about Canadian efforts in interactive graphics, the section shows how postwar researchers interpreted the geometric plasticity of computational representations, and advanced broader claims concerning the relationship between these representations and the objects they described. In addition, materials from the University of Toronto's Dynamic Graphics Project and from Bell Labs in the US highlight a fledgling sensibility where the intimate dovetailing of graphics and interactivity fostered aspirations of immediacy and expression with computers that expanded beyond their instrumentality — in fact recasting them as artistic media. The contemporary artworks in this section hint at how present-day artists, designers, and architects have taken advantage of the geometric and visual plasticity afforded by computational images to embark in aesthetic expeditions, as well to address questions of urban, cultural, and political significance.

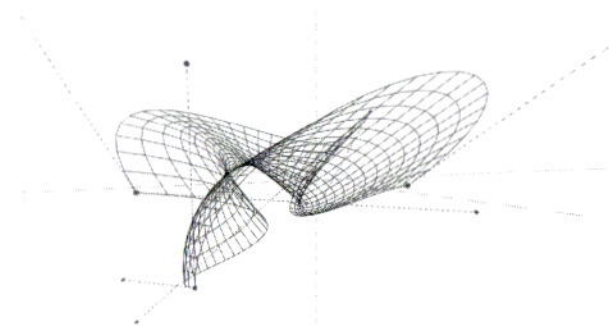

A 3D surface produced using a reconstruction of the Coons Patch, a mathematical technique for surface generation developed by Steven A. Coons in the 1960s.

Alongside the development of numerically controlled machines, interactive computers, and displays emerged new theorizations of the design process. Researchers in computer-aided design drew from artificial intelligence and cybernetics ideas to reimagine design as a collaborative endeavor between humans and machines. The book's third and last section, *Agencies*, showcases materials from research groups and organizations in Canada, Britain, and the US where some of these visions manifested. These include the Architecture Machine group and Lincoln Laboratory at MIT, the Institute for Physical Planning at Carnegie Mellon, and the Systems Design Engineering Institute at the University of Waterloo, among others. In addition, this section includes documents from architectural periodicals, news, and popular media illustrating how computational design researchers were not only confined in their laboratories, but actively sought to capture the imagination of professionals, and of the general public, with their visions of design. Contemporary works on display in this section illustrate how artists, and designers from other fields have used computation to usher alternative modes of engagement with both form and audience — where time, motion, and participation become instruments of aesthetic expression.

In addition to cataloging and contextualizing the materials on display, each of the three sections includes essays and conversations related to its theme. Essay authors come from fields including architectural history, media theory, and science and technology studies. Each essay is a "close reading" of a specific image that links its visuality to its social or technical histories. The conversations bring together scholars and artists, and historical protagonists and contemporary practitioners, to expand the project's scope with other voices that illuminate different geographies and contribute new subjects and critical perspectives.

This book is a snapshot of an ongoing project and conversation. It sketches the confluence, during the second half of the twentieth century, of publicly funded technical innovations in software, geometry, and hardware across institutions in North America and the UK with a technological imaginary of design and creativity we continue to navigate today. Highlighting shared practices, histories, and technical infrastructures, the materials assembled offer a vantage point from which to see computational design as a deeply intertwined cross-disciplinary landscape, to critically reconstruct its visual and intellectual histories, and thus to reimagine its future.

On the Surface

Theodora Vardouli

24

Cutting across the vast category of the digital image, is its instances' steady tendency to perturb the fields that deploy them. This is especially true in domains theoretically and operationally reliant on the production and manipulation of visual material, including architecture. Now and again architectural theorists and critics have made efforts to contend with the transition from drawing — architecture's erstwhile privileged medium — to the production and manipulation of digital images. And although there's a shared sense that the transition matters, it's more difficult to assess *how* and *where* it matters. As is often the case with the study of digital technologies' sociocultural impacts, judging conditions of break or continuity is slippery terrain. In this urgent, if not unwieldy, discourse on digital images, promising accounts emerge from materialist approaches that contend with reconfigurations of architectural labor and expertise and transfigurations of its subjects and subjectivities.

"On the surface," Amelyn Ng writes, "the way we document buildings may still look the same. But something has fundamentally changed in the ambitions of architectural visualization."[1] If Ng traces this change in the managerial and logistical aspirations of data infrastructures that undergird drawings produced by Building Information Modeling (BIM) software, John May locates the difference in the gestural and psycho-cognitive modes of electronic signal processing that renegotiate relationships with history and politics and usher nothing short of a new architectural consciousness.[2] Such invitations to look beyond the deceiving familiarity of digitally-outputted drawings or what May has unforgivingly referred to as "pseudorthography," put forth a clear statement about the locus of digital images' analysis and critique. Whatever the digital image is, has less to do with its surface — its phenomenal appearance — and more with its informational depths.

This is consistent with long-standing rhetorical tropes around computer graphics' and digital computers' advantages in representation and visualization. It is the superficiality of the drawing, its captivity on the thin surface of the paper, that computer graphics seemed to overhaul by replacing the infamous "dirty lines" with clean symbolic descriptions that a digital electronic computer could "understand" and compute with.[3] In architecture, the proliferation of computer-aided design (CAD) software accelerated the production and consumption of

1 Amelyn Ng. 2020. "7D Vision" *E-Flux*. https://www.e-flux.com/architecture/software/337517/7dvision/

2 John May. 2017. "Everything is Already an Image" *Log* 40: 9–26

3 Ivan Sutherland. 1975. "Structure in Drawings and the Hidden-Surface Problem." In Nicholas Negroponte (ed.) *Reflections on Computer Aids to Design and Architecture*. New York, NY: Petrocelli/Charter, 75.

images by making architectural drawings and renderings easier to produce and manipulate. Despite this seeming explosion of visualization, computer graphics displaced the surface of drawing as the container of information.

As Jacob Gaboury has argued, computer graphics shifted visualization's concerns from showing to *hiding*: occluding lines and casting otherworldly fogs over animation clips — as he also discusses in his essay for this book — to make what is computed more akin to conventions of human perception and representation.[4] Francesco Casetti and Bernard Dionysius Geoghegan also remind us that screens are as much about filtering and occlusion as they are about the display of visual information.[5] Even photorealistic images in their persuasive appeal embed, as Lucia Allais argues, an attempt to mediate between the mathematization of the visual world, hidden behind the surface, and demands for immediacy and familiarity.[6] It is the flickering between the phenomenal realm and underlying logico-symbolic structures that constitutes digital images' ambivalent relationship with what Friedrich Kittler described, in his landmark essay on computer graphics some twenty years ago, as a chimeric quest to "gather that which appears."[7]

This ambivalence is perhaps the allure of an unapologetically visual catalog such as *Designing the Computational Image, Imagining Computational Design*: the sense of an expansive hidden world under what appears on the page. In our curating of the visual material for the exhibition and book, however, it quickly became apparent that, parasitic to concerted efforts to ostracize the surface as the realm of representation and operation, work in computer graphics and computer-aided design gave way to a new set of images — paper thin and producing a visual culture of their own. Together with screenshots and computer animation stills, sit such drawings of mathematical abstractions, diagrams of processes, flowcharts, and graphs. They are *inscriptions*, or as Kathryn Henderson would call them, *conscription devices* enlisting multidisciplinary experts in the production of a new way of thinking about the visual and material world, and its design.[8] [9] This is perhaps how the computational image intersects and expands the category of the digital image, by claiming surfaces of various kinds not only as an epiphenomenon of hidden computational structures but as a constitutive element of these structures production.

4 Jacob Gaboury. 2021. *Image Objects: An Archaeology of Computer Graphics*. Cambridge, MA: MIT Press.

5 Francesco Casetti and Bernard Dionysius Geoghegan. 2021. Screen. In M. Kennerly, S. Frederick and J.E. Abel (eds.) *Information: Keywords*. New York Chichester, West Sussex: Columbia University Press, 162-173.

6 Lucia Allais. 2020. RENDERING: On Experience and Experiments. In Çelik Alexander Zeynep and John May (eds.) *Design Technics: Archaeologies of Architectural Practice*. Minneapolis, MN: University of Minnesota Press.

7 Friedrich A Kittler, and Sara Ogger (trans.). 2001. "Computer Graphics: A Semi-Technical Introduction." *Grey Room*: 30–45.

8 The term "inscription" calls attention to the material aspects of scientific representations. See for example Michael Lynch and Steven Woolgar (eds.) 1990. *Representation in Scientific Practice*. Cambridge, MA: MIT Press.

9 Kathryn Henderson. 1991. "Flexible Sketches and Inflexible Data Bases: Visual Communication, Conscription Devices, and Boundary Objects in Design Engineering," *Science, Technology & Human Values* 16: 4.

The bilingual title of the 2021 exhibition at the Centre de design de l'UQAM holds together image, imagination, and the French *imaginaire* — a term we use to denote both imagery and imaginative projection. The coexistence between these terms conveys this project's layered trajectory, one that moves from computational *images* to be directly confronted and reflectively engaged, to a curated *imagery* displaying an emerging visual culture, and to the production of a computational *imaginary* suggesting new modes of creativity and agency within shifting technical, cultural, and political infrastructures. If this book's images forge connective threads across disparate contexts and reveal consistent visual tropes, the captions highlight difference, locality, and context-specificity. Fundamental to the book is the conviction that computational images are materially embodied and socially embedded artifacts produced by irreducibly situated activities.

Expanding the Miller ICA exhibition for the Centre de design de l'UQAM in Montreal confronted us with exciting inflections to the North American geography of the computational image. Canada's investment in data and communications throughout the twentieth century was mighty. As James Patten has described, Canada was a leading participant in postwar developments in digital art spearheaded by strong national institutions, universities, and cultural agencies such as the Canada Council for the Arts, the economic influence of multinational corporations, but also international visibility through the 1967 World Expo.[10] Our efforts to highlight Canada's, often direction-setting, historic contributions in numerical control, computer graphics, and interactive computing unfolded in parallel with a neighboring project at the McIntosh Gallery at Western University in Ontario in November–December 2020. The exhibition *Computational Arts in Canada 1967-1974* curated by Adam Lauder and Mark Hayward was driven by a similar desire to retrieve a remarkably dynamic period of experimentation during the 1960s and 1970s that is often forgotten by contemporary media art histories.[11]

Unlike computer art that came with well-known creative hubs and vocal protagonists, such as Leslie Mezei, Roger Vidler, and Vera Frenkel, Canadian efforts in computer-aided architectural design were more understated and dispersed. The archive presented in the book is similarly aggregatory and partial. It is the collection of utterances as these circulated in leading architectural journals such as *Canadian Architect* and the journal of the

Combinations of the exhibition's bilingual title in the four vitrines outside the Centre de design de l'UQAM. Graphic design: operative.space.

10 James Patten. 2020. Foreword. In Lauder Adam and Mark Hayward (eds.) *Computational Arts in Canada 1967-1974*. McIntosh Gallery.

11 Adam Lauder and Mark Hayward (eds.) 2020. *Computational Arts in Canada 1967-1974*. McIntosh Gallery.

Royal Architectural Institute of Canada (RAIC) between 1960–1980. From this collection emerged dedicated reporters of computer-related developments such as Swiss-trained architect George Banz, who periodically reported on the actualities of Canadian architectural practice vis-à-vis computers' adoption and opined on shortcomings and possibilities. The collection also included well-known architects such as Randle Iredale contemplating the implications of managerial tools such as Critical Path Diagrams in the architectural firm he co-led. The foray into architectural magazines also revealed special issues and dedicated articles discussing developments in the United States, such as the MIT-born Sketchpad, or offering state-of-the-art views of adjacent efforts. Importantly, it also offered leads to other archives to unearth Canadian-born projects such as the computer graphics language GRAPPLE developed by Bell Northern Research.

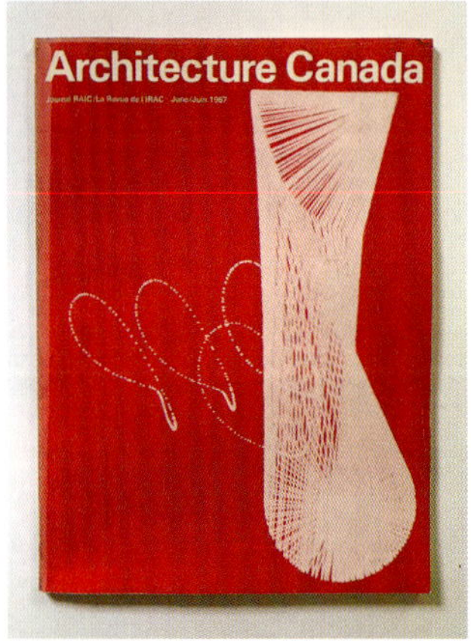

Cover of the June 1967 issue of the RAIC journal *Architecture Canada* featuring a drawing made with Sketchpad. Courtesy of the RAIC Journal.

A vital complement to scanning periodical literature were encounters with historic protagonists who generously offered us access to their personal archives and enlivened, through their narratives, important hubs of activity in computing, design and the arts. Leslie Mezei, the founder of the Computer Graphics Group at the University of Toronto that eventually became the internationally renowned Dynamic Graphics Project, described to us a period of unhindered experimentation, bolstered by easy access to computing time at the University Computer Center and support by Canadian funding organizations. He also immersed us in debates about art and science, the raging Vietnam War making Canada a more desirable place for high-powered US-trained researchers, Marshall McLuhan lecturing down the hall, and the International World Expo of '67 inciting celebration but also critique of Canadian politics and identities. Michael Batty, Professor Emeritus at University College London and leading figure in spatial analytics and urban modeling, talked to us about his time at the University of Waterloo, invited by computational design pioneer Lionel March during his visiting professorship there. He described the University's investment in becoming a world leader in mathematics and computing, its openhanded support of bold research initiatives, and its establishment as a hub in an international network of research excellence.

Support from archivists at the University of Toronto and the University of Waterloo offered access to rich traces of

12 Theodora Vardouli. 2022. "Setting Computer Systems in Motion: Mobilities and Reenactments of the Hierarchical Computer System 2 (HIDECS 2, 1962)" In *Hybrids and Haecceities, Proceedings of the 42nd Annual Conference for the Association for Computer Aided Design in Architecture (ACADIA)*, Philadelphia, PA, USA.

research activity that instantiated, or at times established, such international collaborative networks. Allen Berholtz and Edward Bierstone's adaptation of Christopher Alexander and Marvin L. Manheim's Hierarchical Decomposition System (HIDECS) for Canadian housing at the University of Toronto, also shown as an interactive reconstruction in the Montreal exhibition, is one such example of technical artifacts becoming mobile within research networks.[12] The venue in which the paper on the project was presented, the 1966 Design and Planning 2 Conference themed "Computers in Design and Communication" at the University of Waterloo, also revealed stories of institutional commitments to a reconfiguration of design as a rational process. The University of Waterloo was the birthplace of the Design Methods Group, an interdisciplinary North American "coalition" of researchers bridging design with developments in mathematics, computing, and postwar social sciences. It was also the host of the famed Institute of Design, with its timely ruminations about design discipline and practice and intricate connections with the Expo '67.

Our archives stop before the rise of Montreal as a hub of digital technologies and creativity, hosting major 3D modeling companies such as Softimage 3D, gaming corporations such as Ubisoft, cultural institutions such as the Société des arts technologiques, research creation networks such as Hexagram, and recently the large artificial intelligence research institute MILA, to only sample a part of the city's digital ecology. However, the works capture this pervasive creative energy with compellingly evocative works such as the interactive textiles of Joanna Berzowska, the sono-material installation of Nicolas Reeves, the provocative haptic interface of Jean Dubois, Rafael Lozano-Hemmer's mesmerizing helix-like flow of strings, and studio Iregular's body-merging projection. Expanding the inaugural exhibition are also works by Toronto-based architect and academic Philip Beesley that immerse us in a world of ethereal responsive suspended structures, Canadian data artist Jer Thorp, together with his mother Diane Thorp, dramatizing disjunctions between the infinite computability of weaving patterns and the materiality and finitude of the labor of weaving, and Toronto-based Afghan-born artist Shaheer Zazai who produces intricate carpet patterns one Microsoft Word character after the next.

Just before exiting the Centre de design de l'UQAM gallery and visiting a display of student work produced at UQAM and curated by Nicolas Reeves, the audiences encountered the work of Vancouver-based artist Elizabeth (Liz) Vander Zaag. There they were, projected on the surface of the wall, clips using nascent versions of video editing software inviting onlookers to contend with a baby's view of the world as rendered by a mother through a computer, in *Baby Eyes*, and to follow the artist's television doppelgänger *Digit* as she *Goes to Hawaii, Does the Dishes*, and *Reproduces* – pieces that Gabriela Aceves-Sepúlveda's essay in this book positions in a boisterous feminist art scene in the Canadian West Coast.

Standing in front of the projection, Liz Vander Zaag pointed to the voluptuous curves representing *Digit's* mouth, eyes, and body and recalled the momentous effort it took to produce them. The exhibition, she suggested, is the story of the curve. In looking back at curves of automobiles and aircrafts that early numerical control and computer-aided design work sought to compute with unfailing accuracy, curves of abstract mathematical constructs such as the Coons Patch, curves tamed as straight lines, and curves attempting to trace female bodies in Leslie Mezei's *Bikini Shifted* and *Transformations of a Girl's Face* and in *Digit's* expedition to Hawaii, I have come to think that Liz was right. This is a book about the curve, the technics of its rendering, the politics of its representation, the media surfaces on which it is cast, the disciplinary surfaces on which reverberates, and the material surfaces that it, quite literally, shapes.

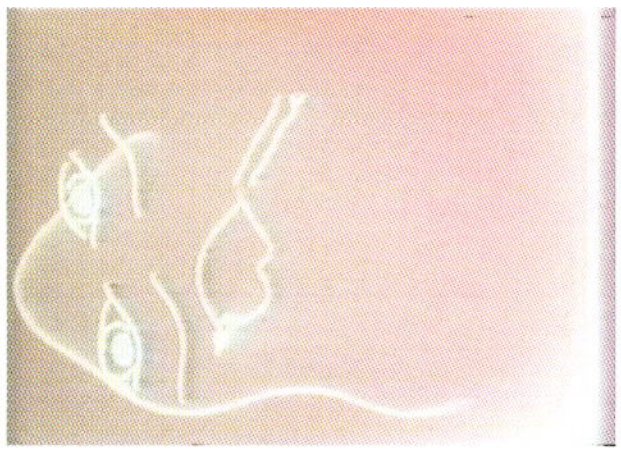

Still from *Digit Goes to Hawaii* (1976) by Elizabeth Vander Zaag. Courtesy of the artist.

Materialities

Archive

Essays

Works

Conversations

Visualities, Page 100 →
Agencies, Page 238 →

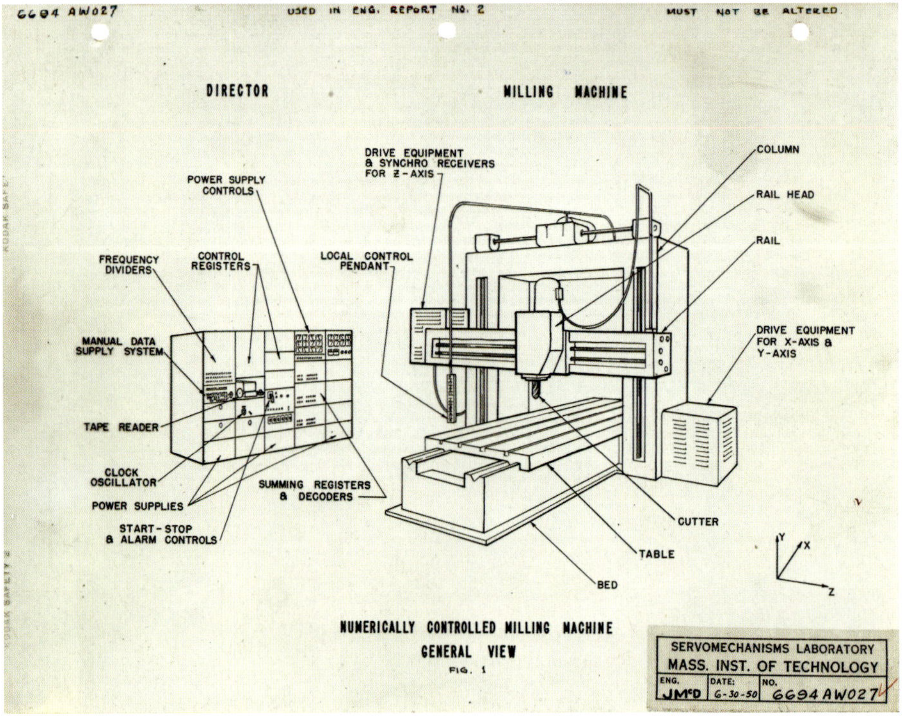

Diagram of the MIT-Parsons milling machine, MIT Servomechanisms Laboratory, 1950, United States

Photograph of the MIT-Parsons Milling Machine, MIT Servomechanisms Laboratory, 1952, United States

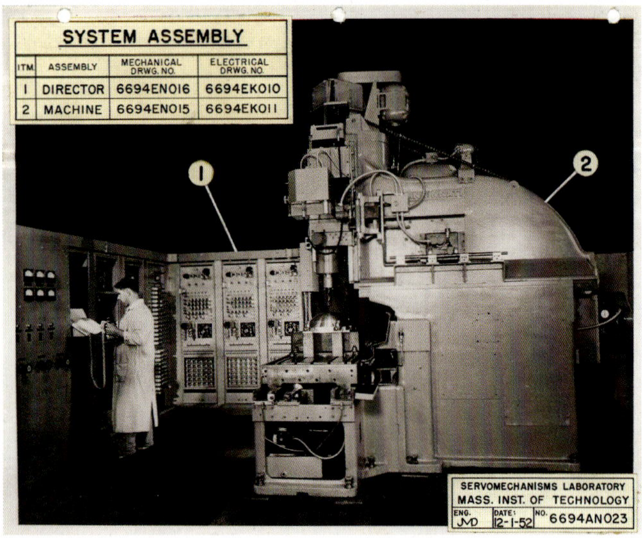

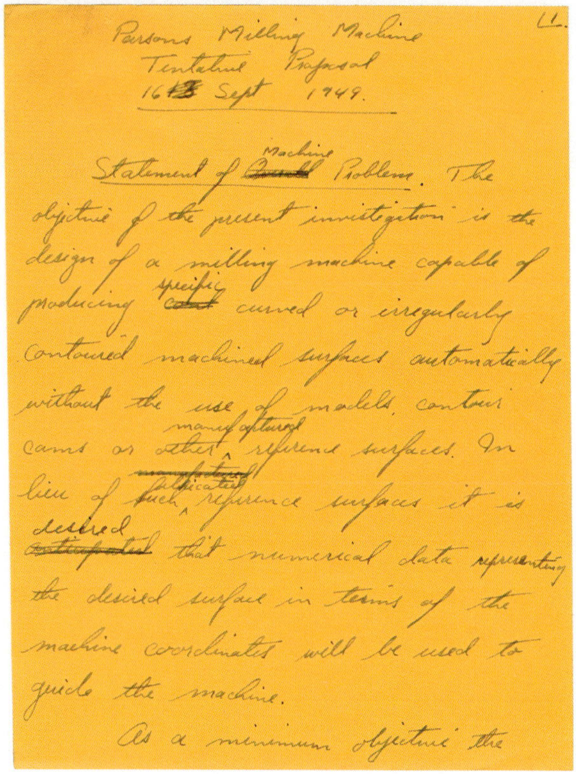
Parsons Milling Machine
Tentative Proposal
16th Sept 1949.

11.

Statement of Machine Problem. The objective of the present investigation is the design of a milling machine capable of producing specific curved or irregularly contoured machined surfaces automatically without the use of models, contour cams or other manufactured reference surfaces. In lieu of such fabricated reference surfaces it is desired that numerical data representing the desired surface in terms of the machine coordinates will be used to guide the machine.

As a minimum objective the

Early notes on the Parsons milling machine, Gordon Brown, MIT Servomechanisms Laboratory, 1949, United States

Established in 1940 under the direction of Electrical Engineering professor Gordon S. Brown, the Electronic Systems Laboratory (ESL) at MIT researched servomechanisms for applications including radar, missile, and gun control. In 1949, John T. Parsons, the vice president of an aircraft company based in Michigan, sought the laboratory's assistance in the development of a numerically-controlled milling machine using punched cards. This collaboration resulted in the laboratory's 1952 demonstration of what is commonly considered the first numerically-controlled machine – a military surplus Cincinnati milling machine driven by instructions stored in rolls of punched paper tape.

Realizing that the process of tape preparation for numerical control was extraordinarily time and labor intensive, researchers in this group began to ponder how to automate it using data processing techniques. In this context, mathematician Douglas T. Ross led the development of the APT (Automated Programming Tool) language, which codified geometric, material, and mechanical aspects of the manufacturing process. The development of this language, and the challenges of automated manufacturing, fostered questions about how aspects of the design process could be automated, foreshadowing the first investigations into "computer-aided design." In 1959, the ESL was renamed Servomechanisms Laboratory, or Servolab.

Courtesy of MIT Libraries

Computer program stored in punched paper tape, Douglas T. Ross, MIT Servomechanisms Laboratory, c. 1948, United States

Before software was stored in disk memory, it was stored in punched cards and paper tape. This paper tape is a facsimile of an original paper tape produced by Douglas T. Ross. In the numerical control research project, each row in the tape contained an instruction or "command" for one of the machine's motions.

Courtesy of MIT Libraries

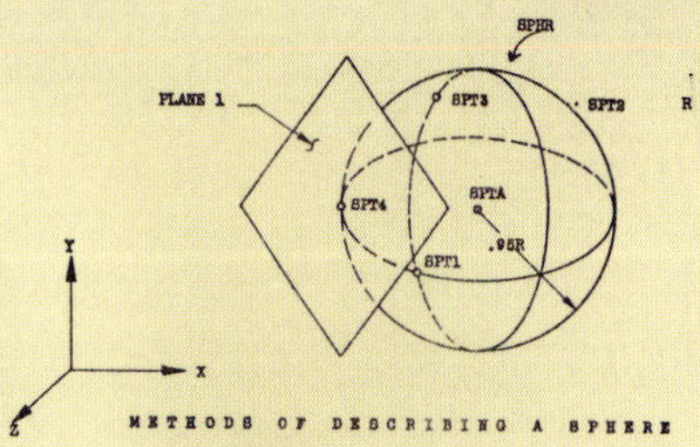
SPHERES

METHODS OF DESCRIBING A SPHERE

SPHR = SPHERE/ X_c, Y_c, Z_c, R   R

SPHR = SPHERE/ CENTER, SPTA, RADIUS, .95

SPHR = SPHERE/ CENTER, SPTA, SPT2

SPHR = SPHERE/ CENTER, SPTA, TANTO, PLANE1

SPHR = SPHERE/ SPT3, SPT2, SPT4, SPT1

SPHR = QADRIC / A,B,C,F,G,H,P,Q,R,D

II Page 10-0

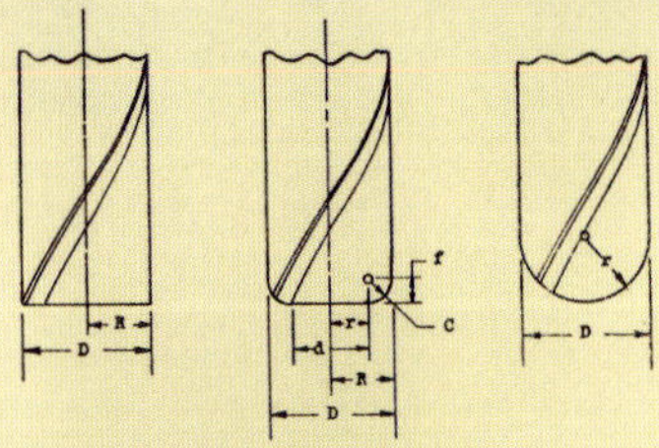
CUTTERS

METHODS OF DESCRIBING CUTTING TOOLS

FIG. 1	CUTTER / D	(Flat End Tool)
FIG. 2	CUTTER/ D, C	(Filleted End Tool)
FIG. 3	CUTTER / D, D/2	(Ball Tool)

NOTE: This is not applicable for Phase 2 production release. All cutters will be ball tool.

II Page 27-0

Methods for describing geometric shapes and cutting tools in the APT language, Douglas T. Ross, MIT Servomechanisms Laboratory, 1960, United States

Precisely describing existing cutting methods, materials, and tools was crucial to the APT effort. These descriptions allowed researchers to automate aspects of the process of calculating the machine's path. These pages, extracted from the "APT Language Dictionary," illustrate the careful parameterization of a milling bit and the parametric definition of basic geometric shapes.

Courtesy of MIT Libraries

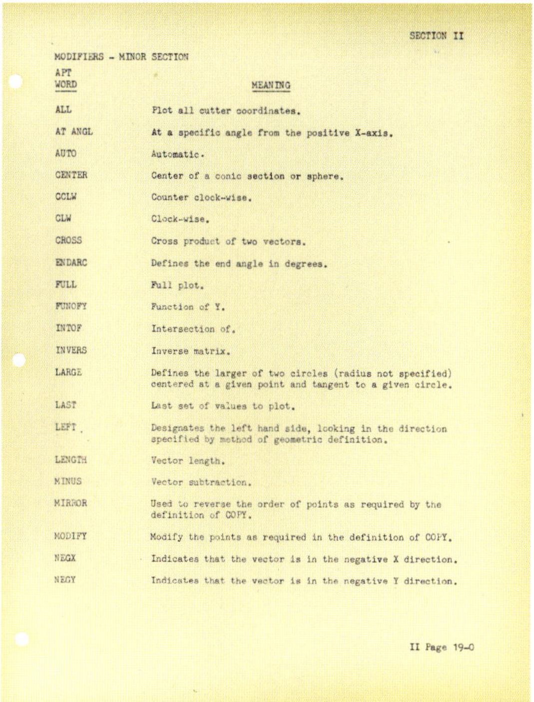

SECTION II

MODIFIERS - MINOR SECTION

APT WORD	MEANING
ALL	Plot all cutter coordinates.
AT ANGL	At a specific angle from the positive X-axis.
AUTO	Automatic.
CENTER	Center of a conic section or sphere.
CCLW	Counter clock-wise.
CLW	Clock-wise.
CROSS	Cross product of two vectors.
ENDARC	Defines the end angle in degrees.
FULL	Full plot.
FUNOFY	Function of Y.
INTOF	Intersection of.
INVERS	Inverse matrix.
LARGE	Defines the larger of two circles (radius not specified) centered at a given point and tangent to a given circle.
LAST	Last set of values to plot.
LEFT	Designates the left hand side, looking in the direction specified by method of geometric definition.
LENGTH	Vector length.
MINUS	Vector subtraction.
MIRROR	Used to reverse the order of points as required by the definition of COPY.
MODIFY	Modify the points as required in the definition of COPY.
NEGX	Indicates that the vector is in the negative X direction.
NEGY	Indicates that the vector is in the negative Y direction.

II Page 19-0

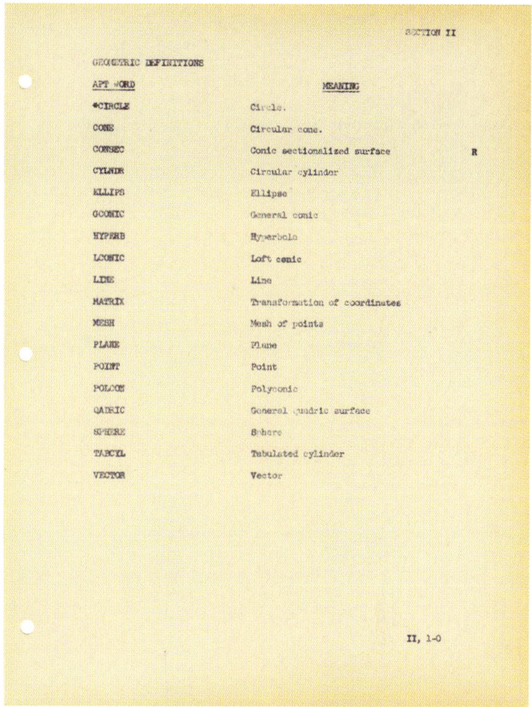

SECTION II

GEOMETRIC DEFINITIONS

APT WORD	MEANING	
*CIRCLE	Circle.	
CONE	Circular cone.	
CONSEC	Conic sectionalized surface	R
CYLNDR	Circular cylinder	
ELLIPS	Ellipse	
GCONIC	General conic	
HYPERB	Hyperbola	
LCONIC	Loft conic	
LINE	Line	
MATRIX	Transformation of coordinates	
MESH	Mesh of points	
PLANE	Plane	
POINT	Point	
POLCON	Polyconic	
QADRIC	General quadric surface	
SPHERE	Sphere	
TABCYL	Tabulated cylinder	
VECTOR	Vector	

II, 1-0

Modifiers and geometric definitions for the APT Language, Douglas T. Ross, MIT Servo-mechanisms Laboratory, 1960, United States

The APT language did not feature high-level abstractions. Instead, it was a "problem-oriented" language focused on describing very concrete aspects of manufacturing machinery. These pages from the "APT dictionary" illustrate how its vocabulary remained close to the basic geometric operations of industrial part design.

Courtesy of MIT Libraries

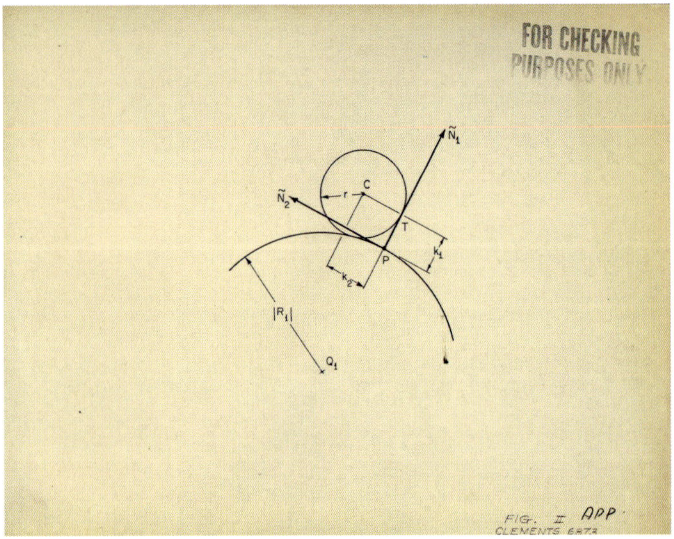

Drawing of a cutting path, D. F. Clements, MIT Servomechanisms Laboratory, c. 1953, United States

A precise understanding of geometric and mechanical aspects of cutting tools was essential to create systems able to automatically calculate cutting paths. This drawing by APT Project member D.F. Clements illustrates the precise parameterization of a milling bit in relation to a curved path.

Courtesy of MIT Libraries

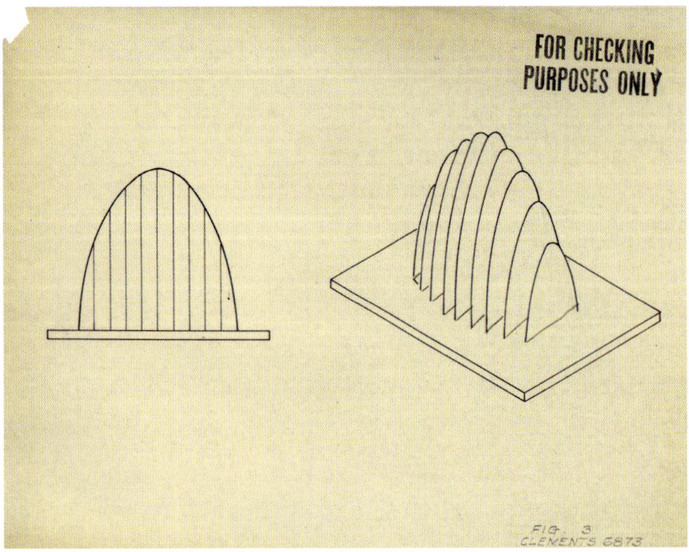

Drawings of a 3D volume subdivided into discrete parts, MIT Servomechanisms Laboratory, c. 1953, United States

Drawn from the archives of the Automated Programming Tool (APT) Project, these drawings illustrate how Servolab engineers subdivided 3D volumes into discrete flat components suitable for numerically-controlled manufacturing. The drawing represents an airplane nose as a series of planes. Aircraft shapes were commonly used as examples, attesting to the militaristic nature of the research, which was funded by the US Air Force.

Courtesy of MIT Libraries

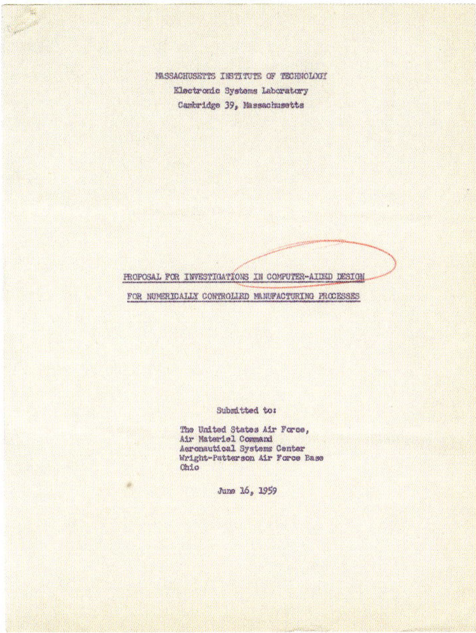

MASSACHUSETTS INSTITUTE OF TECHNOLOGY
Electronic Systems Laboratory
Cambridge 39, Massachusetts

PROPOSAL FOR INVESTIGATIONS IN COMPUTER-AIDED DESIGN
FOR NUMERICALLY CONTROLLED MANUFACTURING PROCESSES

Submitted to:

The United States Air Force,
Air Materiel Command
Aeronautical Systems Center
Wright-Patterson Air Force Base
Ohio

June 16, 1959

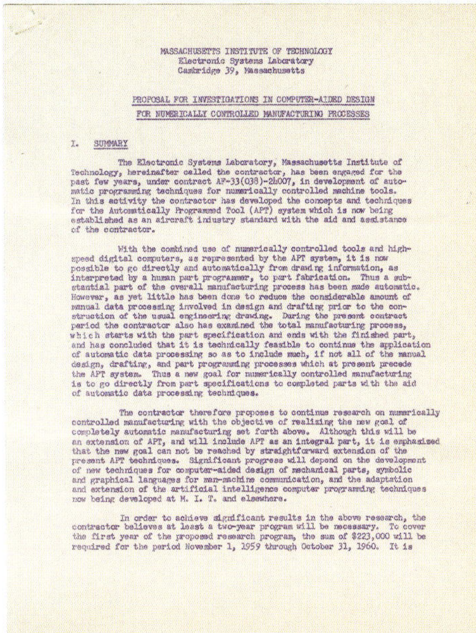

MASSACHUSETTS INSTITUTE OF TECHNOLOGY
Electronic Systems Laboratory
Cambridge 39, Massachusetts

PROPOSAL FOR INVESTIGATIONS IN COMPUTER-AIDED DESIGN
FOR NUMERICALLY CONTROLLED MANUFACTURING PROCESSES

I. SUMMARY

The Electronic Systems Laboratory, Massachusetts Institute of Technology, hereinafter called the contractor, has been engaged for the past few years, under contract AF-33(038)-24007, in development of automatic programming techniques for numerically controlled machine tools. In this activity the contractor has developed the concepts and techniques for the Automatically Programmed Tool (APT) system which is now being established as an aircraft industry standard with the aid and assistance of the contractor.

With the combined use of numerically controlled tools and high-speed digital computers, as represented by the APT system, it is now possible to go directly and automatically from drawing information, as interpreted by a human part programmer, to part fabrication. Thus a substantial part of the overall manufacturing process has been made automatic. However, as yet little has been done to reduce the considerable amount of manual data processing involved in design and drafting prior to the construction of the usual engineering drawing. During the present contract period the contractor also has examined the total manufacturing process, which starts with the part specification and ends with the finished part, and has concluded that it is technically feasible to continue the application of automatic data processing so as to include much, if not all of the manual design, drafting, and part programming processes which at present precede the APT system. Thus a new goal for numerically controlled manufacturing is to go directly from part specifications to completed parts with the aid of automatic data processing techniques.

The contractor therefore proposes to continue research on numerically controlled manufacturing with the objective of realizing the new goal of completely automatic manufacturing set forth above. Although this will be an extension of APT, and will include APT as an integral part, it is emphasized that the new goal can not be reached by straightforward extension of the present APT techniques. Significant progress will depend on the development of new techniques for computer-aided design of mechanical parts, symbolic and graphical languages for man-machine communication, and the adaptation and extension of the artificial intelligence computer programming techniques now being developed at M. I. T. and elsewhere.

In order to achieve significant results in the above research, the contractor believes at least a two-year program will be necessary. To cover the first year of the proposed research program, the sum of \$223,000 will be required for the period November 1, 1959 through October 31, 1960. It is

Proposal for the Investigations in Computer-Aided Design for Numerically Controlled Manufacturing Processes, Douglas T. Ross and Steven A. Coons, MIT CAD Project, 1959, United States

Draft of the first Computer-Aided Design funding proposal to the US Air Force, Douglas T. Ross, MIT CAD Project, 1959, United States

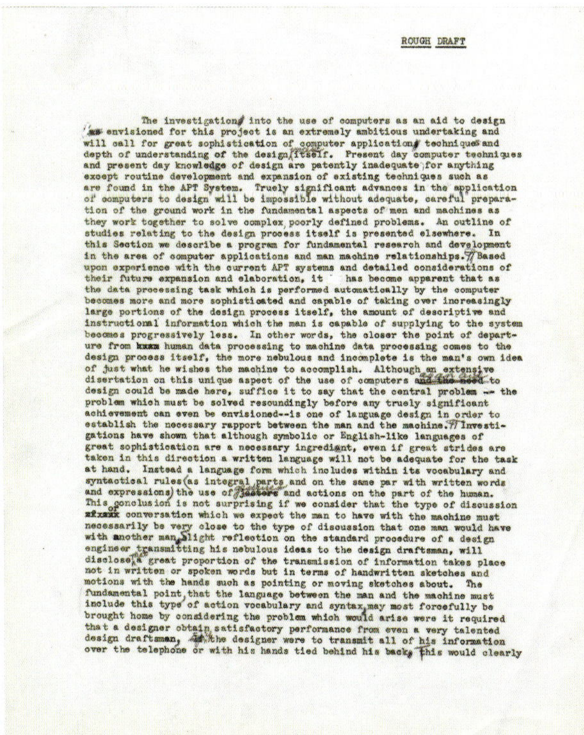

ROUGH DRAFT

The investigations into the use of computers as an aid to design as envisioned for this project is an extremely ambitious undertaking and will call for great sophistication of computer applications techniques and depth of understanding of the design itself. Present day computer techniques and present day knowledge of design are patently inadequate for anything except routine development and expansion of existing techniques such as are found in the APT System. Truely significant advances in the application of computers to design will be impossible without adequate, careful preparation of the ground work in the fundamental aspects of men and machines as they work together to solve complex poorly defined problems. An outline of studies relating to the design process itself is presented elsewhere. In this Section we describe a program for fundamental research and development in the area of computer applications and man machine relationships. Based upon experience with the current APT systems and detailed considerations of their future expansion and elaboration, it has become apparent that as the data processing task which is performed automatically by the computer becomes more and more sophisticated and capable of taking over increasingly large portions of the design process itself, the amount of descriptive and instructional information which the man is capable of supplying to the system becomes progressively less. In other words, the closer the point of departure from xxxx human data processing to machine data processing comes to the design process itself, the more nebulous and incomplete is the man's own idea of just what he wishes the machine to accomplish. Although an extensive disertation on this unique aspect of the use of computers and the need to design could be made here, suffice it to say that the central problem -- the problem which must be solved resoundingly before any truely significant achievement can even be envisioned--is one of language design in order to establish the necessary rapport between the man and the machine. Investigations have shown that although symbolic or English-like languages of great sophistication are a necessary ingrediant, even if great strides are taken in this direction a written language will not be adequate for the task at hand. Instead a language form which includes within its vocabulary and syntactical rules (as integral parts and on the same par with written words and expressions) the use of jesters and actions on the part of the human. This conclusion is not surprising if we consider that the type of discussion xxxxx conversation which we expect the man to have with the machine must necessarily be very close to the type of discussion that one man would have with another man. Slight reflection on the standard procedure of a design engineer transmitting his nebulous ideas to the design draftsman, will disclose a great proportion of the transmission of information takes place not in written or spoken words but in terms of handwritten sketches and motions with the hands such as pointing or moving sketches about. The fundamental point, that the language between the man and the machine must include this type of action vocabulary and syntax, may most forcefully be brought home by considering the problem which would arise were it required that a designer obtain satisfactory performance from even a very talented design draftsman, if the designer were to transmit all of his information over the telephone or with his hands tied behind his back, this would clearly

Servolab members sought domain knowledge about design from colleagues in the department of mechanical engineering. The first proposal to investigate "Computer-Aided Design for Numerically Controlled Manufacturing" was submitted to the United States Air Force by an interdisciplinary team of MIT researchers led by Servolab's Douglas T. Ross and Mechanical Engineering professor Steven A. Coons in 1959. A draft of this proposal by project co-leader Douglas T. Ross further illuminates the project's fundamental concerns with software design and language development.

Courtesy of MIT Libraries

DESIGN AND THE COMPUTER

Steven A. Coons

The technological history of man has witnessed the gradual development of the machine as a slave to extend human powers. All labor that man once performed with the strength and skill of his body has gradually been relegated to the machine. Even the faculties of the senses have been extended in vast amplification by the machine; for instance, the microscope, the telescope, and television have extended the eye's power. Now we have come, within the past twenty years or so, to the final encroachment of the machine upon the activities of man, an encroachment upon his intellectual province. I am referring of course to the rapid development of the modern giant computer. In this development there have been two parallel currents, a rapid increase in the complexity and flexibility of the physical structure of computers, and a concomitant rapid increase in the diversity of applications and the sophistication of techniques that these purely physical developments have suggested and made possible. Far beyond mere numerical problem solving, or mere high speed calculation, the modern computer is capable of modes of operation which do not superficially suggest calculation at all. An excellent example of such an activity of modern computers is in the field of mechanical translation of foreign languages. Incidentally, recent efforts to construct techniques for language translation of a degree of sophistication greater than mere vocabulary search and word substitution has led to a far deeper understanding of the structure of language than we ever had before; this is in a sense an intellectual contribution obtained as a kind of by-product of the united efforts of man and machine.[1]

Early computer programming involved nothing more complicated than preparing a step-by-step list of arithmetical instructions for the computer to follow; it was a single strand of operations to be performed sequentially in time. A significant step was taken when the concept of decision branches was introduced. This meant that the previous single

1. Victor H. Yngve, "Computer Programs for Translation," Scientific American, June 1962.

string of instructions could be woven with other strings into a net, and the logical path of the computer in following such a net could be made to depend upon certain logical decisions at each of the knots of the net. Some of these decisions could be made by the computer itself using a predetermined scale of decision values; other branch points could be under the control of the human operator. Still greater sophistication has been obtained by making the scale of decision values (the way the machine behaves at any branch point) a dynamically varying entity dependent upon past history and results of other computations, rather than upon some static pre-set decision process. This dynamic variation of the branch point decision process makes it possible for the computer to profit by previous mistakes; it introduces the faculty of learning. For example, there is a program written for one of our relatively small computers in which the operator draws a maze on an oscilloscope, and sets a "mouse" in one part of the maze and a piece of "cheese" in another part. The mouse finds his way to the cheese after a tedious series of trial and error experiments, aided only by some rudimentary rules about decisions. But if he is set the same problem again, his path to the cheese is direct and efficient, because on the second expedition all nonproductive decisions have been eliminated. The mouse had "learned" to solve the maze.

In the 1940's at M.I.T. the Servomechanisms Laboratory devised and developed the first automatically controlled milling machine. The controlling information for the machine was introduced in the form of punched paper tape, on which all dimensional information and instructions to the various feeds and cutter speeds was contained. At first the punched paper tape was prepared manually by some human operator who translated, in effect, the detail drawing of the part to be machined into numerical form and then into appropriate patterns of holes in the tape. This was a tedious and entirely mechanical chore, and it was only natural that short cuts in the process began to suggest themselves. The scope of such short cuts began to spread through the fabric of the technique, and it was not long before the computer was involved in implementing them. Subsequently, the Computer Applications Group of the Electronic Systems Laboratory developed in great detail a complete, automatic system for preparing these punched paper "director" tapes from detail drawings; to be sure a human operator

Draft of the article "Design and the Computer," Steven A. Coons, MIT CAD Project, 1962, United States (pictured on previous page)

Steven A. Coons's intellectual stewardship of the CAD Project, along with Ross's, profoundly influenced the evolution of CAD systems, and our current landscape of design technologies. In these documents, Coons uses his distinctive narrative voice to envision design as a human-machine endeavor, and ponders the role of the computer as a "mechanized slave" in the service of creative human designers. In other contemporary documents Coons reflects on the question of computer authorship, pondering the nearby development of computer programs for musical composition. These show how at the root of CAD systems were not just technical but also conceptual redefinitions of design and creativity, and of the roles humans and machines were to play in it.

Courtesy of MIT Libraries

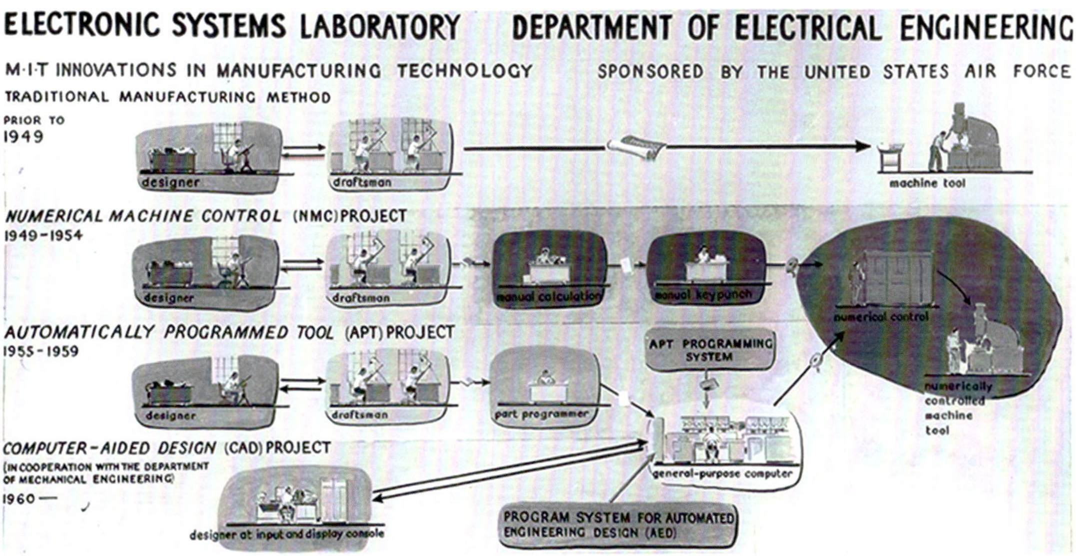

MIT innovations in manufacturing technology, MIT Servomechanisms Laboratory, 1963, United States

Simplifying the design to manufacturing process was the key aim of early numerical control and computer-aided design research. However, as this diagram suggests, the efficiencies of automated manufacturing were premised on considerably more complex sociotechnical arrangements.

Courtesy of MIT Libraries

Images of 3D toolpaths created with the Whirlwind computer using the APT II and APT III programs, Douglas T. Ross, MIT Servomechanisms Laboratory, 1958, United States

Some of the earliest examples of 3D computer graphics were produced by displaying the output of geometric calculations on oscilloscopes. Numerical control researchers at MIT called these drawings "perspective scope plots." This image, produced with the Servolab's Whirlwind computer, visualizes the path of a milling tool in 3D space during fabrication. The curved shapes likely described airplane parts. The APT language had the capacity to produce these images, but was never made available to the system's users outside the laboratory.

Reconstruction of an image from an APT Project report
Courtesy of MIT Libraries

x

Overall view of "Model-making machine," A.P. Armit and A.G. Flutter, Cambridge CAD Group, 1971, United Kingdom

Inspired by his frequent visits to US universities, Maurice Wilkes, the director of the Cambridge University Mathematical Laboratory, started a CAD research group in 1965. Supported by a GBP 50,000 grant from the UK's Ministry of Technology, Wilkes equipped the group with a PDP 7 Station, peripherals, and a display. Aside from important developments in geometric modeling, the group's contributions included a custom "model-making machine" for rapid prototyping, used to fabricate the shoe last illustrated here. The shape, characterized by multiple doubly-curved surfaces, forced CAD Group researchers to confront problems of geometric representation and manufacturing. In the words of CAD Group member Robin Forrest, this shoe last "caused a lot of pain to a lot of people." This shoe last demonstrates the newly found association between image and artifact enabled by computational design and manufacturing methods.

Courtesy of Robin Forrest

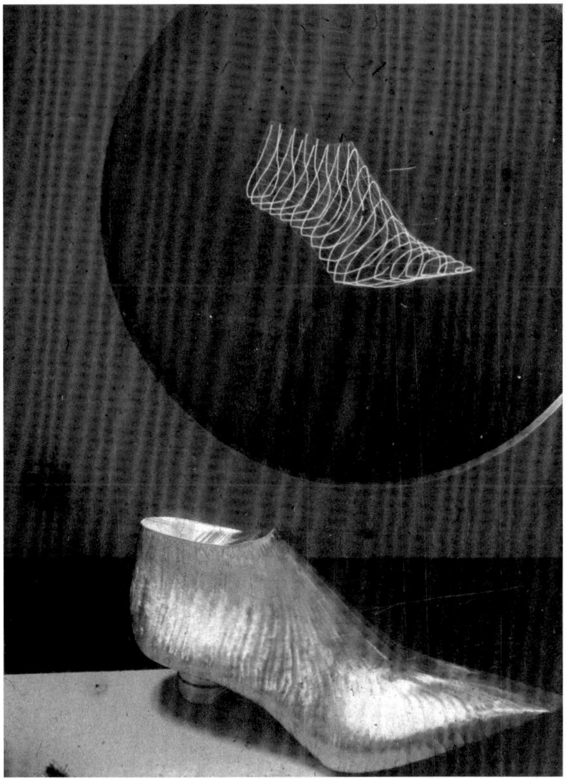

Multipatch model and numerically machined metal last, A.P. Armit and A.G. Flutter, University of Cambridge CAD Group, 1971, United Kingdom

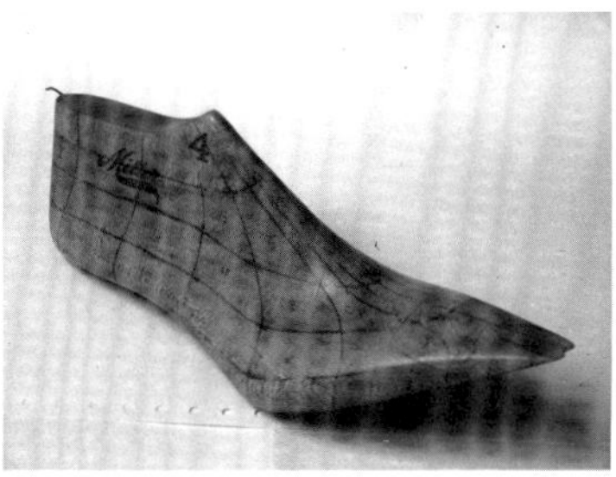

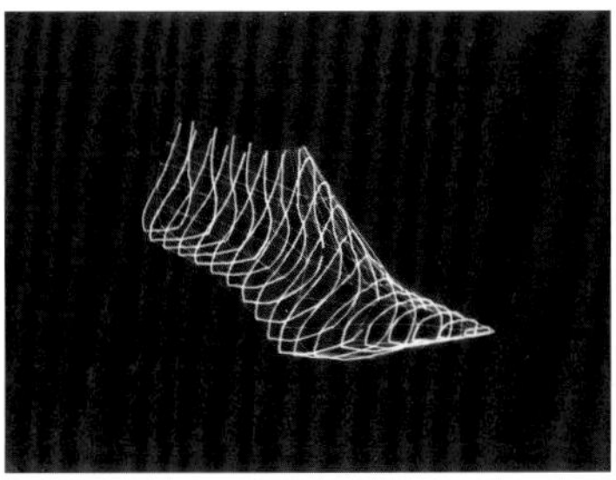

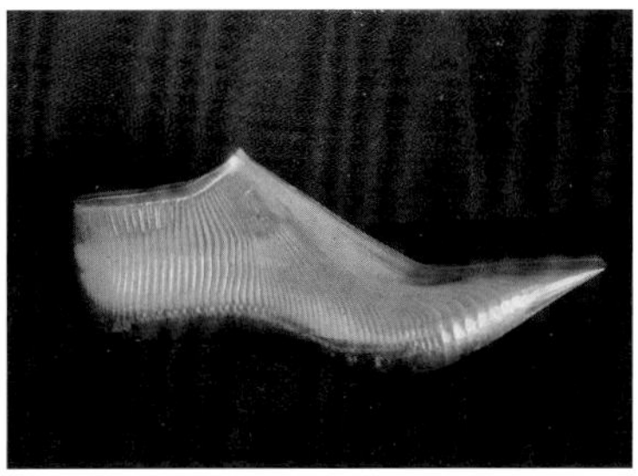

Wooden shoe last, Multipatch model and numerically machined metal last, A.P. Armit and A.G. Flutter, Cambridge CAD Group, 1971, United Kingdom

The UMAC 5, Sperry Gyroscope Co. of Canada Ltd., 1961, Canada

Encased in a glossy gray shell, with one door painted turquoise to match the metal letters prominently featured at the crown, was a pioneering Computerized Numerical Control (CNC) system. Made in Montreal by Sperry Canada, the Canadian subsidiary of the American navigation equipment manufacturer Sperry Corporation, the UMAC 5 stood apart from its predecessors in that it adapted to different machine tools via reprogramming as opposed to hardware and circuitry replacement. As historian John Vardalas has detailed in his 2001 book *The Computer Revolution in Canada* (MIT Press), this was made possible by the integration of a programmable computer with the machine tool, an innovation largely based on the work of University of Toronto Engineering Physics graduate Paul Caden. Despite the excitement about the potential of a fully programmable digital control system, UMAC 5 encountered a variety of obstacles during its development, sometimes due to computer programmers' unfamiliarity with heavy tools and manufacturing processes. Another major obstacle was the lack of an intuitive high-level programming language for the UMAC 5, forcing the use of arduous machine languages. According to Vardalas, because of these and other difficulties, UMAC 5 was perceived as cumbersome and expensive, and Sperry Canada switched to less sophisticated systems after selling only about fifty UMAC 5 systems, primarily to defense contractors.

Courtesy of Ingenium 1985.359

"Canadian Firm Develops New Control System," *Montreal Gazette*, 1963, Canada

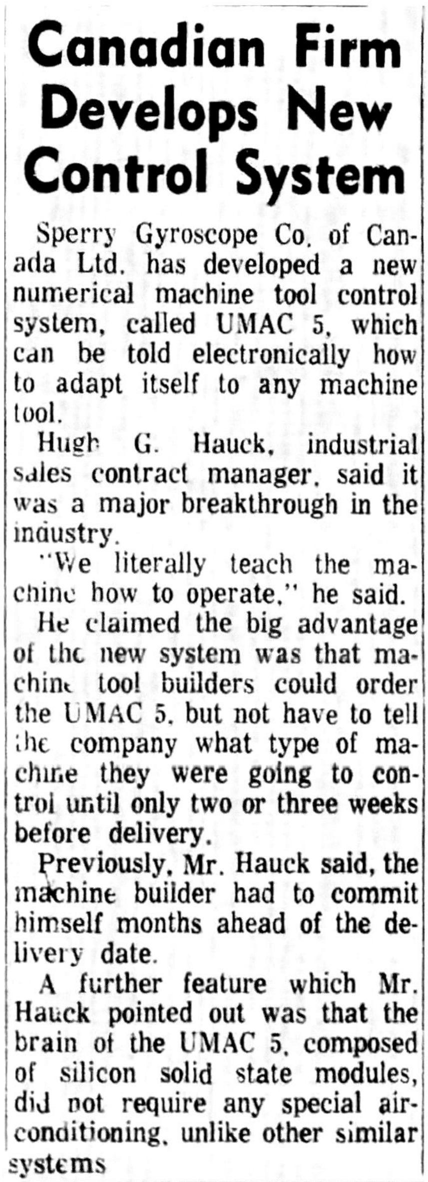

Canadian Firm Develops New Control System

Sperry Gyroscope Co. of Canada Ltd. has developed a new numerical machine tool control system, called UMAC 5, which can be told electronically how to adapt itself to any machine tool.

Hugh G. Hauck, industrial sales contract manager, said it was a major breakthrough in the industry.

"We literally teach the machine how to operate," he said.

He claimed the big advantage of the new system was that machine tool builders could order the UMAC 5, but not have to tell the company what type of machine they were going to control until only two or three weeks before delivery.

Previously, Mr. Hauck said, the machine builder had to commit himself months ahead of the delivery date.

A further feature which Mr. Hauck pointed out was that the brain of the UMAC 5, composed of silicon solid state modules, did not require any special air-conditioning, unlike other similar systems

While UMAC 5 was still under development, Sperry Canada began disseminating a bold vision of a fully programmable commercial Numerical Control system that could adapt to different machine tool requirements. In June 1963, the *Montreal Gazette* quoted Sperry Canada's industrial sales contract manager Hugh Hauck, who described UMAC 5 as a machine that one could "literally teach how to operate" leading to a "major breakthrough in the industry." Although a combination of various funding and technical obstacles did not allow for this vision to be fulfilled, the prospect of software as an infrastructure for controlling manufacturing processes and their tools in a versatile and universal way persisted, and soon after found its expression in other systems.

Pamphlet for Sperry Canada's Automatic Machine Tool Control, Sperry Gyroscope Co. of Canada Ltd., n.d. Canada

Sperry Canada started developing Numerical Control systems in the mid-1950s, based on a series of prototypes by McGill University Mechanical Engineering graduate Peter Herzl (see Vardalas, 2001, *The Computer Revolution in Canada*). The use of punch cards enabled the automation of machine operations by transferring control information encoded in the tape directly to the machine tool. This undated promotional pamphlet conveys some of the technical details of, and key claims around, automatic machine tool control systems.

Courtesy of the Hagley Museum and Library

▲ **ELECTRO-HYDRAULIC VALVE** — This valve, together with the precision Measuring System accounts for the extreme accuracy of the Sperry Automatic Machine Tool Control. Six inch scale shows size of valve.

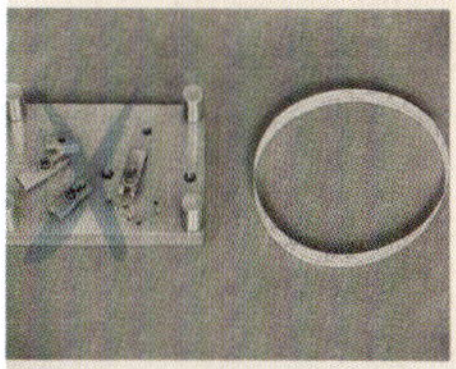

▲ **TAPE MAKING TIME** — Time for making tape to replace tool is reduced to a matter of minutes.

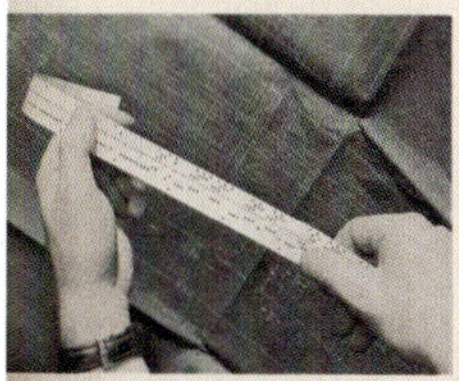

▲ **STANDARD 1″ COMPUTER TAPE** — Can be prepared with a hand punch, special keyboard, adding-machine or typewriter type punch.

Briefly...

HERE IS WHAT THE SPERRY automatic MACHINE TOOL CONTROL *can accomplish*

The Sperry Automatic Machine Tool Control is a device created for the purpose of positioning a table, carriage or tool post within tolerances of ± .0005 inches in 1,2,3, or more axes. On short travels accuracies of ± .00025 inches are obtainable. Motions are repeated over and over again with a repeatability accuracy of ± .0001 inch. Drilling and straight-line milling, turning and grinding can all be controlled by the Sperry Automatic Machine Tool Control in a sequence, determined by programming through a punched control tape. Positioning directly from dials without the use of tape is available as an accessory. The above accuracies are over-all system accuracies experienced with machine tools of reasonable quality. The total electrical accuracy of the control, however, is ± .0001 inches.

HERE IS HOW IT OPERATES

The Sperry Automatic Machine Tool Control activates a table, carriage or tool post at speeds varying from 60 to 200 inches per minute, depending upon application and machine. The positioning speed is maintained right through to final position. Positioning is completely automatic to accuracies normally accomplished with high grade tools and fixtures but without the inherent time and cost consuming set-ups. The desired controlled movement or position is obtained through precision pick-offs mounted on the machine. These pick-offs accept dimensional information from a standard 1″ wide punched tape.

The preparation of the tape is done with standard tape punching equipment readily obtainable from many sources. A few hours instruction to a regular machine operator enables him to produce tapes quickly and accurately directly from working drawings. Using a hand punch, about one minute per position is the time required. Using adding machine or typewriter, tapes can be produced as speedily as expected from normal office equipment. Tape is used in endless loops, eliminating necessity of rewinding or rehandling. Tapes of 2000 positions can be easily handled. Approximately six positions can be obtained per foot of tape used.

KEY COMPONENTS

CONTROL PANEL

The control panel is mounted on a pedestal adjustable to suit operator's height, or at the user's convenience may be integral with the control cabinet. In appropriate positions on the panel are the activating push buttons — on and off; independent table motion in all directions; manual and automatic cycle control. There is also a counter which indicates operation number; two dial lights, one showing green when table is in proper position, one showing amber to warn operator that a change in tool is required, and a red light to indicate off/on.

TAPE READER

The tape reader is a unique device which, by means of low pressure air flow, senses the presence or absence of holes in the tape. The air is at all times blown out of the reading head, so that the head is completely dirt free. Extremely long tape life and reliability under normal shop operating conditions is obtained by this method of sensing.

MEASURING SYSTEM

The measuring system consists of linear electrical scales attached to the machine tool, but independent of the positioning system. The function of the scales can be compared to spacer bars used for positioning in jig boring and other similar operations. They are completely sealed in an oil-tight enclosure fully protected from normal shop contamination.

POSITIONING SYSTEM

An electro-hydraulic system employing specially developed Sperry electro-hydraulic valves provides the positioning system.

ELECTRICAL COMPONENTS

In order to obtain maximum reliability throughout the whole system only the highest grades of electrical components are employed. Those subject to replacement and maintenance are mounted on plug boards, so that no special skills are required for service or inspection. A plug-in test panel is built in to permit quick testing.

SERVICING

A circuit module is shown being removed for replacement. Each module is keyed and can only be inserted in one position. Test panel in bottom centre is simple plug-in system for quick check.

AUXILIARY FEATURES

The tape input can be supplemented by a set of manual rotary switches in order that positioning may be accomplished without having to prepare a tape.

There is provision for the addition of automatic cycle control for the machine tool itself and such auxiliary operating elements as automatic coolant flow and air blast part cleaning.

A tracing attachment is available for machines suitable for this work.

SAVINGS

As an example of the savings effected, one of these Sperry Controls, when applied to a complex, high precision production job saved over $3,000. in four weeks time over the previous conventional way of producing the parts in low quantities. This represents a reduction of 13 hours each on a part formerly requiring 15 hours each to make.

5 *simple steps that make the* SPERRY automatic MACHINE TOOL CONTROL

Two Major Components . . . the Tape Reader, or Cabinet, at left, and the Control Panel, below.

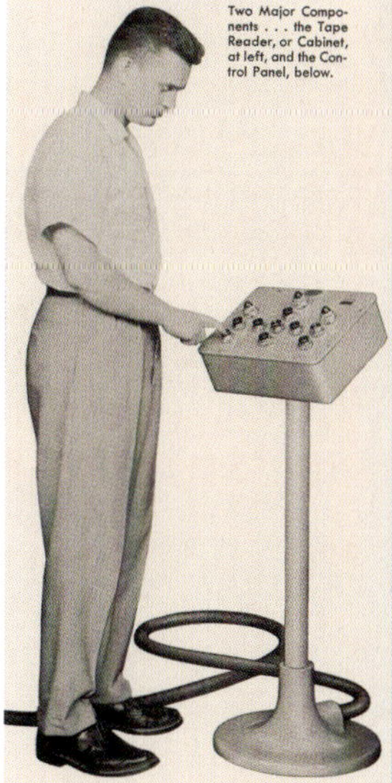

a time and money saver through faster operation and elimination of waste.

1. Tape made in office or shop direct from working drawing.
2. Tape placed in cabinet.
3. Part clamped in position on table.
4. Computation done in cabinet where readings given by linear scales on machine tool are automatically compared to readings given by tape. Valve moves table to command position.
5. System is hydraulically self-locked and ready for operation.

check these important advantages of the... SPERRY automatic MACHINE TOOL CONTROL

- Only two major components
- Highest accuracy and versatility, for full automatic use
- One Sperry-controlled machine can do the work of 3 or 4 conventionally operated machines
- No more costly tools and fixtures
- Damage to expensive parts because of human errors almost nil
- Longer tool life due to elimination of wear normally occurring in guide bushings

EXCLUSIVE SPERRY FEATURES

The tape is read by the machine with a special air-actuated reading head which blows air out of the tape at all times, removing any danger of dirt contamination and allowing considerable dimensional change in the tape without affecting the accuracy of the operation. Entire command block read instantaneously with no complex memory circuits required.

The electro-hydraulic valve combines the high performance achieved by similar valves in missile and aircraft positioning systems with the rugged durability of an industrial, long-life, hydraulic valve.

Although its principal savings result from reduced production time, the Sperry Automatic Machine Tool Control is almost indispensable where low cost, high accuracy components must be produced in limited quantities.

SPECIFICATIONS

CABINET SIZE:
23″ x 18″ x 65″ high

PEDESTAL SIZE:
16″ Dia. Base x 44″ high (Adjustable)

WEIGHT (TOTAL):
Approx. 400 lbs.
Pedestal — 100 lbs.
Cabinet — 300 lbs.

ELECTRICAL INPUT REQ'D.:
115 Volts, 60 Cycles, 350 Watts
(Allowable voltage fluctuation: 90 to 130 Volts)

AIR SUPPLY:
3 cfm 60-120 psi.

SERVO SYSTEM:
Electro-hydraulic

OPERATING PRESSURE RANGE:
0-750 psi.

HYDRAULIC VALVE SIZE:
3½″ x 3½″ x 4½″

MEASURING UNITS SIZE:
5″ x 7½″ x length req'd.

POSITIONAL ACCURACY:
± .0005″ full length of strokes
± .00025″ possible on short strokes

REPEATABILITY:
± .0001″

APPROACH SPEED:
60 to 200 inches/min. depending on machine size.

SPERRY

SPERRY GYROSCOPE COMPANY OF CANADA, LTD.
6011 Cote de Liesse Road - P.O. Box 710 - Telephone RIverside 7-5561 - Montreal, Que.

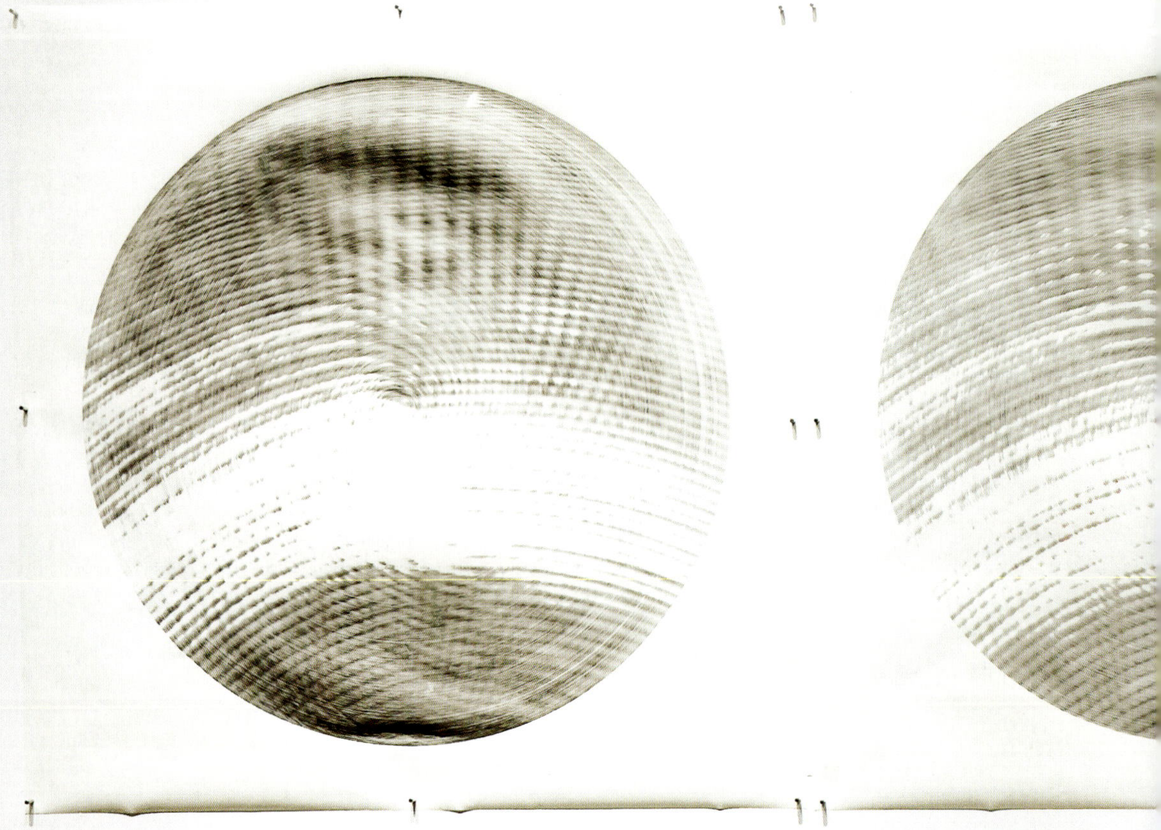

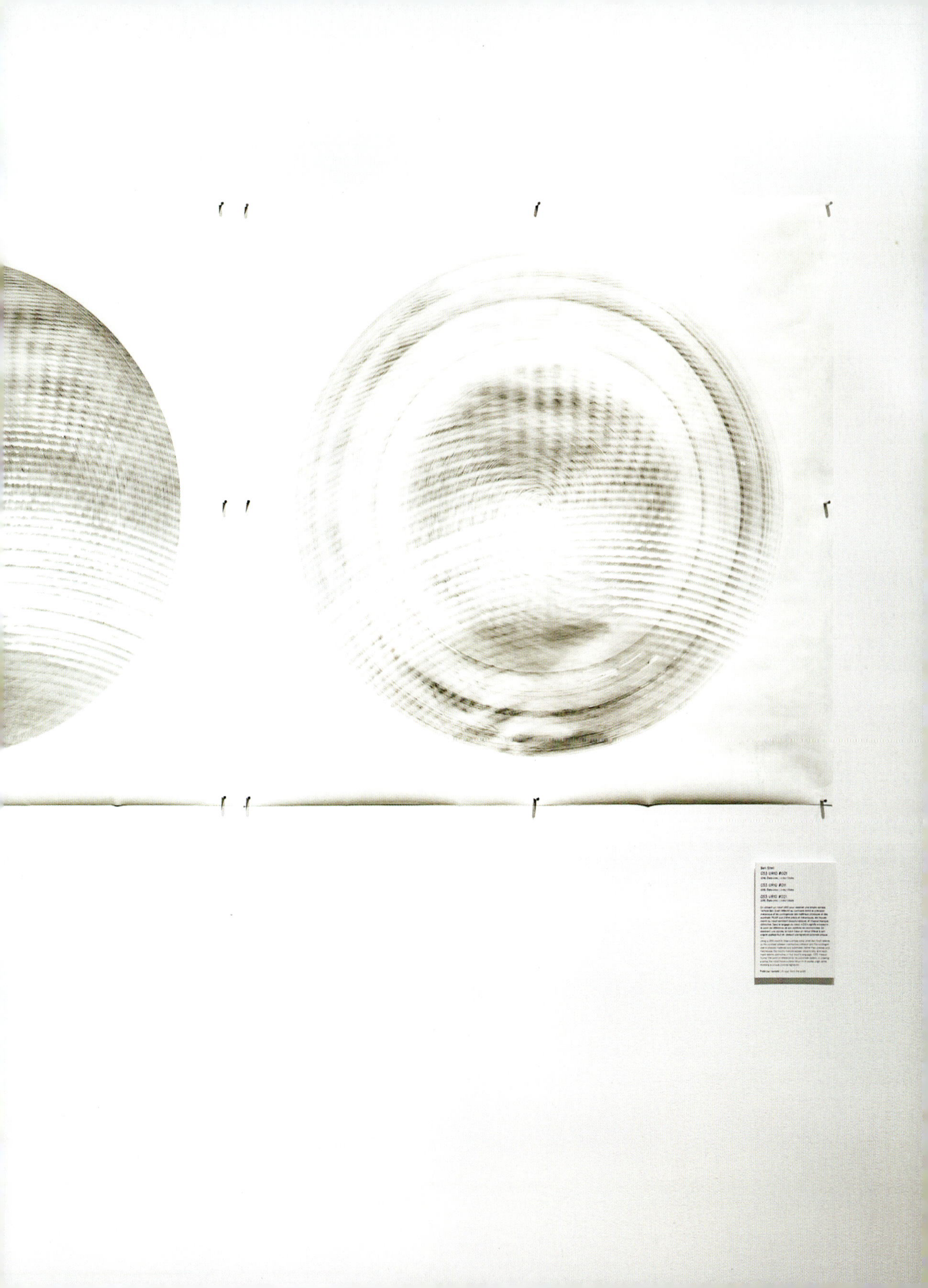

(pictured on previous page)

G53 UR10 #001, #011, #021, Ben Snell, 2018, United States

Using a UR10 robot to draw a simple spiral, artist Ben Snell reflects on the contrast between mechanical precision and the contingencies of physical materials and substrates. Rather than precise and mechanical, the robot's motions appear idiosyncratic, and each mark seems unique. In the robot's language, G53 means "home": the point of reference for its coordinate system. In drawing a spiral, the robot traces a literal return to its spatial origin while revealing a unique pictorial signature.

Robotically painted ink on paper
3.8 in x 3.8 in (1,168 x 1,168 cm) each
Courtesy of the artist

G.L.O. / Graphic Line Object, Kristy Balliet and Kelly Bair (BairBalliet), 2017, United States

G.L.O. is a set of "drawn models" that explore the convergence of the virtual and physical in the drawn line. Developed especially for the Designing the Computational Image, Imagining Computational Design exhibition by United States architects Kristy Balliet and Kelly Bair, the three models reference wall objects — a shelf, a plaque, a tapestry — while alternating roles between three distinct parts: a flat graphic, a thick line drawing, and an object. The architects manipulated the shapes in virtual reality and adapted them to the space of the gallery, incorporating the bodily gestures of drawing into a computational design process.

PLA Plastic and Milled MDF covered with airbrush paint, sponged Gesso, and flocked fibers
Shelf and plaque: 24 x 24 x 16 in (60.9 x 60.9 cm) closed; tapestry: 33 x 20 x 10 in (83.8 x 50.8 x 25.4 cm)
Courtesy of the artists

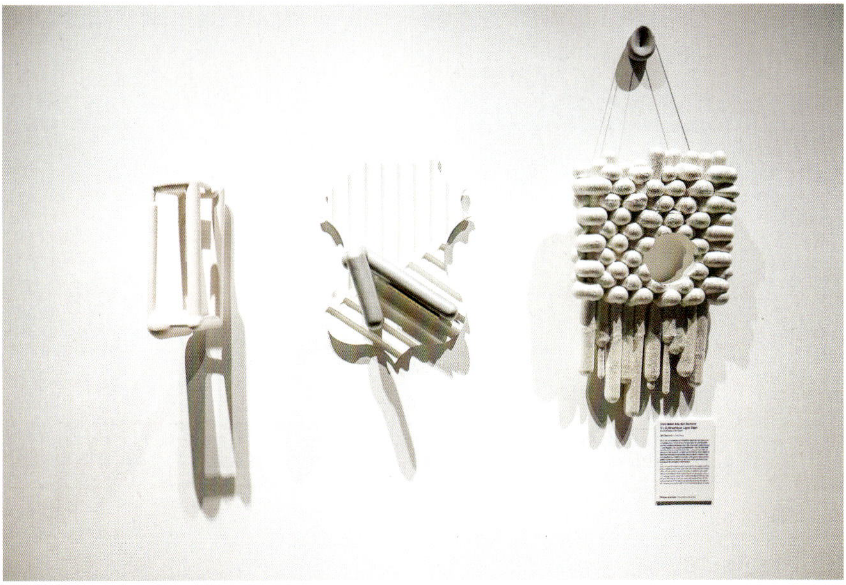

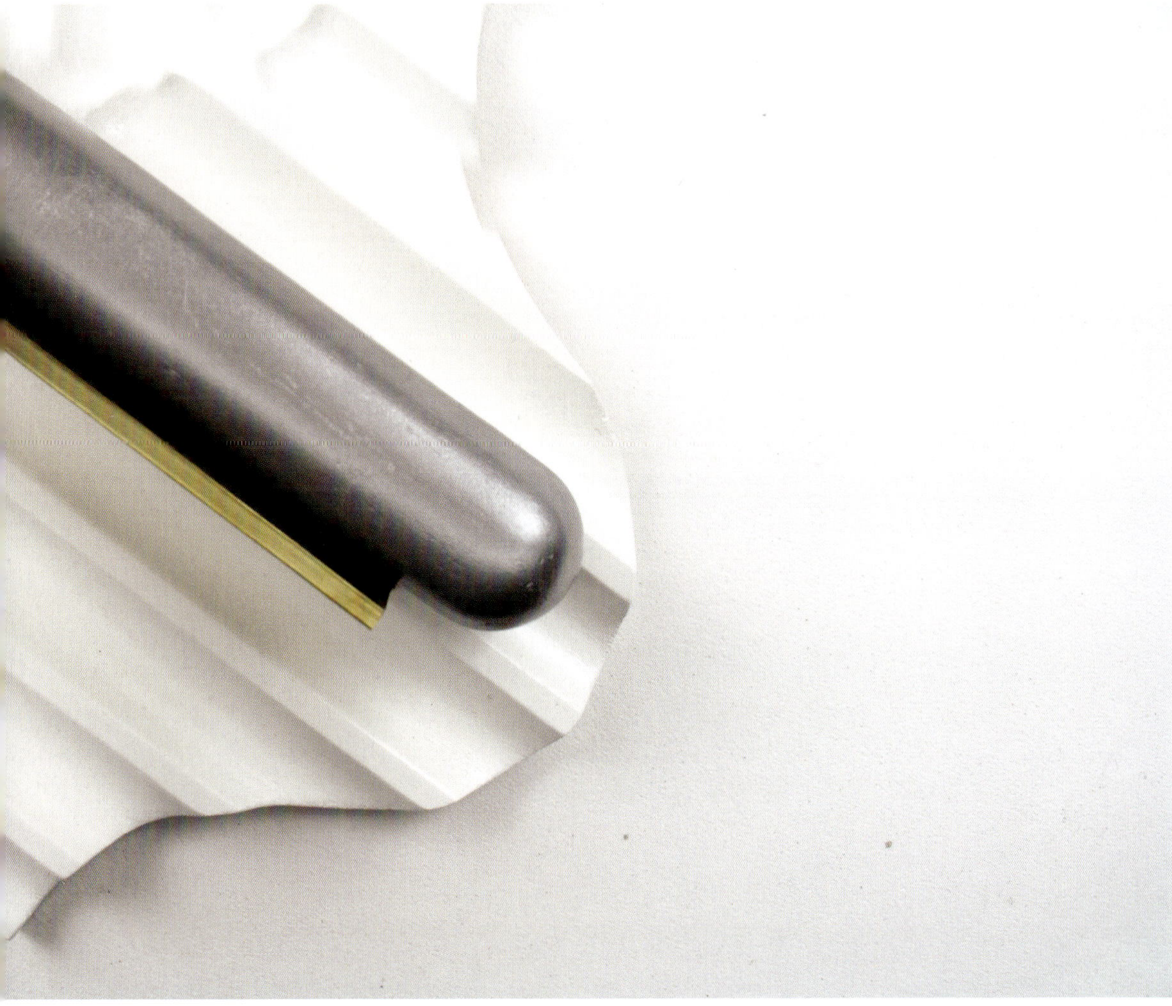

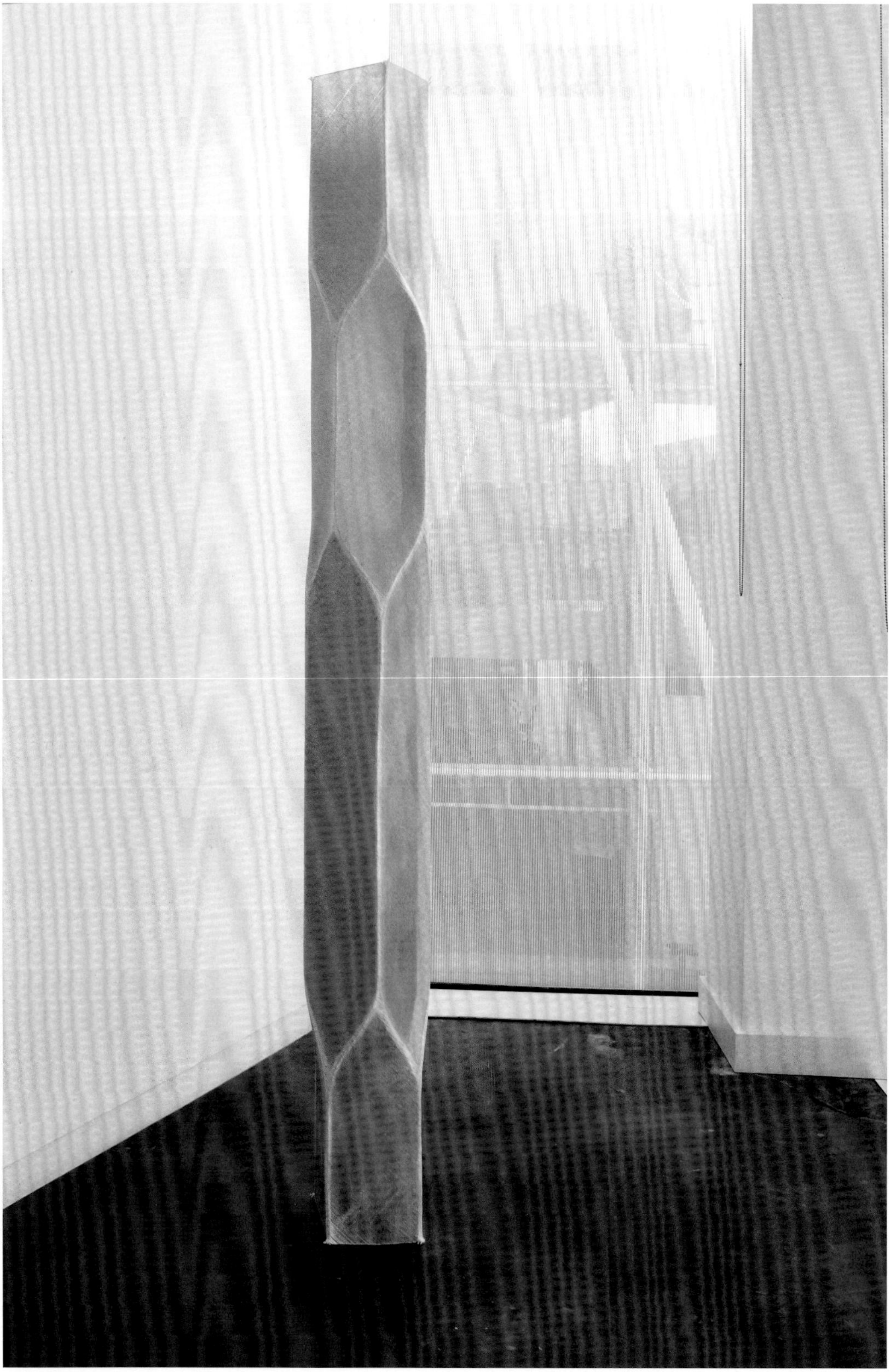

Folded column, Joseph Choma, Design Topology Lab, Clemson University, 2018, United States

United States architect and computational designer Joseph Choma's work explores mathematical approaches to the generation of architectural form, and to its material production. In this folded column, a geometric folding pattern transforms a thin fiberglass surface into a self-standing architectural element. The photograph below illustrates a preparatory paper prototype.

Folded fiber-reinforced-polymer
6 x 6 x 96 in (15.2 x 15.2 x 243.8 cm)
Courtesy of the artist

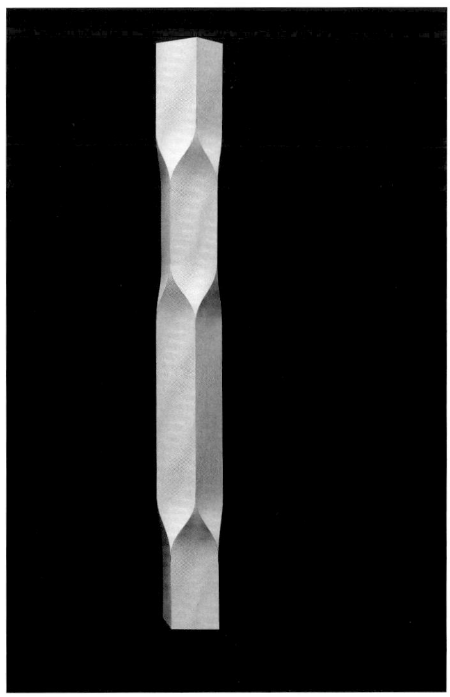

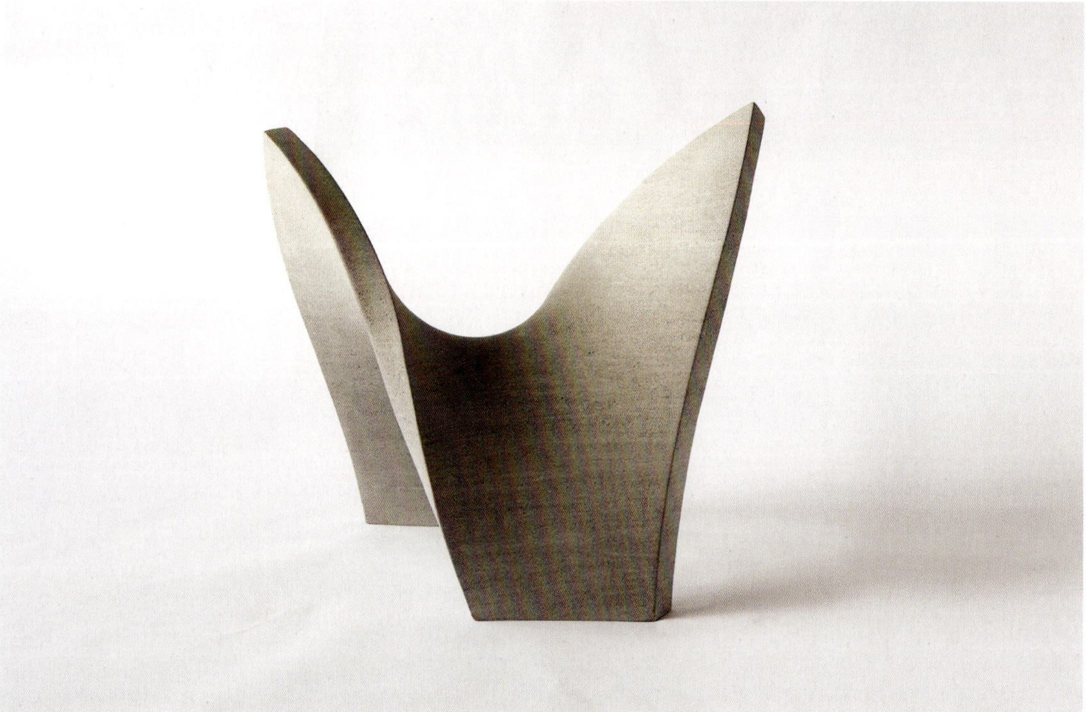

Untitled, Joseph Choma, Design Topology Lab, Clemson University, 2016, United States

Joseph Choma collaborated with the Wisconsin-based company Quarra Stone to robotically fabricate a full-scale physical mock-up of a portion of a sculpture whose shape is defined by the following equation:

$\{ (u,v) \mid (9/4)PI \leq u \leq (15/4)PI, PI \leq v \leq (7/4)PI \}$

$x = u(\sin(u+v)\cos(u)); \; y = u(\sin(u+v)\sin(u)); \; z = v(\cos(u+v))$

Robotically-carved Indiana Limestone
Quarra Stone, fabricator
29 x 19 x 15 in (73.6 x 48.3 x 38.1 cm)
Showcased at the Miller ICA exhibition
Courtesy of the artist

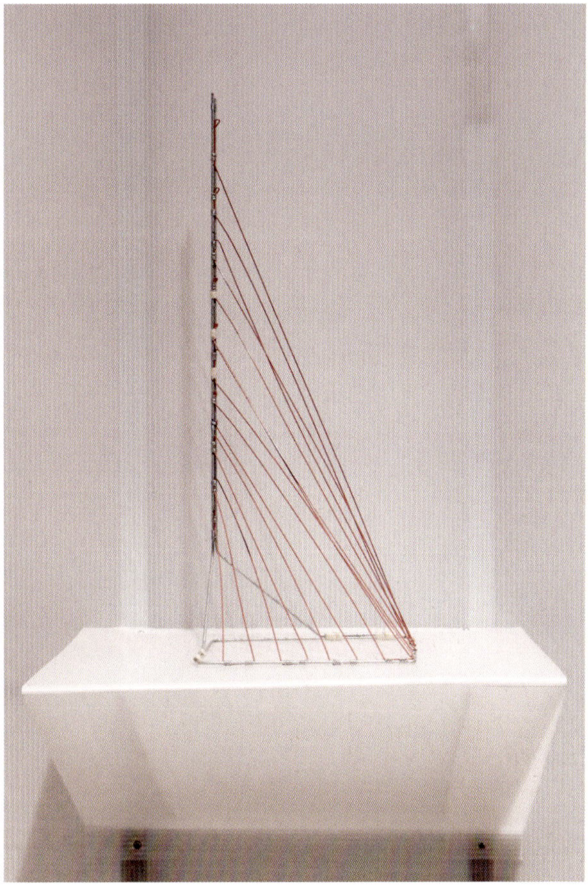

Sympoesis and Explode, Vernelle Noel, 2021, United States

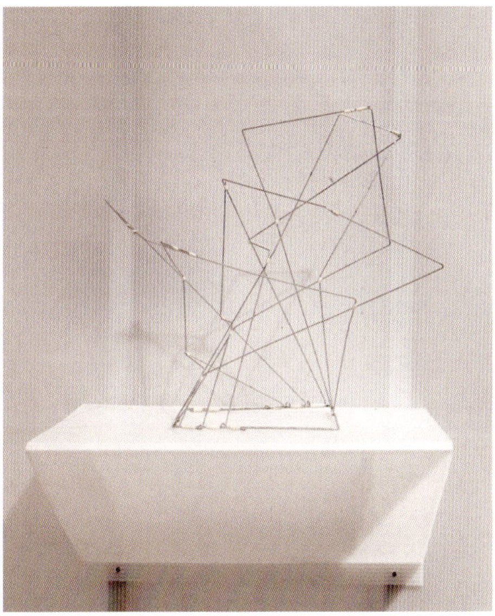

United States-based Trinidadian and Tobagonian architect and computational designer Vernelle Noel combines ethnographic, design, and computational methods to investigate and creatively reimagine craft traditions. Drawing from her study of the craft of wire-bending in the Trinidad carnival, Noel develops a language of material and architectural articulation that results in artifacts that seem both pliable and robust; deeply personal and yet evocative of long-standing material and design cultures. Inspired by Donna Haraway's notion of sympoiesis as "making with others," Noel's pieces draw from and computationally extend a craft tradition.

Bent wire sculptures
18 x 13 x 17 in (45.7 x 33 x 43.1 cm) closed, each
Courtesy of the artist

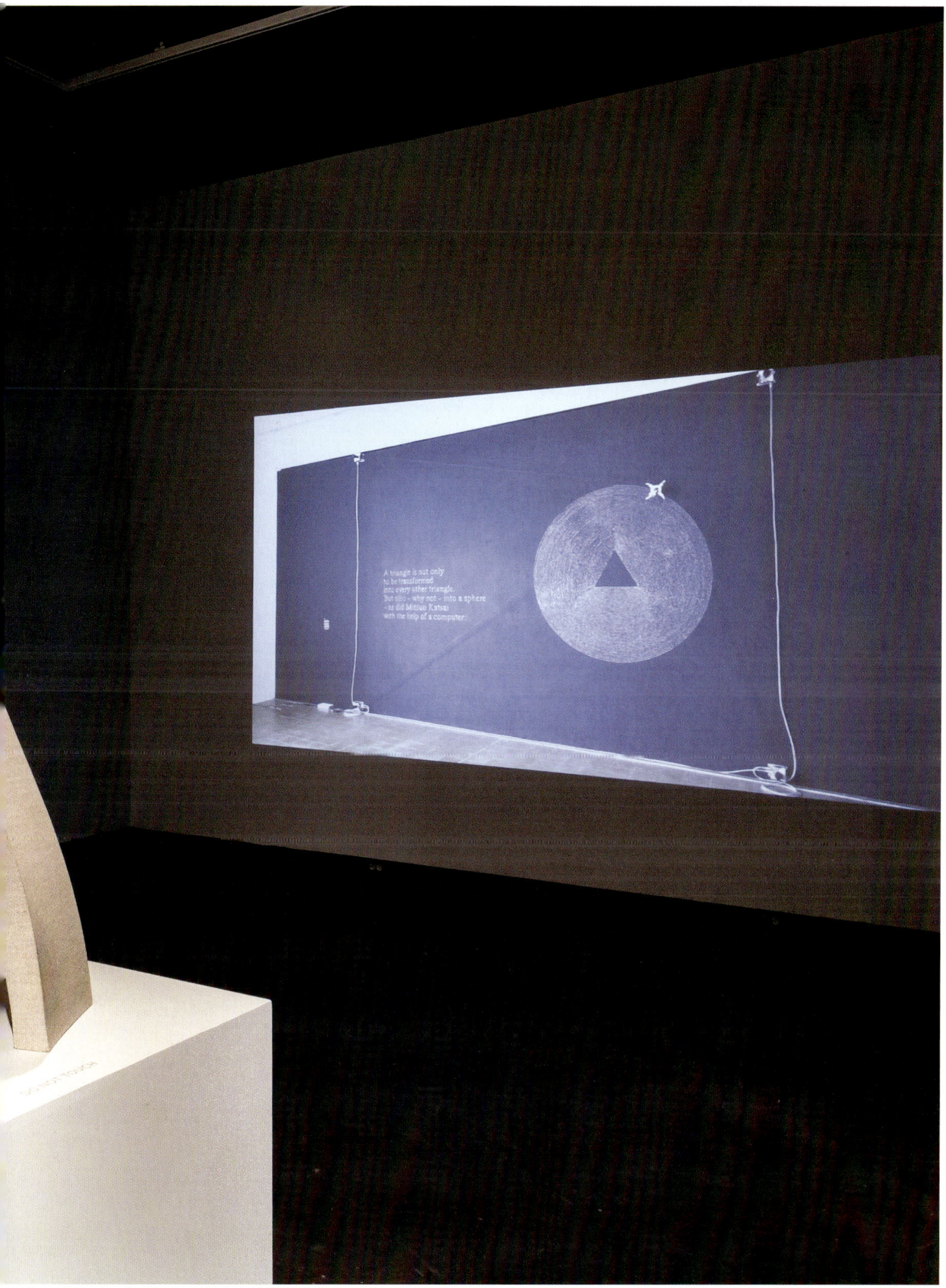
A triangle is not only
to be transformed
into every other triangle.
But also – why not – into a sphere
– as did Mitsuo Katsui
with the help of a computer.
DO NOT TOUCH

Clickspace Time-lapse Drawing Machine, Jonah Marrs, 2015, Canada

Canadian artist and computational designer Jonah Marrs created a custom plotter that he used to print a series of drawings of landmark architectural plans. During printing, he disrupted the process at regular intervals by manually pulling the paper strip. As a result, the drawings show each individual element separated from the rest, revealing the internal order of the image file. The resulting drawings are disjointed and yet recognizable. They evoke the architectural objects while at the same time forcing us to see the usually invisible memory storage and data structures underlying their computational representation.

Custom CNC Plotter built with two CD drives, printing calculator, laptop DVD drive, G-Code, CAM-Software, paper reel, Arduino board, 3x Easy stepper motor drivers, graph paper, pen, acrylic, wire
4.8x 3.5 x 8 in (12 x 8.9 x 20.3 cm)
Showcased at the Miller ICA exhibition
Courtesy of the artist

Clickspace Drawing Series A: O. M. Ungers Marburg Axonometric Time-lapse, Jonah Marrs, 2015, Canada

Custom drawing machine, G-Code, CAM-Software, X-Acto knife, graph paper, 0.1 Micron pen
Seven 2 x 20 in (5 x 50 cm) strips
Showcased at the Miller ICA exhibition
Courtesy of the artist

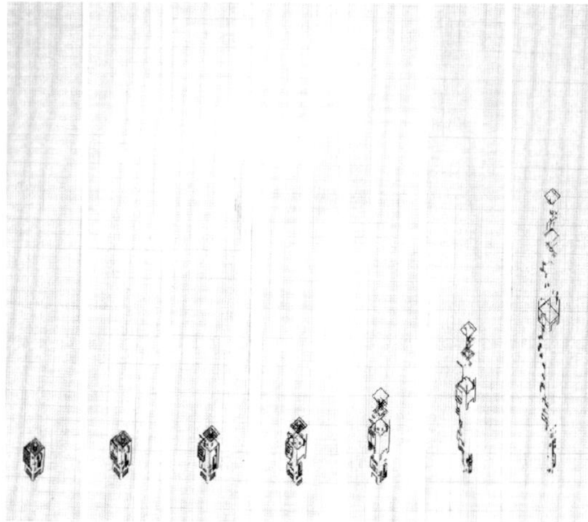

Clickspace Drawing Series D: Villa Savoye Axonometric Time-lapse (top), *Clickspace Drawing Series C: Time-lapse Iconic Plans* (bottom), Jonah Marrs, 2015, Canada

Custom drawing machine, G-Code, CAM-Software, X-Acto knife, graph paper, 0.1 Micron pen
Eight 2 x 20 in (5 x 50 cm) strips
Showcased at the Miller ICA exhibition
Courtesy of the artist

Architectone informatique, Nicolas Reeves, NXI GESTATIO, Université du Québec à Montréal, 2009, Canada

Created by Montreal-based architect and physicist Nicolas Reeves together with his research-creation lab NXI GESTATIO, this architectural sculpture was created by algorithmically analyzing the melody of a traditional song. It illustrates how data processing allows the same data structure to inform different kinds of media. In this case, the same data shapes both an architectural assembly in space and a musical sequence in time. The sculpture, made by stereolithography, uses translucent resins to reveal the object's internal anatomy.

Stereolithography sculpture and audio speaker
15.7 x 15.7 x 47.2 in (40 x 40 x 120 cm)
Courtesy of the artist

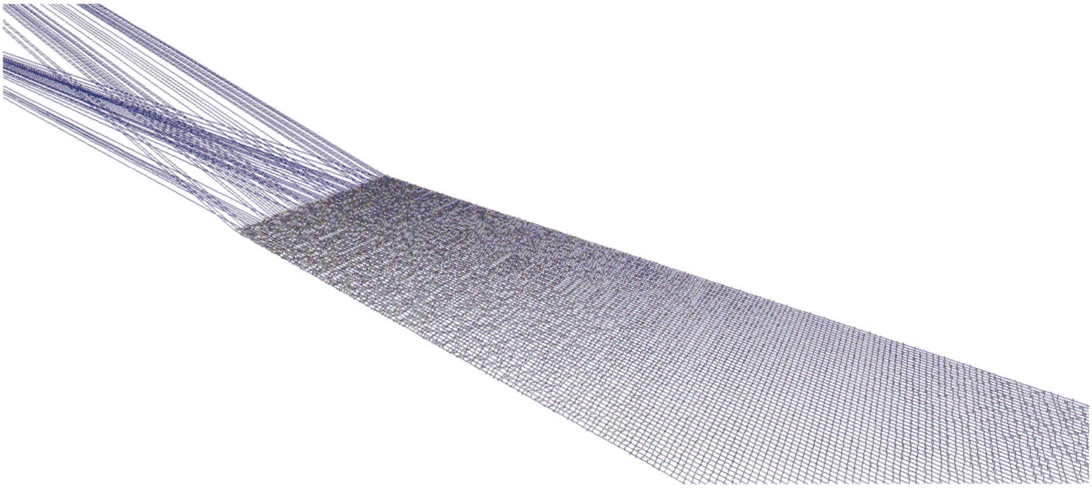

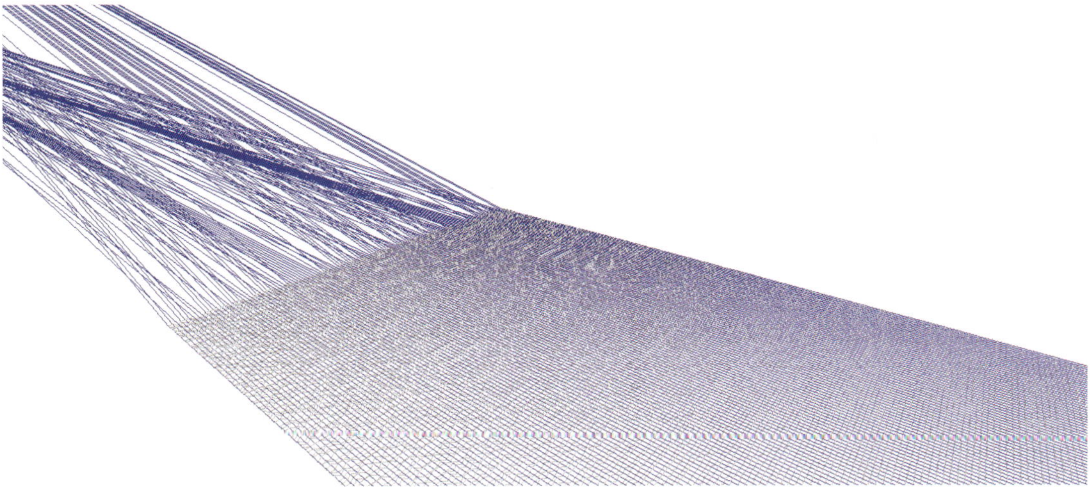

Infinite Weft, Jer Thorp and Diane Thorp, 2012, Canada

A collaboration between New York-based Canadian artist Jer Thorp and his mother Diane Thorp, this piece is a commentary on programming's historical relationship with the Jacquard loom, an intellectual expedition on the mathematics of weaving, and a reflection on textiles as digital objects. *Infinite Weft* explores textile patterns emerging from binary weaving patterns, or "drawdowns," through a software loom. This loom simulator operates on the basis of non-repeating cellular automata drawn from the work of late computer scientist and Bell Labs programmer Ralph Griswold to generate an infinite, unpredictable textile pattern. The carpet on display, handwoven by Diane Thorp, renders material a fraction of this infinite digital pattern.

Fabric and software
250 x 18 in (635 x 45.7 cm)
Courtesy of the artists

(*Infinite weft* pictured on following page)

Binary Image, Visual Latency

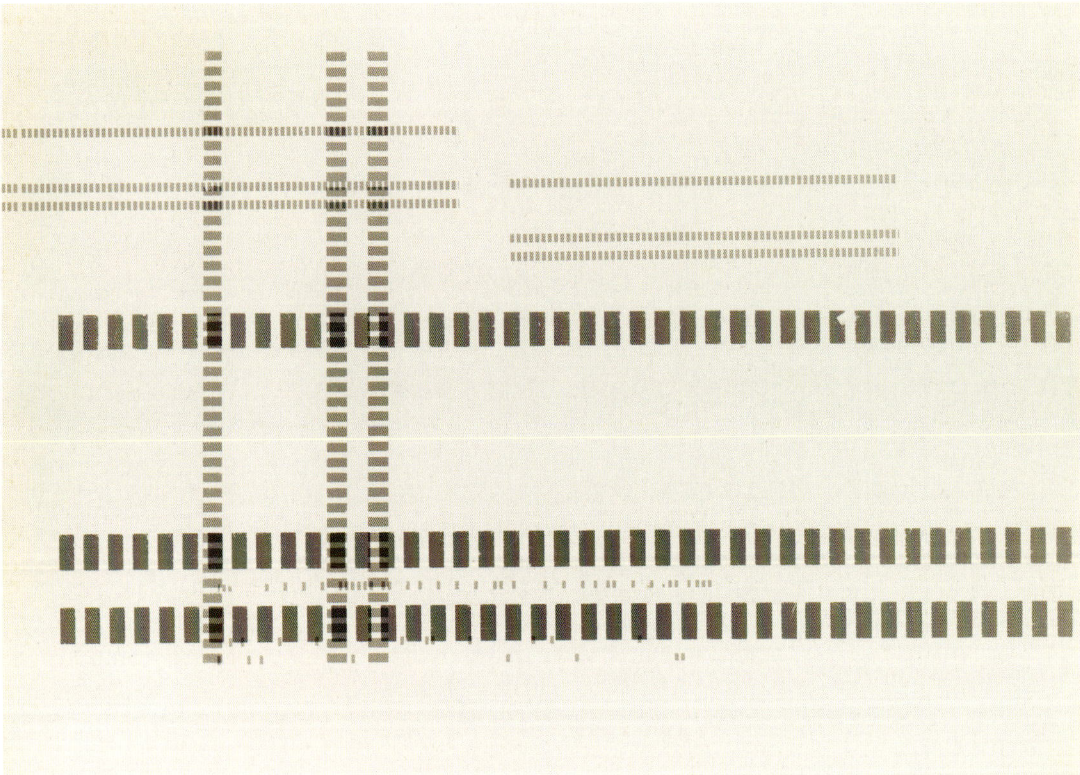

Geraldo de Barros (1923–1998). *Fotoforma*, São Paulo. 1949. Gelatin silver print, 11.8 x 15.1" (30 x 38.4 cm). Acquired through the generosity of John and Lisa Pritzker. Digital Image © The Museum of Modern Art/Licensed by SCALA / Art Resource, NY. © Fabiana de Barros.

Andrés Burbano

Fotoformas is an eclectic collection of experimental photographs produced by Brazilian artist Geraldo de Barros (1923–1998) between 1949 and 1953; even though they all are considered landmarks of experimental photography today, the one featured here is extraordinary. This *Fotoforma* is 30 by 38 centimeters, it has a landscape orientation, and displays a series of black-and-white horizontal and vertical lines; eleven horizontal, and three vertical; each line is not continuous but made out of small rectangles; the rectangles, and therefore the lines, change from tiny to medium size, displaying a grid-like composition. It is an abstract geometric structure made out of a single element, a rectangle. It is an early attempt to transform the binary bit into a primary visual unity, a predecessor of the pixel; this kind of work is rarely seen in experimental photography, indicating a non-optical, camera-less, photographic approach.

What makes a digital image? When confronted with the early history of computer graphics and computational images, we need to deconstruct our preconceptions about instructions, displays, and screens. For example, an inquiry into the earliest generation of computer artists including Vera Molnar, Frieder Nake, Ernest Edmonds, or Waldemar Cordeiro reveals that, in some instances, they created images without seeing them as most computers at the time didn't have screens. These artists needed to understand the machine's operations, the languages to program them, and the algorithms they wanted to implement. They also needed to understand the process of punching their code into cards to control plotters such as the Z64 or the CalComp. In numerous cases, the first time artists saw the images was when those were printed; the entire previous process was abstract. We still don't have a vocabulary to refer to such practices; the closest I can think of is the status of the image while developing an analog photograph when the sensitive paper is exposed to the light, but the chemicals haven't yet touched it. There is an image, but it is invisible: it is a latent image.

A profound examination of algorithmic machines to create images occasionally brings to light earlier examples than the ones of the artists mentioned above. That is the case Geraldo de Barros, who produced the *Fotoformas*. The *Fotoformas* are gelatin silver prints; which was a widely used black-and-white high-quality photography technique at that time; in such a process, a negative image is transferred to a light-sensitive paper constituted of different layers: a paper substrate; an opaque coating of gelatin and barium sulfate hosting the unevenly distributed silver dots of the photographic image; and finally a gelatin cover. The series, a collection of more than seventy photographic experiments, is evidence of Barros's unlimited creativity in every aspect of the photographic process in framing, exploring the camera's qualities, and the double exposure. However, the most compelling and original results were obtained in the darkroom: for instance, by superimposing negatives, drawing over already exposed 6-by-6-inch negatives, scratching and cutting them, or editing them in a physical copy-and-paste process. Today, looking at the Barros negatives is as surprising as seeing the photographic results; the negatives are a stamp of an artist focusing on the materiality of the photographic process.

After examining the relationship between the photographs and the corresponding negatives of the *Fotoformas* series, a mystery is revealed: some pictures have no negatives, the negatives are lost, vanished, or even more, the negatives did not exist. Is that even possible? The first clues to decipher the situation are in the photographic images themselves. Those seven *Fotoformas* that feature multiple sequences of quadrilaterals are examples of non-figurative photography that resembles — or rather anticipates — some of the experiments of the early computer graphics from the 1960s and '70s. At the time Geraldo de Barros produced these photos, he was working part-time at Banco do Brasil, one of the most important banks in the country. Curious as he was of the material culture around him, he started to explore the machinery that facilitated the operation of the bank's transactions, discovering the tabulator machines that the institution acquired — the kind of devices that predate the arrival of the digital computers. Tabulators already stored information and data in punched cards, the same cards used by commercial computers later on. They stored data in the digital format, zeroes are filled rectangles and ones are empty ones. Barros brought them to his studio, then he decided to incorporate the punched cards in his creative process. He took them to the darkroom and replaced the photographic negative with the punched cards in the enlarger; the repetitive sequence of holes projected on the paper with a sensitive coat gave result to an uncommon geometric visual result. Barros didn't stop there: he made multiple impressions on the same paper, changing the distance and the direction of the punched cards, creating a set of abstract photos of refined elaboration. These images are the latent image of the digital image.

I hope the reader will indulge me in venturing to a risky conclusion. Following recent scholarship about the presence of the urban environment in the entire *Fotoformas* series,[1] we can say that the ones made with the punched cards with their rhythmic lines and patterns also depict a city, in fact, one city, the beautiful, chaotic and enigmatic: São Paulo. The South American metropolis lives in these proto computational visual pictures like New York lives in the *Boogie-Woogie* by Mondrian.

1 Danielle Stewart. 2018. "Geraldo de Barros: Photography as Construction." *H-ART. Revista de historia, teoría y crítica de arte*, March. https://doi.org/10.25025/hart02.2018.04.

The Manufacturing Hand: Tactility and Abstraction in Robotics

Emek Erdolu

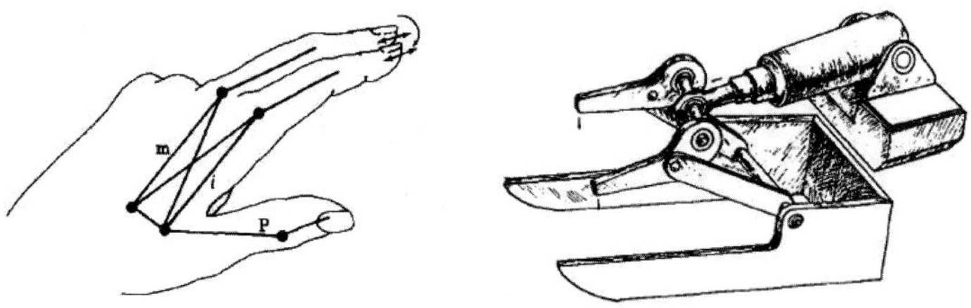

The three-fingered grip (left) and the three-fingered gripper combining the three-fingered and wrap-around grips (right). Reprinted from *Robotics and Computer-Integrated Manufacturing*, Volume 2, Issue 1, Paul K. Wright, "A Manufacturing Hand," Pages 13–23, 1985, with permission from Elsevier.

A diagram in a 1985 paper on robotics depicts a tripod-shaped configuration of a thumb, index, and middle fingers.[1] This "three-fingered tripod" grip, the author tells us, enables gentle and dexterous moves such as those used in domestic tasks, but not stiff and powerful ones, such as squeezing a bolt with a wrench. Those moves require a "wrap-around" grip involving the palm and all five fingers. This full-hand configuration increases power but degrades the move's precision and dexterity. "The manufacturing hand," the robotic gripper developed by the paper's author — Paul K. Wright and his team at the Robotics Institute at Carnegie Mellon University — aimed at combining the dexterity and power of these two grips. Illustrated side by side, the diagram hand and the manufacturing hand display a fascinating rematerialization of the fingers into their mechanical equivalents.

Embedded in these illustrations is a notion of tactility situated in between a poetic description and an abstract representation. When Wright published the paper in 1985, he was a mechanical engineering professor at the Robotics Institute. At the forefront of robotics research at the time, work at the Institute included a number of key manufacturing automation systems such as an autonomous machining line being developed for Westinghouse Corporation. Wright's team in the Institute's Flexible Manufacturing Laboratory developed the manufacturing hand as part of this broader effort. Two years before the paper presented the manufacturing hand to a wider audience, Wright had introduced the gripper in an internal report with the same title.[2] Interestingly, Wright starts his report with a passage from French art historian Henri Focillon:

> *Perception of the world requires a sort of tactile flair ... Surface, volume, density, and weight are not optical phenomena. It is in the hollow of the palm and between the fingers that man instantly assesses these characteristics. Space is not gauged by sight, but rather by hand and foot which impart an indefinable appreciation and without which recognition remains like a delightful landscape of a dark chamber; inconsistent, flat, elusive and chimerical ...*[3]

Focillon's evocative lines describe the human hand as a unique natural instrument connecting the artist to the physicality of the world. It is only through touch and tactile signals that the artist can go beyond the sight of objects, and begin to sense, comprehend, and learn about their physical properties and existence.

1 Paul K Wright. "A Manufacturing Hand." *Robotics and Computer-Integrated Manufacturing,* 2(1) (1985): 13–23.

2 Paul K Wright. "A Manufacturing Hand." *The Robotics Institute 1983 Annual Research Review,* Carnegie Mellon University (1983): 21–31.

3 Focillon's quote is a translation of a passage from: Henri Focillon. "Éloge de la Main [1934]." *Vie des Formes, Suivi de Éloge de la Main,* Presses Universitaires de France (1943): 101–128.

Wright sees this sensorial skill, which Focillon poetically describes and sees as intrinsic to art, also as intrinsic to craftsmanship in a factory. "This subtle relationship between a man and his mechanical surroundings," he says later in the report to carry Focillon's depiction — of the artist's tactile relationship with its surroundings — into manufacturing. According to Wright, this subtle relationship existing in manufacturing had often been "overlooked," while focusing on the software of the machining line Westinghouse and the Institute envisioned. To be "truly unmanned," the system's mechanical components, the computer-controlled arm and its "mechanical hand," which could together simulate the relationship between a worker and its surroundings, were critical. To simulate that relationship, finding the hand's optimized form suited to machining tasks was a key problem.

To search for the optimized form, Wright's team studied the human hand and prehension. They reimagined the hand as a mechanical device and represented the thumb, index, and middle fingers with force vectors. This abstraction enabled them to calculate the force — applied by these fingers to a surface — relative to various positioning of fingers, and thereby evaluate different grip forms in terms of their grip performance. They evaluated the grip performance based on the calculations of grip stiffness and maximum grip force. These operations helped them to reach the final three-fingered form that enabled the manufacturing hand's optimized grip performance. Ultimately, computation of the human hand's motions and of the effect of its touch helped develop the robotic hand's ability to hold twisted shapes with dexterity and without losing power.

The image of the human and the manufacturing hands reminds us that robotics is never only about the robotic devices or the speculative futures they elicit. The field also involves conceptions of skill that inform the technological design of these devices. In the manufacturing hand project, the notion of tactility exists at the intersection of literature, mechanical engineering, and computing; both as a poetic description taken from a literary reference, and a human skill decomposed, represented, computed, and emulated within a mechanical design problem space. The abstract numeric representation allows the researchers to formalize and measure the tactile effects of human grip, and accordingly shape the manufacturing hand's formal and mechanical properties to emulate those effects. Whereas the poetic description becomes a rhetorical device helping to explain that emulation along with its significance for achieving manufacturing automation.

Tracing such conceptions of skill in robotics may help shed new light on the making of robotic technologies. In the manufacturing hand project, such tracing allows us to see how abstraction brings the human and the robotic hands together into a Cartesian world, where their formal and performative qualities become comparable. It allows us to see how abstraction enables a translation of the tactile effects of human grip into those of a robotic gripper. The image is thus emblematic of that abstraction and anthropomorphic translation that underlie the manufacturing hand in the 1980s and, perhaps, many other robotic technologies designed since then.

Olympic Calculations

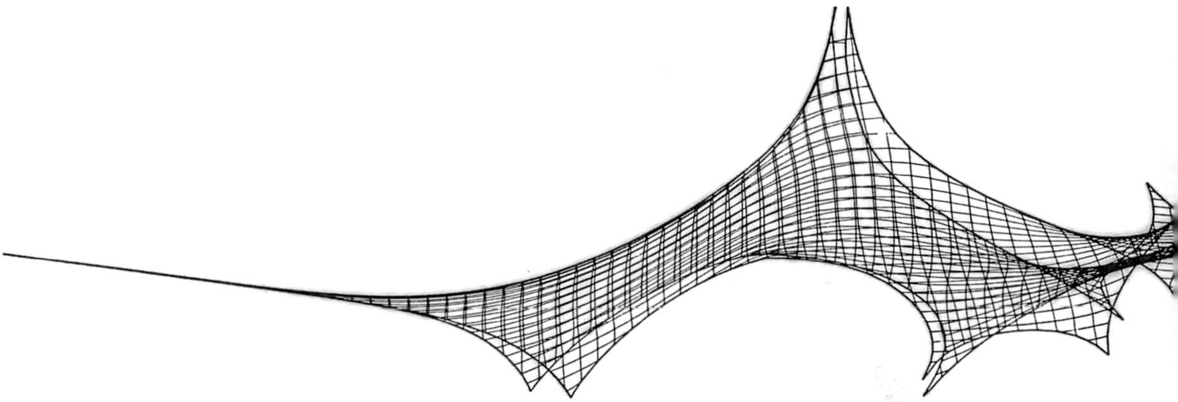

Sean Keller

Computed model of the main entry section of the 1972 Munich Olympic complex, University of Stuttgart, c. 1970. Source: *Zodiac* 21 (1972). Printed with permission from the Institute of Lightweight Structures and Conceptual Design (ILEK), University of Stuttgart.

While, tragically, the 1972 Olympic Games in Munich are now mainly remembered as the site of a terrorist attack, they were also the occasion for a milestone composition of architecture, engineering, and landscape that became a permanent addition to the city. Designed by the firm of Günter Behnisch, this ensemble centers around a 75,000-square-meter prestressed cable net roof covering the main stadium, gymnasium, and aquatics center. Seen here is a plot from a computational model of the highly sculptural main entry section of the roof. Designed and built on an extremely tight schedule, the novel structure was realized through a hybrid design process in which elaborate physical models and new computational techniques — developed by two separate research groups — were used side-by-side to arrive at the final form and specifications of the roof. Ultimately, three-quarters of the roof were built directly from computational models, marking a major inflection point in the history of architecture as physical models gave way to computational design methods.

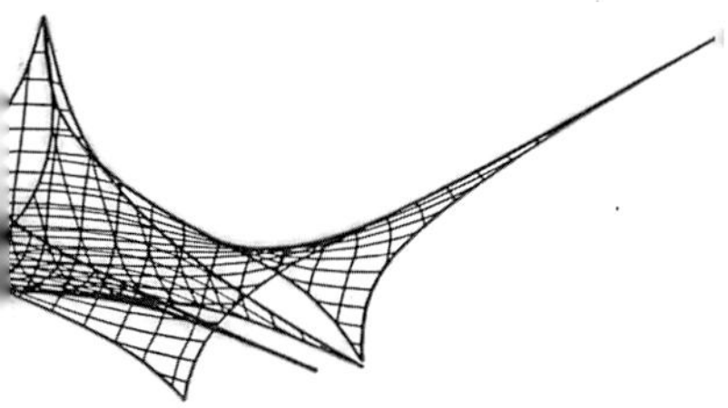

In contrast to the rather casual competition model presented by Behnisch — who had no experience designing tensile roofs — the tensile net system actually presented enormous technical challenges. The roof takes the form of an opposed double-curved — or "anticlastic" — surface so that at any point local curvatures are near-zero. This allows the cables forming the surface to be placed under great tension and become rigid without deformation or shearing. Also, while the Munich roof's varied shape and its system of clamped cables suggest a flexible assembly system, the interdependence of elements in the net and the tensioning which relies on highly precise cable lengths make the construction system more demanding than most others. Yet, while anticlastic surfaces have strict requirements, they do not, except in the simplest cases, have elegant mathematical solutions. Given the ubiquity of complex digital models today, it may be difficult to appreciate the challenge that the Munich roof geometry presented: its form was irregular in three dimensions, incalculable by hand, and yet needed to be absolutely precise. The coordinates defining the roof surface had to be located literally "in thin air." This image represents the culmination of one path to solving this dilemma.

Behnisch's proposal was inspired by Frei Otto and Rolf Gutbrod's West German Pavilion for Expo '67 in Montreal. While Otto was not part of Behnisch's initial team, he eventually joined the sprawling group of architects and engineers working on the Olympic site. Expanding on the processes they had used for Montreal, Otto's Institute for Lightweight Structures at the University of Stuttgart created a host of sophisticated physical models of the roof. As he had for Montreal, Otto turned to Klaus Linkwitz, who headed the University's Institute for Geodesy (IFG), asking him to apply stereo photogrammetry to map the complex geometry of the Olympic roof. Linkwitz did this by treating a model of the roof like a miniature landscape (geodesy is the science of measuring and mapping the Earth). Spurred by the greater technical demands of the Munich project — ten times the size of the Montreal pavilion — Linkwitz's group then went on to produce entirely new research that quickly surpassed Otto's physical modeling techniques.

Hoping to leave the inaccuracies of the physical models behind, Linkwitz and the mathematician Hans-Jörg Schek began working on a "theoretically correct" computational model of the main stadium roof. Their approach was based on the fact that, in an idealized minimal surface net, forces of tension are equal throughout. Although the new computational model still began with an approximate form provided by the physical model, improvements to the geometry were then based on the underlying physics of the net. Mathematically, the problem was cumbersome and demanded electronic calculation. Improvements in the net geometry were made by making iterative adjustments using the method of least squares. The number of simultaneous equations needed was equal to three times the number of intersections in the net, which meant systems of equations with up to 8,000 unknowns. At the end of 1969, the IFG group started writing the computer code to solve these systems, working in Fortran and processing on the University of Stuttgart's CDC 6600, one of the most powerful mainframe computers available at the time: a 60-bit machine typically built with 128k of core memory.

The group's first successes came in early 1970. By fall of that year all nine sections of the stadium were calculated, and later all of the intermediate sections as well, including the entry to the complex shown here. Throughout the process physical plotting was the only form of graphic output available, much to the team's frustration. The final cutting and assembly of the cable net by Arge Stahlbau Dach was based directly on the computer-generated data, presented as large-scale plans and numerical tables — a process that included the computer-driven plotting of an incredible 3,000 square meters of 1:10 scaled construction drawings.

Remarkably, a second group of Stuttgart scientists were simultaneously pursuing yet another path for computational analysis of the proposed roof. John Argyris, who led the Institute for Statics and Dynamics of Aeronautical and Space Construction (ISD) at the University of Stuttgart, was a major figure in postwar engineering, most importantly as an originator of the Finite Element Method of analysis. Having already more than a decade of experience with related engineering problems, Argyris and his research group also begin to collaborate on the Munich roof. The ISD computational method represented the cable net as a "stiffness-matrix" which was put through an iterative "relaxation process" that progressively improved the equilibrium of loads within the net, until reaching an acceptably small range of variation. Beginning with geometry provided by the IFG's survey, their model was able to reach an acceptable state of equilibrium in five iterations. Initially this took three hours of computing time but through improvements this was reduced to twenty minutes on the CDC 6600. Argyris's group would also eventually model all portions of the Munich roof.

In fact, the image shown is not decisively identified in publication, so it is unclear which of the two research groups produced it — an ambiguity that captures the hybridity of this complex design process (context suggests that it most likely came from the ISD group). The historical transition represented by this image is dramatic: the shift from an architectural design process based in physical modeling and drawing to one based on computational representation and form finding. We also see the emergence of a new "anticlastic aesthetic" of complexly curved surfaces that, a few decades later, would become a dominant mode for architectural icons around the globe — though here it remains constrained by a strong structural logic. Deploying early computers to solve a complex problem of geometry and physics, Linkwitz and Argyris helped create a new, and deeply computational, architecture.

Processing Models, Modeling Processes for the HfG Ulm ca. 1952

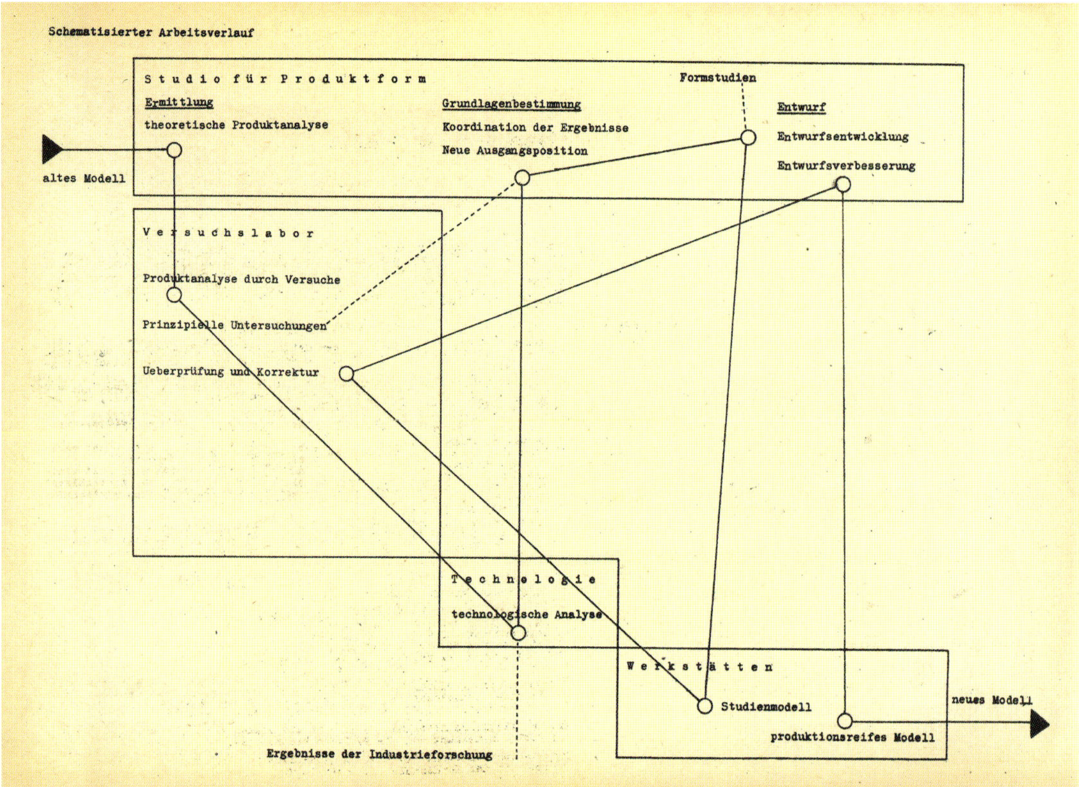

"Schematic work process" diagram from an information brochure of the Geschwister-Scholl Foundation, circa 1951. HfG-Archiv.

Anna-Maria Meister

In an undated brochure from the early days of the Hochschule für Gestaltung (HfG, 1953-1968) in Ulm, a diagram explains to both funding bodies and interested future students the intended ideal process for a product to be developed and shaped in the school.[1] The so-called "old model" ("altes Modell") — namely, the object of design prior to the optimization process prescribed by the diagram — enters the "studio for product form" ("Studio für Produktform") where it undergoes a theoretical analysis probing the assumptions and decisions that defined its shape. It is then handed over to the test center ("Versuchslabor"), where experiments and general testing ("Prinzipielle Untersuchungen") are performed. The next stage, headed simply "technology" ("Technologie") is followed by a return to the studio, where the results obtained thus far are coordinated and prior assumptions are redefined ("Grundlagenbestimmung") for a new "starting position" ("Ausgangsposition"). After a small detour into form studies, the "old model" moves to the workshops where a "study model" ("Studienmodell") is developed, then back to the test center, and again back into the studio. Here, as next to last step, design ("Entwurf") shapes the model before it gets produced as "serial ready model" ("Produktionsreifes Modell") in the workshops. The model then exits the process in its optimized state: as "new model" ("neues Modell"). Black text, lines, and arrows (both dotted and solid) on brown paper, this process is drawn as an unambiguous series of steps (each marked by a small circle connecting two lines) necessarily resulting in the new and improved version of anything that went into it. And while its makers might have thought of tea cups or roofing systems going through this process, the "model" referred to in the diagram applied to any project in any scale.

The HfG became famous for its neo-rationalist product design, which shaped West-Germany for decades long after the school on the hill outside of Ulm had closed its doors. It was also one of the first schools of design to introduce cybernetics to the curriculum, a move that many claim to have provoked the rift in its population between those who believed in the "good design" as the purpose of the school (such as Max Bill or Otl Aicher), and those who were researching processes and sought to automate that design ("Gestaltung"), such as Gui Bonsiepe, Tomás Maldonado, Horst Rittel and others.[2] For the latter, cybernetics then seemed to promise to finally remove the subject — and with it the subjective — from *Gestaltung* altogether. And yet, the school's founders had looked to program "good design" (after all, the school was at one point to be called "Institute for Good Form"[3]) before it even opened its door: a programming not

1 "Aktennotizen Frühzeit," Brochure ca. 1950, HfG-Archiv, Ulm.

2 For an excellent and detailed history of the political background of the HfG both before and after its founding see René Spitz, *Hfg Ulm: The View Behind the Foreground: The Political History of the Ulm School of Design, 1953-1968* (Stuttgart: Edition Axel Menges, 2002).

3 Note that "design" here is the translation of "Gestaltung," not the use of the English term, which was critically debated at the school. For the Institute's name see the notes on conversations between Scholl and Bill in Stuttgart in October 1951, specifically note 7.1951: Institute for "good form" as suggested model for the HfG. Aktennotizen Frühzeit - Ze AZ 6, HfG-Archive, Ulm.

through computer code, but through institutionalized processes and curricular definitions on paper.

In the history of science, three-dimensional models have recently gained new interest as instruments in the production and distribution of knowledge. As "models of the world" in the natural sciences they are studied in their role of staking claims, describing theories, and teaching scientific concepts.[4] At the HfG Ulm, however, the models that the students built were not models *of* the world, but models *for* the world. If "models were central [...] to projects of enlightenment,"[5] the HfG was a truly modern endeavor. When in the 1950s the notion of the model in the scientific sense entered architecture in a more concrete way through cybernetic processes, models became the placeholder for subjective choices — at the HfG neither as theoretical simulation of a projected reality nor as conventional architectural representation, but as physical objects undergoing feedback loop after feedback loop toward an ultimate, optimal form. Using procedures and techniques from disciplines such as the social sciences, computer science or engineering, the model now promised an objectively "good" result. This shift was precisely the source of a longstanding contention between two groups at the school: object-makers and the process-designers, both of which assigned a different role to the subject — the designer. In the former, the subject was necessary to take every decision, mold the shape towards the finished object. In the latter, the subject was needed to amalgamate and translate the tools from the sciences for their use in architecture. After that, the subject's role consisted of the channeling of input into the process that had been created. And yet, the subject was at the heart of the school's design process from its very conception: it was the German subject that was supposed to be educated by the model objects produced at the school, a redemocratization through design, funded by the US occupying forces, grounded in the history of the school's founders in architecture, design, and the resistance against the National-Socialist Regime.[6]

When we look at the drawing, the feedback loops in the model process sketched here were not electronic, digital or scripted — they were enacted design operations on a physical object traveling through several iterations of betterment. "Models" at the HfG oscillated between made object and conceptual method: from "working model" ("Arbeitsmodell") to "model project" ("Modellvorhaben") and back. Over the course of the existence of the school, the school's own approach of combining science, art and practice in one curriculum for design education became known as the "Ulm Model," which was equally (and adversarially) worked

4 Soraya de Chadarevian and Nick Hopwood, eds., *Models : The Third Dimension of Science*, Writing Science (Stanford, Calif: Stanford University Press, 2004), 2.

5 Ibid, 3.

6 It was through Max Bill and Otl Aicher that the direction of the school shifted from adult education to a design school; and Ilse Aicher-Scholl, director of the Volkshochschule (adult education center) in Ulm was the sister of Sophie and Christoph Scholl, the siblings who were members of the resistance group Weiße Rose who were both executed by the National-Socialist Regime in 1943.

7 The term "Ulm model" was used by several of the school's protagonists, not always in agreement. See Otl Aicher, "Die Hochschule für Gestaltung. Neun Stufen ihrer Entwicklung" in *Archithese* 15/ 1975, 12–18; for the discussion of the different perceptions see René Spitz, *Hfg Ulm: The View Behind the Foreground: The Political History of the Ulm School of Design, 1953-1968* (Stuttgart: Edition Axel Menges, 2002), 21-23.

8 German Text: "In diesem Sinn ist die Schule als Modell aufzufassen für den Versuch, die geistige und moralische Krise unserer Zeit zu überwinden." See "Aktennotizen Frühzeit," Brochure ca. 1950, HfG-Archiv, Ulm.

9 *Ulm*. Zeitschrift der Hochschule für Gestaltung, Ulm, issues 6-21, 1958-1968.

and reworked in ever-more meetings and committees toward its optimal form.[7] At the HfG, models were a task and a process toward moral betterment, even for the institution itself. In the same brochure, a few pages after the model process shown in the figure, the school described its own role as that of a "model," not just for design education, but for an approach to overcome the nation's immediate past: "In that sense the school is to be understood as model for the attempt to overcome the spiritual and moral crisis of our time."[8]

If we take the model process outlined above seriously, we might take its mechanics literally straight from the page: not as metaphor for abstract programming, but as a material-testing sequence. Told this way, the story of the model at Ulm is not one of dematerialization away from an analog-material predecessor; neither is it a story of theoretical abstraction of the model concept. Rather, the *physical* model going through the *physical* feedback loops already eagerly performed the scaleless universality of the theoretical one. Looking at the photographs of early models produced at the school, we see them portrayed removed from context, shedding all particularities of size or scale. Still very much material, one might say retrospectively that it was in fact those models who rehearsed physically *and* formally the process of being designed — for any object (or subject) going through that process at Ulm. The elaborate scheme in the figure was neither a curricular diagram (which can be found a few pages earlier in the brochure), nor an aesthetic declaration (as the ones made on the pages of the school's magazine *ulm*).[9] Rather, what was fixed on paper was the attempt to model a process: one not limited to artifacts or buildings, but one that ultimately included students and teachers — even society at large.

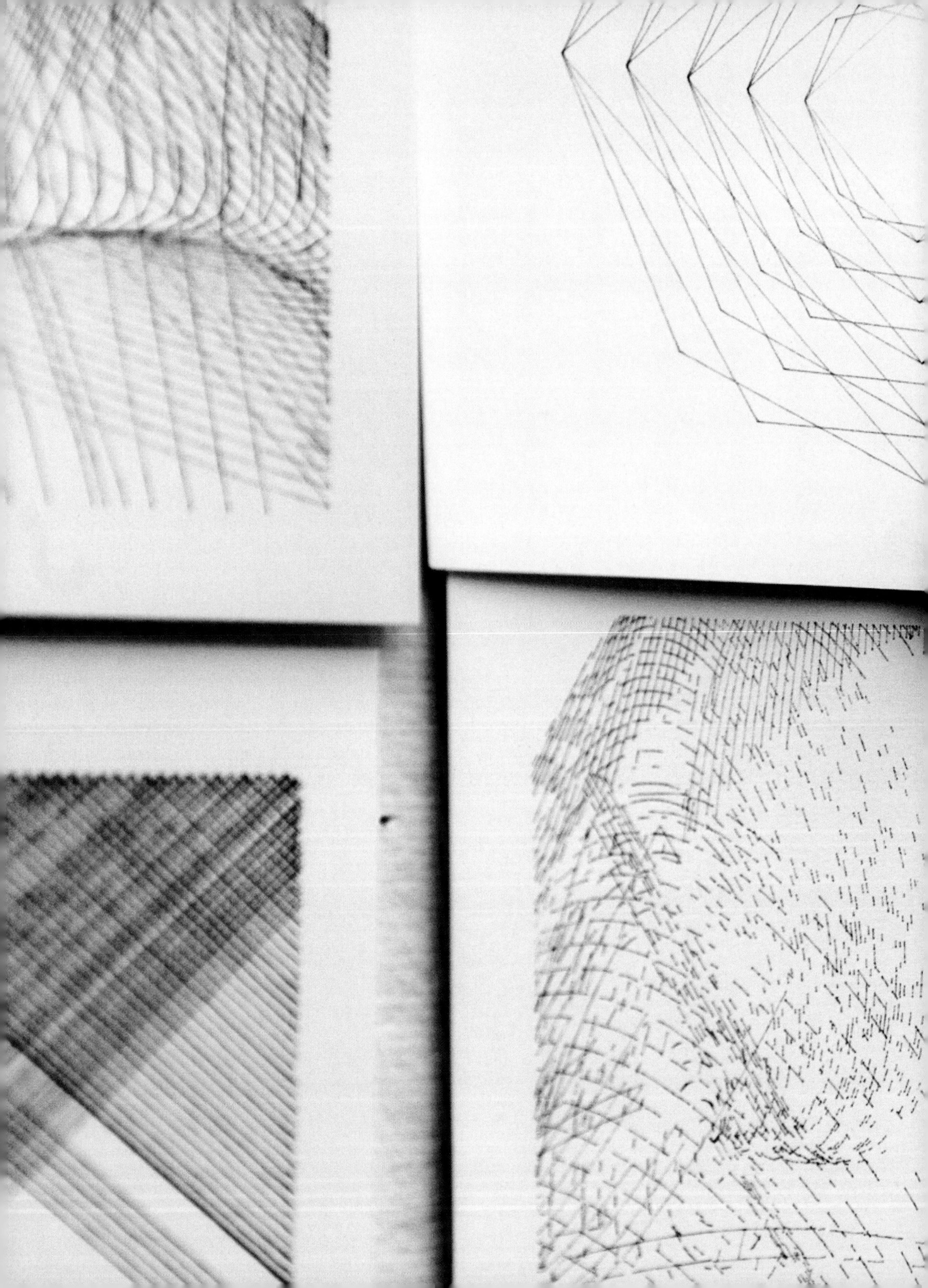

Unsmooth Images: A Conversation about the Materialities of Computational Design

Kristy Balliet
Jonah Marrs
Sean Keller
Nathalie Bredella

Moderated by
Molly Wright Steenson

MOLLY WRIGHT STEENSON: First of all thank you all for four fantastic presentations.[1] I've been heartedly scribbling as they went along, trying to capture dynamics that give us a chance to put everybody in more direct dialogue with each other. You all showed beautiful images, work, artifacts, and there is so much to dig into.[2] One comment I had for Jonah, and this was just something that I was looking at in preparation for the discussion today, is about the notion of an index, which you use to describe your work. I went back and looked at what "index" has actually meant at various points in time. It's first used in the fourteenth century to refer to the index finger. By the sixteenth century it means a wooden pointer which serves to direct or point to a particular fact or a conclusion — a guiding principle. Around the same time, "index" also started to be used to refer to a sign, or a token, of something. And then in 1962, it came to mean a reference to a specific record of a file, including information about its address. It's one of many terms that came into computing from different fields. And 1962 was also a big year for that, as that's the year when architecture starts referring to computing as well. So I wanted to put that word into play a little bit. But I also find myself working back and forth between a

1 The CD-PHI symposium presentations can be viewed in http://lattice.space.

2 Panel discussion at the Computational Design: Practices, Histories, Infrastructures Symposium (Edited for length and clarity), Carnegie Mellon University, October 2017

number of concerns that everybody was talking about. In particular, the relationship between modeling and drawing — not just as techniques, but as epistemologies and worldviews. A notion of lines and objects. A notion of *hinges*, to use Sean's term. Something becomes a hinge for something *else*. And a question of scale, when something is pushed to have a certain scale where it begins and ends — where a line begins and ends, when you inhabit lines.

In Nathalie's presentation, I was really struck by watching the line drawing, the CAD drawing, and then seeing the images of the ellipses. It's a strange moment of back and forth, and I see some points where you, Nathalie, and Kristy are in dialogue with each other. And then, finally, a question of representation. Architects have lately been very uneasy with the word representation. They have been preferring visualization to the extent that Yale has replaced its four-semester drawing course with a four-semester visualization course. Columbia teaches history of visualization, not representation. Architects always like to talk about a crisis. And maybe we could suggest that if there is indeed a crisis, maybe now there's a crisis of visualization, because I think we've come back to representation in some beautiful ways here. So I want to start by asking Kristy and Nathalie to do something maybe a little bit unusual, which is to comment on the notions of drawing, modeling, and the line in each other's work. You'll notice there are microphones right next to you.

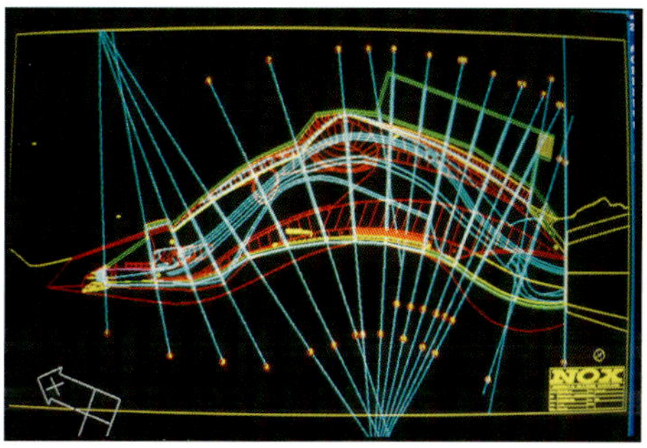

A 1997 CAD drawing depicting the H2Oexpo in Neeltje Jans, Netherlands, by NOX, an architectural firm headed by Lars Spuybroek. ARCH283205. Lars Spuybroek Fonds, Canadian Centre for Architecture, Gift of Lars Spuybroek.

KRISTY BALLIET: Not knowing that I was going to respond to Nathalie necessarily, I also took note of the ellipse — of its ambitions about construction and also its limitations relative to that specific moment in software's historical development. And it's uncanny how this links to conversations about the ellipse and the circle happening in my office for different reasons. What I tried to hint at in my brief presentation is that there is a constant dialogue in my office between Kelly and myself, about the profile of architecture — things that are crisp and legible, with clear references. She would find herself in the camp of the circle, the shape, the primitive. And I tend to be interested in the volume, and in things that are a little less describable, or are more difficult to describe. I tend to find myself interested in the ellipse. And it's that territory between the ellipse and the circle that I think a lot of our work is negotiating. So, it's very interesting to see it in direct contact with the very early and limited forms of computational representation that Nathalie showed in her presentation. I don't know if that's a fair reading, but I think that, certainly when we sketch, model, and draw, there is a tension between things that are very legible, and result from relatively simple computational processes, versus things that have a bit more difficulty built into them.

LOW VOLUME, Kristy Balliet and Kelly Bair (BairBalliet), 2018, United States.

NATHALIE BREDELLA: Something I found particularly interesting is how from the 2D drawing you relate to the three-dimensional space. It's a relationship not only between different scales and different dimensions, but also between different design tools and materialities. In my own work as an architecture scholar, I am interested in exploring this "messiness" and how these moments of translation, from one medium to another, unfold within the design process, and can be interpreted in different ways. For architecture, such a reading is important. How to describe what happens when drawings are used in the context of a construction site, and suddenly materials have an impact on what the drawing tries to communicate? How do ideas about a project — envisaged in a line drawing — unfold within the material practices on site? So, this is also something I found very interesting when seeing your projects, Kristy: how they might aid also in looking in a different way at an architectural design process. The question that [philosopher Bruno] Latour and [architectural theorist Albena] Yaneva have asked: how can you find a theory or a way of capturing what architecture is or how building processes unfold?

MOLLY WRIGHT STEENSON: Something that was clearly present across all of the projects is this notion of scale, and the extent to which something can be bent and broken. I'm struck by a Robin Evans quote from *Translations from drawing to building* that "things can get bent, broken, or lost on the way." I want to address this with both Jonah and Sean, because I think that in the prepared architectural drawings that Jonah presented — and I think of these as almost retrospective John Cage-ian scores for architecture — you definitely see misbehavior. You see things getting bent, broken, and lost. And by contrast, in the work that Sean presented, about Frei Otto and Behnisch & Partners, you actually cannot misbehave in that setting. But to an extent the drawing breaks, and must turn into computation. So, I wondered if you could talk a little bit about that concept, of extents.

JONAH MARRS: Robin Evans is very important to me as well — and kind of a cornerstone of the thinking behind my project. In the olden days, when we did drawings, sketches, and models, we were constantly translating between these different media, and at each of those translation moments there was an opportunity for some kind of creative misunderstanding — or, as you said, of bending and breaking. Now that we have these new digital tools, often these translation moments are sort of taken over by automatic processes which we have less of a connection with. So, my project's aim is to, first of all, acknowledge that these translation moments still exist, but are now machine to machine interfaces and, second, to reclaim this territory for architecture. Sorry, I'm now being bold, but the aspiration was to do that. I'm not saying that it is achieved, but the idea was to reclaim this "translation" territory, and say "these still exist, and while they're now automated we actually have the tools to to engage with them."

Binary bitmaps, Jonah Marrs, 2019, Canada.

SEAN KELLER: It's not a direct answer, but I wanted to come back to your earlier question about representation and visualization. I think I am on the side of representation because one of the observations I draw is that computation introduces the possibilities of representations which are non visual. That's part of my interest in the story of the Munich project. There are representations there which are algorithmic, that involve calculation, that are numeric, and text based, and which can reach out to visual representations or become those things — but don't in every case. In some cases, these simply remain as sets of data, and then become the final project, and that is all part of the working method. I think that this probably has been the case in architectural history for quite a long time — as long as you're not working with measured drawings that is probably true to some extent — but I think computation expands that possibility greatly.

I think there is also a way for us to talk about Frei Otto's physical models [in this sense]. While they are obviously visual — we see them, and they are photographed, and there's something about that that's compelling — they also have a representational aspect which is non visual, but material. They are dynamic material representations of projects, which are performing work which is not visual. They perform a kind of analog of material work, and I think that's something that's quite interesting about them. And you know, in the case of a building like the Montreal Pavillion, where there was no computation involved in its realization, I hesitate to even draw much of a distinction between the models and the realized project. They simply are of different scales, but they perform in quite similar ways. This is dragging slightly away from computation, but I think I prefer this idea of representation as a more general term and come back to Evans, whom we all love. I wouldn't dare to modify the diagram at the end of *The Projective Cast*, but I think there is a non-visual realm of representation which is not represented in that diagram because his concentration is on visual representation, but I think there's something else going on that's quite interesting, that computation then takes up and you are probing the possibilities of.

JONAH MARRS: I'd like to quickly add something. I think that when things go into the computer, it's difficult to visualize them. We have tools like oscilloscopes and logic analyzers, which draw graphs for us about changing voltage over time, so the visualization tools just may have to become more specialized. To me it's fascinating to think of the miniature weights in Otto's model as analogous to elements inside the computer. To visualize these would require something like a giant circuit diagram, or whatever, but I think it's fascinating to think how, with the right tools, we could realize that a physical model is actually still physical inside the computer.

MOLLY WRIGHT STEENSON: And as we consider the various theoretical underpinnings that Nathalie was beginning to put into play, I think underlying everything from a media theoretical sense is a question of forensics. We are considering how things are drawn out, but I think there's also a contemporary question about what happens when the model and the realization are, in fact, the same thing. These are contemporary questions which are certainly in a lot of work going on right now at SCI-Arc. It's a conversation I've had with Aaron Breslin for the last few years, and I think it's something that you see in their work. But there is something else I want to throw into play here, which is that we have two contemporary practitioners and two historians/theorists on this panel, and I want to point out that the Spuybroek project and the Behnisch & Partners and Frei Otto project are very much taking place in certain historical periods. This is something that Sean underscored and, if you consider the role of Behnisch & Partners in West Germany in the 1970s, you know that in postwar West Germany they were the people who designed the Bundestag. Behnisch & Partners carries on and is still one of the major figures in federal German architecture today, so there's an interesting statement there about rationality and calculation that Sean was raising in the end is a new part of German identity in the early 1970s, post economic miracle. Similarly, the Dutch project in 1992 with V2 and media art, the end of postmodernism and the locus of different modes of media and interactivity and under media is also a specific moment.

You two are also working in specific moments right now that are, I think, boundary periods where we see things shift from one to another, and we see the enormity of a line and the inhabitability of a model, or the indistinguishability of a model [from a building].

Should we address some questions? Are there any questions?

AUDIENCE MEMBER: Sean, could you comment on the present-day state and future evolution of computational design in architecture as seen from the perspective of the Munich project?

SEAN KELLER: I don't know that I'm entirely qualified to speculate on the future, but bringing back Molly's question about the periodization, it seems to me that a lot of contemporary work

dealing with computation in architecture shows a desire to "un-smooth": to take the smoothness out of the work and out of the process, and to reintroduce back and forth and integration of physical methods. Or, even if it remains largely digital, to make it clunky. This seems to me something of this moment, after a period where we have been pushing as far as we could towards smoothness. To go back, though, I think that awkwardness and back and forth between the physical and the computational was already present, by necessity, in the Munich project.

This is where I can't speculate on where things will go now. I think it would depend on who you picked today. If you picked certain figures, we would wind up with the perfectly smooth surface and the perfectly smooth execution of that surface. But if you were to pick slightly different figures today, you might get something that was slightly clunky — I mean that in a good way. But this awkwardness was built into the Munich project because they were moving so quickly. And even though they did solve many of the problems computationally, all of those mechanical details were fully worked out by hand, and modeled and cast by hand, and the foundations and all the anchorage points were already in place and cast before they had the finished designs. And they only shifted to acrylic sheets at the last minute — literally in 1971 — when they realized that if they used membranes the color television wouldn't be able to adjust to the lighting conditions. There are all of these things happening on the fly. It's actually a wonderful example of what I think a lot of design practices are kind of looking for today. It's only possible at that scale, because it was funded by the entire national budget and ended up costing ten times as much as the original estimate. It was the equivalent of a $2 billion dollars project today, and that's the only way this could happen at the scale that it happened.

AUDIENCE MEMBER: This is an open question to the panel. Could you please comment on the role of computational tools shaping creative processes?

JONAH MARRS: I think that creative acts involve constraints which, like our tools, become more and more powerful the more

Clickspace Time-lapse Drawing Machine, Jonah Marrs, 2015, Canada.

we are faced with a "blank canvas." It's about limiting the incredible number of possibilities. For me personally, when I enter the world of [Rhinoceros plug-in] Grasshopper, where I can do a million things, I have to start by limiting myself. I have to allow myself to only do a certain number of things. I have to start building in constraints, because the possibilities are too endless. I think it's the same when [in some of my artistic work] I go back in time and limit myself to only using technology from the 1970s, or whatever. So my feeling is that, as the tools become apparently more powerful, to be actually used as creative constraints, human needs need to further constrain them — like a little box within a massive one.

KRISTY BALLIET: I would like to say that the overlap is somewhat uncanny — although probably curated, as Daniel collected us and looked at our work from different perspectives. As you were speaking, I kept writing things, like the "desire for interruption," and whether it's the machine, or two machines that are talking to one another, and then building the desire for interruption in my own work. You know, wanting to almost tie a hand behind your back as a means to interrupt the process starts to become really interesting as a creative limitation. Taking the position of a designer, in different points along my career I've robustly chased after technology, and in other moments I've intentionally been [technologically] naïve. As Jonah indicated, one tactic is to constrain, or bracket. I think limiting what is new may assist the designer's ability to make design decisions in terms of what are you going to bracket. The question is: what are you going to work on? This becomes a big limitation because you're not just tinkering with one or two things, and figuring out where you can maximize something, it's more like the maximum is there and you're interested in using your particular lens to operate within a set of limitations. But sometimes part of the creative process is actually making those limitations.

NATHALIE BREDELLA: And possibly understanding the logic, or the mechanisms, behind the tools might also be a way of finding out about these limitations. I think it's also worth asking, in which historical moments tools or design strategies were developed further — so paying attention to the embeddedness of technological development within the social, economic, and political. That is asking, who is involved and whose interests are part of software development for example?

KRISTY BALLIET: If I could add one thing as an educator, you know, we all have our own histories, and I think I am very pleased, and probably will continue to be, wading in the world of other people's machines that I then use for creative endeavors. But as an educator I continue to feel the pressure — and also the desire — from designers much younger than myself to actually design the machines that do that work. I think that their attitude towards the limitations that they find in the tools are very different from the limitations I find. This is just to say that I loved the drawing that you [Jonah] put up, showing how a sphere could be drawn with seven or so different softwares. I think that in some ways every young designer sees the fact that someone else designed their tools as a limitation, and they want to be able to [go beyond that and] have their mark on how a given tool impacts them.

MOLLY WRIGHT STEENSON: Maybe this phrase "wading in the world of other people's machines" is exactly where we find ourselves here. Please join me in thanking our four fabulous panelists.

Illustrations of graph-theoretic concepts and architectural arrangements, 1980

Charles Eastman
Obtaining the pseudo-geometric dual of the graph G.
Parametric site planning patterns.

Visualities

Materialities, Page 34 ↑

Archive

Works

Essays

Conversations

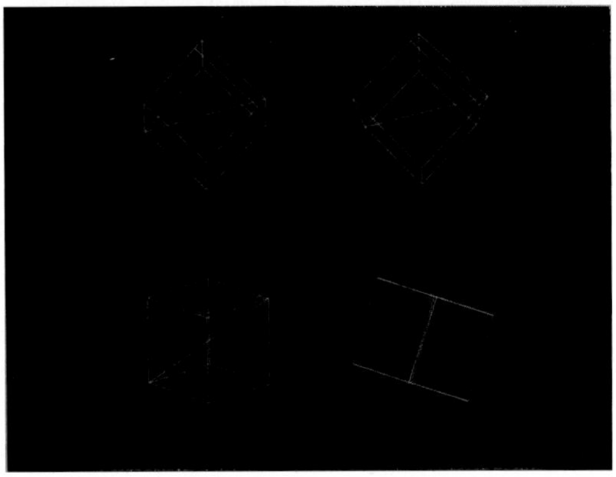

A house and cubes created using Sketchpad III, Timothy E. Johnson, MIT CAD Project, 1963, United States

Following the development, by Larry Roberts, of the four-dimensional matrix transform, which encoded the homogeneous coordinates of perspective geometry in matrix form, CAD Project member Timothy E. Johnson extended Ivan Sutherland's "Sketchpad" with the capacity to represent 3D objects. To allow users to view an object from different angles at the same time, Johnson divided the screen in four quadrants – an innovation later known as "viewports" which is still a key feature in most modeling interfaces today.

Courtesy of MIT Libraries

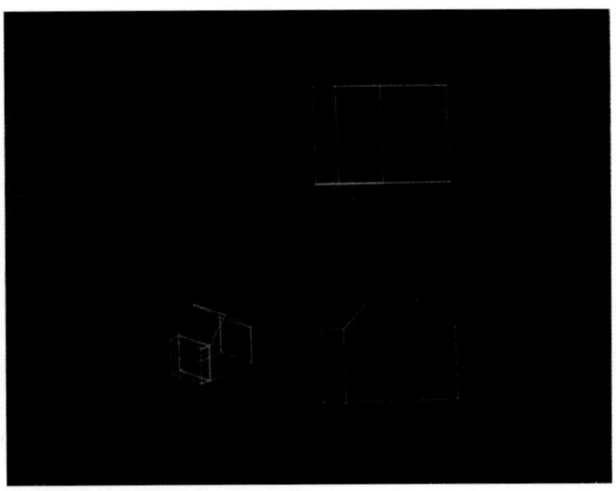

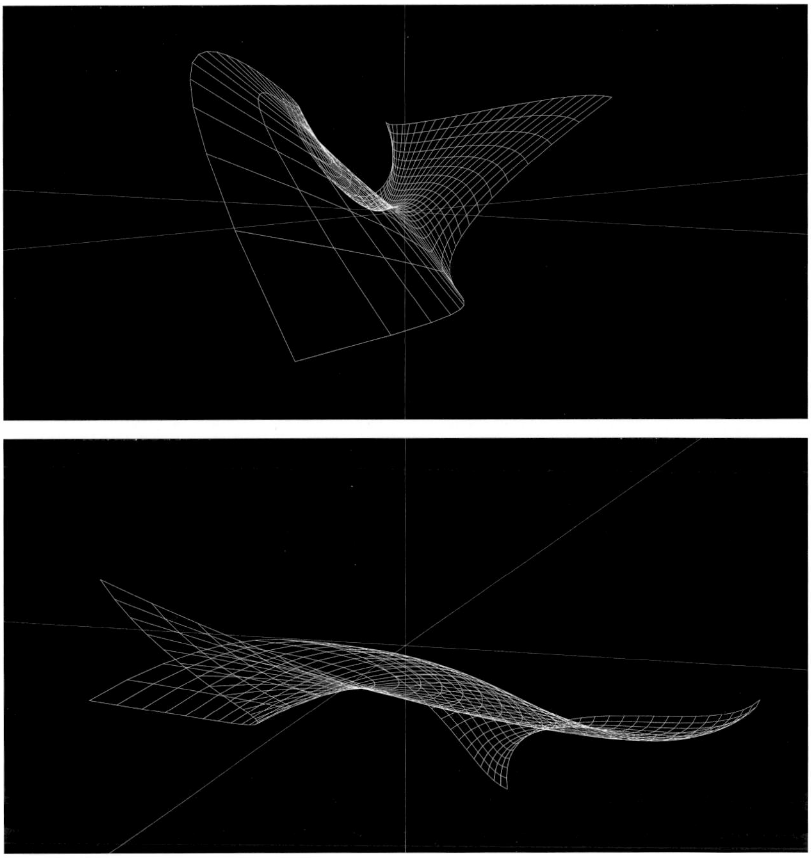

"Coons Patch," Steven A. Coons, MIT CAD Project, c. 1967, United States

The "Coons patch" is an early mathematical technique to calculate curved surfaces from any set of "edge" curves. Developed in the 1960s by Steven Coons, a professor of mechanical engineering at MIT, this technique attracted the attention of aircraft, car, and ship design industries because it showed the potential of the computer to serve as a design environment for complex shapes. Coons's technique was first a non-parametric interpolation of a "patch" between four edge curves. Later, he developed it further using parametric methods based on a set of polynomials. This interactive installation developed at the Computational Design Laboratory at Carnegie Mellon University demonstrates Coons's technique. It allows visitors to manipulate a "Coons patch" by editing the coordinates of the points in cubic curves, and to experience its geometric plasticity.

Reconstruction by CMU Computational Design Laboratory, 2017 (updated 2021)

(Coons Reconstruction Installation pictured on next spread)

Images structurées
Structured images
Interaction et intelligence
Interaction and intelligence

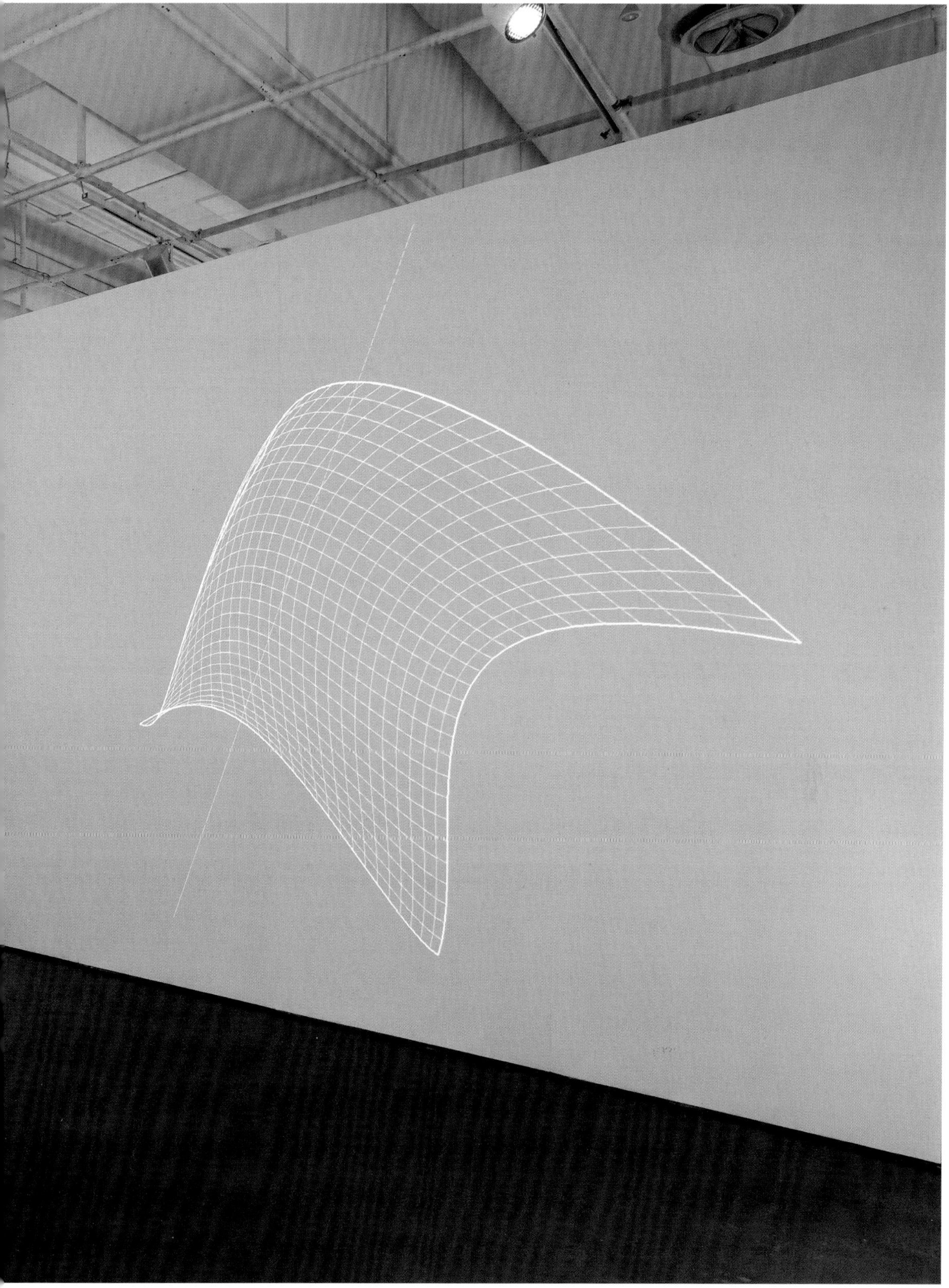

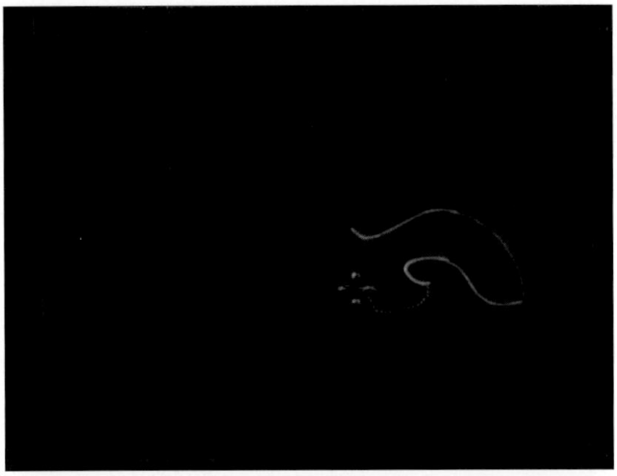

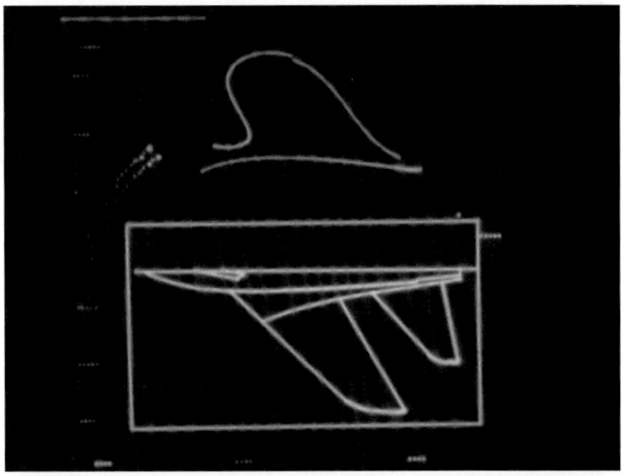

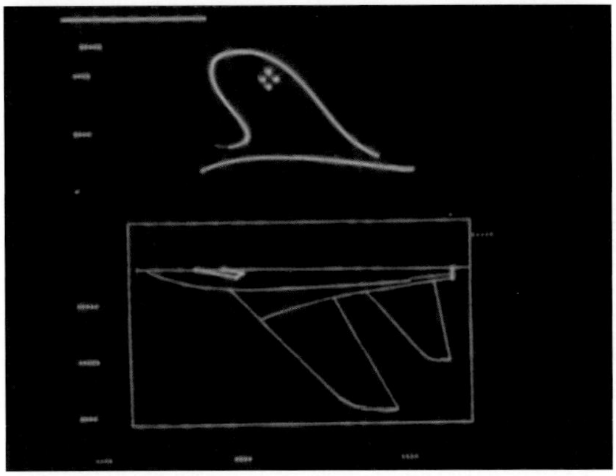

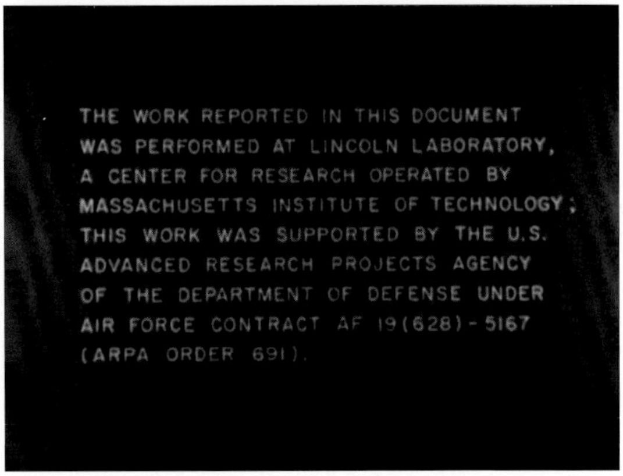

Freehand Curve Sketching, Timothy E. Johnson, MIT Lincoln Laboratory, c. 1963, United States (left)

Surface generation by computer, Steve A. Coons and Ford Motors Co., MIT Lincoln Labs and Bell Labs, c. 1967, United States (right)

Early efforts to harness the potential of computer graphics rested on an alignment of industrial, academic, and governmental supports. This collection of films from 1967–1968 illustrates this alignment. With the ARPA-funded MIT Lincoln Labs as a common thread, these three films show how computer graphics served a variety of purposes, including airplane design for defense, industrial design for car manufacturing (at Ford Motors Co.), and scientific visualization for research at Syracuse and John Hopskins universities — the latter with the notable participation of Bell Labs computer graphics pioneer K. C. Knowlton. While the development of computational design and manufacturing methods was linked to national security concerns in the US, Lincoln Laboratory members collaborated with multiple other institutions and organizations, exploring applications of computer graphics across diverse domains.

Courtesy of Timothy Johnson

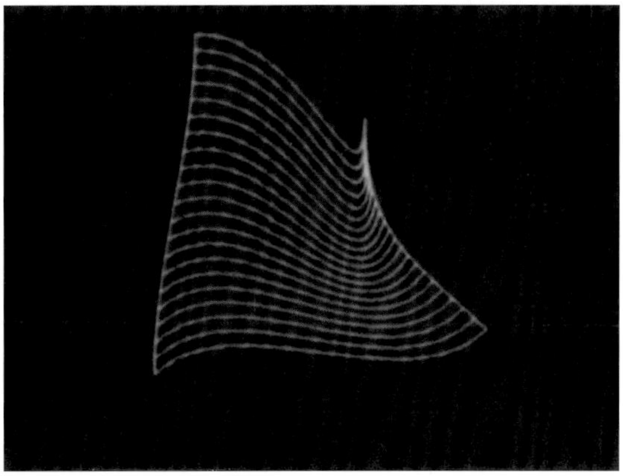

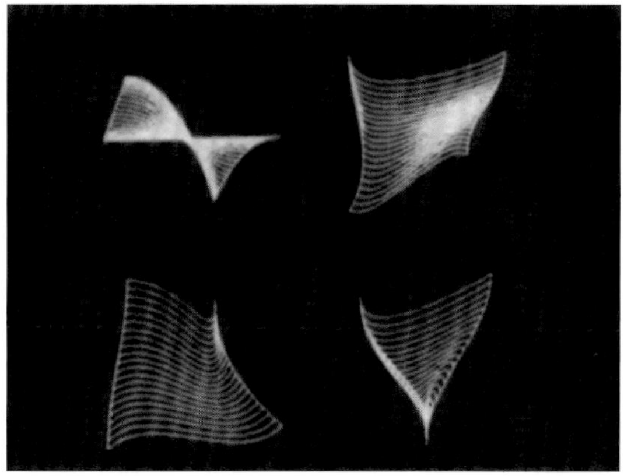

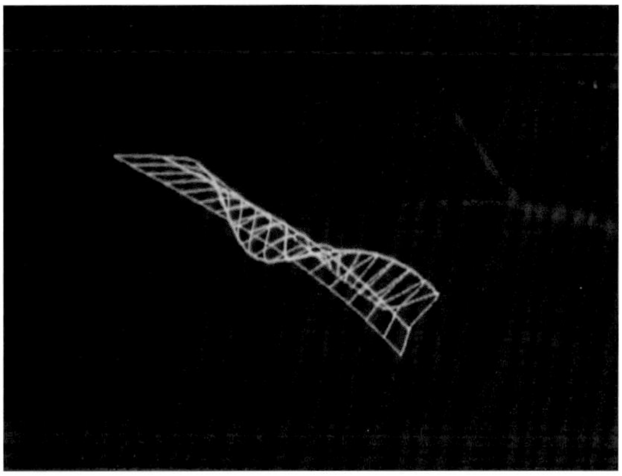

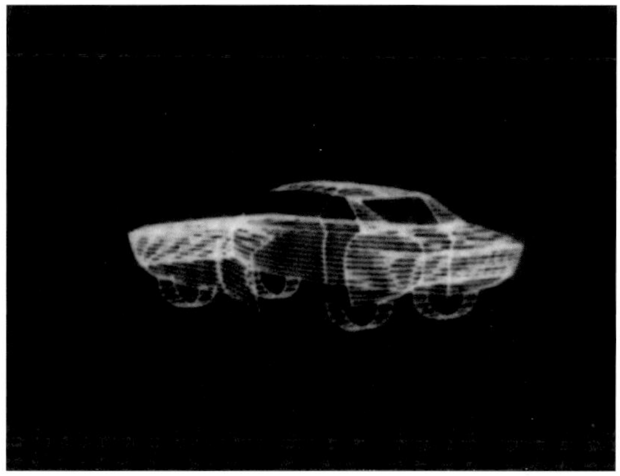

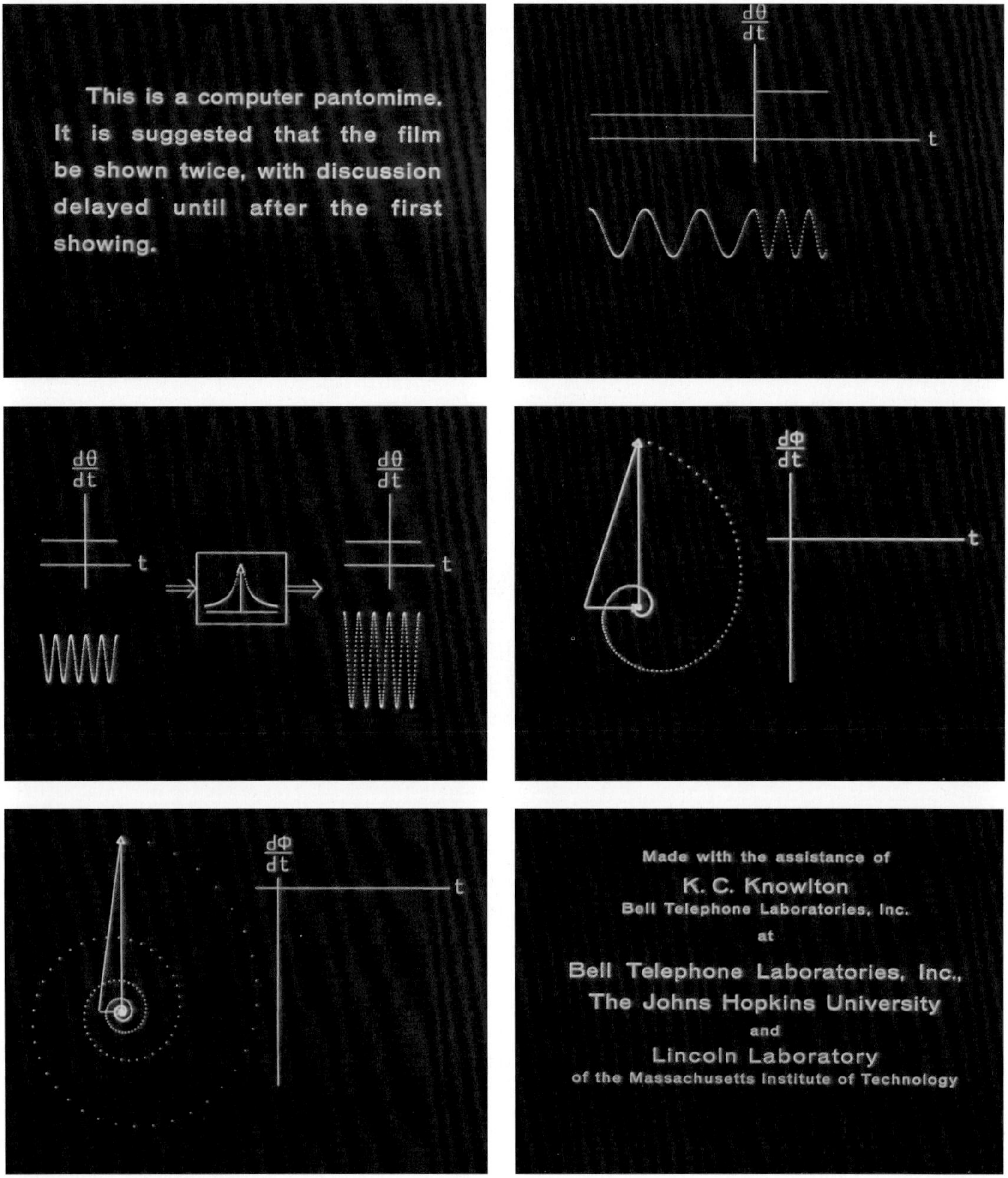

Response of a resonant system to a frequency step, Donald D. Weiner and William H. Huggins, Ford Motor Co., 1968, United States

Courtesy of the Computer History Museum

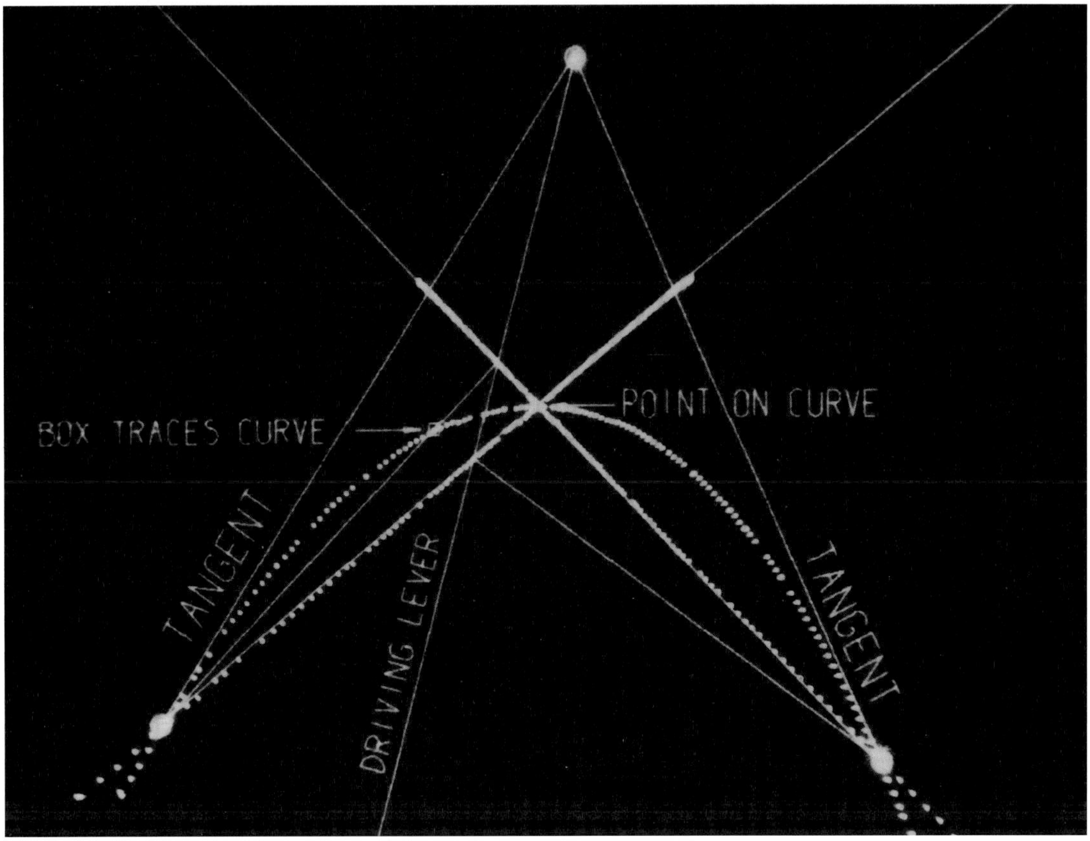

Conic drawing linkage, Ivan Sutherland, MIT Lincoln Laboratory, c. 1963, United States

Ivan Sutherland's Sketchpad system innovatively allowed users to establish geometric dependencies between different elements, a feature that remains central to many of today's modeling systems. For example, a geometric element could be set to remain at a fixed distance from another by creating a geometric "linkage" between the two. Sutherland called linkages "by far the most interesting application of Sketchpad." This photograph, which was included in Sutherland's dissertation, shows a special kind of linkage developed by Sutherland to illustrate Sketchpad's capacity to constantly find the intersection of two lines on a specific point on a curve, even when changing the drawing.

Courtesy of MIT Libraries

Flying Carpet, William Fetter, Boeing, 1963, United States

This computer-generated drawing, intriguingly titled "Flying Carpet," appears to describe a doubly curved surface with a series of tightly packed lines following the same direction. It resembles contemporary images of the "Coons patch" photographed on the screen of the TX-2 computer or PDP displays in Project MAC terminals. However, its astonishing level of detail and intricacy raise questions about how it was produced. A version of this drawing appeared in the journal *Architectural Record* in January 1965, where it's credited to graphic designer William Fetter, Boeing's art director at the time and who is credited with coining the term "computer graphics."

Courtesy of MIT Libraries

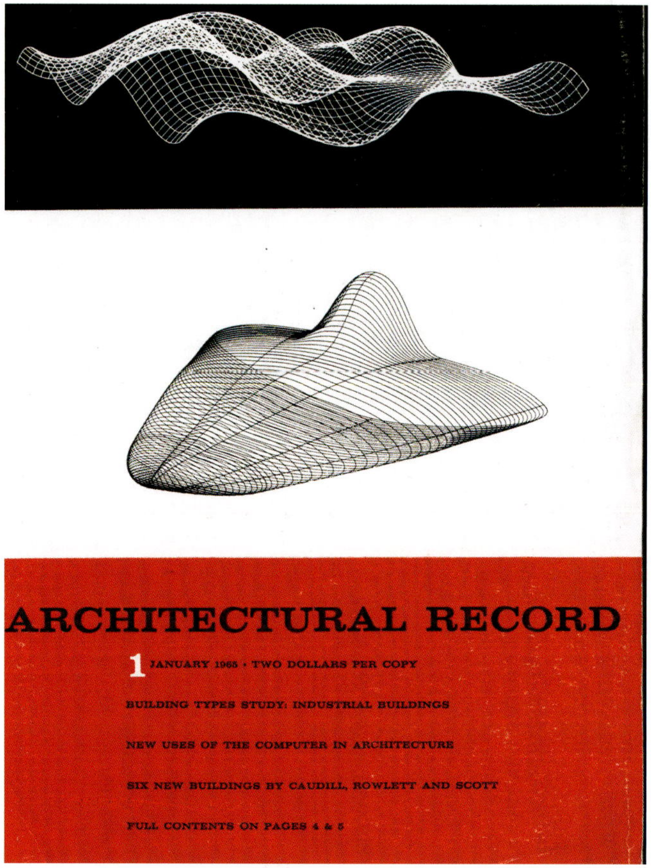

Steven A. Coons and Douglas T. Ross during a MIT CAD Project progress meeting, Photographer unknown, MIT CAD Project, 1960, United States

These two rare polaroid photographs capture the two leaders of the MIT CAD Project — mathematician Douglas T. Ross (seated) and the self-taught mathematician and designer Steven A. Coons — during one of their weekly progress meetings.

Courtesy of MIT Libraries

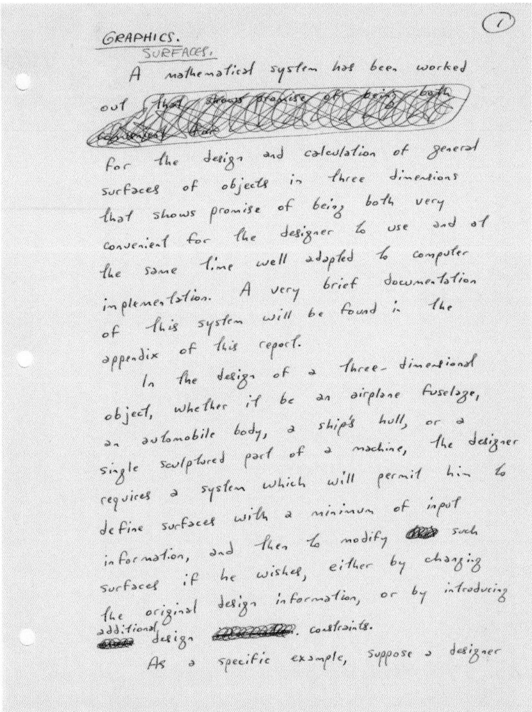

GRAPHICS.
SURFACES.

A mathematical system has been worked out for the design and calculation of general surfaces of objects in three dimentions that shows promise of being both very convenient for the designer to use and at the same time well adapted to computer implementation. A very brief documentation of this system will be found in the appendix of this report.

In the design of a three-dimentional object, whether it be an airplane fuselage, an automobile body, a ship's hull, or a single sculptured part of a machine, the designer requires a system which will permit him to define surfaces with a minimum of input information, and then to modify such surfaces if he wishes, either by changing the original design information, or by introducing additional design constraints.

As a specific example, suppose a designer

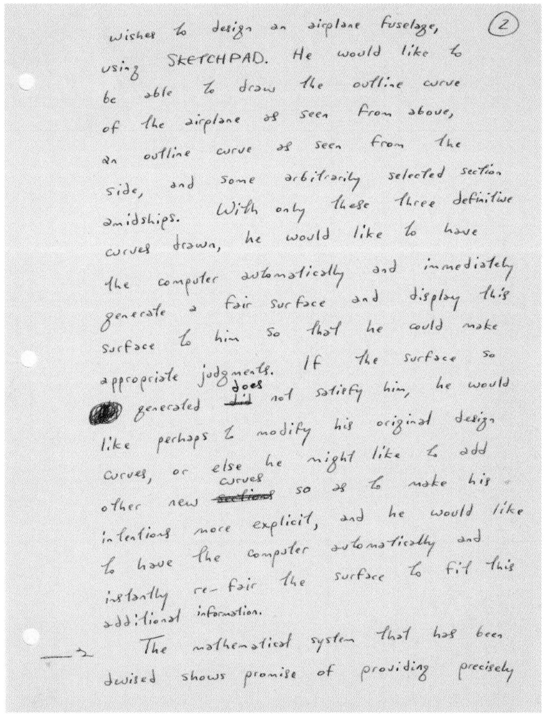

wishes to design an airplane fuselage, using SKETCHPAD. He would like to be able to draw the outline curve of the airplane as seen from above, an outline curve as seen from the side, and some arbitrarily selected section amidships. With only these three definitive curves drawn, he would like to have the computer automatically and immediately generate a fair surface and display this surface to him so that he could make appropriate judgments. If the surface so generated does not satisfy him, he would like perhaps to modify his original design curves, or else he might like to add other new curves so as to make his intentions more explicit, and he would like to have the computer automatically and instantly re-fair the surface to fit this additional information.

The mathematical system that has been devised shows promise of providing precisely

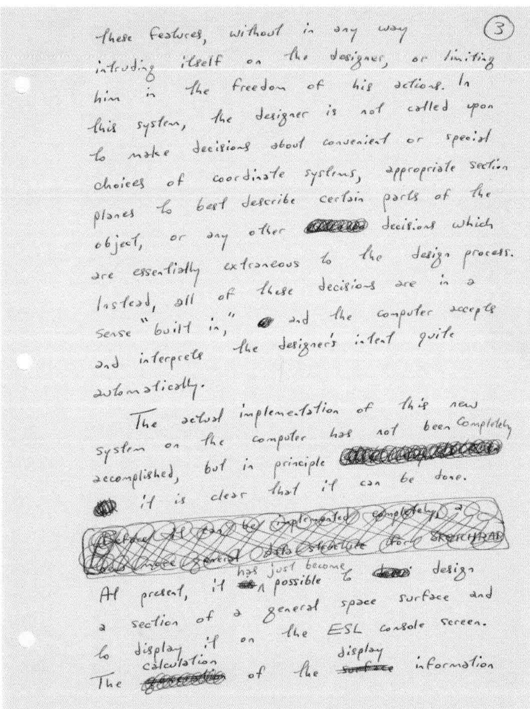

these features, without in any way intruding itself on the designer, or limiting him in the freedom of his actions. In this system, the designer is not called upon to make decisions about convenient or special choices of coordinate systems, appropriate section planes to best describe certain parts of the object, or any other decisions which are essentially extraneous to the design process. Instead, all of these decisions are in a sense "built in," and the computer accepts and interprets the designer's intent quite automatically.

The actual implementation of this new system on the computer has not been completely accomplished, but in principle it is clear that it can be done.

At present, it has just become possible to design a section of a general space surface and to display it on the ESL console screen. The calculation of the display information

Handwritten draft of "Surfaces" article, Steven A. Coons, MIT CAD Project, c. 1963, United States

An early draft of Steven A. Coons's would-be classic work on "Surfaces for Computer-Aided Design," where he presented his technique for surface interpolation: the "Coons patch." In these four initial pages, Coons uses his signature expositive style — accessible and rich in examples — to describe his technique's potential applications, and how it could be implemented as part of Ivan Sutherland's "Sketchpad."

Courtesy of MIT Libraries

A drawing made with "Sketchpad," Author unknown, 1967, Canada

Starting in the second half of the 1960s, *Architecture Canada* — the journal of the Royal Architectural Institute of Canada (RAIC) — featured an increasing number of articles on computing and information processing. This issue includes an article by Timothy Johnson of the MIT CAD Project introducing architects to computer graphics and the "Sketchpad" system. The image on the cover is a time exposure of a moving crank and follower mechanism drawn with the system.

Courtesy of the RAIC Journal

Netherlands stamps designed with "Sketchpad," Author unknown, 1970, Canada

The Royal Architectural Institute of Canada (RAIC) periodicals disseminated not only claims about the potentials of "Sketchpad," but also the striking visual language that emerged from the system's outputs. This clipping displays an intricate series of postage stamps featuring "Sketchpad" line-drawings alongside a prediction for the system's role as a "future design partner for architects."

Courtesy of the RAIC Journal

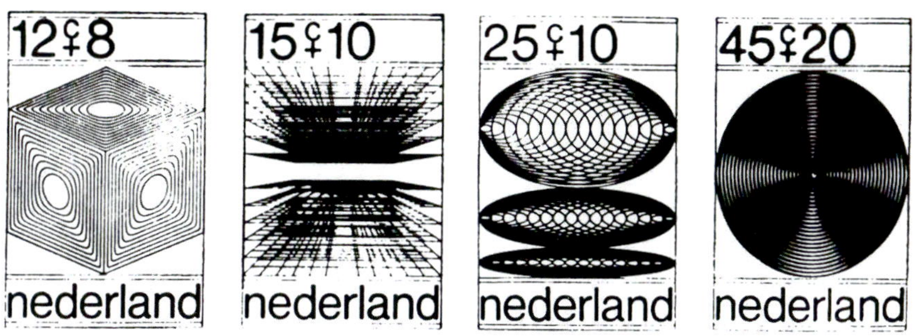

Netherland Stamps

The sketchpad computer is predicted as a future design partner for architects. The same machine produced the intricate drawings for these postage stamps.

General view of Type 340 display with PDP7 and Titan teletypes, Photographer unknown, Cambridge CAD Group, c. 1972, United Kingdom

Supported by a GBP 50,000 grant from the UK government, Cambridge University Mathematical Laboratory director Maurice Wilkes started a Computer-Aided Design research group, and organized a laboratory with the PDP 7 Station, peripherals, and display seen in this photograph. Many of the pieces shown in this section were produced using this equipment.

Courtesy of Robin Forrest

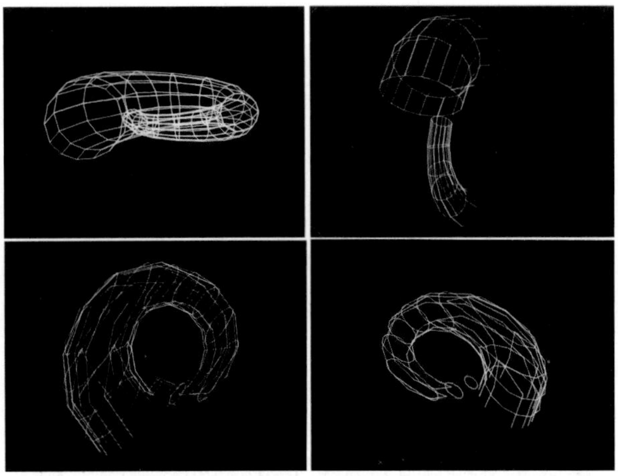

Patch model of pump volute, P. J. Payne, Cambridge CAD Group, c. 1972, United Kingdom

Multipatch joining was a software technique developed by A. P. Armit at the Cambridge CAD Group in the late 1960s. It made it possible to produce smooth curved surfaces by aggregating parametrically defined surface sections or "patches," enabling designers to model more complex shapes. The images are from a model created by P. J. Payne using Multipatch.

Courtesy of Robin Forrest

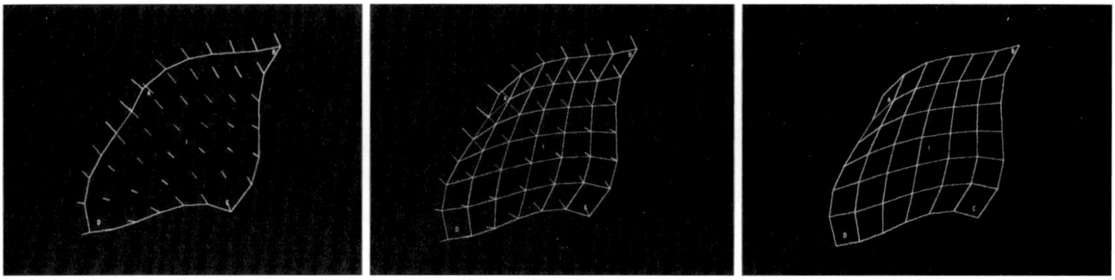

Patch visualizations using parameter lines and surface normals, P. J. Payne, Cambridge CAD Group, c. 1970, United Kingdom

Courtesy of Robin Forrest

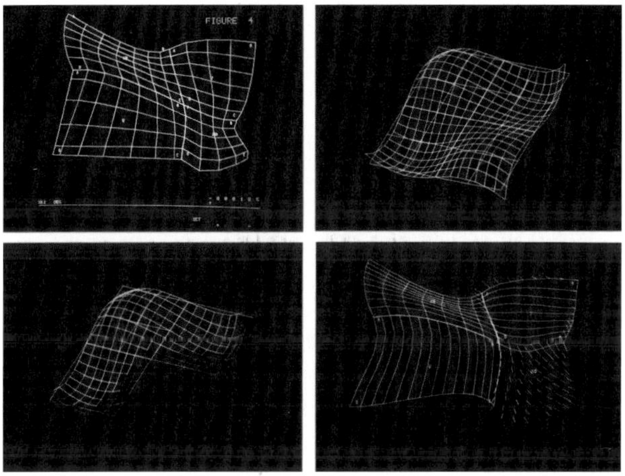

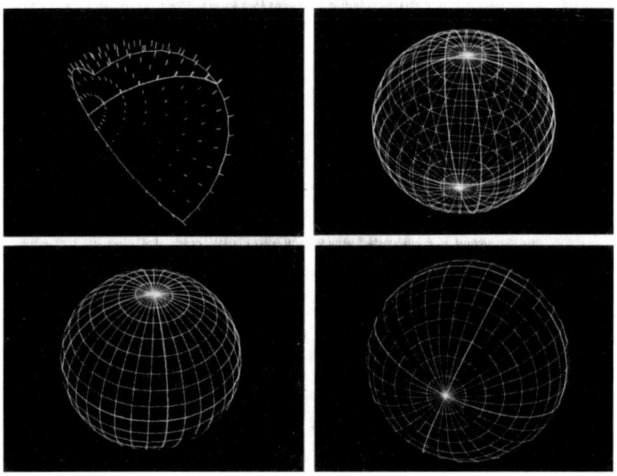

Joining surface patches using Multipatch, P. J. Payne, Cambridge CAD Group, c. 1970, United Kingdom

Spherical patches with parameter lines and surface normals, P. J. Payne, Cambridge CAD Group, c. 1972, United Kingdom

Courtesy of Robin Forrest

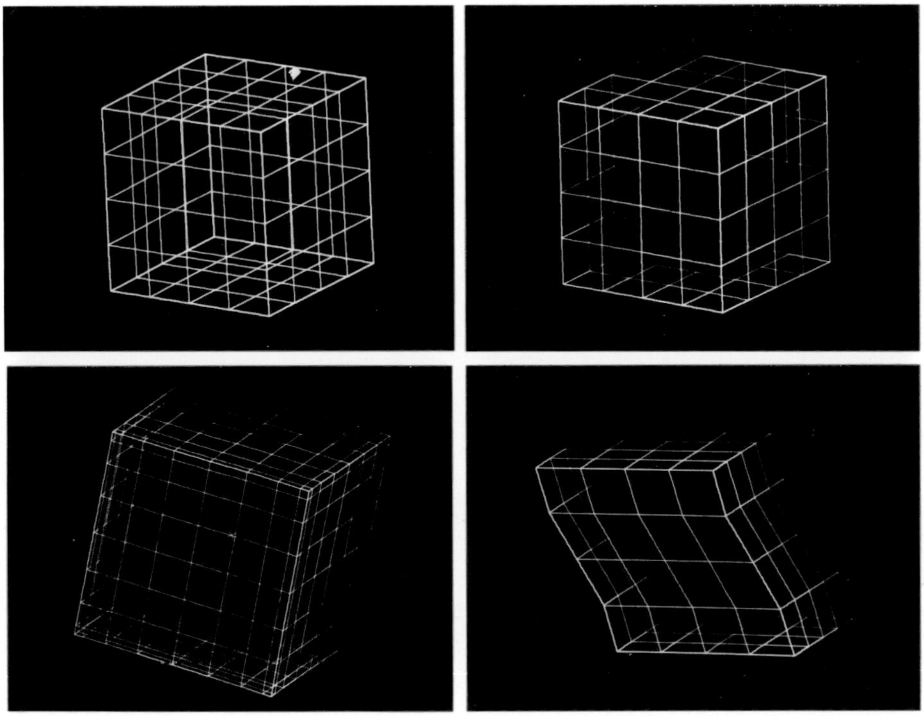

Cubes with different parameter settings and depth-modulated intensity, P. J. Payne, Cambridge CAD Group, c. 1972, United Kingdom

Computational images are parametrically flexible because of their numerical structure. Exploring this new plasticity, researchers at the Cambridge CAD Group generated programs to represent and manipulate different shapes. Later, the group developed GINO, a graphics package which laid the foundations of what later became GL, a standard language for computer graphics.

Courtesy of Robin Forrest

Primitive solids and test part in the BUILD solid modeling system, Ian C. Braid, Cambridge CAD Group, 1974, United Kingdom

Simple pocket design in the BUILD solid modeling system, Ian C. Braid, Cambridge CAD Group, 1974, United Kingdom

A pivotal development in computational descriptions was Ian Braid's BUILD system, which he developed as part of his PhD dissertation under Charles Lang's advice at Cambridge in 1973. BUILD offered a new type of representation for geometric modeling: the boundary representation, or 'B-Rep,' which became the foundation for many solid modeling systems. Notably, B-Reps made it possible to calculate intersections between non-planar surfaces, enabling a wide array of operations of significance to design. More generally, it conceptualized computational descriptions in a broader way, opening the door for future developments assigning different attributes and data indexically to a geometric model.

Courtesy of Robin Forrest

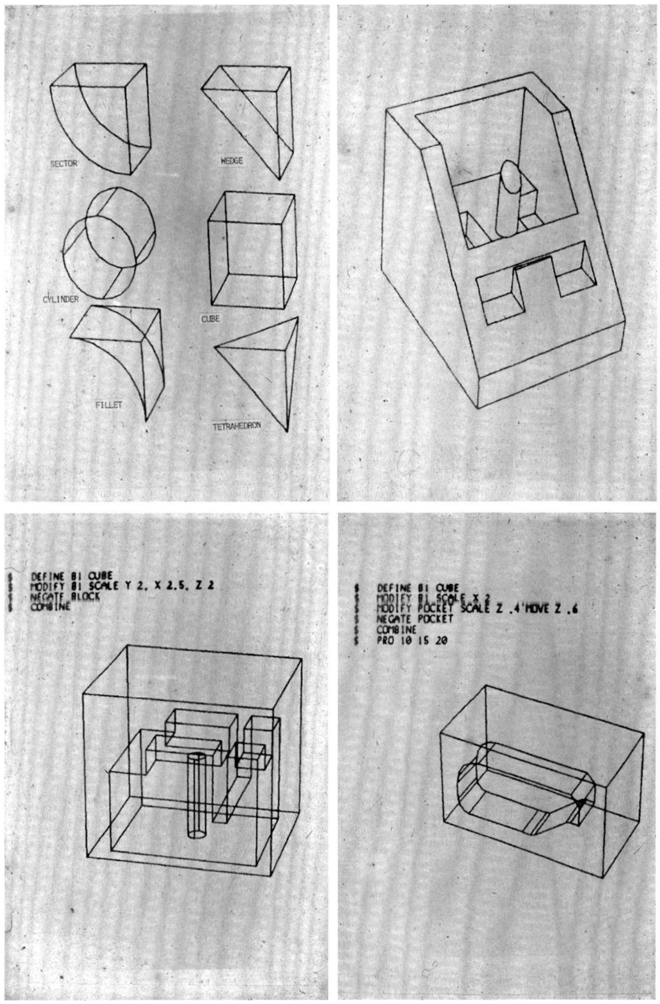

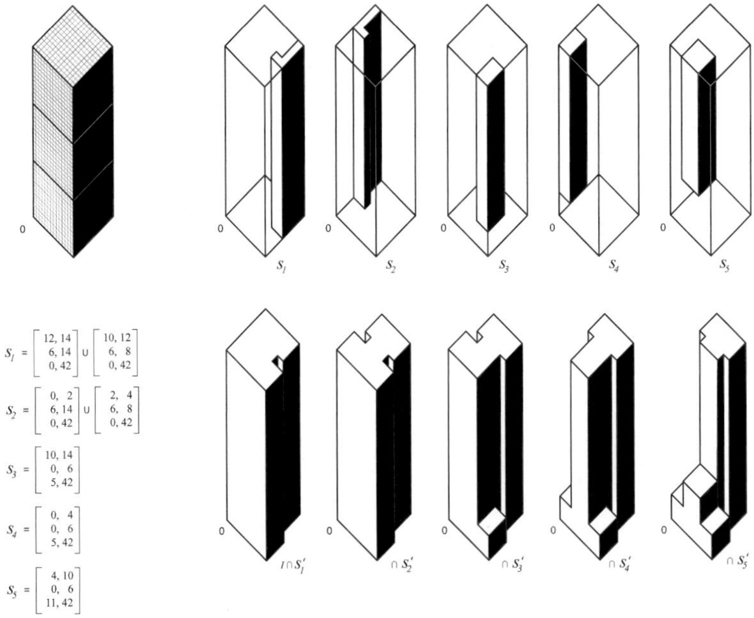

The development of the block form of the Seagram Building (architect: Mies van der Rohe) by the subtraction of volumes from a notional building envelope, Lionel March and Philip Steadman, Cambridge CAD Group and LUBFS, 1971, United Kingdom

Collaborations between architects, mathematicians, and engineers became common in research universities in the US and the UK during the postwar years. This image, a procedural diagram of Mies van der Rohe's Seagram Building in New York, is an example of such collaborations. CAD Group member (and former student of Steven A. Coons) Robin Forrest produced the mathematical model for one of the chapters of a volume edited by two mathematically-inclined architects at the University of Cambridge's Center for Land Use and Built Form Studies (LUBFS): Lionel March (the center's director), and Philip Steadman. Alliances between members of the two groups sought to develop computational methods to study aspects of the built environment. If architectural form could be represented mathematically, they imagined, it could be analyzed (and manipulated) in logical and rigorous ways using the computer. In an interview, Forrest recalls: "Lionel March asked me for a version [of one of his technical reports on transformations and matrices] for one of his volumes and, being interested in modern architecture, I thought the Seagram Building would provide a recognisable model to illustrate the chapter. I cannot claim it is accurate, but it looks approximately correct!"

Reconstruction of a diagram in Lionel March, "A Boolean Description of a Class of Built Forms," in The Architecture of Form, *Cambridge Urban and Architectural Studies 4, ed. Lionel March (Cambridge, UK: Cambridge University Press, 1976), 41-73.*

The Utah teapot (wireframe), University of Utah, c. 1976, United States

In 1974, University of Utah student Martin Newell produced a dataset with the spatial coordinates of a regular teapot purchased at a hardware store. He used the teapot because it featured different types of curvature, making it useful for exploring problems of geometric modeling and lighting. Newell made the dataset publicly available, and the "Utah teapot" became a benchmark of 3D graphics. This photograph is a rare, low-resolution, version of the Utah teapot – most likely developed at the University of Utah in the mid-1970s.

Courtesy of the Computer History Museum

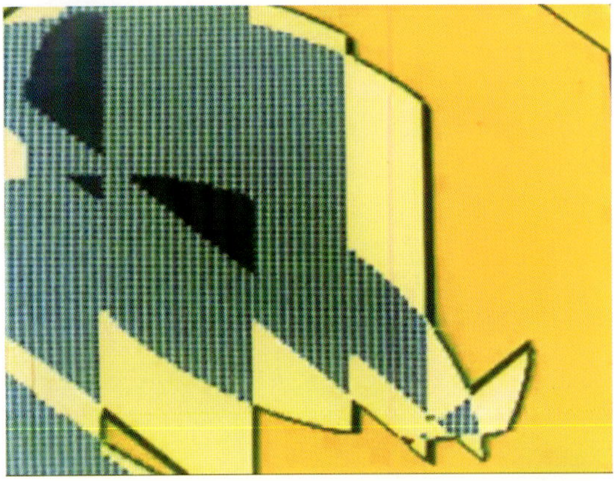

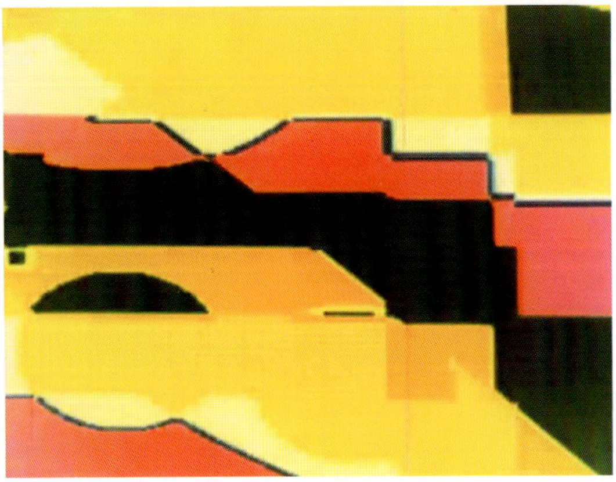

Metamorphosis, Lillian Schwartz, Bell Labs, 1974, United States

Pixillation, Lillian Schwartz, Bell Labs, 1970, United States (upper right)

Color tests, Author and date unknown, United States (lower right)

Lillian Schwartz was a resident artist at Bell Laboratories for nearly three decades, starting in 1969. During this period, she produced pioneering films using computers, sometimes in collaboration with Ken Knowlton. In contrast with her contemporaries at the MIT Lincoln Labs and at other industry laboratories, Schwartz's films are not concerned with efficiency or precision, but explore instead the aesthetics of the computational image through textures, movement, and sound. Along with the MIT Lincoln Labs, Bell Laboratories was a key center for the early development of computer graphics in the US. An essay by architecture historian Olga Touloumi included in this section explores this piece in greater detail.

Courtesy of the Computer History Museum

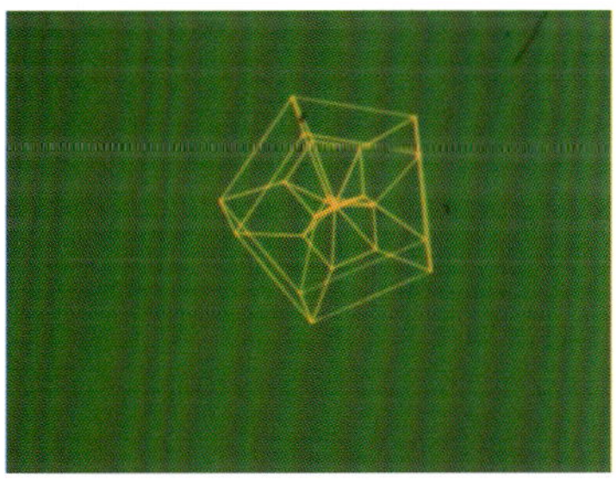

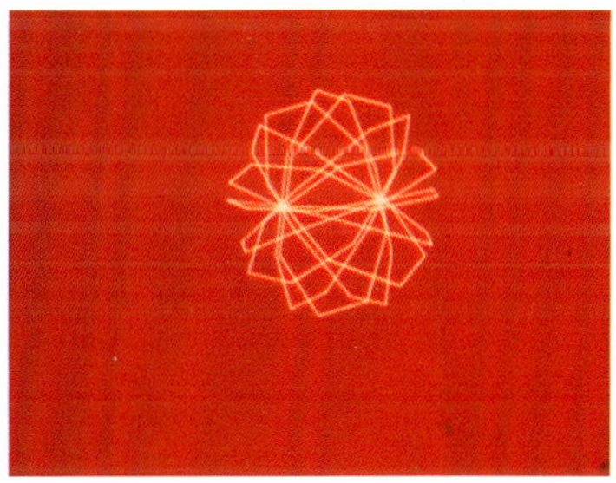

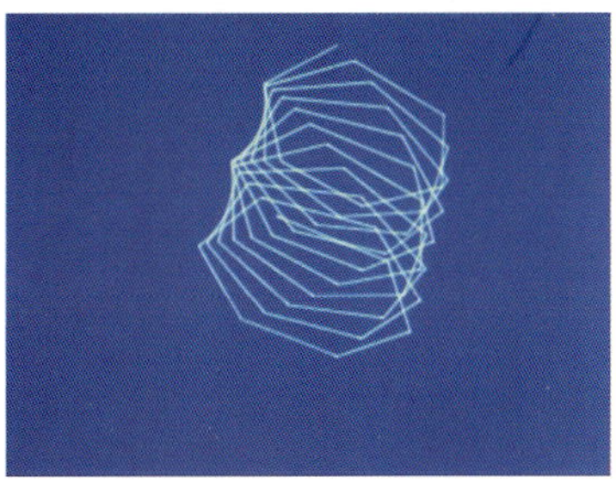

(*Pixillation* pictured on next spread)

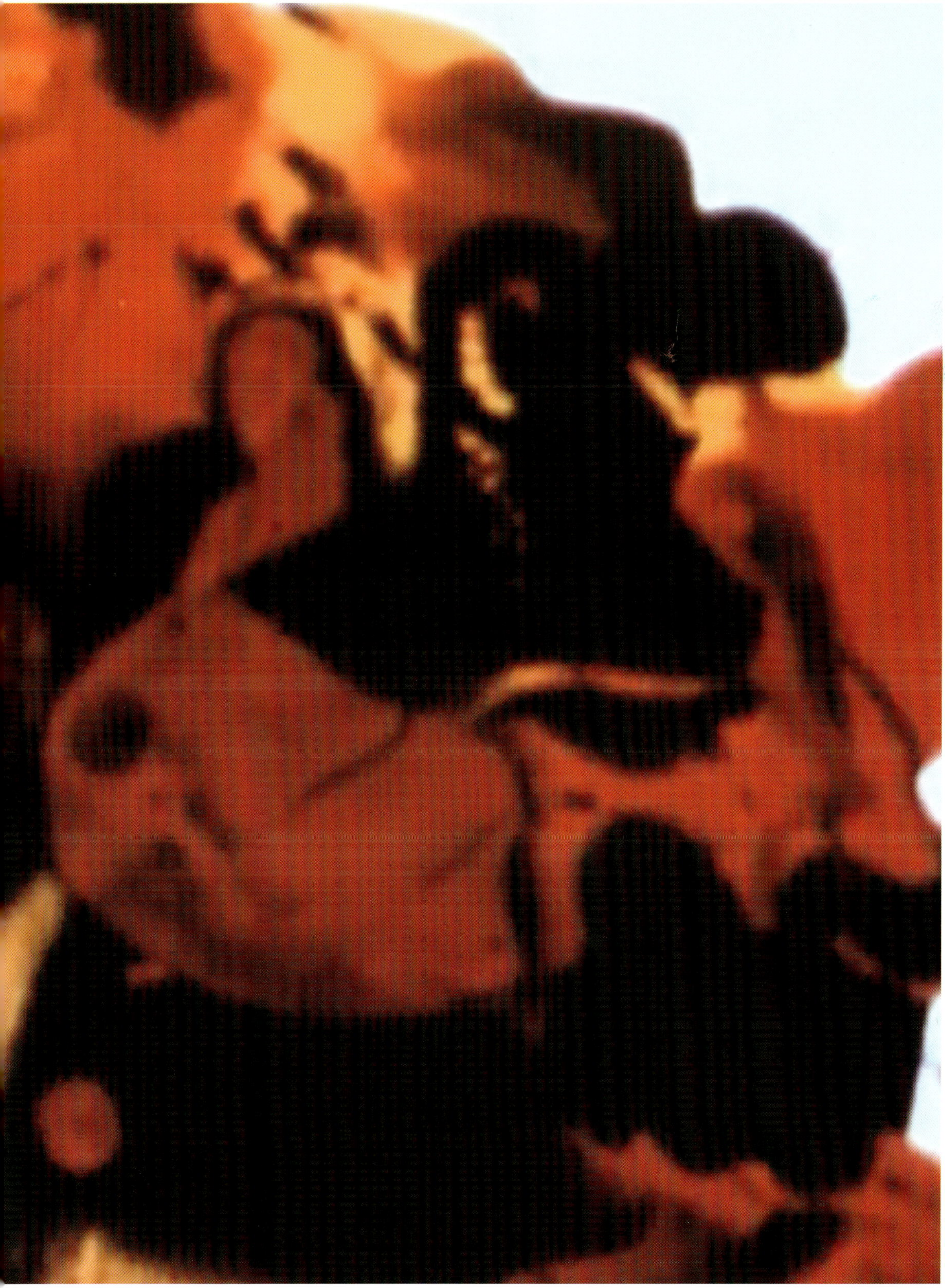

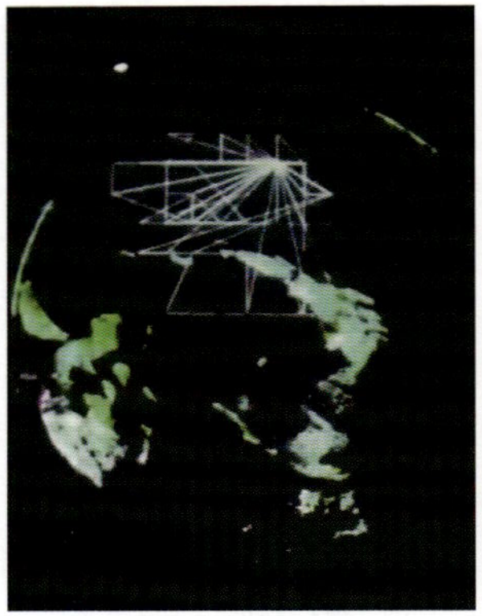

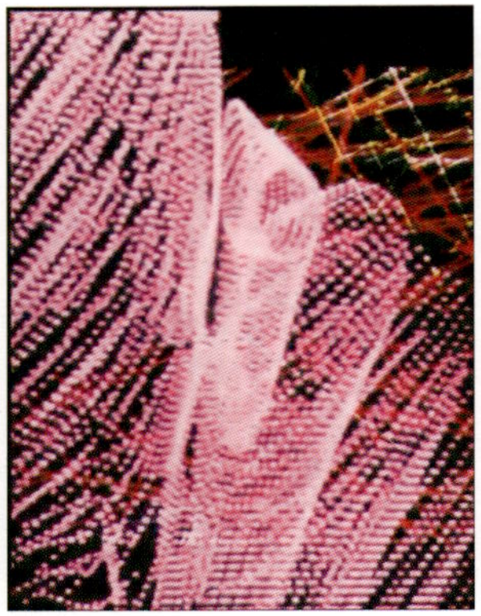

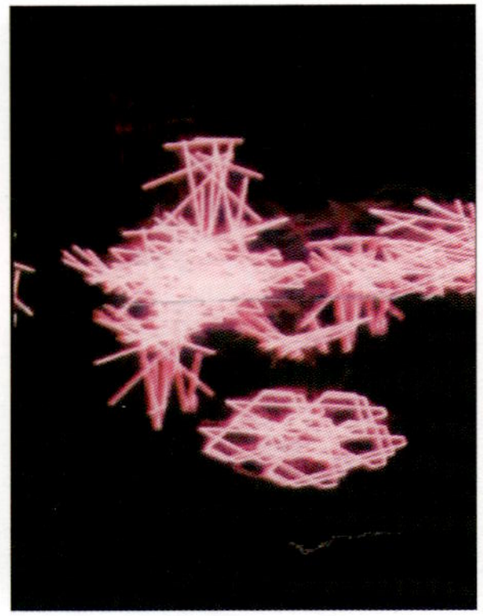

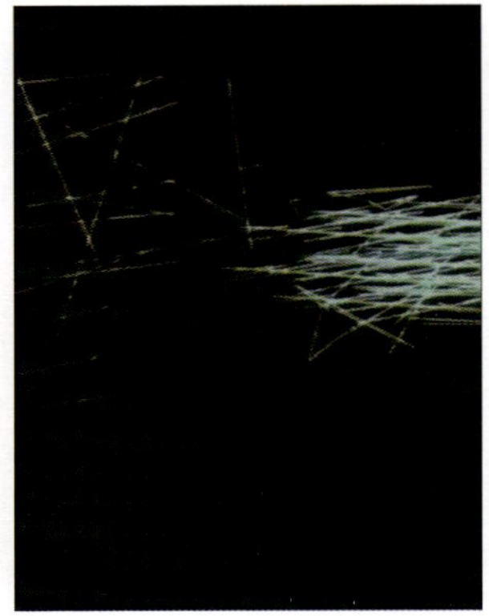

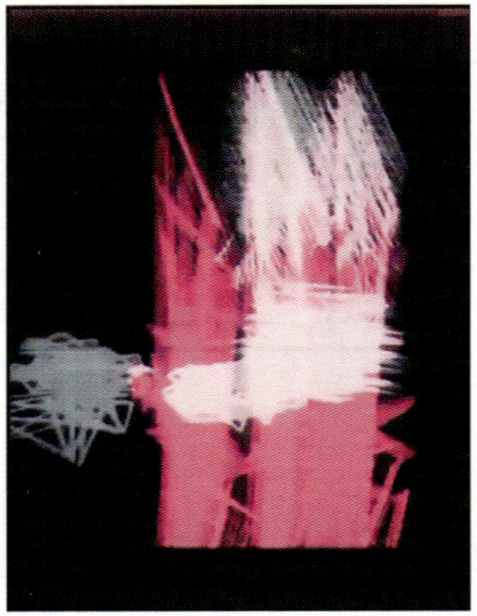

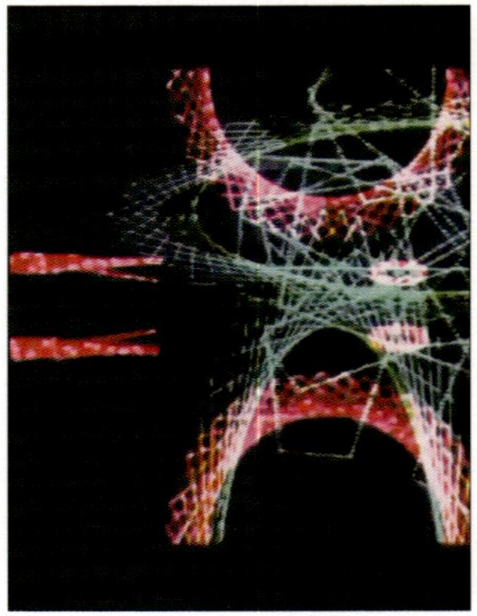

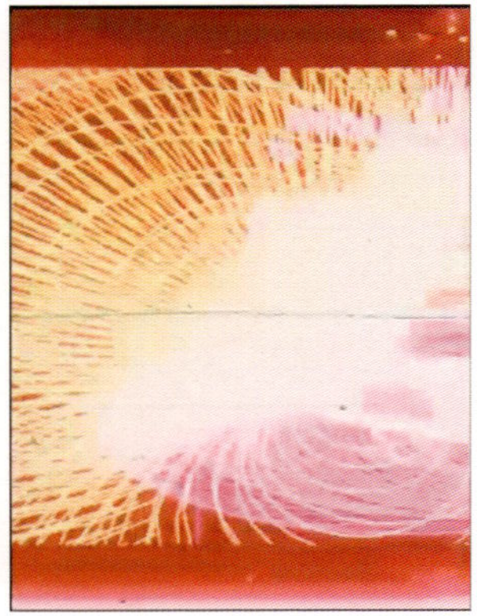

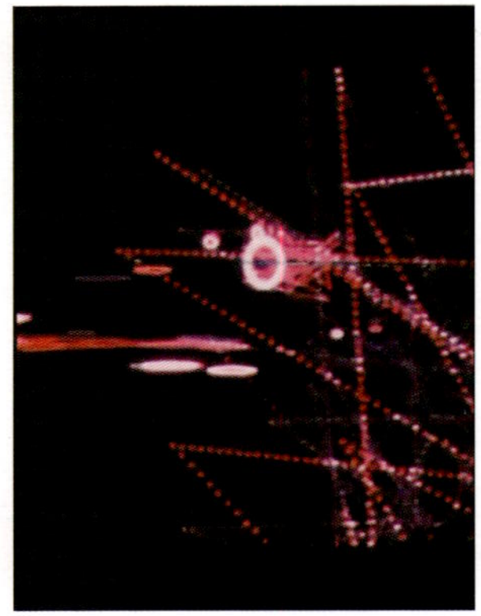

Cybernetik 5.3, John Stehura, 1969, United States

This film by United States computer art pioneer John Stehura combines algorithmic methods with live film and photography to produce an intriguing, atmospheric result. In an interview with media art theorist Gene Youngblood published in his book *Expanded Cinema*, Stehura explained the computational logic behind the artwork: "....when the image gets near this mathematical point it will either get brighter, or darker, or be altered in such and such a way, like enlarge, or burst into points, or diminish into infinity. So that's the reason for the randomness. When the images go into the metamorphosing fields, their mathematical order, while specified, becomes too complex and appears to be random. Once all the rules in the program were specified, I simply turned it on to see what would happen. If I liked the results, I'd leave it."

Courtesy of the Computer History Museum

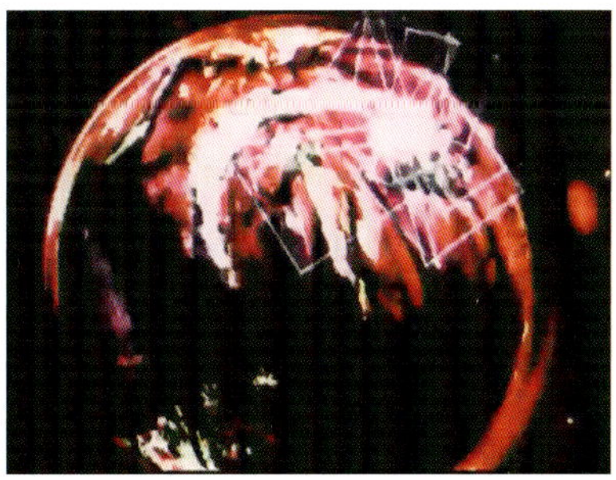

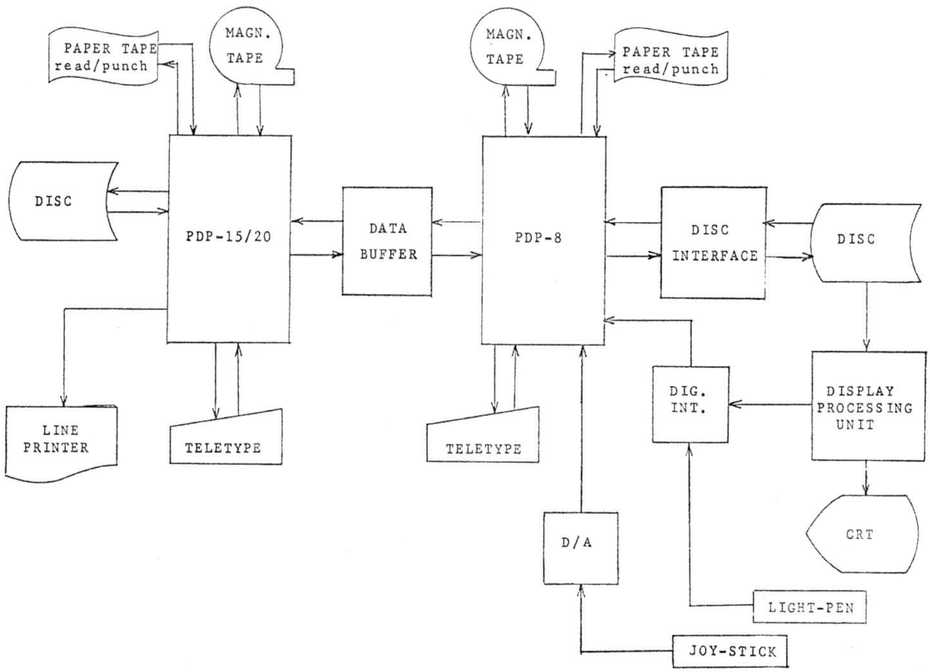

The McGRAPH system, A. S. Malowany, K.C. Campbell, T. McNeil, McGill University, 1973, Canada

It is almost impossible today to imagine a computer without a screen that dynamically displays graphic elements in response to various inputs from its users. And yet, just fifty years ago, interactive graphics were considered a complex technical problem. Researchers worked on the development not only of the computer languages that would allow interactive graphics to be programmed, but also on the hardware that would allow them to be displayed. This diagram illustrates the complexity of interactive graphic displays by depicting the "architecture" of the computers, storage devices, and input/output devices of McGRAPH, a general purpose graphic display system developed by mechanical engineering researchers at McGill University to perform the seemingly simple task of refreshing images on a cathode ray tube (CRT) display from files stored on a buffer disk.

Courtesy of the National Research Council of Canada

McGRAPH implementations of FORTRAN and GRAPHICS 2/GRIN2, A. S. Malowany, K.C. Campbell, T. McNeil, McGill University, 1973, Canada

Flexibility and adaptability were key mandates in the development of computer graphics display systems. McGRAPH was envisioned as supporting implementations of a wide array of programs, from pattern recognition, to system modeling and optimization, and to computer-aided design. On the left are two screenshots of a Regression Analysis Program developed using FORTRAN and applied to analyze different data sets by Canada Ciment Lafarge and the Montreal Children's Hospital. On the right are two screenshots from the implementation of GRAPHIC 2/GRIN2, an interactive graphics language based on a directed graph data structure developed by Bell Telephone Laboratories. GRIN2 had initially been developed for an arrangement similar to that of McGRAPH, in which a PDP computer with a DEC display were feeding off a mainframe computer. In McGRAPH, however, the mainframe was a PDP-15/20 instead of a GE 635 time-shared computer originally used by Bell.

Reconstruction from A. S. Malowany, K.C. Campbell, T. McNeil. 1973. "The McGRAPH System." Proceedings of the 3rd Man-Computer Communications Seminar. *Ottawa, ON: 30.1-30.5.*

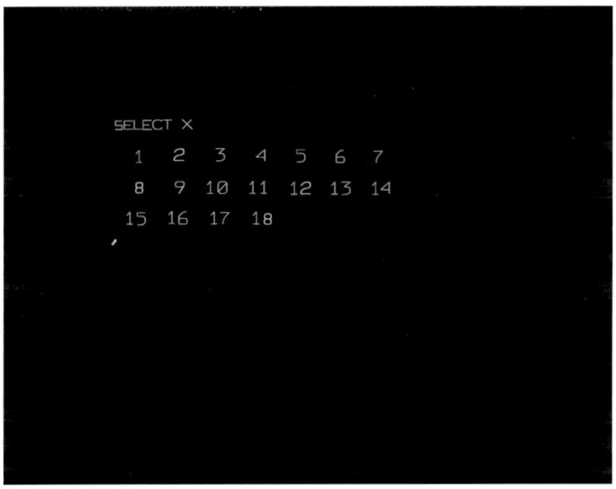

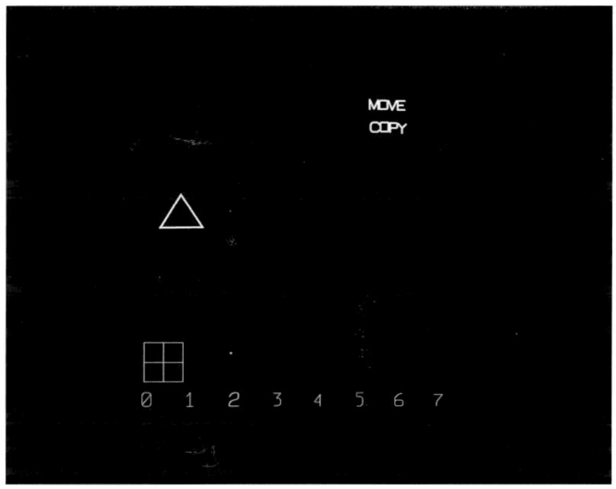

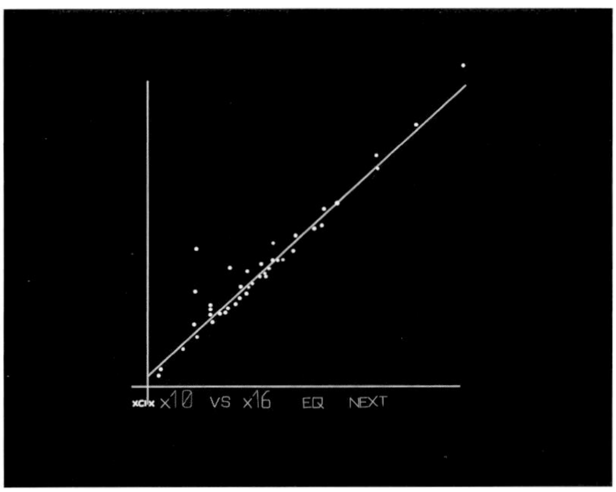

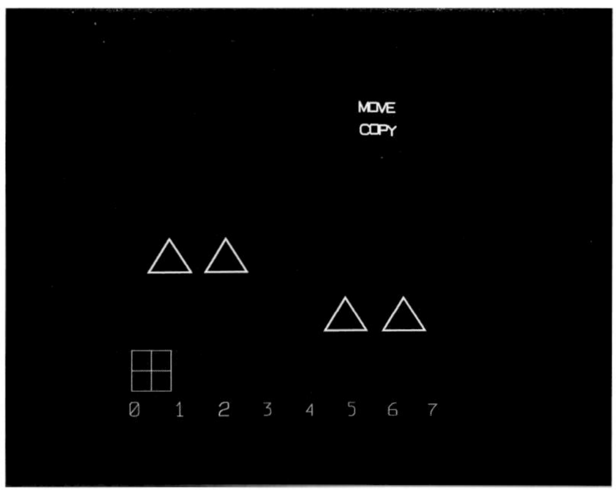

GRAPPLE functions, D.L. Williams, Bell-Northern Research, 1973, Canada

GRAPPLE primitives, D.L. Williams, Bell-Northern Research, 1973, Canada

Bell Northern Research (BNR) developed GRAPPLE (Graphical Application Programming Language) in early 1972 under the leadership of Graeme Scott who was managing BNR's computer technology center. Its aim was to make computer graphics accessible to non-programmers by enabling the direct manipulation of images through intuitive commands, without requiring the manual encoding of images as numbers. GRAPPLE involved a series of "primitives" corresponding to typical drawing and input-output operations such as SET (the pen), MOVE (the pen), DRAW, VECTOR and others, which could be nested into more complex "functions" and given mnemonic names.

Reconstruction from D.L. Williams 1973. "Graphics Application Programming Language." Proceedings of the 3rd Man-Computer Communications Seminar. *Ottawa, ON: 5.1-5.7.*

Command	Description	Syntax / Example	Drawing
$RECT	DRAW RECTANGLE	$RECT(X,Y), $RECT(700,200),	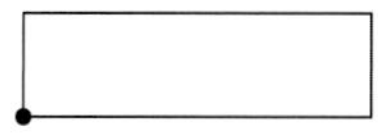
$CIRCLE	DRAW CIRCLE	$CIRCLE(RADIUS), $CIRCLE(150),	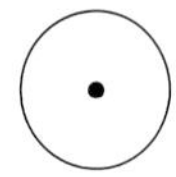
$ARC	DRAW CICULAR ARC	$ARC(RADIUS,ANG1,ANG2), $ARC(250,0,120),	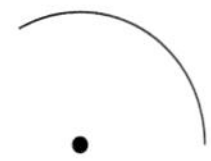
$ELIPSE	DRAW ELIPTICAL ARC	$ELIPSE(XRAD,YRAD,ANG1,ANG2), $ELIPSE(400,150,0,270),	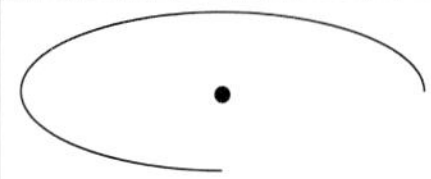
$TMARK	DRAW AXES WITH TICKMARKS	$TMARK(DX,NX,NNX,DY,NY,NNY), $TMARK(30,20,2,20,12,3),	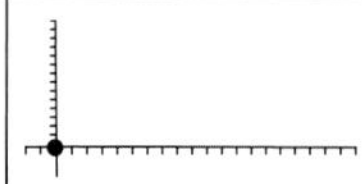
$GRID	DRAW RECTANGULAR GRID	$GRID(DX,NX,DY,NY), $GRID(100,7,50,4),	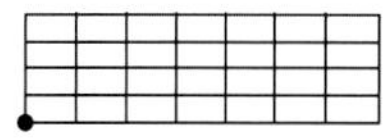
$SHADE	SHADE A RECTANGULAR AREA	$SHADE(X,Y,DELTA), $SHADE(700,200,20),	

Command	Description	Syntax / Example	Drawing
D	DRAW ABSOLUTE LINES	D(X1,Y1,X2,Y2, ,), D(700,0,700,300,300,300),	
V	DRAW RELATIVE VECTORS	V(DX1,DY1,DX2,DY2, , ,), V(300,100,200,-100,200,200,0,-200),	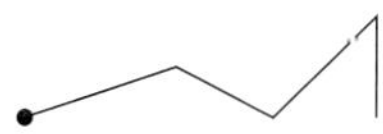
R	DRAW RELATIVE RADIALS	R(DX1,DY1,DX2,DY2, ,), R(700,100,700,200,300,200),	
X	DRAW RELATIVE ORTHOGONAL LINES FROM X AXIS	X(DX1,DY2,DX3,DY4, ,), X(400,200,200,-200,100,100),	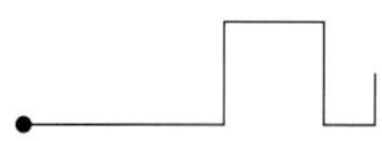
Y	DRAW RELATIVE ORTHOGONAL LINES FROM Y AXIS	Y(DY1,DX2,DY3, ,), Y(200,700,-200,-500,100,300),	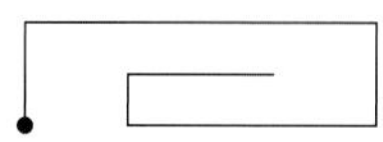
S	SET PEN ABSOLUTE	S(X,Y), S(200,100),X(200,20),	
M	MOVE PEN RELATIVE	M(DX,DY), X(200),M(200,100),X(200,20),	

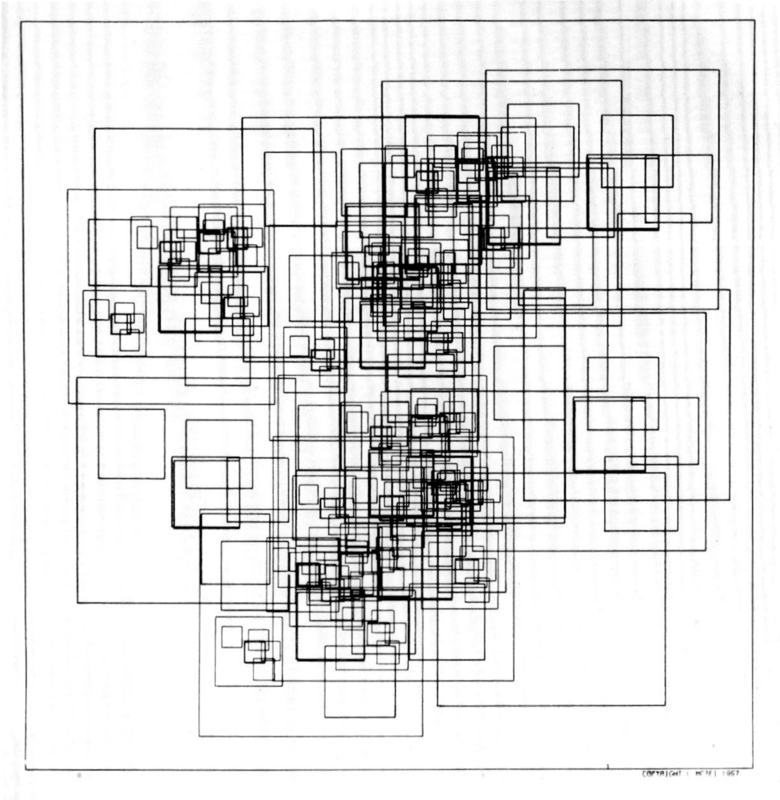

Squares within Squares, Leslie Mezei, Computer Graphics Group, University of Toronto, 1967, Canada

Leslie Mezei is widely recognized as one of the founding figures of computer art. Mezei graduated from McGill University in 1953 with first class honors in mathematics and physics, and joined the University of Toronto Computer Science Department in 1965. Two years later, he established the Computer Graphics Group and started experimenting with creating computer art using SPARTA – a FORTRAN-based programming language developed in an IBM 7094II of the University of Toronto Computer Center. These four pieces are original prints of Mezei's explorations, applying SPARTA commands such as MOVE, SIZE, ROTATE, FRAME, RDSTP (random distort points). These works correspond to three of the four "genres" of computer art that Mezei identified through extensive surveying of international activity in this emerging field: geometrical arrangements (in *Squares within Squares*), plots of mathematical equations, experiments with controlled randomness and stochastic processes (in *Babel Shook*), and topological transformations of representational images (in *Beaver Scaled* and *Transformations of a Girl's Face*). Beneath the playfulness of these works' themes which engage topics of communication, gender, and national identity, is a striking demonstration of computer graphics' capacity to render manipulable the mathematical structures underlying the visual world.

Courtesy of the artist

Babel Shook, Leslie Mezei, Computer Graphics Group, University of Toronto, 1967, Canada

Transformations of a Girl's Face, Leslie Mezei, Computer Graphics Group, University of Toronto, 1967, Canada

Beaver Scaled, Leslie Mezei, Computer Graphics Group, University of Toronto, 1969, Canada

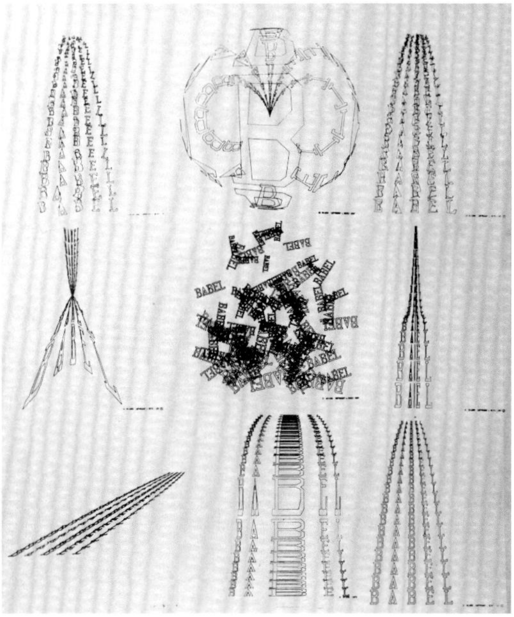

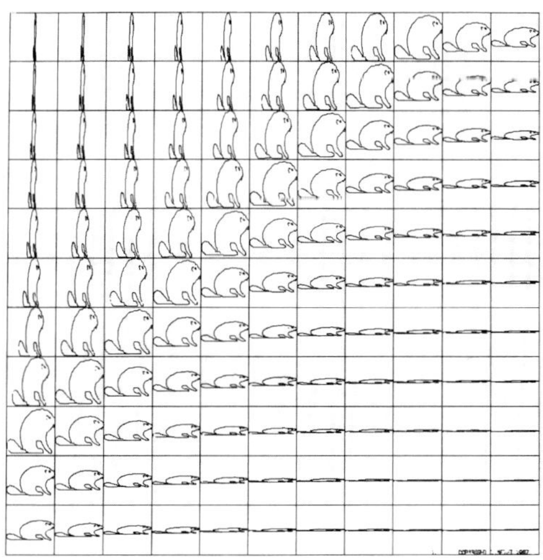

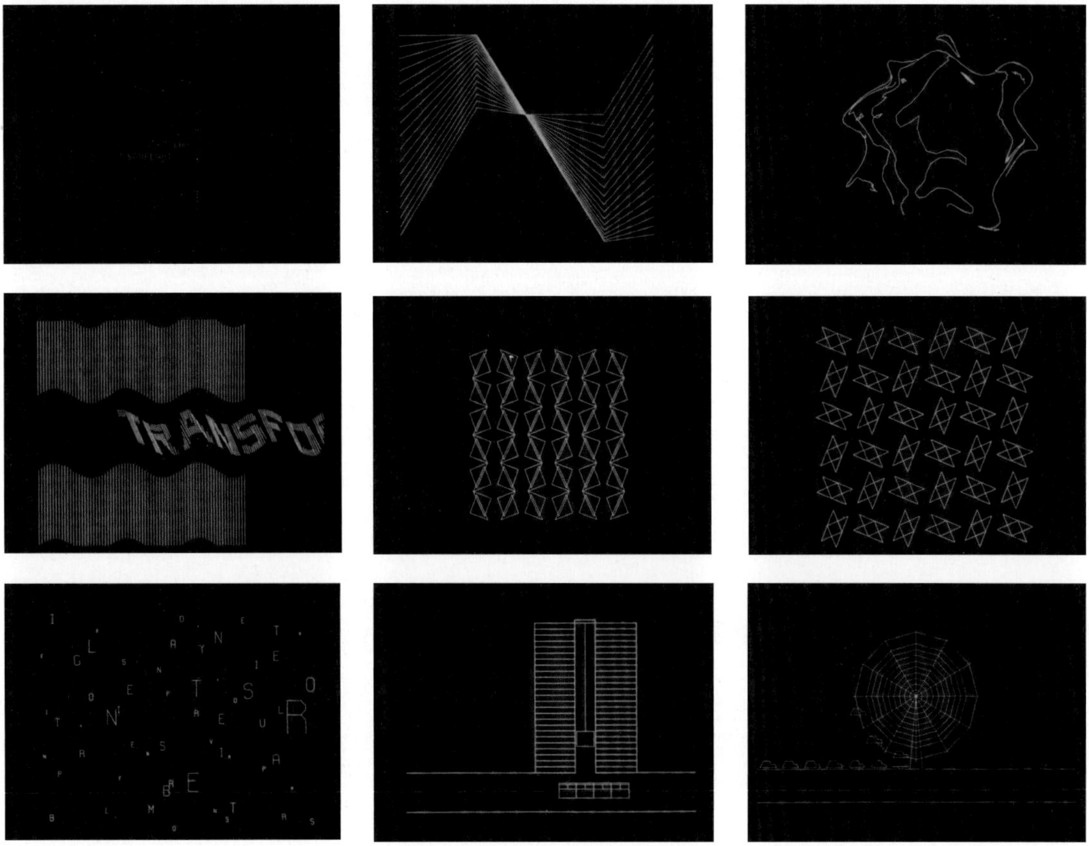

Samplart, Various artists, Computer Graphics Group, University of Toronto, 1971, Canada

From May 1971 to June 1972, and with the support of the Canada Council for the Arts, Leslie Mezei brought various artists and designers to the University of Toronto to experiment with the ARTA animation system. *Samplart* is a sample of these works created with the assistance of computer programmer Tom Britton. The participants included Lillian Schwartz, Georges Singer, Julian Rowan, and Jekabs Zvilna, and several students. These works were produced through the IBM 2250 graphics display unit at the University of Toronto's Computer Research Facility, attached to a System 360/44, with 16 mm film output from a Calcomp 835 microfilm plotter. The film score is a sampler of computer-performed music produced by James (Jim) Gabura using PIPER — a system for real-time music writing and editing using computers and analog synthesizers.

Courtesy of the artist

Art from Computers, Leslie Mezei and Aletta Schaap, Computer Graphics Group, University of Toronto, 1971, Canada

Conceived and written by Leslie Mezei and animated by Aletta Schaap, the film *Art from Computers* was produced by the Ontario Educational Communications Authority (now TVO) for the program *Adventures in Mathematics*. In a teacher's guide accompanying the video, Mezei described the film as not only providing an aesthetic experience, but also cultivating an eye for the different types of mathematical relationships that abound in the visual world. Computer graphics, in that context, were the medium for materializing art made possible through the use of mathematics: from complex arrangements of elemental geometric units, to smooth line patterns generated by equations, to transformations and distortions of familiar figures using various mappings.

Courtesy of the artist

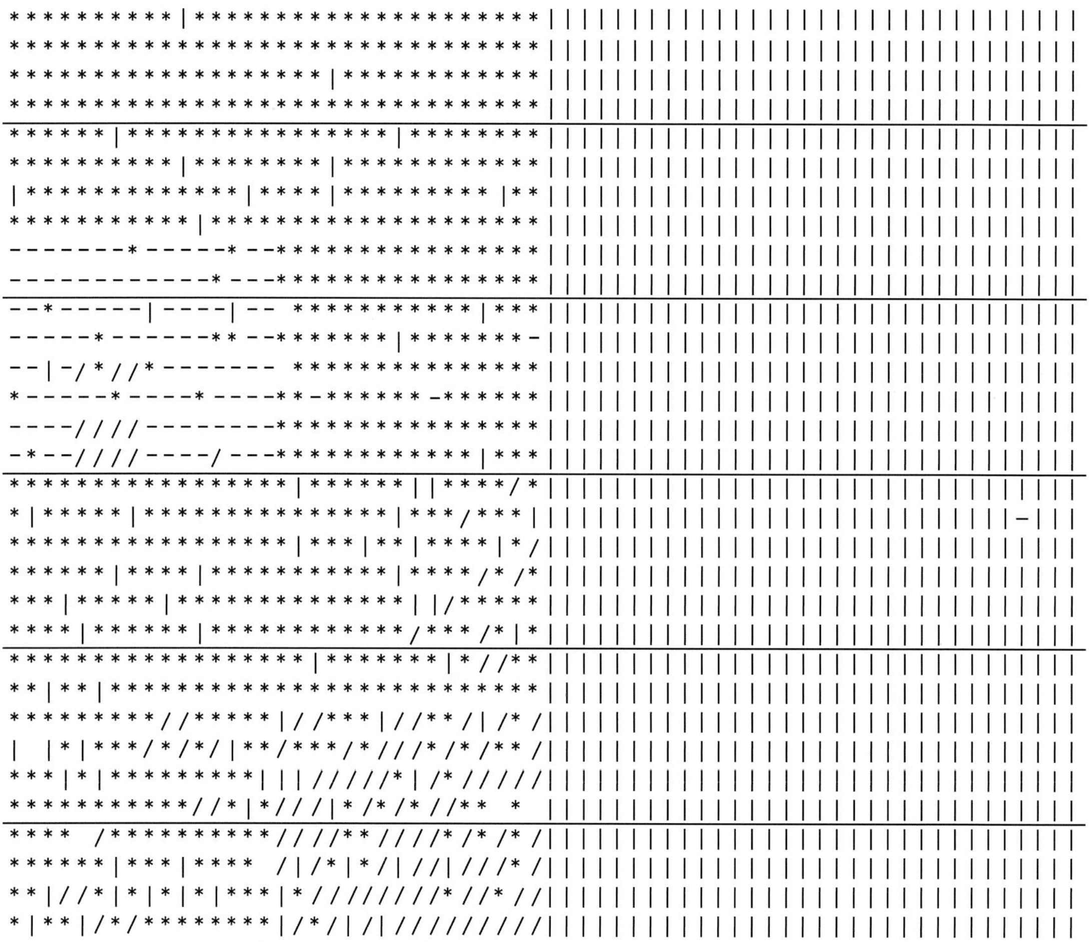

Generative Aesthetics I. Experiment 4a.5, Frieder Nake, Computer Graphics Group, University of Toronto, 1968, Canada

While pursuing postdoctoral research under the supervision of Leslie Mezei at the University of Toronto, Frieder Nake wrote a program that generated a line-printer output that was based on elements like * + - / instead of colors. He then associated these abstract symbols with colors. The printer symbols made it possible to generate large numbers of experiments. The only two print-outs realized by hand were *Experiment 4a.2* and *Experiment 6.22.*

Reconstruction from Frieder Nake. 2012."Information Aesthetics: An heroic experiment." Journal of Mathematics and the Arts. *6 (2-3):65-75.*

Generative Aesthetics I. Experiment 6.22, Frieder Nake, Computer Graphics Group, University of Toronto 1968–69, Canada

Courtesy of the artist

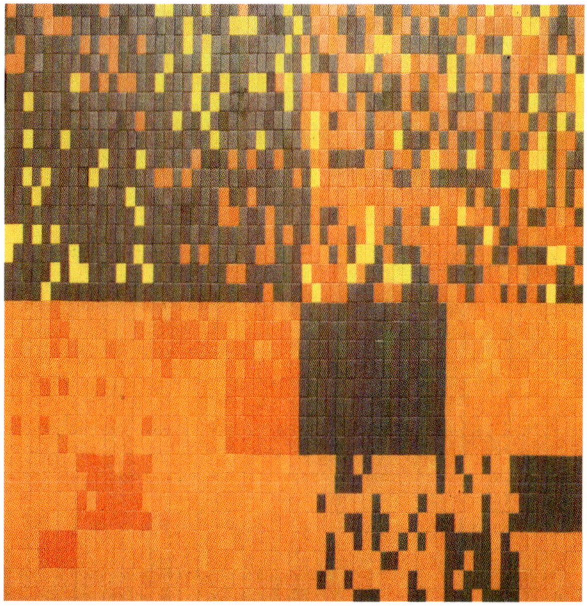

Generative Aesthetics I. Experiment 4a.2, Frieder Nake, Computer Graphics Group, University of Toronto, 1968–69, Canada

This work was realized based on the visual code on page 134 Nake and his students attached small rectangles of colored cardboard onto a large hard board (128 X 128 cm) following the position and sequence of the symbols outputted by the line printer. Nake's mother destroyed *Experiment 4a.2* when he went to Vancouver. *Experiment 6.22* (page 131) is currently featured in the collection of Museum Abteiberg in Mönchengladbach, Germany.

Courtesy of the artist

Walk-through Raster, Frieder Nake, 1972, Canada

This work was published in *Art Ex Machina*, a portfolio of six silk-screen prints of computer-generated images and statements by prominent computer artists Manuel Barbadillo, Hiroshi Kawano, Ken Knowlton, Manfred Mohr, Frieder Nake, and Georg Nees, edited and published by Gilles Gheerbrant in Montreal, Canada.

Courtesy of the artist

Napoleon Portrait, Frieder Nake, 1969, Canada

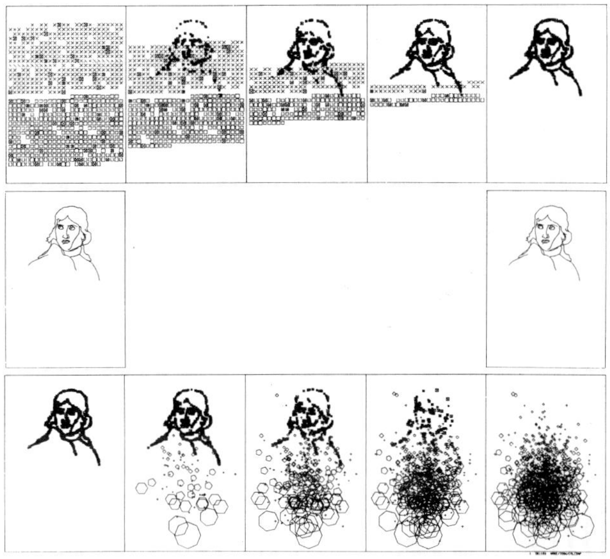

In 1968, the German curator Klaus Hoffmann sent a postcard of an unfinished portrait of Napoleon by Jacques David to 100 artists, including Frieder Nake, and asked them to finish the painting. Instead of completing the unfinished work, Nake rather "destroyed" it: he took the unfinished portrait as a "gestalt" and had it transformed into a line drawing, which was then transformed into little square points, which, in turn, were re-assembled step by step in two different directions: structure and chaos. The structure stood for the French central state, the chaos for Napoleon's wars.

Courtesy of the artist

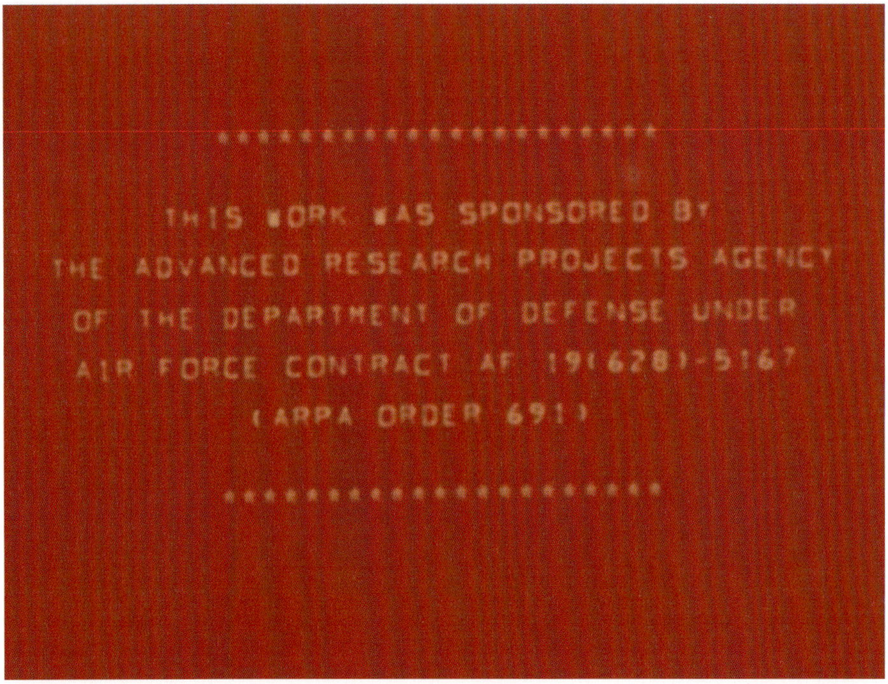
****
THIS WORK WAS SPONSORED BY
THE ADVANCED RESEARCH PROJECTS AGENCY
OF THE DEPARTMENT OF DEFENSE UNDER
AIR FORCE CONTRACT AF 19(628)-5167
(ARPA ORDER 691)
****

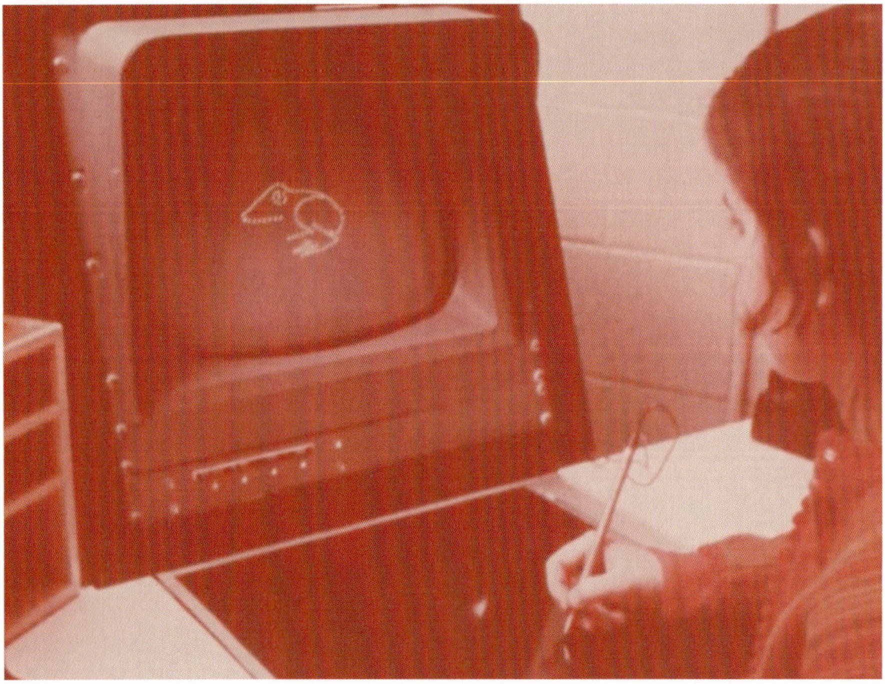

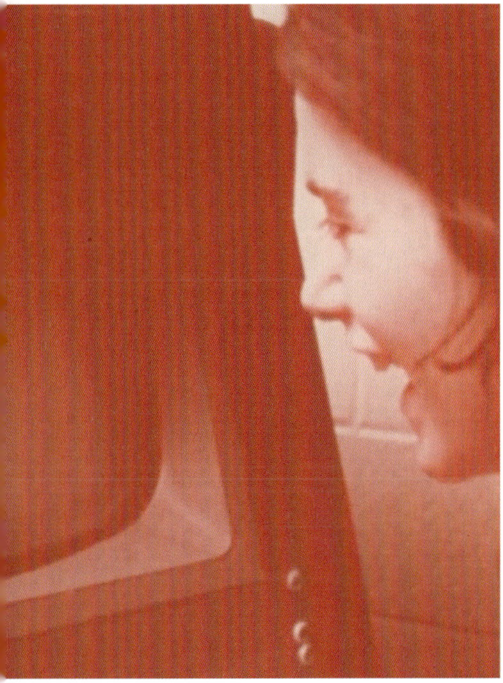

GENESYS: Computer animation system, Ron Baecker, Project MAC, c. 1970, United States

GENESYS was an interactive computer animation system developed by Ronald Baecker, co-founder of the Dynamic Graphics Project at the University of Toronto. Baecker developed GENESYS at MIT as part of Project MAC (Project on Mathematics and Computation), a major collaborative endeavor to implement and explore the potentials of time-sharing computer systems. Opposite to animation systems that required their users to write a movie in a programming language, such as Ken Knowlton's EEFLIX or EXFLOR, GENESYS allowed for free-hand sketching of the animation aiming for a spontaneous, real-time interaction.

Courtesy of the author

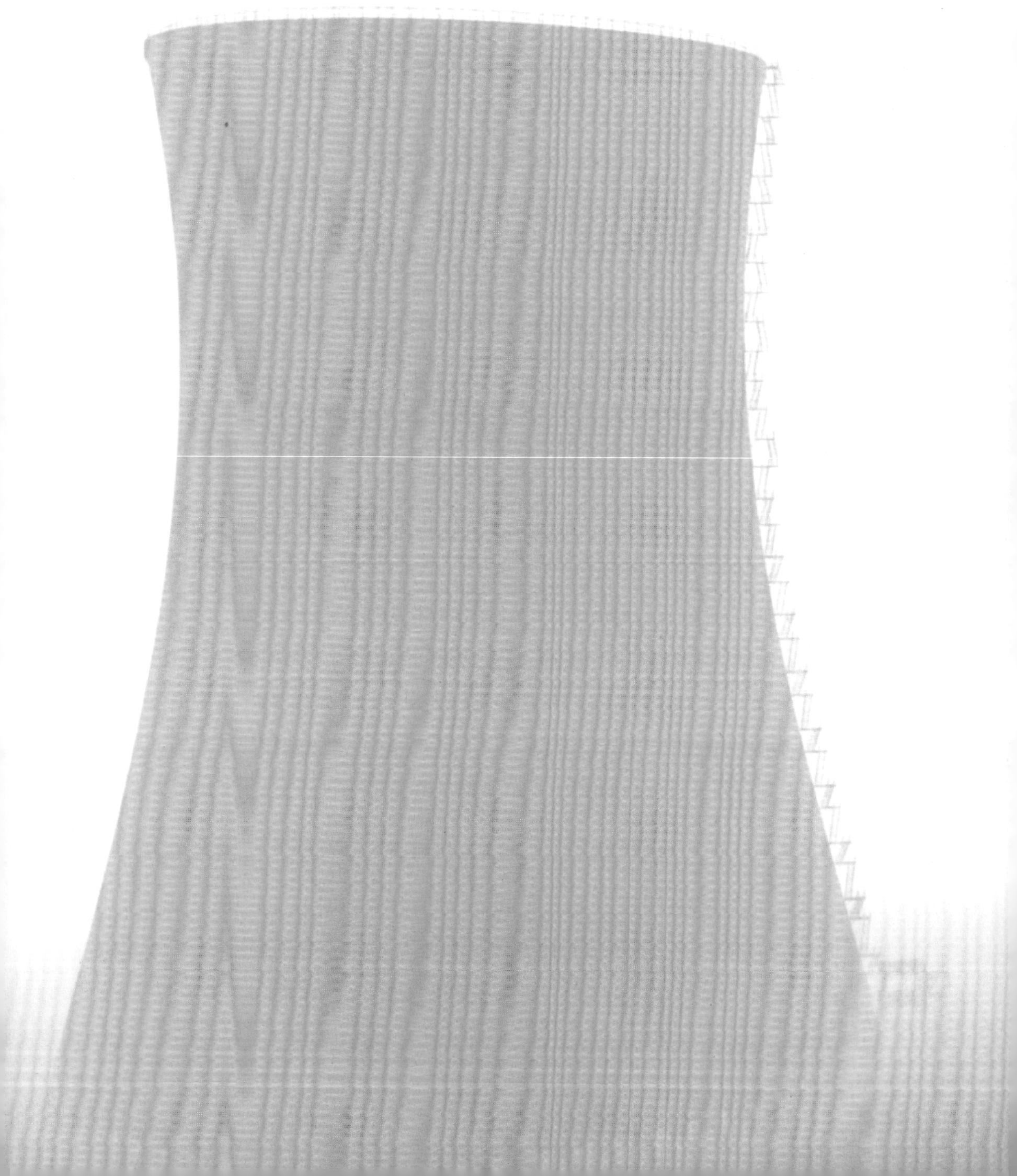

(pictured on previous page)

Z, Alan Warburton, 2012, United Kingdom

This film by British multidisciplinary artist Alan Warburton is composed entirely of z-depth images — a ghostly black & white data format native only to CG animation. The z-depth image works similarly to radar or MRI scans. It interprets objects within a scene according to distance: those closest to the camera are black, those furthest away are white (or vice versa). Details are lost at either end of the spectrum, and are revealed within the middle distance. Functionally, this allows CGI artists to pull camera focus in post-production by using the monochromatic shades in the z-depth pass. The z-depth image is thus usually an unseen, intermediary step in the calculation of realistic CG imagery. By exposing it and focusing our attention on it, Warburton offers us a glimpse of the complex and structured nature of the contemporary computational image. An essay by media historian Jacob Gaboury on this piece is included in this section.

Digital video on screen, 3 min. loop
Courtesy of the artist

Indeterminate Set, Dana Cupkova, EPIPHYTE Lab, 2017, United States

This lenticular print created by Slovak-born, US-based architect Dana Cupkova in collaboration with Maranatha Dawkins and Colleen Clifford represents the topography of a flooded landscape. Each curve is assigned a color value based on the element's numerical description encoded in a digital file. The result evokes the aesthetics of indeterminacy of early computer art, and yet its rooting in geographical analysis data make it a unique representation, or portrait, of a landscape.

Lenticular Print
20 x 30 in (50.8 x 76.2 cm)
Courtesy of the artist

Abstraction II (Unsmooth), Andrew Heumann, 2011, United States

In these four pieces, United States artist and architect Andrew Heumann investigates algorithms commonly employed by CAD systems, playfully subverting them to make visible the traces they leave on architectural work. *Abstraction II (unsmooth)* explores subdivision, a process to recursively divide a geometric shape into successively finer meshes to achieve smoothness. Dating back to 1978, Catmull-Clark is the first general algorithm for mesh subdivision. It recursively applies weights to each initial mesh vertex location to generate new vertex positions. This piece depicts a form that has been recursively subdivided according to the Catmull-Clark algorithm, with the values in the weighting function altered so as to produce a jagged, complex spikiness instead of smoothness.

Digital print
12 x 12 in (30.5 x 30.5 cm)
Courtesy of the artist

11-House / 1.8%, Andrew Heumann, 2016, United States

For decades, architectural researchers and practitioners, and technology companies, have sought to automate aspects of architectural practice. In this piece, Heumann selects eleven plan drawings from a large pool of automatically-generated versions of the "Revit Basic Sample Project" — a model that ships with Autodesk's ubiquitous BIM software — and playfully explores them through automation. The final piece post-processes the generated drawing sets into a composite uniting the linework from all eleven plans. Here, the artist uses automation to create ambiguity. The resulting drawings demand the affective human labor of interpretation and reflection.

Digital print
12 x 12 in (30.5 x 30.5 cm)
ourtesy of the artist

Ayo, Andrew Heumann, 2017, United States

Numerous software tools for 3D modeling and rendering feature a technique called "Ambient Occlusion" — an approximate simulation of the lighting of an object given uniform, diffuse illumination. Its effect is soft, yielding no hard shadows, and can frequently be seen as an underlay in architectural diagramming work. It allows the expression of three-dimensional volume without any reference to a specific context or lighting condition — it is the most "generic" lighting possible. This piece applies ambient occlusion to sequentially deeper voids cut in a surface, and then exposes their "soft" geometries by rendering isocontours on the brightness values, also known as isophotes.

Digital print
12 x 12 in (30.5 x 30.5 cm)
Courtesy of the artist

Four Fights, Andrew Heumann, 2017, United States

This piece celebrates a phenomenon normally regarded as a glitch, error, or mistake: the "Z-Fighting" that occurs when two polygonal mesh faces occupy the same space, overlapping precisely. The beautiful and varied patterning that occurs is the consequence of several interacting systems: floating-point arithmetic, the system of approximate-but-fast mathematics used by the computer; rasterization and fragment rendering by which a 3D polygon model is transformed into 2D screen space; and the "Depth Buffer," an invisible rendering channel which represents the distance of each element in the scene from the virtual camera.

Digital print
12 x 12 in (30.5 x 30.5 cm)
Courtesy of the artist

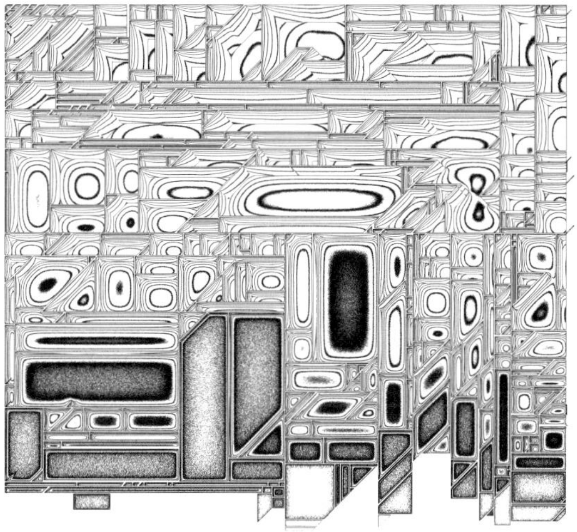

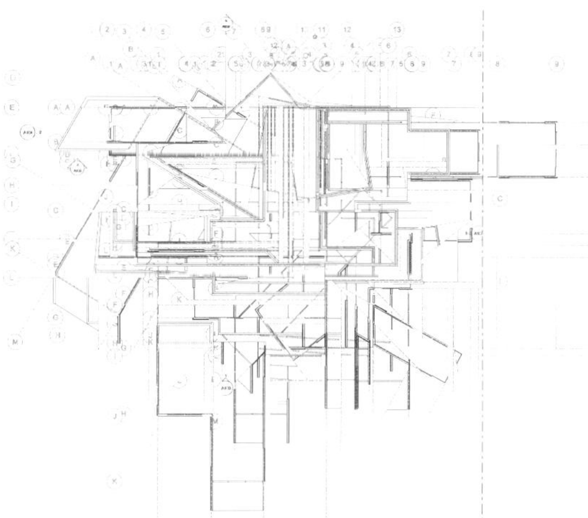

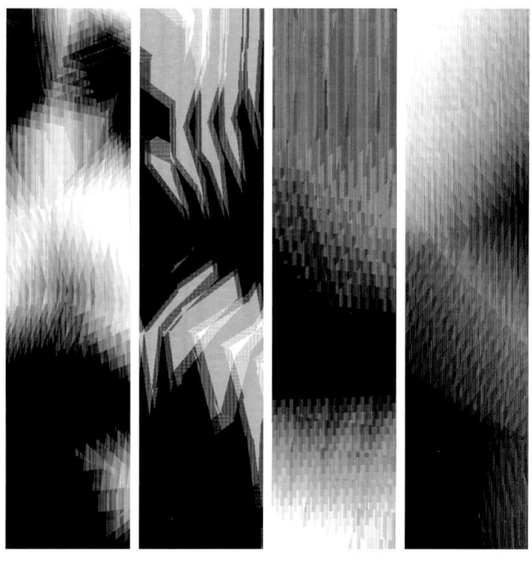

Icosphere ink (left), *Ink sphere* (right), Zach Lieberman, 2016–17, United States

One of the United States' foremost new media artists and educators — and a leading figure in the creative coding community — Zach Lieberman combines the development of new programming tools for creative exploration with playful experimentation of time-based and interactive systems. This selection of works, developed using Open Frameworks, a C++ library he co-initiated and continues to develop, illustrates Lieberman's astute understanding of (and playful engagement with) computational form, color, and geometry.

Digital video on square screen
26.5 x 26.5 in (67.3 x 67.3 cm)
Courtesy of the artist

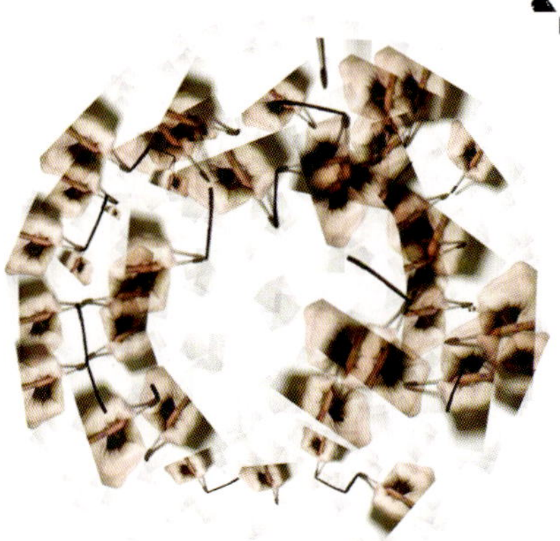

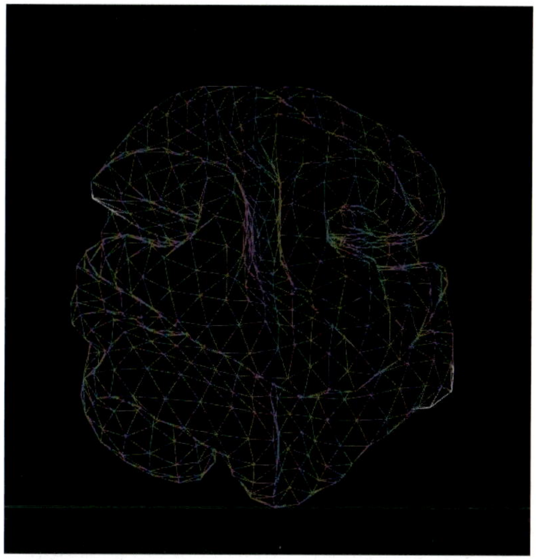

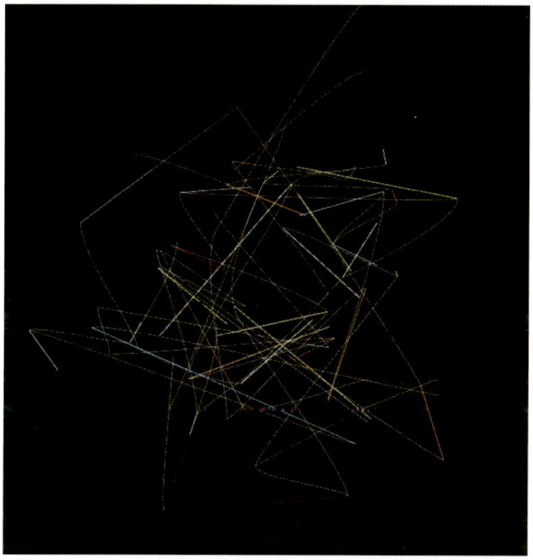

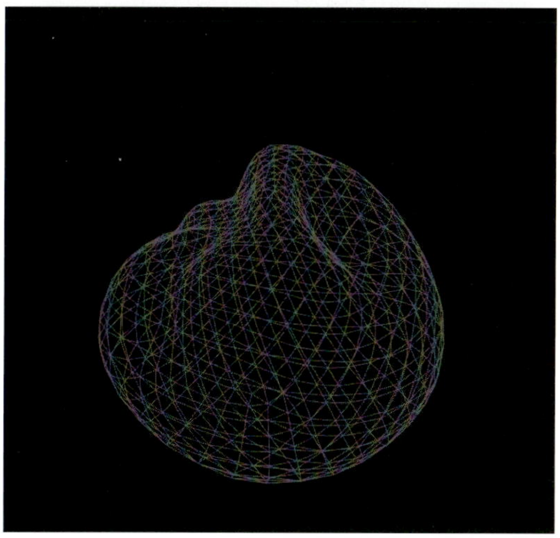

10x10 cubes with random lines (upper left), *3d blob / movement study* (upper right), *Cube with curves* (middle left), *Puffball* (middle right), *3d blob / contour travelers add energy* (lower left), *More trails* (pictured on following spread)
Zach Lieberman, 2016–17, United States

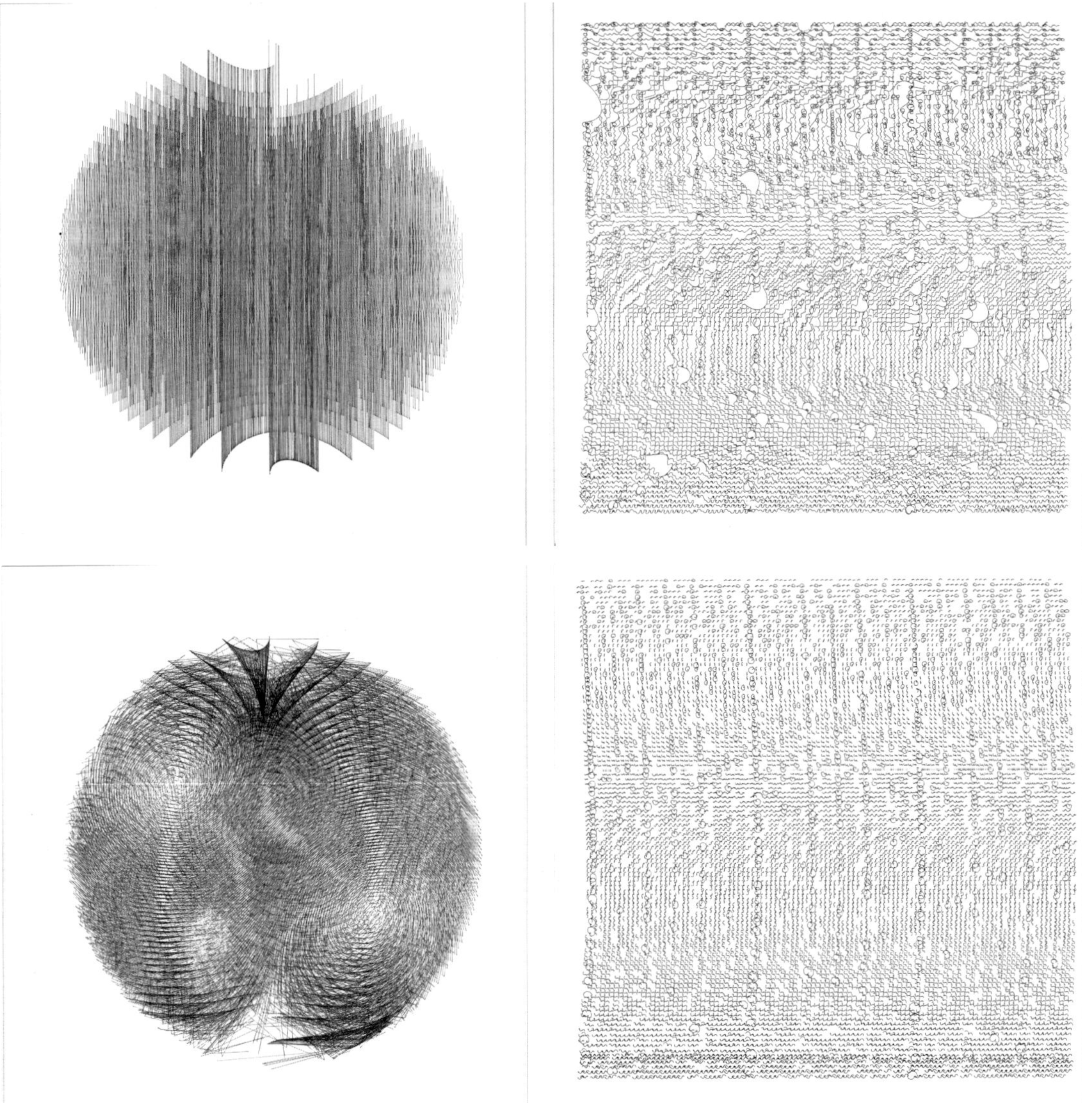

Curves created in two dimensions, Unrelated on Paper 1-4, Carl Lostritto, 2017, United States

United States architect and computational artist Carl Lostritto's visual practice explores contingencies in both the materiality of physical media – plotters, markers, substrates, ink – and algorithmic processes. Combining stochastic processes and geometry, and wet ink and bits, his works evoke earlier expressions of computational aesthetics, while leading us to rethink the act of drawing, and the nature of points and lines, through a distinctively architectural eye.

Ink on paper, gel pen and vintage Hewlett Packard 7475A plotter
11 x 11 in (27.9 x 27.9 cm) each
Courtesy of the artist

Synclastic and anticlastic (series), Joseph Choma, Design Topology Lab, Clemson University, 2021, United States

In this series of computational drawings, architect and computational designer Joseph Choma explores geometries that evoke Frei Otto's tension-only or compression-only soap bubble structures. However, instead of simulating the physics of tensile structures, Choma generates the shape by iteratively modeling mathematical expressions — an approach he calls "materializing mathematics."

Digital print
16 x 16 in (40.6 x 40.6 cm) each
Courtesy of the artist

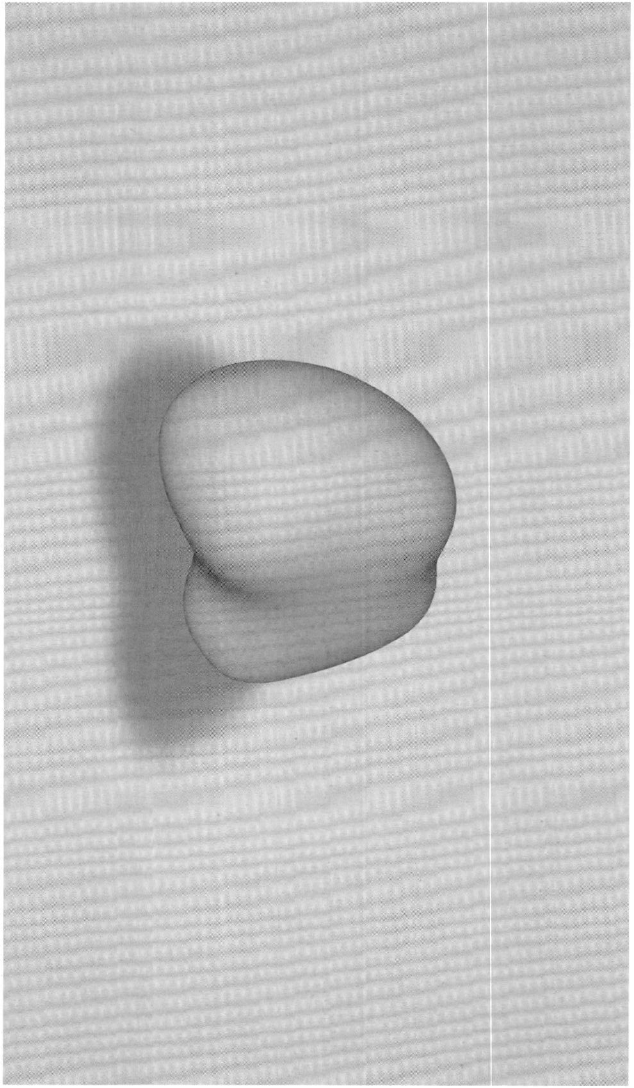

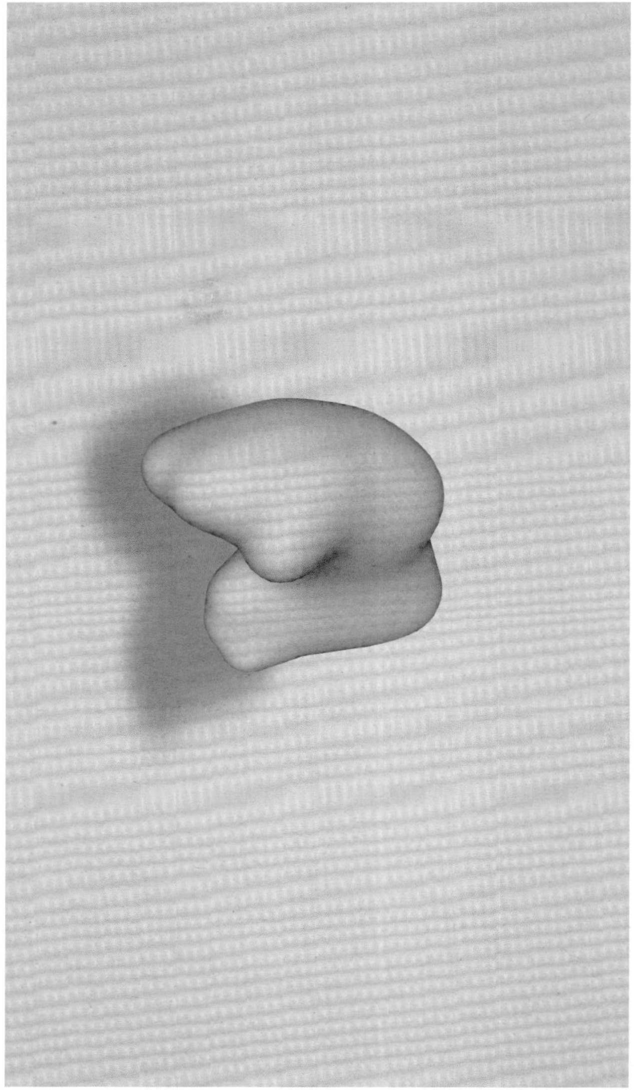

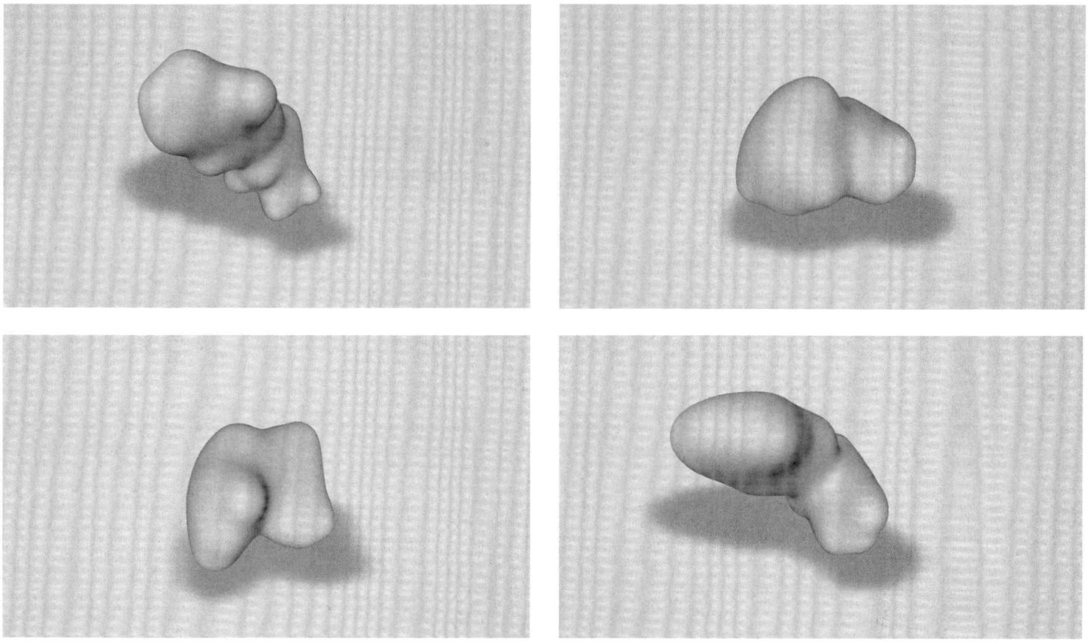

Merce's isosurface, Golan Levin, 2009, United States

Four artists — Brian Knep, Golan Levin, Casey Reas, and Sosolimited — were invited to independently repurpose United States dancer Merce Cunningham's dance performance data into new digital forms. *Merce's Isosurface* is Golan Levin's remixing of these data, which returns a mortal coil to the disembodied datapoints of Merce Cunningham's performance. The video uses the digitally captured coordinates of Cunningham's fingers and knuckle joints to structure a smooth field of simulated energy. The result is a twitchy, fleshy blob, animated by Cunningham's own movements, which dances in the liminal territory between pure abstract form and medical information visualization. The source motion capture data from the LOOPS project (2001–2008), a digital portrait of Merce Cunningham, by artists Marc Downie, Shelley Eshkar and Paul Kaiser released open source by The Cunningham Foundation and OpenEnded Group. The LOOPS project was funded by the LEF Foundation, and the four remixes were commissioned by the 2009 Boston Cyberarts Festival. Software, Art, Remix Concept: Golan Levin; Motion capture data: Courtesy OpenEnded Group and Cunningham Foundation; Mocap parsing code: Lucas Walter, Bioviewer; Metaball code: Andreas Jönsson, Angelcode; Mocap file conversion: Moshe Mahler, CMU Graphics Lab; Developed in openFrameworks. The artist thanks George Fifield of the BCF, and to the other artists involved.

Digital video on screen
2 min. 17 sec. loop
Courtesy of the artist

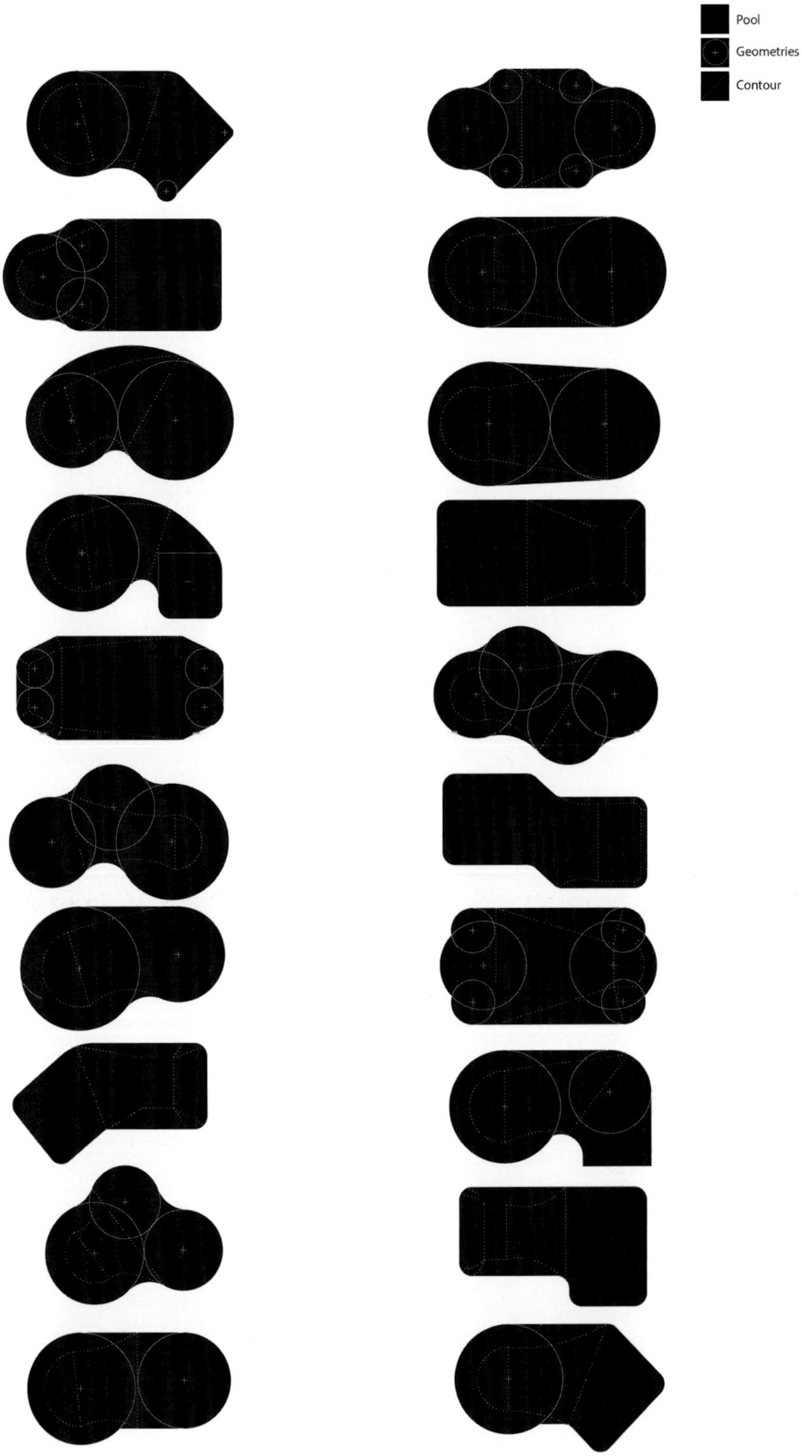

Pool Shapes and Proportions

LOW VOLUME, Kristy Balliet and Kelly Bair, 2018, United States

In LOW VOLUME, United States architects Kristy Balliet and Kelly Bair reconsider the conventional ratios and relationships between yard, deck, and pool/water in a house. The deck overtakes the pool volume and adopts its material properties resulting in a formal spill of surface decking that houses a kidney shaped pool within its folds. The kidney shape is tilted, obstructing the view of its profile from above. The pool is experienced in elevation and section, an effect furthered by the pool's placement within the already sunken front garden. In *LOW VOLUME*, the relationship of the house with the ground is ambivalent. In recombining architectural elements and their functions, and modeling unexpected spatial dependencies, the team conceives an architectural process where spaces are as reconfigurable as variables in a computer program.

Architectural model and three framed drawings
Model: 13 x 33 x 12 in (33 x 83.8 x 30.4 cm);
Drawings: 24 x 24 in (60.9 x 60.9 cm) each
Courtesy of the artists

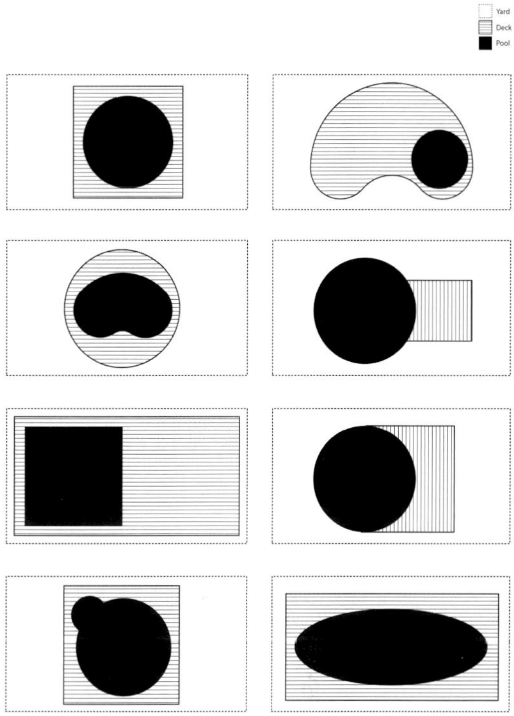

Yard to Deck to Pool Relationships

Avena + Test Bed, Benedikt Groß, 2013, Germany

This piece, an exploration of agriculture and digital fabrication by German computational designer Benedikt Groß, resulted from close collaborations with agriculture experts, engineers, a tractor driver, a videographer, and a pilot. Groß transformed a tractor into a sort of printer which, guided by algorithms, planted a variety of plants over a field of 11.5 hectares. The piece explores computational method's capacities to enable sustainable and biodiverse farming ecosystems for the production of both food and biofuels.

Digital print and video on screen
Print: 8 x 5.33 in (20.32 x 13.5 cm); video: 4 min. 53 sec. loop
Courtesy of the artist

Formations in Bodoni Baurer, Kyuha Shim, 2017, United States

In this computational typography project, computational designer Kyuha Shim demonstrates how type can be made flexible by introducing random variations and autonomous, form-giving behaviors. The piece interrogates the notion of craftsmanship, suggesting it may be defined both by direct engagements with a medium and indirect simulations of logic. Utilizing real-time data, a graphic designer shifts from authoring form to authoring a process of formation.

Interactive projection (dimension variable)
Courtesy of the artist

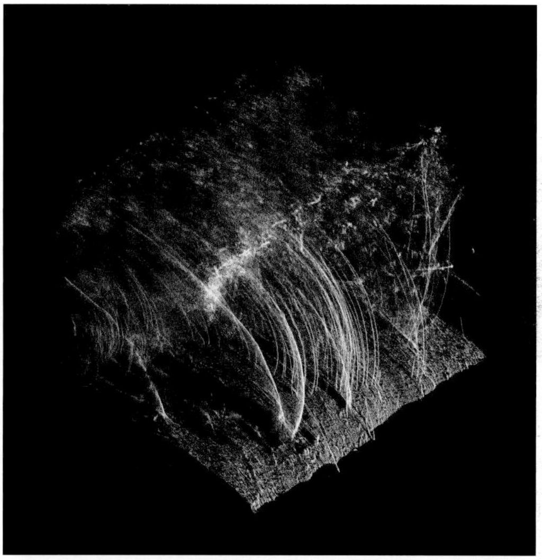

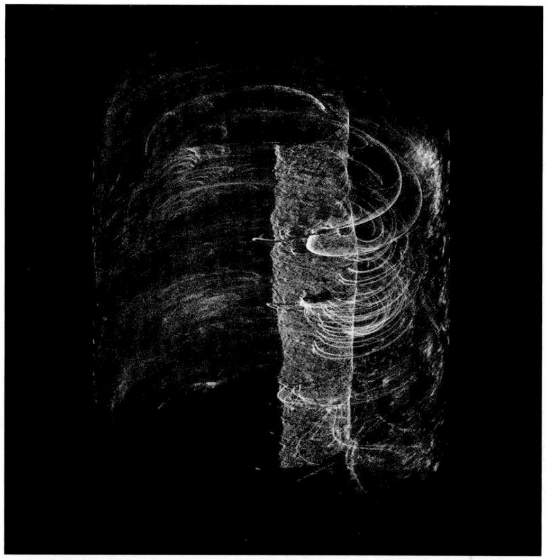

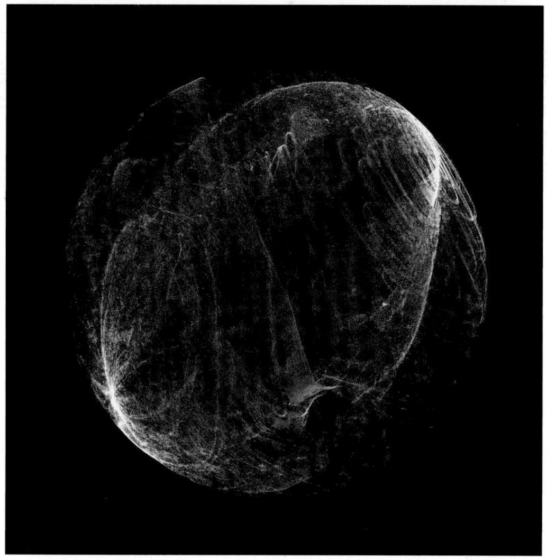

Untitled, Ben Snell, 2017, United States (also pictured on previous page)

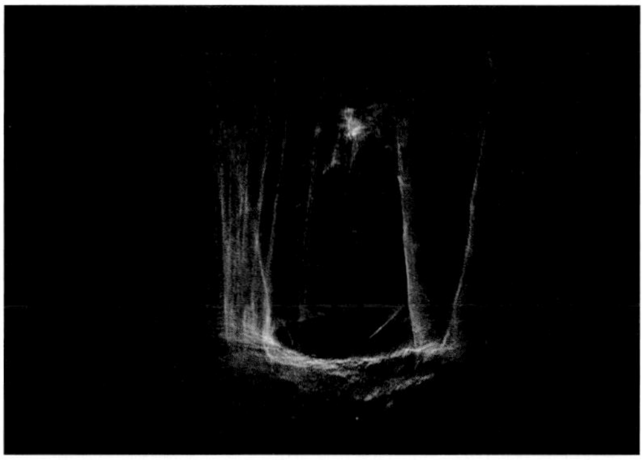

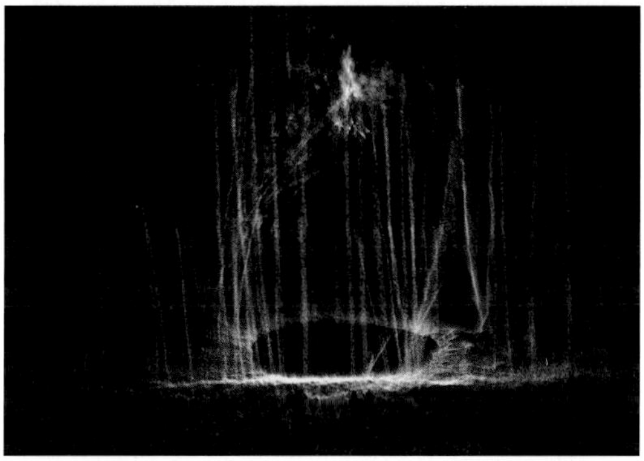

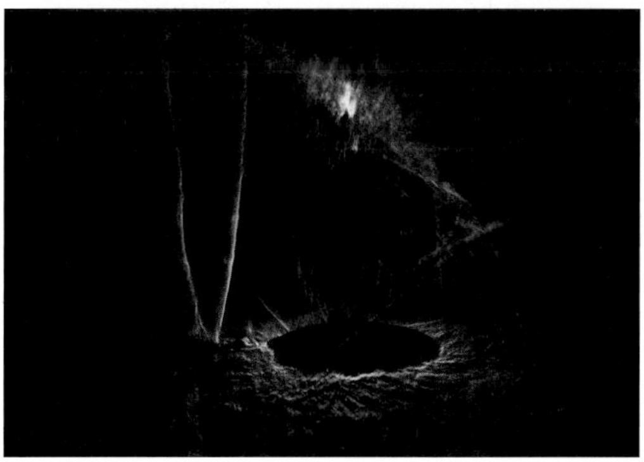

LIDAR is a range-sensing technology typically employed by the government and military to survey land from above. By measuring the time of flight of modulated pulses of light, depth can be extracted from a scene, often to very high precision. Here, United States artist Ben Snell brings this device deep within a bamboo forest in the Blue Ridge Mountains of Northern Virginia. Setting up a conversation with this piece of technology, out of the context in which it normally belongs, he explores how it sees the world. From a single capture stem myriad interpretations of the same scene: variations of coordinate mappings. Some look like the world as we know it; others may be unfamiliar, appearing impossibly distorted. Together, they reveal the full space of possible realities: those already imagined and those yet to be. Two forests with all but one of the same dimensional projections bear substantial resemblance: They are structurally different, yet contain the same raw material. The ravine situated between these forms epitomizes the breadth of a latent space where illuminating new vantage points reside.

Two digital prints and video on screen
Prints: 22 x 13.75 in (55.9 x 34.9 cm); video: 6 min. loop
Courtesy of the artist

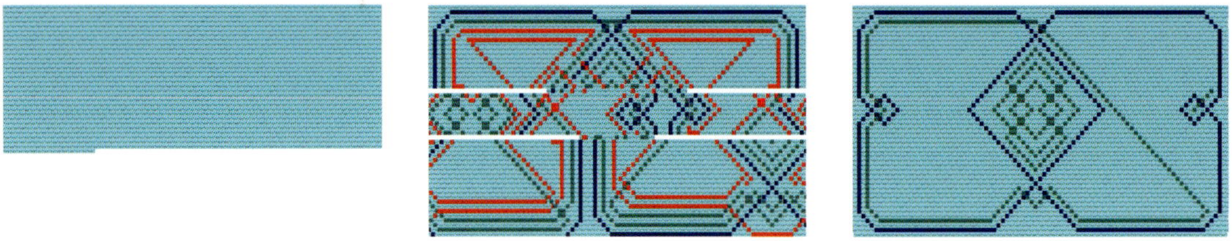

Trajan pro, Shaheer Zazai, 2014, Canada

Digital video on screen
6 min. 15 sec. loop
Courtesy of the artist

Resident, Shaheer Zazai, 2017, Canada

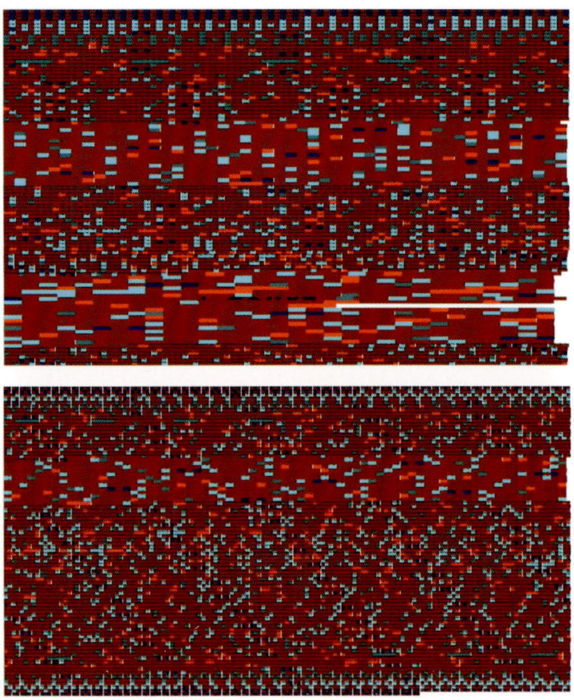

Toronto-based Afghan-Canadian artist Shaheer Zazai generates intricate and ornate patterns by arranging characters and symbols in Microsoft Word. Printed on watercolor paper, Zazai's works playfully leverage the constraints of a pervasive commercial software to produce visually striking pieces with ambivalent evocations of cultural identity – a throughline in Zazai's work. Zazai's composition of images from discrete characters in Microsoft Word is reminiscent of early computer output devices such as line printers. However, Zazai's process videos reveal a different sensibility that operates through arraying and modifying discrete characters and symbols in a layered manner. Select commands and page movements produce unexpected visual effects that re-enchant the humdrum word processing software.

Digital video on screen
1 min. 9 sec. loop
Courtesy of the artist

44NS10F, Shaheer Zazai, 2019, Canada
MFPTN1, Shaheer Zazai, 2019, Canada

Digital print, Microsoft Word
17 x 22 in (43.2 x 55.9 cm)
Courtesy of the artist

Binary bitmaps, Jonah Marrs, 2019, Canada (pictured on the following spread)

Paris-based Canadian computational artist and designer Jonah Marrs created this series of bitmaps using binvis.io, a software developed by Aldo Cortesi to visually analyze binary files (digital files which do not comprise text, such as computer programs). The software assigns visual values to a sample of a binary file's contents to facilitate its analysis. The four bitmaps displayed here result from interpreting files in formats commonly used in computational design such as .STL, .DXF, and .3DM. The results offer an unusual glimpse of the structures that underlie computational images.

Digital print
24 x 12 in (60.9 x 30.5 cm)
Courtesy of the artist

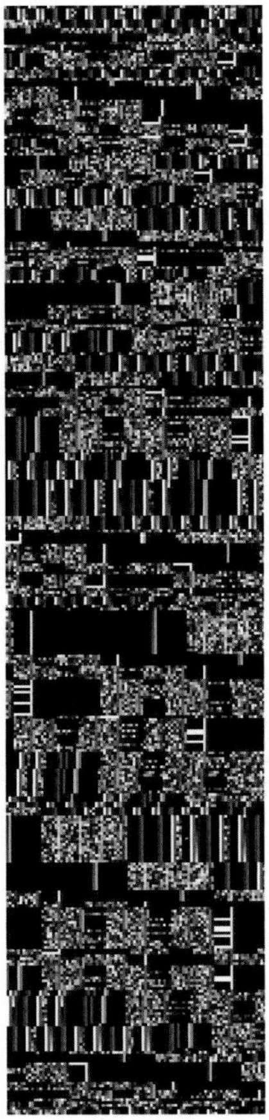

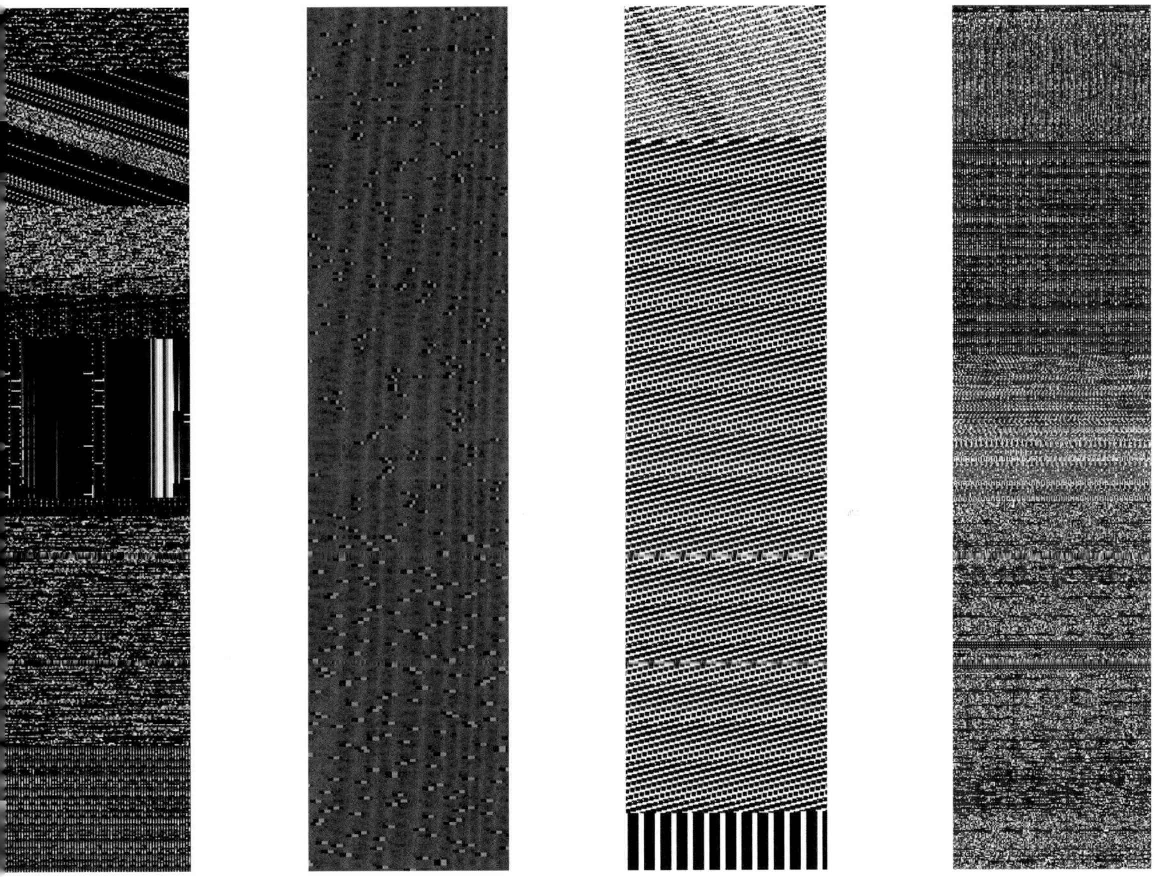

Materialities of Shiny Surfacing with Chrome

Akshita Sivakumar

Shader Ball

Procedural Chrome

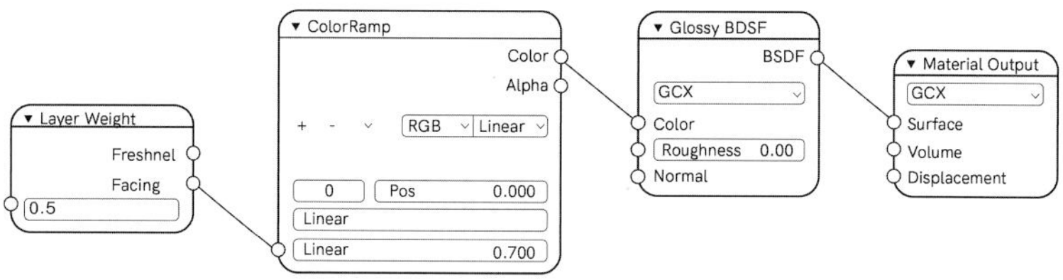

Wireframe Diagram . Blender

Cycles Procedural Node Setup

From top to bottom: "Shader Ball," Blender wireframe diagram, and "Suzanne the Monkey." "Shader Ball" reproduced under Creative Commons Attribution and with kind permission from Robin Marín (a.k.a. tuqueque); Blender wireframe diagram by the author; "Suzanne the Monkey" reproduced under General Public License and with kind permission from Willem-Paul van Overbruggen (a.k.a. SLiD3).

Suzanne the Monkey. Blender

Chrome Surface

1 For more on the generation of computational complexity within the rendering domain see Alvy Smith. "Plants, Fractals, and Formal Languages." *ACM SIGGRAPH Computer Graphics* 18 (July 1, 1984): 1–10. https://doi.org/10.1145/964965.808571.

Shiny surfaces reflect more than their environments.

Let's begin with this image of a chrome ball, a wireframe diagram, and a monkey. The material shader ball is a test geometry used in computer graphics material texture libraries to depict what a particular texture looks like on a curved surface. The wireframe diagram is an abstraction of the logic behind how geometries are surfaced to produce a chrome effect using procedural textures in Blender3D, an open-source computer graphics suite. Suzanne the monkey is a standard reference object within Blender, here surfaced in chrome.

Digital surfaces developed through procedural techniques are not merely technical accomplishments. Surfaces in architectural design have long been a site of cultural communication where meaning is made, and social values are reflected and negotiated — from Potemkin village-like facades to the latest nanocoating to strengthen building materials. Chrome surfaces have variably but surely materialized modernist aphorisms of newness, reflectivity, lightness, and durability. One only needs to look at the oft-valorized chrome-plated cruciform columns that Mies van der Rohe designed to achieve the lightness of the German Pavilion in Barcelona and Villa Tugendhat in Brno or look to the trade catalogs of the 1930s to see the surfeit of chrome's use as a signifier of mass-produced modern life; shiny utility made durable. While chrome may have faded from its peak modernist desirability, the process of electroplating this thin layer of chromium onto a metal substrate is nonetheless still popular among built environment products like plumbing and lighting fixtures. Digital representations of these objects employ techniques that reproduce the language of computer graphics in terms of abstraction, flexibility, and efficiency. They effectively occlude other kinds of work produced in their representation.

Chrome surfacing in the Blender environment is achieved in one of two ways. *Image texturing* maps a reference photograph of a chrome surface onto a digital model of an object. The increasingly popular process of *procedural texturing* develops a material computationally and relies almost entirely on mathematical equations and algorithms. Mathematical functions compute color and intensity values at every pixel "on-the-go." In the field of computer graphics, proceduralism has long held promise for its features of adaptability, flexibility, control, and infinite difference, that can be produced on demand. In 1984, Alvy Ray Smith, the co-founder of Lucasfilm's computer division and Pixar called this process of computationally generating visual complexity "database amplification,"[1] where complex detail is generated from limited parameters. Image texturing and procedural texturing involve different logical, material, and gestural practices within Blender. To develop a good material texture through image texturing requires scoping out an ideal physical sample of the material, photographing it at a very high resolution in a way that lends itself to complex mappings in various lighting conditions, and making it available within material texture libraries, which can take up large amounts of storage. Procedural texturing on the other hand requires an understanding of the mathematical procedures that simulate material properties like color, roughness, and reflectance, to enter data values to produce the desired effect. As the wireframe diagram indicates, it is from such a data-processing pipeline — where various procedures are connected to but don't permanently alter the input object — that Suzanne becomes shiny.

However, surfacing with procedural textures isn't merely a result of abstractions and mathematical equations. Considered within the communities that use them also points to the operations of surfacing that are dependent on co-producing knowledge in ways that are far from procedural.[2] A situated and embodied approach to analyzing these processes that attends to *who* does the work, *how*, and with what epistemic resources debunks the illusion that these computational images are merely technical accomplishments to reveal they are also social accomplishments. By expanding the site of the surfacing process, a taxonomy of *attuning* work emerges. Attunement here is the socially constructed perceptual and technical awareness upon which further knowledge is built, and effects are achieved. The text of a video tutorial hints at how material conditions and knowledge production practices converge in the Blender software environment. The tutor begins the tutorial for procedural chrome by pulling up a photograph of a chrome-plated motorcycle on the "chrome-plating" entry on Wikipedia:

> *...Wikipedia is my first choice if I'm researching materials because there are images of the material, [a] description of how the material [is] manufactured, and [also] how it behaves. Chrome is a shiny, glossy material, and because it's a plating...and the plating is really thin, it has something special; it has something like a color ramp, and the color ramp is from white to black. If [the chrome] is not facing directly[at] you, it [looks] black. It's because [of this thinness that] the reflection behaves like it is going through a little bit like a Fresnel... or something like that.*
>
> *Ok...let's jump into Blender right now.*

2 For more on how shared understanding is constructed in-situ between human(s) and machine(s), see Lucy Suchman. *Human-Machine Reconfigurations: Plans and Situated Actions*. 2 edition. Cambridge; New York: Cambridge University Press, 2006.

Rather than starting with a wireframe diagram of the procedural logic, the tutor begins with the photograph, and for the next minute we — the tutor and the anticipated audience — spend some time collectively studying the perceptual and material properties of how light reflects off the chrome surfaces of the motorcycle. He then moves on to pair the observations with a sequence of shaders in Blender to create a similar effect computationally, periodically referring to the motorcycle photograph on which we have been mutually calibrated. He then adds procedures in the following order to develop the effect of chrome:

> LAYER WEIGHT$_3$ - COLOR RAMP$_2$ - GLOSSY BSDF$_1$ - MATERIAL OUTPUT$_4$

These acts of attunement between human-machine interaction that occur within seemingly mathematical operations include gauging, matching, and anticipating. A tutor may *gauge* "real-enough" like in the vignette above, by finding ways to establish a common baseline of the physical properties, behaviors, and manufacturing techniques of chrome plating to balance visual accuracy with physical accuracy; "shiny but not too shiny." They *match* sense perceptions to the mathematical jargon within procedures to make them understandable to a user. For instance, they may pair a shader category like Glossy BSDF (Bidirectional Scattering Distribution Function) — a probabilistic mathematical function for light scattering — and its unitless input parameters with corresponding phenomena in the observed, physical world. Tutors *anticipate* the technical configurations of the end user's machine and recommend settings of procedural techniques to accommodate various levels of computational power and memory capacity.

This partial and contingent taxonomy of attunements destabilizes oppositional categories of abstract/material, digital/physical, visual effects/real, analog/digital computation, or even objects/environment. It provides a foil to typical texture libraries of material swatches to include the co-produced actions of *gauging*, *matching*, and *anticipating* that accompany them. It prompts the question: What allows designers of the built environment to think the materialities of chrome surface rendering and chrome surface plating apart? This line of questioning draws into relation two surfacing processes that although analogous in visual effect are worlds apart in process and material effect. The taxonomy further mushrooms out when attending to the work of making legible the conditions of life of those involved in the process and impacts of chrome plating. Chrome plating is a toxic and extractive process. *Sympathizing*, *calibrating*, *adjusting* are few attunements that synchronize efforts between community members and technical experts within the control apparatus of modeling, monitoring, and sensing to make this toxicity of chrome legible. These attunements counter the insatiable desires for shiny chrome parts for everything from aerospace components, plumbing fixtures, to collector cars; a desire for chrome to look "just right." The taxonomy of human and machine interactions expands into a more copious set of social, technical, and cultural accomplishments that are not devoid of politics. They expose and challenge surfacing's agonistic complicities with modernity's impulse for standardization, abstraction, flexibility, and efficiency.

Shiny surfaces reflect, refract, and diffract more than their environments; it is for us, designers of the built environment to decide what we choose to attend to.

Digit Goes to Hawaii (1976) and Baby Eyes (1984)

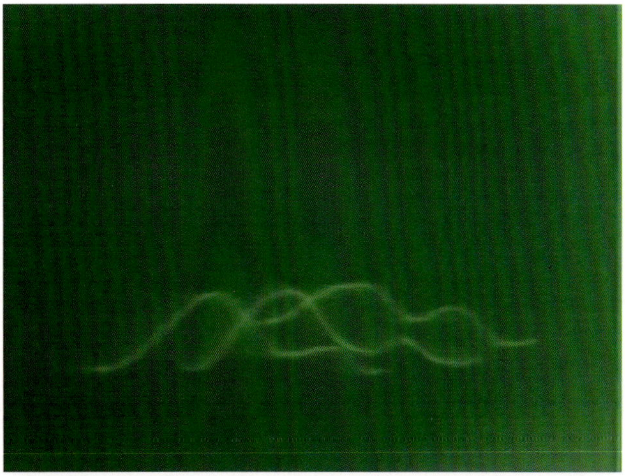

Elizabeth Vander Zaag, *Digit Goes to Hawaii* (1976, 2.5 min). Still image.

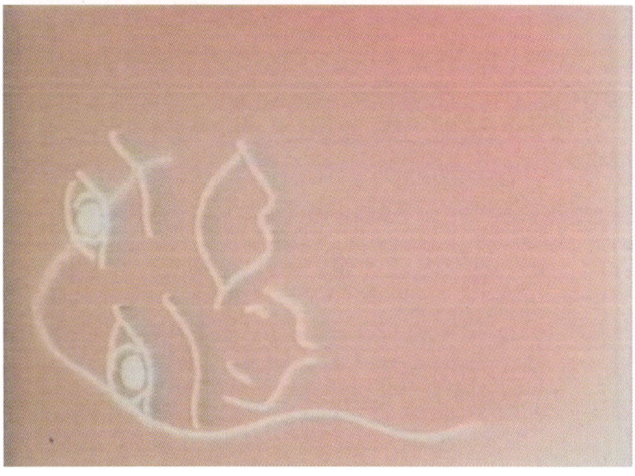

Digit Responds. (1979, 2.5 min). Still image.

Gabriela Aceves Sepúlveda

In *Digit Goes to Hawaii* (1976, 2.5 min) Elizabeth Vander Zaag introduces Digit, a female computer-generated character and the protagonist of a program of short videos that appeared in the experimental television program *The Gina Show* broadcasted in Vancouver Cable 10 from 1978–1981.[1] In the video, Digit appears as three bright wavy lines overlapping each other on top of a green background. Using GRAX, a computer animation software developed by Jerry Barenholtz, Vander Zaag animated the lines by making them move slowly from screen left to right to the rhythm of the sound of ocean waves.[2] To achieve the green color overlay of the video, Vander Zaag ran the animation through a colorizer built at the Audio-visual Department at Simon Fraser University (SFU).

Digit Goes to Hawaii represents Vander Zaag's experimental attitude towards technology and her unique position bridging the artistic and academic worlds of the era. Vander Zaag's approach combined drawing, performance, video, sound, and computer graphics to construct a distinct aesthetic language that described women's lives through technology. As a video technician at SFU, she gained access to equipment, resources, and research on the latest developments in computer and creativity including the work developed at the *Sonic Research Studio*, managed by Barry Truax, and the *Kinesiology Lab* directed by computer scientist Tom Calvert, where Barenholtz developed GRAX. At the *Kinesiology Lab*, researchers were beginning to create motion capture technology to represent human movement realistically. The achievement of an accurate simulation of reality guided the design of these systems. Vander Zaag's parallel involvement with artist-run-centers in Vancouver (including PUMPS Center for the Arts, the Western Front and the Video In, now VIVO Media Arts) gave her a unique position to question this scientific focus and creatively explore the potential of computer systems to simulate reality, before the advent of the personal computer.

Every week and with limited access to computers, Vander Zaag improvised and took turns presenting Digit at *The Gina Show* as an animated character or as her artist persona as she performed in front of the camera. Through a combination of drawings, performance, spoken word, synthesized sound effects, and video images, Digit manifested as either the artist's digital off-spring or as her alter-ego. Each of the short videos that form part of *the Digit Series* includes a sound mix of audio effects and the artist's voice detailing Digit's digital adventures or reflecting on Vander Zaag's own life. By intersecting the personal with the performative, Vander Zaag blurred the distinction between the object and subject of representation, a strategy employed by

1 For more on *The Gina Show*, see Allison Collins, *"The GINA Show Archive: Vancouver Memory in Motion."* Accessed April 5, 2020. *http://www.theginashow.orgallery.org/about/*

2 For more on the development of GRAX, see Jerry Barenholtz, *Towards A New Animation Technology* (MSc Thesis, University of British Columbia, 1978), viii-ix.

other feminist artists to place themselves at the center of their work and assert themselves as the agents of their narratives.

Before appearing as a digital construct in *The Gina Show*, Digit appeared as Vander Zaag's art persona at the PUMPS's *Lotto-Logic Theater*, a paid art performance event at the Manhattan Apartments in downtown Vancouver. In the performance, Vander Zaag recited some of her findings on the binary logic of computers, a theme that she avidly researched at the time.[3] Vander Zaag's act at the *Lotto-Logic Theater* was in tune with Vancouver performance practices of the era involving the creation of over-the-top personas referencing popular commodities or invented identities as evidenced in the work of artists such as Vincent Trasov, Eric Metcalf and Kate Craig.[4] This performance style was a direct response to the social lives of the artists and resonant to the collaborative impetus that characterized Vancouver's artist-run culture at the time. Vander Zaag's *Digit* was a pun on *Gidget Goes to Hawaii*, a popular television sitcom starring a teenage girl looking for love on the beaches of Malibu. The satirical appropriation of Gidget was not only a comment on the search of heteronormative love but an investigation on the limits of Self and the slippages between Self and Other amidst rapid technological change.

In other episodes of the series, the messy and fraught relationship between reality and simulation, artist and creation, becomes more apparent. In *Digit Responds* (1979), Digit materializes over a pink background. Digit's wavy line drawings animated using GRAX now resemble a pair of eyes and eyebrows, a mouth and fragments of the silhouette of a woman's body. The output to video is accomplished using a betacam camera to record the CTR monitor that the artist rotated 90 degrees. The rotated shapes float through the screen from left to right as we hear the voice of the artist poetically unfolding *Digit's* emergence:

> *Digit responds by enabling her, right create program. Initially she has a lot of information unloading to do. Why do I have to be green? I like pink. This analog video interface is ridiculous. I am digital. And please do not let that betacam tube put me on my side like this.*[5]

The poem chronicles the emergent relation between the artist and her art persona, and the contrast between digital and analog-born images. In the process, both the artist and Digit "take turns at being Sentinels,"[6] watching each other and also witnessing how computers were increasingly opening up new formats for artistic ex-

3 Zoom interview with the artist, 18 March 2021.

4 On performance practices in Vancouver see Marina Roy, "Corporeal returns: feminism and phenomenology in Vancouver Video and Performance, 1968-1983" In *Canadian Art* Vol. 18 (2), Summer 2001: 58.

5 Elizabeth Vander Zaag, *Digit Goes to Hawaii* (1976), Elizabeth Vander Zaag Fonds. VIVO Media Arts, Vancouver (excerpt).

6 Ibid.

7 Ibid.

8 See Donna Haraway, "A Cyborg Manifesto: Science, Technology, and Socialist Feminism in the 1980s," in *Cybercultures Reader*, ed. David Bell and Barbara M. Kennedy (London: Routledge, 2000). 291–323.

perimentation in conjunction with traditional art forms (analog video and drawing). The poem ends as Vander Zaag tells us: "Gone is the genius, but that will change."[7] In taking turns at being one and the Other and asserting the demise of the Genius, Vander Zaag also gives voice to our unrelenting preoccupations with the challenges that digital technology presents to artistic authorship and subjectivity. Vander Zaag's use of drawings, sounds (including the artist's voice) and her presence are strategies that bring nuance to the act of creating art with computers, rendering this act as neither based in the artist's full control or the independence of an algorithm. The artist, a woman, is always mediating the art of creation. In doing so, Vander Zaag opens up a space for a critique of the male-dominated fields of art and technology. That is, if the Genius is being challenged, Digit and Vander Zaag are both witnesses and enablers of this challenge and the changes to come.

Through these weekly experiments with Digit, Vander Zaag constructed a sense of self that was inseparable from her tools. Much like other feminist video artists, Vander Zaag developed an embodied relation with technology. In doing so she questioned the dominant ontology of early and current digital systems, which treat numerical value as the underlying principle of nature, thus rendering its reproduction via algorithmic models possible. In contrast, Vander Zaag's feminist sensibility expressed how the attempt at simulating reality via computer systems was fraught and messy. Digit was not a simulation of the artist nor an independent digital construct. Digit was Vander Zaag's offspring (her creation) and her artist persona. It existed both inside and outside the mainframe. It was simultaneously a drawing, a numerical value, a code, a voice, and a body; a digital construct that extended into the personal life of the artist as it pretended to be independent from her. Throughout the *Digit Series* Vander Zaag investigated her position as an artist vis-à-vis a computer, anticipating the reconfigurations of subjectivity through technology formulated by Donna Haraway in the mid-1980s.[8]

As *The Gina Show* came to an end, Vander Zaag productions became more deeply oriented by her own life experiences as an artist-mother. Echoing the concerns of other feminist artists for understanding the process of subject formation as evidenced in Mary Kelly's *Post-Partum Document* (1976), Vander Zaag began to explore the pre-verbal stage of her newborn child. In the single-channel video *Baby Eyes* (1983) she investigates the potential of technology in mediating mother and child relations and the capacity of the computer to describe human perception. Using Ko Nakajima's *Aniputer* to draw onto video images, Vander Zaag imagines how her baby daughter perceives the world.[9] The composite visuals and the use of overlaid graphics, a mixture of analog and digital-born images, points to Vander Zaag's interest in the reflexive capacities of video prevalent amongst video artists at the time.[10] These capacities included video's potential to disrupt the act of viewing through feedback loops, and creating and manipulating images via electronic signals rather than through chemical processes.

The video includes images of herself, her baby, natural landscapes, and home interiors; all manipulated through a wide array of visual effects. At some point, we see the artist speaking directly to the camera, as a new mother she ponders how her infant perceives the world. This scene is followed by a series of close-up images of the baby's face looking at the camera through a layer of colorizing effects and squiggly fluorescent drawings, reminiscent of characters of an imaginary pictographic language, thus expressing the impossibility of ever really understanding how an infant perceived the world. Each image fades in and out of view to the rhythm of a soundtrack created using a pitch shifter to process and mix the non-verbal expressions of her newborn baby and the artist's own voice singing lullaby's. Echoing Vander Zaag's earlier explorations in the *Digit Series*, here the human offspring sees the world as a cyborg. The computer interface mediates the infant's vision. But this exploration is not guided by a scientific impulse of enhancing human capacities or obtaining a true simulation of human perception. It is guided by the artist's imagination and her playful use of the *Aniputer*. Vander Zaag's particular blending of images, use of direct address and graphic effects that rupture multiple image layers, combined with the intimate content of her videos also signal Vander Zaag's adherence to Brechtian defamiliarization and distanciation techniques. As Griselda Pollock has argued, both are identified as critical approaches in the work of feminist artists to disrupt conventions of representation.[11] In addressing her infant's perception, Vander Zaag moves a step beyond mere visual representation and continues to speculate on the role of technology in subject formation and the complex process of apprehending the world through sound images.

The layering of analogous and digital images to produce richly-textured images combined with a synthesized soundtrack seen in *Baby Eyes* became key in Vander Zaag's aesthetic sensibility. Vander Zaag's exploration of the female voice continued through various interactive works expanding into her teaching and research on the visual sense of language to explore subjective and cultural sensibilities through interactive systems.[12] As others have noted Vander Zaag's hybrid method of mix-

9 For more on the presence of Nakajima in Vancouver see Jesse Cumming, "Art and Technology between Canada and Japan, 1967-1985." Accessed April 15, 2021. https://www.vivomediaarts.com/archive/video-communication-switched-on/

10 On video as a reflexive medium see Yvonne Spielmann, *Video: The Reflexive Medium* (Cambridge, MA: MIT Press, 2008).

11 Griselda Pollock, "Screening the Seventies: Sexuality and Representation in Feminist Practice — A Brechtian Perspective." In *Vison and Difference: Femininity, Feminism and the Histories of Art* (London and New York: Routledge, 1996), 155-199.

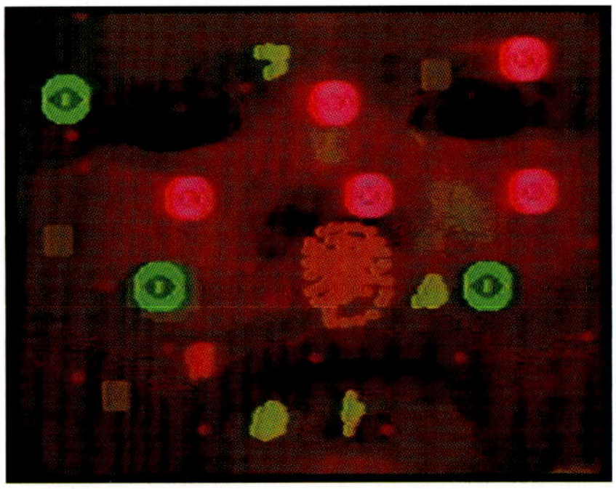

Elizabeth Vander Zaag, *Baby Eyes* (1983, 2.5 min). Still image.

Elizabeth Vander Zaag, *Baby Eyes* (1983, 2.5 min). Still image.

ing analog and digital sources and her unique position in academic, professional and artistic milieus offers an alternative path to the histories of computer art in Canada.[13] It points to a feminist orientation towards digital art production that circumvents the male-dominated universe of early computer art and the computer industry. In the *Digit Series* the computer becomes an extension of the artist, a daughter and an alter-ego. In *Baby Eyes* it mediates and enables an understanding of mother-daughter relations and human perception. In both, the computer is a tool to explore, mediate, imagine and intervene in the dynamic process of subject formation.

12 See Vander Zaag research published in *Mother Tongue: A Study of Participant Affect in an Interactive Installation* (VDM Verlag; Dr. Müller, 2011).

13 See Katherine Stein, "Creative Metamorphoses"; and Anne-Marie Trépanier "An Infinity of Solutions: Tactics of Technological Resilience in the Videos of Elizabeth Vander Zaag." In *Vulnerability Part 2* (Montreal: Ellen Gallery, Winter 2021). Accessed March 18, 2021, http://ellengallery.concordia.ca/wp content/uploads/2021/02/Ellen_Terms_Vulnerability_Part2.pdf

Depth and Historical Vision in Computer Simulation

Jacob Gaboury

Stills from the film *Z*, Alan Warburton, 2016. Printed with permission.

In a short video work from 2012, simply titled *Z*, British artist Alan Warburton explores the function of perspective as a technique for the production of historical vision in computer simulation. Opening on an empty screen of pure white, the work follows a virtual camera as it tracks forward along the z-axis, revealing an eerie scene of shaded objects that emerge from this blank field into the middle distance before disappearing into a sea of black as they move behind the camera and beyond our vision. Over the course of its three-minute runtime we watch a seemingly deserted cityscape materialize before us, moving through empty office buildings, past makeshift tent encampments, and alongside military tanks frozen in time. The scene appears to capture a dynamic moment in the history of a city emptied of its inhabitants. We might even mistake the scene for a static landscape were it not for the swirling particle effects of paper and trash that occasionally blow past as we continue our relentless movement forward. The work foregrounds the impermanence of any single perspective by refusing us a totalizing image of the space we inhabit, and we are therefore left with an impartial vision that ultimately disappears into the same sea of white with which it began. While this work is striking in its simplicity, there is also a larger argument at play here. Much of Warburton's work engages with and aestheticizes the labor of digital image production, with particular focus on 3D modeling and visualization. In *Z* the artist makes this same gesture, creating a kind of readymade video work from a rendering "depth pass," one of the many visual passes made in the production of realistic three-dimensional scenes, used to capture and measure distance in 3D computer simulation.

Distance has always posed a unique challenge for computer graphics. Indeed, one of the earliest and most vexing problems for graphics researchers was known as the "visibility" or "hidden surface" problem, in which a computer must determine whether or not an object or surface in a given scene should be visible to the viewer, or if it was in some way occluded by another surface that lies between it and the viewer. Put another way, the computer has to be programmed to understand depth as a relational quality between objects in a scene, since by default the computer possesses full knowledge of all objects in their totality, and therefore must preemptively subtract that which should be invisible such that it might be made legible. For computer-generated images, the visibility problem lays bare the surprising challenge of simulating the inaccessibility of the invisible, a property that hinges on the proper simulation of depth as a relational form. For well over a decade, graphics researchers struggled to find an accurate and efficient algorithm for this problem, a calculation that could be made in software that was scalable and did not restrict the form and type of objects it could simulate. Ultimately, it was hardware that provided a lasting solution that would grow into an industry standard still widely used today.

In his 1974 PhD thesis at the University of Utah, future Pixar co-founder Ed Catmull proposed a graphical workstation with a built-in grid of random-access memory that could be used to store the depth value of all visible objects in a scene, an object he called the z-buffer, named after the depth axis in three-dimensional image space. Rather than try to calculate the relational position of all objects in a scene for every image or frame of a simulation, the z-buffer simply stores its depth as a numerical value along the z-axis to be compared with the depth value of other objects in a scene. As an object or camera moves and transforms, the buffer makes a simple numerical check, adapting to display whichever surface is most proximate to the viewing position. The z-buffer now serves as the de facto solution for the visibility problem and has remained relatively constant over the past forty years, and yet it also marks the beginning of a much larger transformation in the simulation of visual depth.

While its initial value was hidden surface removal, over the past forty years the z-buffer has become an important tool for 3D imaging as a whole and is essential for the production of the depth map used by Warburton in *Z*. Functioning almost like a radar image or MRI scan, depth maps interpret three-dimensional objects according to their relative distance in a scene, with objects appearing lighter the farther they are from a virtual camera. For digital rendering in film and visual effects, this depth map is an essential tool for manufacturing depth effects in post-production, such as object focus and blur. And yet, unlike most computer-generated images, these depth map images are not meant to be seen or interpreted by a viewing subject and are not representational in the strictest sense. While we can view these images they are, for all intents and purposes, not for us. Their visualization is incidental to their function. Their gradient shade is not an abstraction or interpretation produced so that we can better understand the function of the buffer, it is an indexical trace of the data stored in the buffer itself, a number for every pixel corresponding to object proximity within that pixel, scaled from the darkest black to the lightest white. This is data visualization in the purest sense, where the image we see corresponds directly to what the computer sees, to what is stored in the bitmap itself. An incidental image. While historically computer graphics have been understood as those visual images rendered out from the computational materiality of software, hardware, and code — abstracted into a representational form that is legible to a viewing subject — in the depth map we are viewing an image bereft of that abstraction, in which each pixel corresponds directly with a bit value stored in a physical buffer. Just as the computer reads this buffer to register depth information, we too read the gradient to determine the appearance of a scene deprived of all visual information save the relational proximity of every object to our viewing position.

Thus, what seems an exceptional object to us is a rather mundane and everyday part of the rendering pipeline for any computer graphics artist. In showcasing the depth pass in *Z*, Warburton produces a kind of selective vision that reflects the work's broader theme, which is the production of historical narrative. As he notes in his artist's statement, "*Z* is about how we make sense of the clutter of current events, how we create epochs, and how, in an era of intense global change, we are affected by a kind of long-term myopia that obscures us to the larger forces at work." Depth here is a function not only of vision, but also a means of reflecting on the limits of what can be made sensible in the broadest sense — a process mirrored in the culling of visual information that is the precondition for digital image production itself. While this is true of all history, it is particularly true of the history of technology, and of computer graphics as a subfield that simultaneously embeds and occludes the very objects that materially structure and enable it.

Topology, Crystals, and A Multitude of Futures

David Theodore

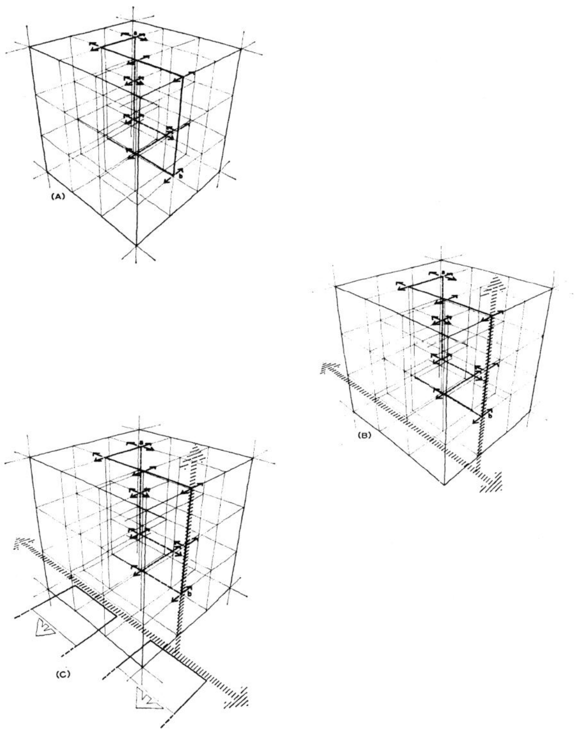

Fig. 7. Communication lattice in health sciences facility. Each strand in lattice represents a communication path. A. Two points *a* and *b* can be connected by many paths, each finding different node points in complex. B. Addition of through communication spine provides users with bypass system. This would connect to each of the vertical strands in the lattice, here symbolizing elevator banks. C. Subsystems may have independent lives and independent extension requirements. These are attached to main system in such a way that its chief characteristics are not affected.

Communication lattice in health sciences facility diagram from *Design Strategy for Flexible Health Sciences Facilities*, John Weeks and Gordon Best, Health Services Research: HSR, 5(3), 1970. Republished with permission of John Wiley & Sons - Books, permission conveyed through Copyright Clearance Center, Inc.

In 1970, British architects John Weeks and Gordon Best presented a three-dimensional communication lattice diagram at the annual conference of the American Hospital Association. Published later that year in *Health Services Research*, the diagram set out organizational principles for the planning and design of future flexible health sciences facilities. "Flexibility" was vexed terminology, signaling contemporary anxieties about obviating obsolescence. Planners and architects, they argued, now had to understand growth and change as the "prime forces" in design for complex buildings such as hospitals.[1] Growth and change were the only constants, the "positive and major design parameters."[2]

The diagram combined two scientific topics, the lattice structure from crystallography and topology from mathematics. Both were old news by the time Weeks and Best drew the diagram, codified towards the end of the nineteenth century.[3] In adopting them, Weeks and Best followed the practice, newly relevant in postwar Britain, of borrowing scientific concepts and repurposing them for art and architecture. The ideas of D'Arcy Thompson, for instance, were debated and promulgated among the Independent Group, an assembly of avant-garde artists Weeks exhibited with just after World War II.[4][5] And his business partner, Richard Llewelyn-Davies, used his position as head of the Bartlett School of Architecture to incorporate scientific research models into architectural education.[6]

In postwar Britain, architects engaged scientific images for architectural rhetoric — the ability to convince clients and publics of the value of particular design concepts — and for architectural inspiration — metaphors or images that could help control design development. The lattice diagram drew on science for both issues, but it also purported to arise from scientific research itself. With the advent of the National Health Service and the Hospital Plan, doctors, administrators, operational research scholars and others had turned to closely grained, data-based studies to make substantive propositions for hospital design. Existing data about hospital work, especially nursing, was repackaged through operational research and building science. A popular tool was the so-called traffic study, which, as its name suggests, tracked the movement of people, services, and materials.[7]

In hindsight we can see in the lattice diagram — and in hospital planning — the congelation of the information age. A key factor was computation. The electronic, stored-program computer and the flexible, research-based health centre came of age together. At the National Institutes of Health, research funds pushed for explorations of computerized diagnostics, management,

1 John Weeks, and Gordon Best. "Design Strategy for Flexible Health Sciences Facilities," *Health Services Research* (1970): 263–284, 284.

2 Ibid.

3 Alma Steingart. "The Axiomatic Aesthetic." *In Computer Architectures: Constructing the Common Ground*, eds. Theodora Vardouli and Olga Touloumi (London: Routledge, 2020), 194–213.

4 D'Arcy Wentworth Thompson. *On Growth and Form* (London: Cambridge University Press, 1917).

5 Sam Gathercole. "Art and Construction in Britain in the 1950s," *Art History* 29, no. 5 (2006): 887–925.

6 David Theodore, "Treating Architectural Research: The Nuffield Trust and the Post-war Hospital," *The Journal of Architecture* 24, no 7 (2019): 982–998.

7 David Theodore, and Theodora Vardouli, "Walking instead of Working: Space Allocation, Automatic Architecture, and the Abstraction of Hospital Labor," *IEEE Annals of the History of Computing*, 43, no. 2, (2021): 6-17.

imaging, and architectural planning. Although Weeks and Best manipulated data mostly through hand-drawn tables, graphs, and diagrams, their work engaged the two sides of computing: computers could be engaged for architectural design and planning, and the building itself had to make room for computers and computer-based communication equipment and organization.[8]

Unlike many artists and architects who borrowed from science, however, Weeks and Best proposed neither to make buildings that looked crystalline nor to optimize form through topological aesthetics. Weeks and Best promoted the concrete meanings of the diagram; the mathematical abstraction was a means to an end. For example, they criticized the diagrams and ideas proposed by US-based researchers British architectural scholar Sheila Clibbon and University of Pennsylvania internist Marvin L. Sachs.[9] "It is unclear," Best and Weeks wrote in 1971, "just what technological implications—if any—their ideas have."[10]

In other words, the lattice did not matter (beyond tapping into scientific rhetoric) for the kinds of buildings it evoked. The abstraction mattered more. They insisted that "the model provides a framework within which potentially flexible medical facilities can be specified: it does not 'create' flexible buildings."[11] Instead, the diagram visualized a reversal of the "conventional" relationship between program and design, and whose advantages were: that "it is translatable into building for a wide variety of physical situations, and while it may be distorted, its topological characteristics remain constant."[12] A topological crystal would allow planners to manipulate flexibility, shaping and making feasible future plans.

This reversal was a rallying cry for hospital planners of the era. Washington DC-based consultant Gordon A Friesen, for example, proselytized industrial engineering over architecture: you should not ask the pilots and passengers about their needs and aggregate the results to design an airplane. Instead, design the airplane according to best scientific principles and then train the pilots how to fly them.[13] Best and Weeks added a further sophistication: evidence of the past few decades showed that present needs and best practices could not predict future ones. "If the inputs change radically in nature," they wrote, "the system either breaks down or modifies itself in an unpredictable way."[14]

The idea that a diagram can control the planning and construction of hospitals reached a crescendo in postwar United Kingdom. Earlier attempts to coordinate structures and services without determining form had led Weeks to the idea of indeterminate planning. Weeks proposed a series of strategies, such as the use

8 Alise Upitis. "Alexander's Choice; How Architecture Avoided Computer Aided Design c. 1962," Arindam Dutta, ed., *A Second Modernism: MIT, Architecture, and the 'Techno-Social' Moment* (Cambridge, MA: MIT Press, 2013), 474–505.

9 S Clibbon, and M L Sachs. "Like-spaces Versus Bailiwick Approaches to the Design of Health Care Facilities." *Health Services Research* 5, no.3 (1970): 172–85.

10 Gordon Best, and John Weeks. "The Search for Flexibility in Hospital Design: A Perspective on the Work of Clibbon and Sachs," *Architectural Record* 150, no 3 (1971): 66, 258.

11 Weeks and Best. "Design Strategy for Flexible Health Sciences Facilities," 277.

12 John Weeks. "Multi-Strategy Buildings." *Architectural Design* 39, no. 10 (1969), 536–540.

13 Don DeMicheal. "We're Practicing 20th-Century Medicine in 19th-Century Hospital," *Actual Specifying Engineer* 21, no. 4 (1969). Reprint in Library and Archives Canada, MG 31 B 51 Vol. 3.

of a two-level "main street": as in the linear main street of a village, buildings could be added or removed from the main street of a complex building without disrupting ongoing activities.[15] Later, in a project for the University of Ottawa in Canada, lines became nets capable of extending in three dimensions. The lattice took form in a proposal for Memorial University in Newfoundland, also in Canada, literally crystalizing lines of communication, but also imagining them as nets capable of topological deformation and reformation.[16]

The lattice diagram proposed to make co-extensive architectural, nosocomial, and informational concerns. The concept of historical change sparked the possibility of obsolescence. The diagram addressed unfolding possibilities, linking the routines of hospital life to the new world of the computerized information age: new frontiers (outer space), new terrors (hydrogen bombs), and new subjects (the airline passenger). Weeks and Best's last word was optimistic: the lattice diagram would allow architects to design buildings "within a strategy that will allow the development of a multitude of futures."[17]

14 Weeks and Best. "Design Strategy for Flexible Health Sciences Facilities," 274.

15 John Weeks. "Indeterminate Architecture," *Transactions of the Bartlett Society* 2 (1963-4): 83-206.

16 Weeks and Best. "Design Strategy for Flexible Health Sciences Facilities," 281.

17 Ibid., 284.

Metamorphosis (1976) by Lillian F. Schwartz

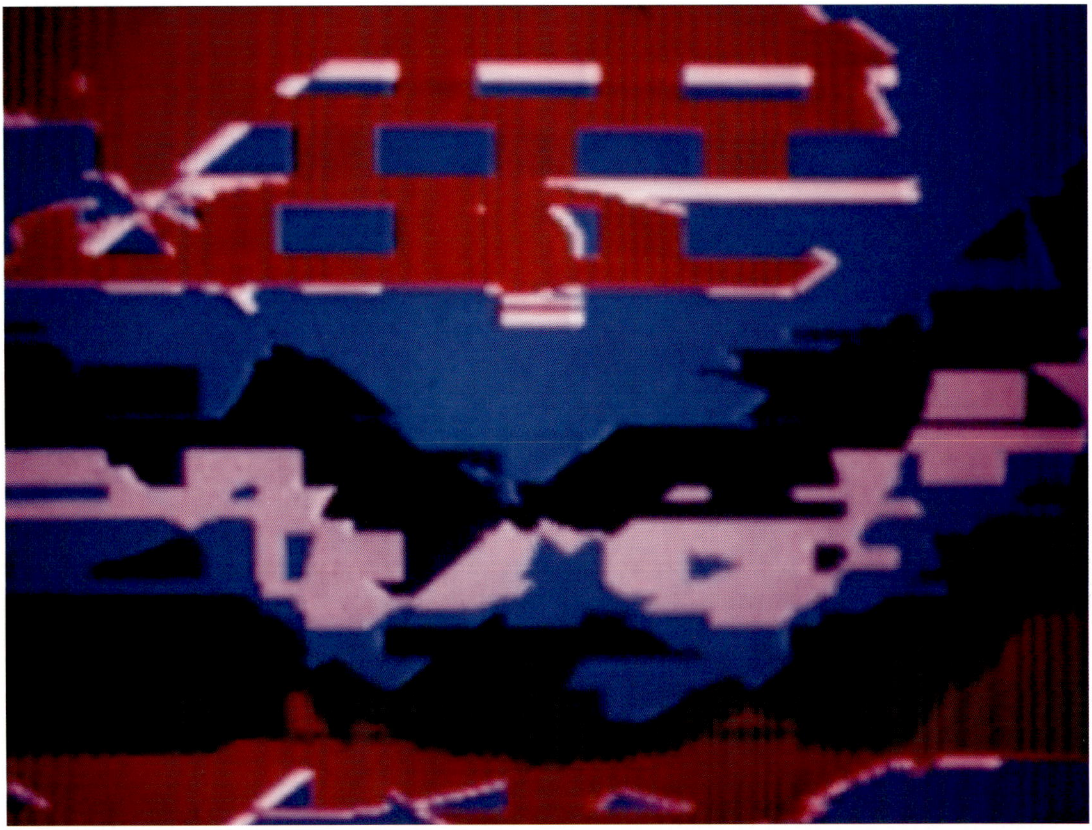

Still from the film *Metamorphosis*, Lillian F. Schwartz, 1976. Printed with permission.

Olga Touloumi

Planes of circles, grids, dots, and lines emerge, move and overlap in Lillian Schwartz's *Metamorphosis*, creating ever-shifting color strata in an animated abstraction that reminds the viewer of early twentieth century experiments with filmic abstraction. Lines glide across the screen; circles appear and take over, celebrating their flickering existence with intense purple, blue, pink, and red hues. A study in visual perception, the animation experiments with visual expressions of depth by means of overlap and intermittent black frames, until everything dissolves into a colorful tapestry that brings the metamorphosis of the initial squares and circle into a resolution.

Lillian Schwartz produced *Metamorphosis* (as she tellingly called her film) in 1976 using the Bell Labs computer infrastructure — a mainframe, magnetic tapes, and punch cards. Similarly to her earlier work (Pixillation, UFO, Olympiad — to name a few of her film animations) *Metamorphosis* combines computational and filmic tools. In collaboration with Ken Knowlton, the computer engineer behind the programming language BEFLIX and EXPLOR, Schwartz programmed black and white output images, adding color in post-production with filters she created on Bruce Cornwell's optical bench.[1] She controlled hues, saturation, and brightness with a joystick, meanwhile a "random number generator" chose colors.[2] The pace and rhythms of the animation reinforced Antonio Salieri's violin overtures, gesturing toward a synaesthetic, even if environmental, ambition to immerse her viewer in a milieu of shifting geographies of abstraction.[3]

Schwartz arrived at Bell Labs in 1968. Her introduction to the world of art and computers was atypical, since she lacked the formal training of an artist or an engineer, the two types of professionals qualifications allowed to enter the Bell Labs in the 1960s. She grew up in Ohio, where she recycled material for her collages; trained to be a nurse; married a pediatrician; moved with her family and worked as a nurse in occupied Japan. There, she experimented with punch cards for the first time and used calligraphy to bring her polio-paralyzed hand back to life.[4]

The pass to Bell Labs arrived after her participation at the 1968 exhibition "The Machine at the End of Mechanical Age" that K. G. Pontus Hultén curated at the MoMA.[5] There the interdisciplinary collective Experiments in Art and Technology (EAT) had issued a competition for works in the intersection of art and technology, promising them a place within MoMA's exhibition and access to the Bell Labs' arsenal of tools and expertise.[6] Schwartz's entry, the installation "Proxima Centauri," and the translucent lightscapes of her pillared dome caught Leon D. Harmon's attention, who

1 Lillian Schwartz, *The Computer Artist's Handbook: Concepts, Techniques, and Applications* (New York, NY: Norton, 1992), 113.

2 Ibid., 133.

3 Ibid., 193.

4 Ibid., 34.

5 K. G. Pontus Hultén and Museum of Modern Art, *The Machine, As Seen at The End of the Mechanical Age* (New York, NY: Museum of Modern Art, 1968), 198–99.

6 John Beck and Ryan Bishop, *Technocrats of the Imagination: Art, Technology and the Military-Industrial Avant-Garde* (Durham, NC: Duke University Press, 2020), 77–106.

introduced her to Bell Labs and their research programs on visual perception.[7]

At the time a whole new art scene was brewing inside Bell Labs, a predominantly white and male space. Bell Labs electrical engineers Billy Klüver and Fred Waldhauer, in collaboration with artists Robert Rauschenberg and Robert Whitman had created EAT to explore the meeting of art and technology. Bell Labs provided the engineers and infrastructure and EAT the artists. The goal was to create "an international network of experimental services and activities designed to catalyze (...) cooperation between artists, engineers and scientists, and members of industry and labor."[8] In placing the artist within the laboratory, EAT promised to fuse the prerogative of technological progress with art and creative imagination centered on humans, while endowing artists with technique and tools.

The collective hoped for a productive exchange but conditions on the ground revealed a complex ecology of bureaucrats, engineers, funding, and protocols. Most of the time, administration kept these collaborations and their research under the rug and away from the public eye, exposing institutional priorities.[9] Bell Labs considered art production outside the bounds of its commercial work and research, maintaining a dichotomy between art and engineering. Artists were creative and playful partners but useful only to the extent that they served and reinforced the technocentric vision and projects of Bell Labs. In an effort to suppress the presence of artists in their labs, the administration restricted access to its facilities during evenings and weekends, when research divisions seized their work.

The collaboration between artists and engineers also problematized the attribution of authorship. Who was responsible for the final work of art? The artist who brought in the vision or the computer engineer who programmed the computer? In their writing, computer graphics pioneers such as Michael Noll, for example, praised computers for being artists' creative "partners" and "collaborators" but also conditioned the quality of computer art upon one's mastery over the tool.[10] Upholding mastery and professional training in programming created an exclusive set of criteria that maintained gender disparities already present in engineering environments.

Lillian Schwartz contested such conversations over mastery, while asserting her authorship. She had no interest in reinforcing with her art the professionalized realms found in Western European and North American institutions. Similarly to other women in her field, such as cybernetic art curator Jasia Reinhardt and electronic music composer Laurie Spiegel, she advocated for the blurring of such boundaries, arguing that such fusion created openings for women to enter the field.[11]

7 Hultén and Museum of Modern Art, *The Machine*, 204.

8 E.A.T., "Experiments in Art and Technology October 1966 – May 1969," E.A.T. Proceedings, No. 9, May 19, 1969; and Helen M. Franc and Anne Coffin Hanson, "The Machine as Seen at the End of the Mechanical Age," *Members Newsletter*, No. 2 (Nov/Dec 1968): 1–3.

9 Carolyn L. Kane, "Digital Art and Experimental Color Systems at Bell Laboratories, 1965–1984: Restoring Interdisciplinary Innovations to Media History," *Leonardo* 43, no. 1 (2010): 53–19.

10 A. Michael Noll, "The Digital Computer as a Creative Medium," *IEEE Spectrum* 4, no. 10 (October 1967): 89–95.

For decades Schwartz produced work at the margins of Bell Labs. Her residency status came with no salary or employment benefits; Bell Labs did not grant her a dedicated office space, while limiting her access to Bell Labs equipment and expertise only after official working hours. Solidarity took the form of tutorials, technique exchange, and consulting with female mentors and fellow engineers and artists, building a support network within a world of men.[12]

Schwartz was interested in the liminal space that the cross-over between engineers and artists created, a liminal space that made it possible for her to enter Bell Labs. Her projects and overall vision pushed engineers to create new programming languages, as Knowlton admits in his own recollections. The computer, her "collaborator," enticed her to relinquish artistic control. She challenged disciplinary and technical boundaries. "I do not have it [the computer] particularly under control," she says in the documentary *The Artist and the Computer* that John K. Ball produced for her in 1976. "I think the computer is most intimidating to those who are already set in their methods," she noted.[13] She claimed the process of drawing on the computer "blind." There was always a time lag "among input, an image appearing on a monitor, manipulation of the image, and output," as she explained.[14] Throughout her career, she continued enlarging the use of computers in visual fields, pioneering later digital humanities tools for art history, most notably in her research on Leonardo Da Vinci's *Mona Lisa* and *Last Supper.*[15] Computers, she argued, "can aid both the analysis of a work of art and the decision-making steps in the creative act."[16]

In *Metamorphosis*, Schwartz introduced computerized randomness not only as a tool for visual innovation, but also as a strategy that allowed her to undermine professional expertise and authorship. In her animations, she delineated new ways of working and producing together with computers and engineers. But most importantly Schwartz used computers to resist the predetermined disciplinary and institutional boundaries that initially marginalized her, turning them into tactical tools for groundbreaking computer art.

11 María Fernández, "Detached from HiStory: Jasia Reichardt and Cybernetic Serendipity," *Art Journal* 67, no. 3 (Fall 2008): 6–23.

12 Stefanie Wuschitz, "Feminist Hackerspaces: A Research on Feminist Space Collectives in Open Culture" (PhD, Technischen Universität Wien, 2014), 164–70.

13 Schwartz, *The Computer Artist's Handbook*, 27.

14 Ibid., 32.

15 Lillian Schwartz, "Computers and Appropriation Art: The Transformation of a Work or Idea for a New Creation," *Leonardo* 29, no. 1 (February 1996): 43–49

16 Ibid., 49.

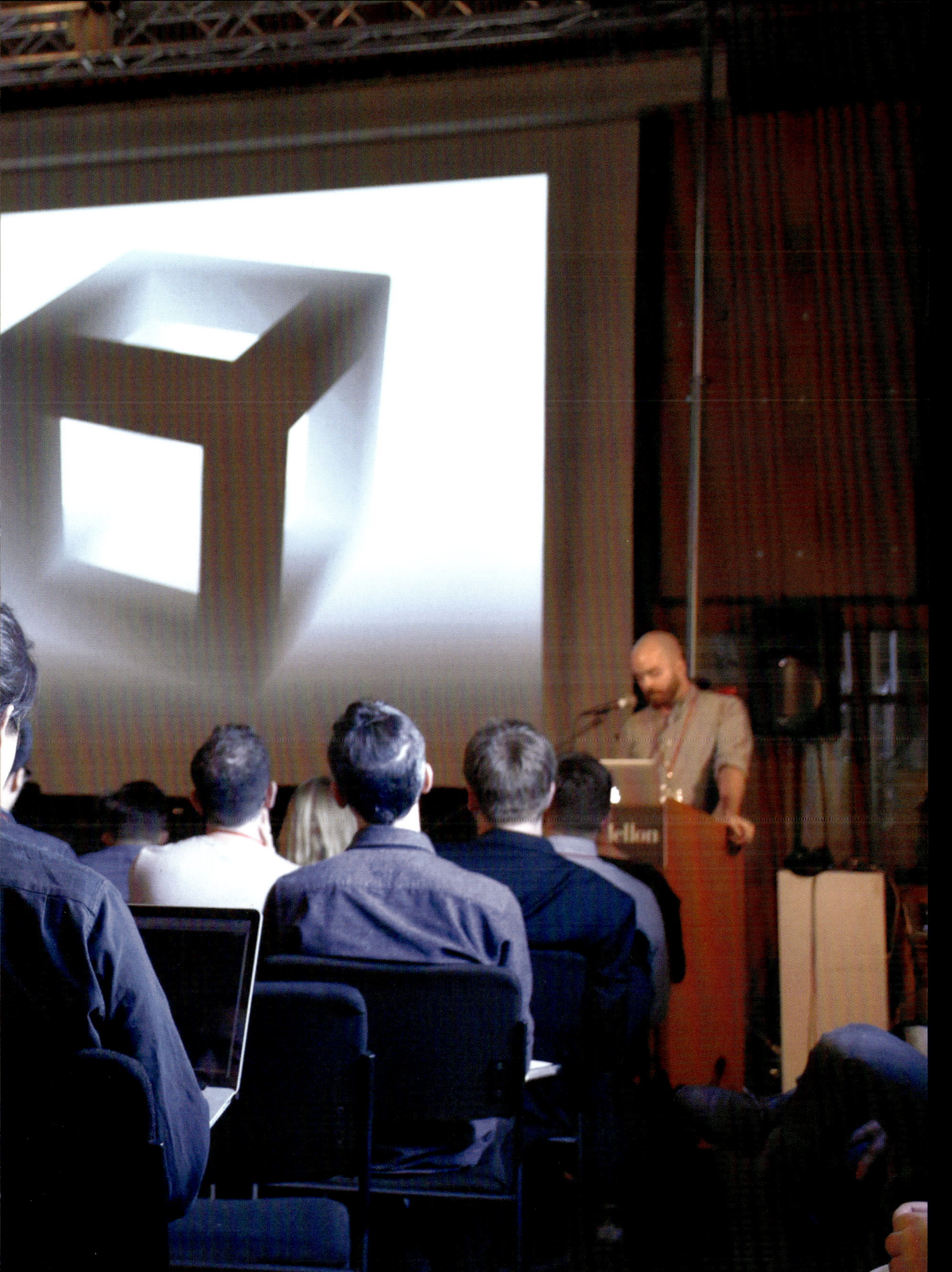

Interfaces of the Self: A Conversation about the Structures and Histories of Computational Images

Joseph Choma
Carl Lostritto
Theodora Vardouli
Jacob Gaboury

Moderated by
Olga Touloumi

OLGA TOULOUMI: Thank you all for the wonderful presentations.[1] I will condense my questions and observations into one to make sure that there is enough time for questions. This was a very provocative set of presentations that made me think about the limits and boundaries of visualization, as well as the various terms that we use — representation, visualization, drawing, simulation, animation. At times it seems that we might lose sight of the differences among those terms, but they are not the same. Because you are all arriving to this conversation from very different disciplinary positions — you are practitioners, theorists, and historians of architecture, or design or media studies — there is an opportunity here to discuss the problem of images from a wide variety of perspectives. What is the work of the computational image? What can we learn from these images and the fields they are talking to? What is it that your images *structure* and how are they *themselves* structured? This way we can start unpacking images, representations, visualizations — what they are and what they are not.

1 Panel discussion at the Computational Design: Practices, Histories, Infrastructures Symposium (Edited for length and clarity), Carnegie Mellon University, October 2017

CARL LOSTRITTO: The artist is, in a way, a consumer of images. I walk into a museum as a selfish person aiming to consume what I perceive to build up my own discipline. So, for me, it's not so much about the image leading to knowledge, but about the image leading to a sort of personal reflection. Something that I have to exercise my own methods and processes on so that whatever is happening in the image, I can do. It's in a way very childish. It's sort of like I look at an image and I think, "how can I do that?" This is why Jacob's investigation of the z-buffer is so fascinating. I'm a real curmudgeon about thinking students or architects should actually have to craft their own algorithms for resolving depth like some people think all architects should hammer a hammer. I think they should be like, well, you take your z-buffer for granted, but there's also things called binary space partitioning trees, which are really cool graphs and they force you to understand and operate in the context of depth. It's not so much that I want to buy a machine that can do it for me, but I want to bring everything into my own practice. So, again, I think that's looking at images as an artist: assuming that my discipline is personal and so everything has to be sort of filtered by my own interests. It sounds very selfish. I don't like the way it sounds, but it's the honest truth.

Stills from *Z*, Alan Warburton, 2012, United Kingdom. Discussed by Jacob Gaboury at Computational Design: Practices, Histories, Infrastructures.

JOSEPH CHOMA: At Clemson University I typically coordinate the second-year undergraduate studios. In the Fall, the studio is rooted in computational thinking, and by midterm students essentially have just a collection of artifacts. I call them "objects and drawings to think with." And that's how I would think of this question. Whether it's a rendering, a drawing, a simulation, or an image, if it's something you can think with, then I think it's of value. For one person it might be about how the artifact was created. For someone else it might be about how to find opportunities within the artifact itself. If you can think with it, if it creates opportunities, then it's of value. And it's not about a problem and a solution, but about exploration. Where I don't find value is when students purely represent something for the sake of it being represented. There's no longer a design decision, or a lesson learned. It becomes pure instrumentation, pure recording. It feels like the game is over. If you're not actively engaging in a reflective way, like how you are describing it, then it's no longer an object to think with, and there's no value in it anymore.

THEODORA VARDOULI: In my case, I am almost fetishistic about my image. I'm using the graph as a vehicle by which to piece together the larger history that I'm interested in — and Alexander is one chapter in that history. The project, of which my presentation today is a part of, is talking about a larger transaction between mathematical modernism and architectural modernism as the context in which the computational transitioning of architecture occurred. Again, this is very situated within research universities and specific groups — I'm not trying to make a general claim about what computation is in architecture and so on — but I know that some of the first computational theories and implementations of computers happened within specific sites and that there were specific techniques of representing and calculating that facilitated them. So, I'm really trying to use these techniques to assemble different kinds of rhetorics and discourses, and do a cross-institutional and cross-geographic history of the introduction of computation in architecture. So, the graph in my story is this ambivalent object that architects who subscribed to that project of structural abstraction as the epitome of postwar modernism used to furnish the architectural discipline with an abstract basis. It's ironic that a picture actually was used as the facilitator of this iconoclastic project. So, in answer to your question, yes, I think in my case the image is more of a vehicle. By looking at its specific properties, the way that it was drawn, and the things that were said about it, I'm trying to recreate a specific cultural and epistemological moment in architecture.

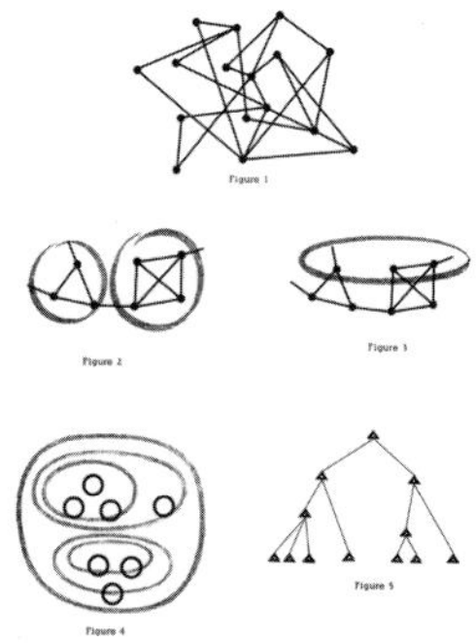

Image discussed by Theodora Vardouli at Computational Design: Practices, Histories, Infrastructures: *Graphs, subgraphs, and trees, "picturing" the design problem's structure.* Christopher Alexander. 1962. Source: "Information and an Organized Process of Design." In *New Building Research* Spring 1961, 115–24. Washington, D.C: National Academy of Sciences - National Research Council, 106.

JACOB GABOURY: First, I just noticed this is a bejeweled microphone, I just wanted to point that out. Now, a lot of the archival material that I work with are images that have been wholly decontextualized from the space in which they were first rendered. In particular because the moment in which they were rendered predates the file formats and the ways in which we produce, print, and save images today. So, what initially drew me to some of this work was realizing that this *thing* that was so legible to me as a digital image was, in fact, produced with a camera strapped to the screen of an oscilloscope — an oscilloscope that took around two minutes to create a simple raster image. In my work I take an image and unpack those objects that enable it and, in doing so, perhaps limit and restrict it — or produce a set of affordances that then carry on historically into the present. But that connection is often [not well understood]. The historical lineage of those connections would inform and make us better historians, designers, architects, and so on. So, in some ways I'm interested in problematizing the relationship between images and objects, and that's why the book is called *Image Objects* — not to plug my book!

And I think that it works in the other direction as well. A lot of the objects that many of you are interested in are, in some senses, images. The way some of you may look at a building and determine the kind of CAD program that was used to produce it for example. The flattening goes both directions — there's a way in which objects are embedded within visual apparatuses, but also a way the affordances of visuality become a product of what we think of more normatively as objects.

ANDREW HEUMANN: I see, especially in the work of Joseph and Carl — and maybe a little bit in the work of Alexander that Theodora discussed — a sort of purism, or an attachment to a particular set of restrictions about how things are generally thought out. I wonder if you could speak to the value of that purism.

JOSEPH CHOMA: Maybe I should just go backwards and just say why I got interested in mathematics. Before I went to MIT I was really just a digital guru. I was fully immersed in the most cutting-edge digital tools at that time — or at least that's what

I'd like to think. But at some point I realized that depending on which tool I used, I had a particular bias. And I found that I would click a lot of buttons — I knew how to click them really well — but I didn't always know what was behind those buttons. So, I thought okay, maybe I have to learn computer science, to understand what's behind them. When I learned computer science, I learned that there are still hierarchical heuristics embedded within those systems, and that maybe I had to go even further. So, I started looking at mathematics, which led me to Joseph Fourier's 1800s "Fourier Series." Which is essentially what I showed today, but bringing that from signal processing to the control of three-dimensional shapes. The strange thing with math is that mathematicians make proofs and then they just move on. But when you stop and you say "well, hold on a second," if you don't just move on and instead try to understand it as a tool, there's actually a whole spectrum of other opportunities that we're missing out on. [In design] you can't just calculate with mathematics. You have to manipulate it like anything else. So that's something that I became interested in and obsessed with. It's a very tight constraint. Mathematics is a transparent tool unlike many digital black boxes, but it's very biased. When I teach my students I don't actually teach them mathematics, but I do teach them computational thinking and rigor, and design experiments — very similar to the way Josef Albers defined design experiments. So for me it's just a bizarre expertise at this point, and now I'm starting to find that I have enough control over it that I should start to tackle other real world problems like structure, materiality, long span structures. So I'm now trying to overlay those as other constraints, to try to elevate my understanding of what I can do, and to make new opportunities.

CARL LOSTRITTO: In some ways, fanatical purism to me gives me license to care about making beautiful things without feeling guilty, or being accused of being an aesthetician — and... that's it.

——— OLGA TOULOUMI: Can I speak to that a little bit before taking more questions from the audience? I had initially decided not to indulge in a psychological reading of your work, but your responses tempt me. Throughout the different presentations I kept thinking that we are talking about a fetish — technique as fetish. There is a fetish of the real, which comes across in the z-buffer that Jacob discussed, where "depth" is the whitest element on the screen (an enlightenment that is actually obscuring the work of the tool) — I might be stretching hermeneutically my interpretation; or at the exhibition, where we had the "petit objet" of the Sketchpad — the three-dimensional experience. So, there seems to be a fetishization of the computational image and the structured image. And if I wanted to push the limits of that, the desire to control the tool echoes Hegelian ideas of dialectics, where it is unclear who is actually controlling what.

CARL LOSTRITTO: I got to do the fetish response thing, because, to me, there's a matrix where one column ranges between fetish and fashion, and the other between craft and virtuosity and I think it's very easy to be on one side or the other. But I think implicit in Andrew's question is an idea of disciplinarity that I think allows me to say that I'm a little bit immune to the psychological problems of getting obsessed with my own work, because there's a discipline to it. So, I sleep well at night. My therapy needs to be about the discipline of architecture as an overbearing parent I can't get away from. It's the way I was raised, and yet I'm not totally comfortable with it — but that's my problem.

THEODORA VARDOULI: I had a comment about the question before, but maybe I'll fold it in the answer to Olga's question. I plead guilty to this kind of methodological fetishism. And I'm using Arjun Appadurai's use of the term, which is that you can be really very fetishistic about the objects that you decide to follow, because they enliven the context through which they circulated. In my case, I think the graph has been really productive as a catalyst of this transaction between mathematical modernism and architectural modernism. I think it's important to appreciate that this question of purism had disciplinary stakes for architecture. But it was also a much broader cultural narrative in the postwar. In mathematics there was a very particular model of discipline that was being promoted which was based on axioms. It was completely self-enclosed, and it was built around its own internal rules. They would talk about the internal beauty of mathematics, and so on. Questions of autonomy in architecture have been rehashed multiple times, but I think the fact that Alexander was a mathematician, or that Lionel March was a mathematician, or that half of the Land Use Built Form Studies people studied under the new math teachers, [suggests that] there is a kind of cultural transaction that I think we need to appreciate when we're talking about intellectual histories of architecture during this period. There were interactions between architects and mathematicians that were very situated, and real. So, I guess being fetishistic sometimes as a historiographic method can allow you to appreciate objects as catalysts of communications between disciplines that we may be unlikely to see otherwise.

DANIEL CARDOSO LLACH: Regarding the issue of the CAD reconstruction which came up in Olga's question about fetishism: I think it's certainly there, but I'd like to frame it by noting an emerging tradition in the history of science, and in studies of science and technology, of doing historical reconstructions — I am thinking of the work of Lawrence Principe and others in the history of alchemy, as well as other examples in STS. The concept is to not only engage with our objects of study through documentary descriptions, or visual representations, but to also be able to access their gestural, sensual, and material dimensions. In other words, to use "making" methods to approach historical questions. So the aim of the Sketchpad and other CAD reconstructions in the exhibition is precisely to approximate the gestural and sensual aspects of past design technologies, and to consider these aspects as worthy subjects of historical reflection. So I think I am agreeing to an extent, but I'm also saying that there is a deliberate methodological approach — and I think this in some ways aligns with Theodora's answer — as software reconstructions allow us to experience and explore these systems in other ways, and to ask new kinds of questions about them.

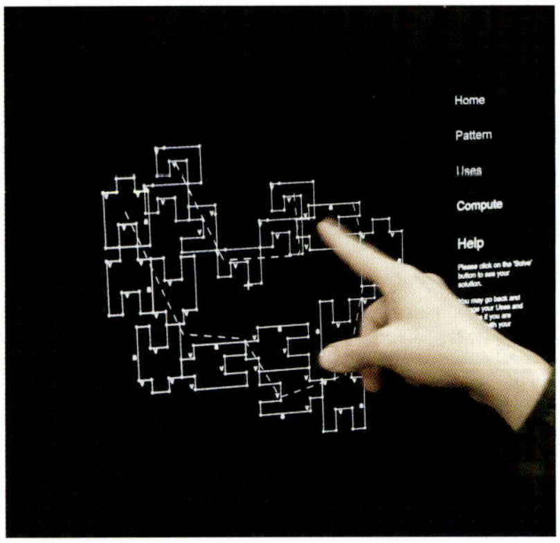

Reconstruction of CISP: Computer Implemented Site Planning, Christos I. Yessios, Institute for Physical Planning, Carnegie Mellon University, 1972, United States. Reconstructed by the Computational Design Laboratory, CMU, 2019 (updated 2021). Photo by Hasrhavardan Kedia.

ANN BURDICK: I am really interested in the image as an interface between human and machine, and in the issue of time — thinking about the potter, and about modeling within three-dimensional environments, and the notion of the WYSIWYG. And I wonder if you could all talk about the image as an interface between human and machine.

CARL LOSTRITTO: Joseph discussed the idea of a sketch as an interface between human and the self. I am not fully certain this is true, but I believe that there exist an order of magnitude more [digital] images today than will ever be seen by humans in all of human history. So, there are way more images that work as interfaces between machines. But in our culture we are way more accustomed to images being interfaces between human and human, so the interesting territory is when images mediate between humans and machines. One of the reasons why I like drawings is that they are a little bit stuck. Unlike a digital image that is a data structure, a drawing cannot be edited on those terms — so in a way it defies the interface notion as it requires perception. That's why I find the discourse about coding to be not necessarily vocational but actually potentially poetic, and quite interesting. The operational territory of the interface is the body of text that is the code, and then there's a drawing. And the role of images isn't actually clear in that, you know, paradigm of code to drawing. I think that was a partial answer, but that is the best I can do.

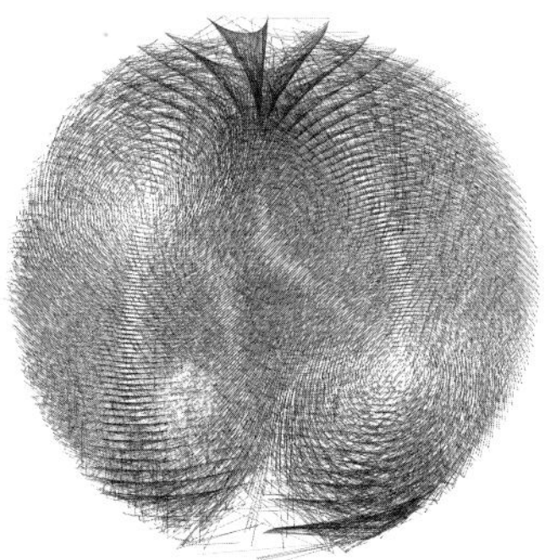

Curves created in two dimensions, *Unrelated on Paper*, Carl Lostritto, 2017, United States.

JOSEPH CHOMA: Personally, in my work — whatever you want to call it: drawings, sketches, graphics, images, mathematical sketches — the math is actually there, so we can look at the equation. In theoretical mathematics lines don't actually exist, only points exist. How is that true? So I don't know if I buy that model. The first thing I'm taught as an architect is how to draw a line. When you get into applied math you start to get into surfaces and other definitions. So, for me, when it comes to rendering things graphically, I am essentially deciding subjectively how I want to record that mathematical object, or boundary definition. If I render it as a solid surface, it would feel very fixed, like "it is what it is." An object. Conversely, if I render it as a wireframe, I can get inside, and cut it using traditional orthographic methods. So, I subjectively choose to do a wireframe drawing because I like the fact that I can look inside and outside at the same time. And it is subjective, but I think it also allows for a reading that might be unpredictable. So, while I'm working with mathematics on the computer, there are times when I'm working through sketching — literally writing equations and imagining what those combinations are doing.

Something happens differently when I tacitly start to type in the code. It happens very quickly and it's hard to explain. The process there was not the true process — it was much more tacit and back and forth. And then, at some point I just stop and I make a drawing — what I call a drawing where I guess you [Carl] could say a recording. And when I look at it, I may say "wow, you know what? There's this weird gnarly texture that's happening here and I'm really interested in that" or "actually I really like the fact that it anchors to one side." And then other things emerge that sort of question the actual objectness of the model or its ideas. So I like the idea of doing something whenever I can do something that will open up ideas.

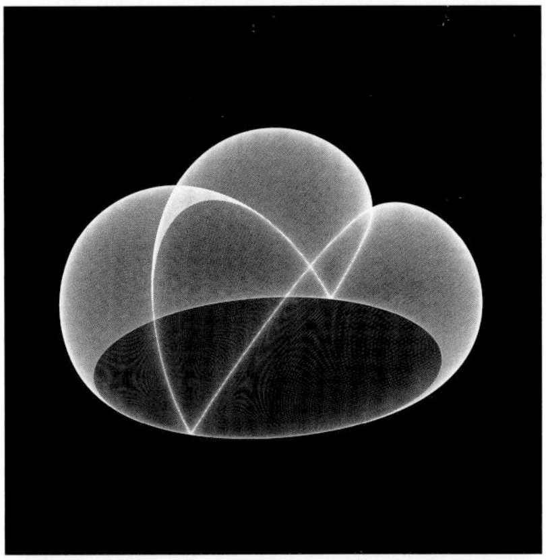

Synclastic and anticlastic (series), Joseph Choma, Design Topology Lab, Clemson University, 2021, United States.

JACOB GABOURY: What's interesting about computer graphics is that it falls into a very long history of optics and human vision that in a certain mathematical sense are very well described and understood. So, a lot of histories of computer graphics emphasize the moment when perspective was first introduced at MIT in the early 1960s, but I think this is in fact an incredibly uninteresting moment in the history of computer graphics. Perspective is essentially a mathematical calculation that is extremely straightforward and well-known — I mean, sure, it's being displayed on a screen. But the interesting thing to me is the way computer simulation interfaces not only capture vision but also larger ontological questions about how we understand the world. Computer simulations by necessity are incredibly narrow and deep. They simulate very few things extremely well. But they are limited. It's a bit like — and I hate to do this, and I do it far too much — the Rumsfeld, Žižek, thing about known knowns, and known unknowns. So, there are things that we can see and understand very well, like optics, that can be simulated well. So, there's a sort of interesting interplay between the human and the machine. There are things that we understand exist, but we can't get them right quite yet, but we have this sense that eventually we'll get there. But in a kind of "new materialist" sense, or in a larger kind of philosophical materialism, or ontological sense, there are potentially things in the world that we do not understand and don't know that we don't understand, that are outside the simulation. And if we believe those to exist, then this sort of teleological thrust of, really all of the history of technology — particularly computation and especially computer graphics — that we will somehow achieve a perfect simulation at some point in the future, falls apart immediately. But nonetheless, it persists in the way in which we develop, market, sell, and use these tools ourselves. So, I think it's interesting to think about what kind of ontological claim computer graphics makes about the function of the world, as enframed for us, which is sort of the larger kind of Heideggerian question about technology. So, there's a lot there, maybe. But vision especially is a wonderful example precisely because we have hundreds and hundreds of years of history of mathematically modeling our own vision and perception in this way.

THEODORA VARDOULI: I'd like to add something about the graph. One of the aspects that has been analytically really fruitful is to think of it as an interface between the rational and the empirical, or between the abstract and the concrete, even in the history of mathematicians writing about graphs. For example, the first book on graph theory, which I think was written by Denes König in the mid-1930s, went to great lengths to say that even though graphs can be drawn, they are really abstract mathematical structures, they are not visual entities. They are not geometry — they are abstractions. And then in the '70s, people like Frank Harary, for instance, who is another graph theorist, went to great lengths to say that graphs are visual. He even had a taxonomy in the University of Waterloo, and had students classify graphs as "sexy" or "pretty" or "ugly" or "beautiful" and so on. And it's fascinating to me how architects kind of moved between the two ends of that spectrum, mobilizing either the abstract aspects of graph theory, or the visual ones. So, for example, we have early Alexander making iconoclastic declarations claiming the graph as the technique that delivers them. And then we have people like Yona Friedman, who uses the graph as a kind of intuitive tool for participatory design. So visuality works as a kind of register of the human, and then the question of how its mathematical underpinning relates to the visual world — how an object works as an interface between the two — has been analytically productive for me.

OLGA TOULOUMI: Any last questions? Okay, so I would like to thank the panelists for a great discussion.

Imagination Machines: A Conversation with George Stiny

Moderated by
Daniel Cardoso Llach
Theodora Vardouli

DANIEL CARDOSO LLACH: We're excited to welcome George Stiny to reflect on the Shape Grammar enterprise that he has spearheaded since the late 1960s; on the different types of research that it has generated; and on the role of the visual in a numero-centric culture.[1] Instead of thinking of computers as "aids" to design, George's work conceptualizes design itself as a form of visual calculation. Shape Grammars offer a view of design as an open-ended manipulation of shapes through the application of visual rules. They also speak of design as an irreducibly sensorial practice — as a cycle of perception and action (of seeing and doing). Premised on the notion that design cannot be reduced to symbolic transactions, Shape Grammars can be seen as a critique of software-based approaches to computational design. And yet, the mathematical scaffoldings and procedural logics of Shape Grammars have also enticed many other researchers to explore a contrasting sensibility: one focused on codifying and automating design — and perhaps this ambivalence is a key to their power. Today, Shape Grammars remain a vital theoretical scaffolding for computational

George Stiny, *Blooms Day* (1968) as installed in the Miller Institute of Contemporary Art, 2017. Photo by Tom Little.

1 Digital.Visual.Material Symposium, (Edited for length and clarity), virtual event, May 2021

designers, a seemingly intractable technical problem for digital computing, and a useful analytical and generative device with practical applications across different design fields.

THEODORA VARDOULI: After inventing Shape Grammars in the late '60s, George has been exploring their sweep in art and design ever since. He is the author of *Pictorial and Formal Aspects of Shape and Shape Grammars, Algorithmic Aesthetics: Computer Models for Criticism in Design and the Arts* with James Gips, and *Shape: Talking about Seeing and Doing.*[2] In his next book, *Shapes of Imagination: Calculating in Coleridge's Magical Realm*, which we might talk a little bit about today, he discusses how Shape Grammars subsume English poet Samuel Taylor Coleridge's imagination and fancy, and Oscar Wilde's advice to see things as in themselves they really are not.[3] Today we'll have an open-ended conversation and we hope to engage the audience through a question and answer period.

DANIEL CARDOSO LLACH: We'd like to start by looking at the painting *Blooms Day*, which is one of the exhibition's key pieces. The painting itself is generated procedurally following Shape Grammar-principles. It's composed of twelve triangular canvases which can be arranged in multiple ways. You painted this a while back, in 1968. We believe this is a few years before, or perhaps concurrent with the formulation of the theory of Shape Grammars. Is this so?

GEORGE STINY: This was before. I actually knew what Shape Grammars were formally around three years before the paper, and at that stage in my life — I've since corrected this lapse — I wasn't terribly good at the formalism — all the little symbols that you have to write out in order to write a scholarly paper — so I asked Jim Gips to help me with that. That's why it's the Stiny-Gips paper, but the Shape Grammar idea was prior to the paper. Gips did his PhD at Stanford in computer science, and I did mine with a marvelous person at UCLA, Sheila Greibach, who looked at what I did and said, "well, it's not exactly my thing, but go do it."

2 See George Stiny. *Pictorial and Formal Aspects of Shape and Shape Grammars*. Interdisciplinary Systems Research 13. (Basel: Springer Basel AG, 1975); George Stiny, and James Gips. *Algorithmic Aesthetics: Computer Models for Criticism and Design in the Arts*. (University of California Press, Oakland, CA, 1978); George Stiny. *Shape: Talking about Seeing and Doing*. (Cambride MA: MIT Press, 2006.)

3 See George Stiny. "The Critic as Artist: Oscar Wilde's Prolegomena to Shape Grammars." *Nexus Network Journal* 17 (January 4, 2016): 1–36. https://doi.org/10.1007/s00004-015-0274-4.

DANIEL CARDOSO LLACH: Can you tell us a little more about the making of this painting?

GEORGE STINY: At the time I was keen on the word play in James Joyce. The original arrangement of the painting was a six-pointed star, and that's why I named it *Blooms Day*. You were supposed to trace through it the same way that [Leopold] Bloom would trace through Dublin. And the paths — when you use your eye, and you use things that today I would call identity rules — were equally as strange, bizarre, and random, and actually fit quite well into *Ulysses*. It reminded me, of course, of the *Odyssey*, and getting from Troy back to Ithaca, and encountering sirens, and all these other strange and wonderful things along the way. It was meant to be arranged in the way Daniel arranged it here, and I hope in his next exhibit he rearranges it in yet another way, so that it fills up the wall in whatever way you choose. The panels all connect together — because of the way silk screening works, and the way the overlap rules work. It's really amazing all the things that you can see. That's what this is trying to do. I'm trying to capture the visual, and how we interact with the visual, and how interacting with the visual doesn't preclude interacting with it computationally. I can show that everything that I see in this painting corresponds to a rule that I can also show you. Today, that's what my preoccupation is. How you can pick stuff out in all sorts of weird ways to restructure the object over and over and over again, and come to different aesthetic conclusions about what it is.[4]

George Stiny, *Blooms Day* (1968) as installed in the UQAM's Centre de design gallery, 2021.

DANIEL CARDOSO LLACH: Could you help us understand a little better the intersection, or the interaction, between your artistic practice and your theoretical work?

GEORGE STINY: When I started out doing this, I remember saying to myself: "Look, I can see these things, and I can see that they change, and I can see that they do all sorts of stuff, and I'm going to write out what the mathematics is that lets me do that." That was my goal in doing a PhD I thought there were different ways of doing it. One involved minimal representations, where you picked out the smallest bits that had to do with the way parts interacted. And I said, "Well, I know how to do that, so I won't do it first; instead, I'll start out with the other part." The other part was these maximal bits, and that's the way I do it now with maximal elements. These are just fused elements that have certain common geometrical properties. It turned out that once I saw how to do that, I didn't need to do the minimal bits, because they just fell out with embedding. They fell out by applying rules. The whole idea was to start with what my eye did, and then invent the mathematics. As luck would have it, the mathematics turned out to be some really nice modern stuff that has to do with generalized Boolean algebras and Stone spaces, and things that people still talk about today in mathematics departments. But that was just luck. As far as I was concerned, it didn't matter. I was going after the mathematics that made my eyes work. Everybody else was busy taking existing mathematics, and making visual materials correspond to that mathematics. That's what Gips did when he wrote out his PhD He went at it the way computer scientists are supposed to go at it. Instead, I went at it saying: "Look, I want to be an artist and that's what really interests me." And I said to myself: "I also like maths, and I'm pretty good at it, so what does the math look like that lets me see the way I see?" That's why I talk about the things that I talk about. In order to get that, you need the "embed-fuse" cycle.[5] That's exactly what I think Coleridge was after and, in his own way, I think it's exactly what Wilde was after when he was talking about what a "beautiful form" is. Certainly it's implied in his aesthetic formulas to "see things as in themselves they really aren't." Occasionally I see people who pick up Wilde's aesthetic formula as a kind of incantation. Well, I took it seriously. And if you take it seriously, you just get Shape Grammars. One of the reasons that my recent work has been so focused on the work of Romantics — both painters and poets — is because it's as artsy as you could possibly get, and therefore as far away from computation as you can possibly get. What I'm trying to show is that it's still calculating. I've used

4 See "Two Exercises in Formal Composition." *Environment and Planning B: Planning and Design 3*, no. 2 (December 1, 1976): 187–210. https://doi.org/10.1068/b030187.

5 In Shape Grammars, "embedding" refers to the act of seeing something in something else. For example, seeing chevrons and triangles in a star is to "embed" in the Shape Grammar sense. "Fusing" refers to the act of seeing the whole again — rather than a collection of discrete units — in the result. The "embed-fuse" cycle is the basic conceptual machinery of Shape Grammars. During the symposium, Stiny related Shape Grammars and the embed-fuse cycle to the English poet Samuel T. Coleridge's notion of "imagination" — as opposed to "fancy": "Coleridge talks about imagination and fancy in terms of 'esemplastic power' which is the ability to fuse things together so that where they had divisions before, those divisions disappear." Access the full recording at http://www.lattice.space. (Editors' note.)

the word calculating and computation differently. Computation being computers, and calculating being what you do when you apply rules in terms of embedding and recursion. I can't imagine a wider gap to try to fill and yet Shape Grammars do it in a very straightforward, very direct way. I've been saying that for fifty years, and Coleridge has been moaning and groaning about imagination and fancy for 200 years, and neither of us have anybody paying any attention. So, I'm in good company. I've got 150 years to go!

THEODORA VARDOULI: We thought it would be wonderful to get a little closer to the context in which Shape Grammars came to be, and this idea that you just described, which was that you were seeing something and you felt that you would use mathematics to talk about what you're seeing, and to allow you to see more. I'm wondering about this kind of bringing together of mathematics and art, and how this idea was received at the time — if it was met with resistance, if it has been met with resistance since, or if you felt that you were part of a larger project of really using math as a way to illuminate creativity?

GEORGE STINY: I find it strange, because it's mostly been met with incomprehension. The incomprehensibility comes from saying that recursion isn't the heart of calculating, and that the embedding relation is. And that within embedding I can do the zero-dimensional stuff that's symbolic, but I can also do the visual stuff that's not symbolic. When I say that most people look at me and I can tell that it's just not clicking. It has to do with their expectations and education. From my point of view, a lot of people have been "educated out" of this. My own kids, when they went to school, were taught to discretize everything almost instantly. When my little daughter went into kindergarten the teacher gave her a ruler. On one side of the ruler was the alphabet, and on the other side — in discrete little cuts — were the numbers one to six, for six inches. I asked the teacher: Why are you doing this? And she said "I wanted them to see that the world could be made out of a finite number of little things that you can combine." I almost went berserk and had to be kind of pulled out of the room. It's that kind of incomprehension that's greeted this subject.

Certainly there have been a lot of people that have supported Shape Grammars very strongly. At UCLA Sheila Greibach was one of them. She wasn't a visual person. I used to show her something visually that I could do instantly and she'd say, "well, you have to write that out in symbols for me to understand it," so I would go back and I tediously write it out in symbols, which is how I learned mathematics. And she'd look at it and say, "oh, I understand that"; then she would make some suggestions that were symbolic that I'd translate into visual stuff. Another great person who I miss a lot was Lionel March, who was probably one of the most numerical people I've ever met. He could do mathematics in a numerical way that I still find staggering. He was marvelous. He supported Shape Grammars enthusiastically, and in many ways this went very counter to what he was trying to do at the Centre for Land Use and Built Form Studies, with Leslie Martin and the group at Cambridge. And certainly counter to what Serge Chermayeff was trying to do at Harvard with Chris Alexander. Alexander's *Pattern Language* is fancy on steroids. It's exactly what Coleridge was railing against.

It took me a long time to figure out what was going on. You do this stuff and you have the feeling in your soul, or your heart — or wherever it is — that it's not what anybody else is doing, but you don't quite know how to say it. It's taken me fifty years to get to the "embed-fuse" cycle, and to Coleridge, Wilde, and all these guys, to say it in a way that I think is elucidating and fits that tradition. I certainly didn't have this conception of it in 1972, or 1968, and I certainly didn't have it when I did the *Shape* book in 2006. All the machinery was there in 1975, but it wasn't presented in a way where it captured an idea that had been around long enough that was right, which was Coleridge's imagination and fancy. Of course, Coleridge didn't know any mathematics. He was a great inventor of words, and a pretty good poet — especially a good inventor of words, "esemplastic" was one of his inventions. Namely, imagination — esemplastic power — redividing and fusing. Fusing and redividing are Coleridge's terms.

THEODORA VARDOULI: One thing that we find particularly striking from *Algorithmic Aesthetics* is this link that Shape Grammars provide between analysis and generation, which is quite unique.[6] We're wondering about this idea. And then — and this may be an irritating question — about your choice to call shape grammars Shape Grammars, and whether this was a critique of Chomsky or was influenced by Chomsky at all.

GEORGE STINY: I have a lot of fanciful — as opposed to fancy — stories on that. The first thing regarding analysis and generation is that, in my mind, they were never different. I always thought they were the same thing and all you were doing was emphasizing one thing or the other. My paper "Two Exercises in Formal Composition," which came out before the *Algorithmic Aesthetics* book, really captured that idea because one of the exercises was constructive — synthesis, putting things together. The other was analysis — applying identity rules to cut things up in different ways. If you look at what the calculations were doing that did both of those, they were indistinguishable. You couldn't tell them apart. So, from my point of view, from a Shape Grammars point of view, it seemed ridiculous to make a distinction that was hard and fast. It always seemed to me that once you realize analysis is construction and construction is analysis, you get a lot farther. Certainly, if you look at the way Shape Grammars work in the "embed-fuse" cycle, when you do embedding, you're doing analysis. It's just that you don't do it once. You do it over and over and over and over again. You think to yourself, "why is he doing that?" but you're doing it because you're reanalyzing every time you do it, which was Coleridge's point. I mean, that's what he's talking about when boundaries diffuse, and then you redivide. So, you're constantly putting things together and then redividing them. Most people do this once or twice, and in Shape Grammars, you do it every time a rule applies. The analysis/synthesis stuff really predates the algorithmic aesthetics. There's no way I could talk about it unless I said they were the same, I just don't see the difference. The other distinction that I don't see is between generation and evaluation. They're the same thing as far as I'm concerned. You evaluate something when you don't want everything to have a

6 George Stiny, and James Gips. *Algorithmic Aesthetics: Computer Models for Criticism and Design in the Arts.* (University of California Press, Oakland, CA, 1978.) http://www.algorithmicaesthetics.org/

high value, and when you want everything to have that value, you generate it. Going back and forth between the generating and the evaluating is really remarkably straightforward. The rules you're using to evaluate, you translate into shape rules and you're off and running. That's just another manifestation of analysis and synthesis-type stuff, where the rules are doing the analysis, and they're doing the synthesis. They're doing it both together glove in hand, hand in glove without distinction. But again, that's one of the reasons that Shape Grammars tend to be looked at with suspicion. A lot of classical distinctions evaporate and they're very, very hard to maintain if you're willing to accept the "embed-fuse" cycle. I find that exciting. If you're wedded to a certain kind of epistemology — to use Theodora's favorite word — or maybe an ontology, then you're in a real bind.

Why are shape grammars called Shape Grammars? It's very simple. They originally were called Shape Grammars, because that's what happens in linguistics. The model that I had in mind initially was Chomsky's. I took a couple of his classes when I was an undergraduate, and the one thing that impressed me was the generative power of a grammar — that you can get all these sentences. The transformational part I thought was kind of klutzy, but the basic grammar part I thought was really elegant. I went on to do theory of formal languages and other stuff. So that's where the name came from. Subsequently, in later years, I realized that it was really a change from Chomsky and linguistics because shapes are not grammatical in the syntactic sense. So really, the term is ironic — I say this in the *Shape* book — because there's not a syntax of shapes. In order to have a syntax, you need to have parts, atoms, and elements, and there are none in shapes. It was a radical departure from Chomsky, which I enjoy even to this day. If I look at Chomsky's stuff now, he's got this minimalist theory where you put the units together in a context-free way. He's got the no tampering rule proviso which states that if you put A and B together, you can't change A or B, because they're together. The Shape Grammarist says, "Well, gosh, that's kind of limited! I can take two squares and put them together — square A and different square B — and get triangles." The Linguist says, "this is not thought," and the Shape Grammarist says "well, that's perception... that's seeing." What is really interesting is that the stan-

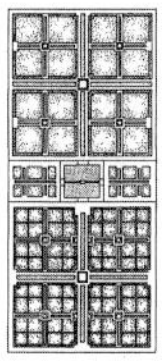

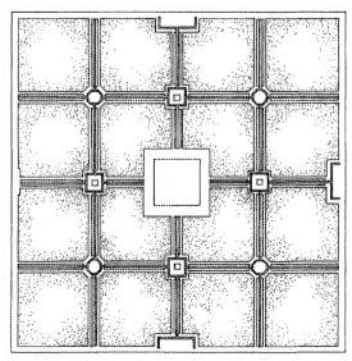

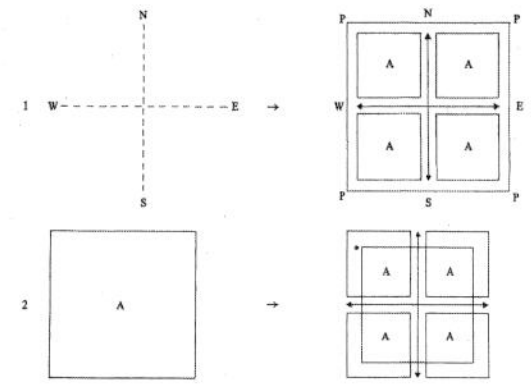

dard linguistic notion of grammars is a special case of Shape Grammars. In my case, it's when things have zero dimensionality and go together like points. If you pump that up a little bit and go to one or two dimensions then you get Shape Grammars. Interestingly, Alberti, who's one of my heroes — I think he really got it right — talks about what architecture is as the graceful pre-ordering of lines and angles. The lines and angles are spatial relations, and that they're lines and that they're on a plane makes them one-dimensional in two space. So, Alberti has already pumped the thing up one dimension, and the minute you do that, you get an entirely different world to play in, and it's the world of the designers, the world of the artists, it's the world of the painter, it's the world of the poet. It's not the world of the linguist, which is not to say that I don't want linguistics. You want language to do something for you, you want to be able to use it to think, but at the same time, you don't want to forget that there's a lot more in the world than putting two words together, so that they satisfy the no-tampering proviso, which, from a Shape Grammar point of view, is just an unproductive restriction.

7 In "The Grammar of Paradise" Stiny and architectural theorist William J. Mitchell study the formal rules for generating Mughal gardens. See G Stiny, and W J Mitchell. "The Grammar of Paradise: On the Generation of Mughul Gardens." *Environment and Planning B: Planning and Design* 7, no. 2 (June 1, 1980): 209–26. https://doi.org/10.1068/b070209.

8 Elizabeth B. Moynihan, *Paradise as a Garden: In Persia and Mughal India*. World Landscape Art & Architecture Series. (New York: G. Braziller, 1979.)

DANIEL CARDOSO LLACH: Maybe this is a good moment to think about the foundational role that "seeing" plays in Shape Grammars, and in the view of design that Shape Grammars propose. We are really curious about what the work of "seeing" is, and what it is that we do when we see. We are hoping that you could walk us through the process of making a Shape Grammar and help us see in the way that Shape Grammars ask us to see. We're proposing that we look at this paper which is one of your best-known works — a collaboration with Bill Mitchell where you look at the Mughal gardens in Lahore and other places.[7] Could you tell us about how this grammar came about? How was it *made*? Or how did ***you*** make it? What kind of work did it entail? Was drawing involved?

GEORGE STINY: It was a drawing in Elizabeth Moynihan's book [*Paradise as a Garden: In Persia and Mughal India*].[8] Bill was enthusiastic about Mughal designs, and I looked at them and said, "Oh, I can do this because the recursion is obvious." It's just squares inside of squares and it has a functional aspect to it that's very nice. You've got a square, and you can put four little squares in it. It had to do with the way irrigation worked in these gardens, because you'd have these canals and what you wanted to do is flood the green area. So, the canals are like capillaries in your body and you'd want them to be dense enough so that you could get blood everywhere. In the *char-bagh*, it was to get water everywhere. You'd have this canal system and you divide it so that when you flooded the canal, enough water would dump out of the canal and cover the ground area. The bigger the thing is, the more cuts you need to have. The fourfold division is just the Four Rivers of Life — north, south, east, and west — and all that kind of mythology. All of this, to be perfectly honest with you, was done visually. I only read Moynihan's book after I did this. I paid no attention to it at all — I just looked at the drawings. And I don't know whether the drawings are true or not. Jim Westcoat, who just retired from MIT, is an expert on Mughal gardens and he used to tell me, "you got it wrong," and I said, "Well, that wasn't the point. The point was to show you can calculate this stuff." It's one of those funny cases where he did the scholarship — and it's admirable scholarship — but he didn't want to embrace the way you might calculate it, and the way someone might think about it in this visual sort of way.

DANIEL CARDOSO LLACH: Maybe to build a little bit on that, I think it would be wonderful if you could tell us a little more about what challenges you encountered in trying to convey the importance of the visual calculation and the visual in general in a culture that is so numerical and focused on digital calculations, such as MIT.

GEORGE STINY: I'll make two comparisons. The first one is that to get my students — Theodora, you and others — it takes about three years to get you to see what these strange things are doing, with no guarantee that you're going to go away and do them. It takes a while just to have it seep in. The other great irony is that algorithmic aesthetics does do information processing in the normal way. It's very much in the information processing tradition, that was at a high point in 1978, and is still very much at the high point. It was very much in that tradition. My students find that very easy to understand, and I get so irritated, because they come up with really good questions and it just it's very straightforward, but I show them something that is simpler — namely, a rule, which I think is an aesthetic system itself because it allows you to see something, and to do it, which is the effector and the receptor in the algorithmic aesthetics — and I show them how that works and that takes a long time to get a response. I apologize to all my students that may be watching this, but this is what I think of when I go home and I pull my hair out — which I don't have anymore to pull out — and say: "My God, it took me a long time to get that one across." And yet here's algorithmic aesthetics that everybody found very clear... I mean, I was really staggered. They read it in my seminar a couple years ago, the comments were great, the insights were great, and it was just this information processing model. It fits with what you thought and what you know, from computers, and yet today I wouldn't do it that way. I'd say, "well, here's a rule, and this captures everything." It allows me to *see*; that's the embed part, and it allows me to *do*; that's the fuse part — and then I can do the cycle over and over and over again. So, instead of having a normal machine cycle with units that get moved around in a database, I've got this "embed-fuse" cycle. It gives me this imagination. That's the part I really want to get across today, rather than the algorithmic aesthetics, which I'm happy people are picking up again, I think that's wonderful. [Computer scientist and AI pioneer Marvin] Minsky taught it at MIT for a couple of years, and in those days nobody was interested in aesthetics. So, I'm really glad that you're picking it up again. There's a lot of interesting stuff in that book. Even though today I would discard it. I mean, it's not my favorite thing, but at the time, it was exactly right and it's still fresh today. The ideas in there still stand up to the examination in the light of today. It's just that what goes on in Shape Grammars is so much more interesting, from my point of view.

DANIEL CARDOSO LLACH: It's almost as if the idioms of information theory became useful to communicate these ideas, but at the same time hid part of the complexity — the actual sort of materiality you're trying to get at.

GEORGE STINY: Right, and I guess I'm sharing the frustration Coleridge must have in his grave, that it's 200 years on and people still don't understand what imagination, or fancy, is. I knew about imagination and fancy in the 1960s, and the reason I know that is because I have a book on Coleridge and I was thumbing through it after I went back to it recently, and here was the passage underlined with a big star next to it. So, I knew about it, but I didn't know what to do about it. Now I've got it, and know what to do about it, and it's still as hard to get people to understand. Being a quasi-scholar, I immediately went out and tried to figure out what everybody else was saying about it. It was weird. Nobody had any sense of what poor old Coleridge was talking about, which is why 200 years have gone by and it still doesn't work. The only person who really kind of got it right was I. A. Richards in a little book called *Principles of Literary Criticism* and he has these six kinds of imagination and the last one is Coleridge's.[9] He runs amok saying how wonderful it is, and talks about it in another book on Coleridge. My problem with Richards was that I had to read it as an undergraduate, and I hated it. I now know why: because he wanted to have a scientific view of art, and his scientific view of art was psychology. Yet, inside the book was this wonderful chapter on imagination. I probably didn't get that far as an undergraduate, because I just couldn't stand it.

9 I. A. Richards, *Principles of Literary Criticism*. A Harvest Book, HB43. (New York: Harcourt, Brace, 1962.)

DANIEL CARDOSO LLACH: This might be a good moment to open up the conversation. We want to make sure that people have the chance to converse with you and formulate questions.

BENAY GURSOY: George, it's always very inspiring to listen to you. Not everyone approaches Shape Grammars the way you do, in the sense that not everyone is focused on embedding and recursion. There are a lot of people who use Shape Grammars for different reasons. So, I wonder what your thoughts are about these different applications of Shape Grammars?

GEORGE STINY: My thought is that everybody should use them for what they want to use them for. They provide a remarkably different way of thinking about things, and they make a lot of stuff that's hard, very easy. My sense is that the visual enterprise is a way of doing things that is as rigorous as a Turing machine but allows access that's direct because it suits the eye. So, you don't have to divide things up into symbols, you can just do it in terms of what you're looking at. I see Ramesh Krishnamurti here, and I should have mentioned that he was the very first person to make computers do this stuff.[10] To this day, the techniques that he used are the ones that people are using. It was a marvelous piece of work. He tells me that some of the maths I do today are bad because you can't do them on a computer, and I look at him like he's nuts, but that's beside the point. I wanted to point that out, because Ramesh is a very important figure in this entire enterprise. But to get back to your question, I think people should try them out for anything. What I'm interested in is engaging the world with my eye.

MIT has the motto "Mind and Hand." And if you think of mind as representation or language, and hand as hand, you get a certain model of the world — and that's the MIT model of the world. It's numeric. It's representational. It's logical. I think of the world in terms of a model that's Eye and Hand. The irony is that the eye subsumes the mind in Shape Grammars, because the eye requires multi-dimensional elements and the mind is a Turing machine and it's perfectly happy with zero dimensional stuff (0's and 1's). So, when I say the model should be Eye and Hand — the artist's formula — it really subsumes "Mind and Hand" which is the scientist's and the engineer's formula, and together they make the world. I think what's interesting about Eye and Hand is that it's an ambiguous or experimental world where you can try stuff out, which is why I want people to try anything they want to try. The reason you do that is because it's easier to calculate with the devices that we have in computers, and you want to do it over and over and over again. But if you don't know what you're doing you better do it Eye and Hand.

10 See R. Krishnamurti, and C. Giraud. "Towards a Shape Editor: The Implementation of a Shape Generation System." *Environment and Planning B: Planning and Design* 13, no. 4 (December 1, 1986): 391–404. https://doi.org/10.1068/b130391.

Shape Grammars allow you to do both. I want people to *get over* the zero dimensionality of stuff, but I don't want to *get rid of it*. I think it's marvelous and wonderful. It's just that there's a lot more there than just that.

——— THEODORA VARDOULI: I think George, as Daniel Rosenberg wrote in the chat, many of your students have been influenced by the general sensibility of your approach. Matthew [Lee], you're at McGill and the second-year undergraduate studio right now is very much inspired by some of the Shape Grammar ideas. Not so much in how to use the computational formalism, but precisely thinking about what it means to train yourself in a constant re-formulation — like you were discussing, George. How do we stop over-verbalizing and start to look with the intention to discover new things? I think many of your students have been influenced by this approach. It's making it into architectural pedagogy in one way or another, either with or without the computational machinery. The fundamental idea of how you train yourself to constantly look for new ways to look at things, I think, has been very influential for many of us.

GEORGE STINY: Well, thank you for saying that, Theodora. I have to say two things. One, I really liked the mathematics. It's really pretty. But, having said that, I would much rather people use their eyes than get hung up on the mathematics. The mathematics make it just weird enough that it's outside of what you learned in school, and the weirdness is kind of an impediment. It's a threshold that's difficult to get over, and is really kind of irrelevant — although pretty. I'm enough of a mathematics person that I like it and don't want to diminish it, but I'm more of a visual person. I'd rather see the art and the design in the sense that you're constantly changing what you're seeing and taking advantage of that. If that's presented just informally, as far as I'm concerned, that's all to the good. Not everybody has to do the math — except for Ramesh! I have to say one other thing — possibly in closing — something I hear from architects in my department at MIT is, "well, you know, we're treated like second-class citizens in the Institute. Nobody takes our ideas seriously." And I'll say to them: "MIT is a funny place. It's very macho, despite, you know, wanting to make it less macho these days. And you've got to show everybody that your math is stronger than their math." And they'll say: "What do you mean?" And I'd say, "well, look, here's Shape Grammars, and they subsume Turing machines, and everybody else's math. And so here, I've got my math — it's bigger than your math! — and then they'll take you seriously." The problem is that everybody in architecture at that point walks away. They don't want to hear about it. But the only way you're going to get that kind of academic respect, at least at a place like MIT, is to play that kind of math card. It's a stupid thing to say, but that's one of the reasons I don't want to diminish the math, even though I don't think it's necessary in pedagogy, whether it's in architecture, art, or anywhere else. This is my beef with MIT, although it's not mine but for some in my department. I get along fine.

——— DANIEL CARDOSO LLACH: Maybe this is a good moment to close — but not before thanking George for a wonderful journey through some of the key ideas in Shape Grammars. It's been a delightful overview of some concepts behind the theory of the visual *enterprise*, as you like to call it. We are all very excited to have you join us. Thank you.

——— THEODORA VARDOULI: That was great, George, thank you so much. It was such a pleasure to have the chance to talk to you today.

Computer Art and Information Aesthetics: A Conversation with Leslie Mezei and Frieder Nake

Moderated by
Theodora Vardouli

THEODORA VARDOULI: In our conversations so far, the computational image has figured both in its entanglements with digital electronic computers and within a broader context of thinking about the entwining of art and mathematics.[1] We also discussed the political, social, cultural, and material contexts that encompassed such efforts to bring together images and code.

I could not see a more fitting and exciting way to continue the conversation than with Leslie Mezei and Frieder Nake, both leading figures in theorizing, experimenting, producing, and also teaching "computer" or "algorithmic art," to use the terms they introduced. Leslie Mezei is a Holocaust survivor from Hungary who graduated from McGill University in 1953, with first class honors in mathematics and physics. He became an Associate Professor of Computer Science at the University of Toronto in 1965, where he established the Computer Graphics Group (later Dynamic Graphics Project, or DGP) in 1967. Mezei was the leading scholar of the early years of the field of computer art, with many talks and publications including the landmark article "The Electronic Computer as an Artist" (*Arts Canada*, 1964) with Arnold Rockman, an annual bibliography from March 1967, and a regular column in

1 Digital.Visual.Material Symposium, (Edited for length and clarity), virtual event, May 2021

Arts Canada from April 1968 for two years. Mezei started producing his own computer art in 1967 using his SPARTA language, and animations with ARTA, which have been exhibited and published internationally. Frieder Nake has been a Professor of Interactive Computer Graphics at the University of Bremen since 1972 and founding figure of the Joint Bremen Program in Digital Media. He is one of the foremost scholars on aesthetics and information theory and in the mid-1960s he was one of the first to create software for aesthetic objects ("computer art"). His record of publications and lectures is extensive and wide-ranging, on topics ranging from probability theory to computer graphics, Human Computer Interaction, semiotics, theory/critique of computer science, digital media, art and art theory. Nake has held a number of visiting positions all around the world and his work has been exhibited internationally in museums including the Tate, the Victoria and Albert Museum, and many more.

It is such a pleasure and honor to have you both here today. Let's kick off our conversation with a question about the technological context of your early work. Today, the ubiquity and ease of access of digital computers makes us forget how inaccessible, large, and difficult to use they were just a few decades ago. To set the stage for our audience, would you be able to reflect on your first encounter with computers, your perceptions, and first impressions? And then could you tell us the story of how you came about with the very bold idea, which you both pioneered, of having these large and onerous machines produce art?

FRIEDER NAKE: **The first computer I ever saw was at IBM. I was a young student and after my first semester I spent a summer at IBM Germany, which was located very close to Stuttgart where I was studying. And the situation was fantastic. I came there in the morning, the boss of the Computing Center welcomed me saying, "sit down in this room and wait a minute." I waited, nothing happened. It was essentially an empty room with tables, chairs, shelves. After a while, I took a brochure from the shelves and started reading it. It described how to use their computer, which was in the next room and soon I would see it, how to force it to calculate the square root of a number. Then finally somebody came and said: "Okay, now we will show you** the computer." Fantastic! I didn't understand a thing because you could not understand a thing. But I realized something about this large machine that spread out into the entire room, full of boxes, magnetic drums and so forth running around. I realized I had the chance to do something that would force that computer to do what I want it to do. And I have never left this position. As I had time, they allowed me to do whatever I wanted. So, I learned how to program and then wrote a program, what is called an "eternal calendar." Whatever, it is not important now. But I realized, when you train yourself to think very clearly, very precisely, then it's simple to use that huge machine, of which, in technological terms, I didn't understand a thing. Technologically, I'm totally ignorant. So, my first meeting with a computer was with a huge machine whose capabilities, most likely, were less than what your smartphone now is capable of doing. And that was an entire room. You now carry it in your pockets.

LESLIE MEZEI: For me, this is like a life review of that part of my life. I'm going to share some appreciations, some admissions, and maybe some regrets. In 1954, I got a job at Ontario Hydro and there was only one computer in Canada, it was called a FERUT at the University of Toronto, built by Ferranti electronics at the University of Manchester, and Alan Turing was actually involved with its design. A real Turing Machine! Two rooms full of diode tubes, which blew out regularly. Then, at Ontario Hydro, we got a UNIVAC, which had a giant mercury tank that was the memory. And I became a hotshot programmer. I moved to Confederation Live, where they had an IBM 705. And in 1965, I joined the University of Toronto.

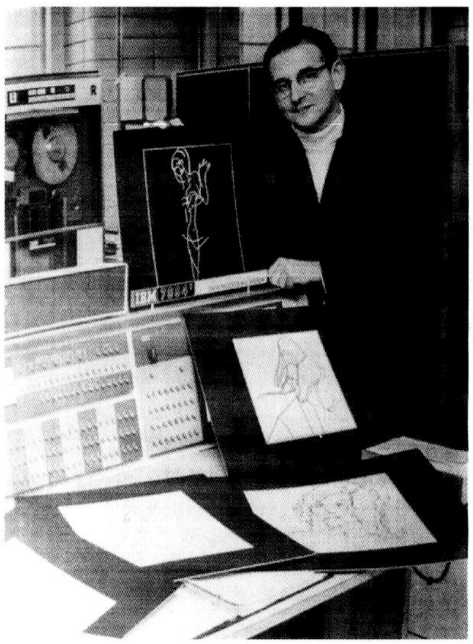

Leslie Mezei standing in front of an IBM 7094 at the University of Toronto, with prints of *Bikini Shifted* and *Transformations of a Girl's Face*, 1968.

In fact, this picture is about the time that Frieder [Nake] joined us for a year. There I am in front of the IBM 7094 with some of the computer art that you will see later. Now to the second part of the question: It was in conversations with Arnold Rockman, who was a good friend — an artist and a sociology professor — that I became interested in computer art, in graphics, and in becoming an academic. In articles such as "The Electronic Computer as an

2 Leslie Mezei and Arnold Rockmann. 1964. "The Electronic Computer as an Artist." *Canadian Art*. 21 (6): 365–367.

Artist,"[2] we reviewed what was being done at universities and industrial labs, what was planned by them, and also talked about mathematical theories of aesthetics like Birkhoff's, Fibonacci numbers, Golden Mean, Le Corbusier's module, and so on. Not that I ever got to actually do any work in that area. I saw the computer and its graphic output as new tools, not as a competitor with artists. I personally looked for art as pleasing pictures — I knew nothing about art to tell you the truth. In my own work, I selected the most pleasing ones out of various experiments.

FRIEDER NAKE: The only thing I can add to what I said before is that programming is trivial. Forcing a machine to do something must be trivial, especially, machines that are more semiotic than they are mechanical. The mechanical machine, a car, is much more difficult than the semiotic machine, the computer, because we are semiotic animals. We are dealing with signs all the time. And, therefore, that's our field. Mechanics is already much more difficult. You can easily be killed by some mechanical machine.

When I moved into that field, I hesitate saying this, at least when I was pushed, when I was pulled, when I came, when I entered into that field, when I did something forcing the computer to produce drawings, that was the time when we did not allow ourselves to speak of art. We spoke of aesthetics only. Aesthetics is the theory of perceiving. There are many ways that we perceive. Animals do it in a different way, and plants. But if we want to acknowledge that something that we have done ourselves or with the help of a machine is art, then that means that it offers some kind of value, some kind of emotional reaction. Since we do not know what art really is, we hesitated and in fact, decided, no, we are not going to talk about art. We will talk about aesthetics, about our way of perceiving these things.

The first exhibition [of computer art] was in Stuttgart in February 1965 at Max Bense's Institute of Philosophy with Georg Nees's work, and the second in April '65 in New York with A. Michael Noll. Michael had signed a complicated contract with the Howard Wise Gallery about what they were going to do when something gets sold. Nothing got sold. I never did anything like that when I had, a little later, my first exhibition in 1965. Some graphics were sold for hardly anything. But then I just didn't care. When I first met Michael, I asked him why he had done the contract. If he had not done it, maybe somebody would have bought something. I told him he should not do such official things. Art is a field that we don't really know. Now with computers, we must know precisely. The two don't exist nicely next to each other. It's us, Leslie, you and perhaps me also, who brought the two together: the machine that is made for utmost precision, on one hand, and art that is always open for anybody to comment on. It always remains open. This is our field, I believe.

3 Frieder Nake. 1971. "There Should Be No Computer Art." Bulletin of the Computer Arts Society. No. 18: 1-2; Reprinted in: A. Althena and L. van der Velden (eds.) *The Anthology of Computer Art* (Amsterdam, Sonic Acts, 2006), 59–60.

——— THEODORA VARDOULI: That's wonderful. There are several historians and scholars who have argued that art helped humanize computers, at a time when computers were seen as military instruments or as unimaginative calculators. At the flip side of that (and you have written critically about that, Frieder[3]) is the transformation that computers brought upon art, the figure of the artist as a creator, and the art market. Could you reflect on the bi-directional transformative effects of the collision of computers and art that you were just describing?

FRIEDER NAKE: Theodora, that is a great and complex issue that you raise. But I will not hesitate to say a few things. First of all, the fact that people are a bit afraid of the computer should make us curious. As many workers know very well, the computer always comes with a danger of them losing their job, first of all. So, computers are a kind of machine that we do not understand. The "ordinary" people in the room, at least, in the mid-1960s did not understand that machine. Now, to humanize that machine, I believe, is the wrong way to go. We, in my opinion, cannot but use computers or leave them alone. The human element stays with us. The machine remains in the world of machines. The computer is that kind of machine that takes over some of what we are good at, namely, *semiotic processes*. However, the computer can never deal with the full range of signs (the stuff of semiotics). As soon as we put something into the computer via sketching or typing, it loses all of its real semiotic character. It is reduced to what is called the "syntactic" component. [Charles Sanders] Peirce has thought about the basis of what we do, when we speak, when we sing, when we dance, when we paint, and so on in terms of signs. The sign to him, is, first of all, something that appears and that we perceive by our senses, by several of them in parallel. The sign is first a sensory appearance. But now, something fantastic is happening because we as humans cannot *but* interpret. The sign appears somehow, and we immediately interpret it. Interpretation is the human way of existence. Much later in the development of culture, we take signs and input them into the computer. However, the computer immediately gets rid of all the interpretation. The reason for this is that computer is a computer because it does, indeed, deal with signs, but it always reduces their interpretation to one and only one; what the computer is doing, for us amounts to a total reduction of what we are doing.

LESLIE MEZEI: It was the age of C.P. Snow's "Two Cultures,"[4] and I saw these two cultures as something to help bridge. I was neither a scientist really, nor an artist, nor an aesthetician. I was interested in novel applications of computers. I was impressed by Norbert Wiener's *Human Use of Human Beings*[5] — the use of cybernetics for people. One of your questions was about how the idea of computer art was accepted. In our 1964 article ["The Electronic Computer as an Artist"], Arnold Rockman was worried that there was going to be opposition from the visual arts. I was invited in 1966 to the Annual Meeting of the American Society of Aesthetics in Santa Fe, New Mexico. I was housed in a room of six with several philosophers and they had so many questions they wanted to talk about that there was no time to sleep. I also spoke at a conference at the New York Metropolitan Museum of Art, which was reported in a major article in *The New York Times*, and later at the Detroit Institute of Art. I also published an annual bibliography on visual computer art. And then had a column in *Arts Canada*, on art and science. So there was a lot of interest. I collected a set of the products of most of

4 Charles Percy Snow. *The Two Cultures and the Scientific Revolution*. (New York: Cambridge University Press, 1959).

5 Norbert Wiener, *The Human Use of Human Beings: Cybernetics and Society*. (Garden City, NJ: Doubleday, 1954).

those who were involved in early visual arts by computer, and some of their statements which didn't get published, and that manuscript with 64 illustrations is going into the archives of AGO (Art Gallery of Ontario). This will make available the first decade of computer art to researchers and students. Especially important are the programmatic statements of many of the "computer artists" about what they were hoping to achieve. Much of that is yet to be fully accomplished.

——— THEODORA VARDOULI: Frieder, you talked before about a distinction between aesthetics and art and the fact that you were using "aesthetics" rather than art. I am also curious about distinctions you may make between *information aesthetics* (measuring kind of a statistical aesthetic value in the tradition of David Birkhoff and Max Bense) and then *computer art*, which is more tied to the generative as opposed to the analytical aspects of using mathematics to understand and produce art. How does this distinction between the "analytical" and the "generative" manifest in your work, if at all? The same question goes to Leslie.

FRIEDER NAKE: My thinking in the 1960s about these issues was totally different than it is now. I was a believer in information aesthetics. That has to do with the kind of thinking and theory (should I say, philosophy?) that I came from. Max Bense, in fact, took up Shannon's simple mathematical concept of information. This concept of information has nothing to do with what we think of when we speak of "information" in the formal way of Shannon's. That is reduced to measuring the frequencies of the elementary signs appearing in an arrangement. That is the only thing you have to know: what are the frequencies of signs appearing in an arrangement. That's the most trivial thing you can ever come up with. However, it was not bad to have such a measure. It may, however, have been bad to apply to art. But why did Max Bense do this? He had lived through Nazi times in Germany. And his philosophy after the war was that we cannot, and we don't want to, allow for any emotion anymore. Because the Nazi propaganda, to a large extent, relied on arousing emotions in people. Therefore, Bense decided, no emotions whatsoever and he and his students took up the information measure by Claude Shannon.

A second important approach by the Bense group was taking up theory from David Birkhoff, who in the mid-1920s, had come up with what he called an "aesthetic measure." Birkhoff applied his theory to simple polygons. For example, the square got a higher value or, better, measure, than the triangle. Does that tell us anything? No, not really. You take a square and you base it horizontally. But now you tilt it a bit. Aha! What a sensation for our perception! Something aesthetic has happened. Birkhoff's measure was not capable of coping with this, at least not easily. This was already outside of his theory.

Leslie, I did not start on such issues as this in Toronto. But I wrote the program for this in Toronto. There were two inventions in it. I took things like the measure of surprise and the measure of dominance, as defined by information aesthetics researchers and I told my program things like this: "I want blue to have the following measure of dominance. And I want yellow to have the following measure of surprise, and more such." Then the program calculated a probability distribution for the colors it was to use. The result of the calculation of the distribution didn't tell me much.

But in addition, I came up with an invention that, at the same time, some other people in the United States invented. It is called a "quad tree": you divide the entire image into four parts, and each of the four parts into four parts, and so on and so forth. You start with the probabilities for blue and yellow and red and orange in the whole image, and then you divide them into the quarters and into their quarters again, and so on and so forth. The entire process of distributing the colors in the image becomes a totally rational mathematical process. I didn't even tell the program that, perhaps, I wanted to have a lot of blue. I only said I wanted blue to have a measure of dominance of 0.8, let's say. So, you can approach something totally rationally and, perhaps, get something not uninteresting.

With some friends, I actually realized by hand two rather large images (1.5 meters squared). We glued small colored cardboard elements onto a hard board, and there we had the computer-generated work of art. I believe, we were proud. With good reason: We had taken the generative steps using what the information aesthetics people had only defined analytically (see pages 134-135).

The *Napoleon Destroyed* is another work I did in Toronto. In 1968, an art critic from Germany, sent a postcard of an unfinished painting of Napoleon by Jacques David to 100 artists and asked them to finish it. I was not an artist, I was a mathematician, but I still got this postcard. Everybody did something and they sent their postcards back, and an exhibition was arranged (see page 137).

For my part, I decided: "No, I will not finish it, I will destroy it." And I destroyed it in two directions. In the figure, read the top row from right to left; read the bottom row from left to right. In the top row, Napoleon's outline is dissolved into little squares that also show little crosses. You see them appearing step by step, causing the outline to more and more disappear in the structure. In the bottom row, however, the figure is gradually dissolved into polygons that are thrown into the little window. As they find their new locations farther away from their original positions, the polygons' sizes increase. In result, Napoleon's image dissolves into chaos. That's Napoleon. The French state — that's structure. The Napoleonic Wars — that's chaos. I see some beauty in this. Leslie, I wrote that program in Toronto, but I guess I never told you. [Laughs] This is fantastic because, Theodora, you gave me a chance to tell Leslie what I was doing while he was giving me shelter.

LESLIE MEZEI: Our lab attracted many different people. It was not only the age of trying to become humanistic, but it was also an interdisciplinary age. The University of Toronto Faculty of Arts and Science had a department of interdisciplinary studies for a while, which dissolved in the 1970s when money was running short. We attracted people like Stafford Beer, the cyberneticist, who gave the 1973 CBC (Canadian Broadcasting Corporation) Massey Lecture on "Designing Freedom." He tried to design a democratic participative communication system for Salvador Allende in Chile. I'll talk to you about the poet Pedro Xisto in a moment. We had the French composer Pierre Schaeffer, whose work many consider a sort of early

Scale of Randomness, 1967.

Oscillating Wastebasket, George Olszewski, 1968.

computer music. And of course, Ron Baecker, who was a co-founder of the Dynamic Graphics Project (DGP) that continues to this day and has been very successful. Bill Buxton started the early computer music work there, and both he and Bill Reeves got honorary PhDs at the same time from the University of Toronto. Bill Reeves was our PhD student who started particle systems: fire, grass, and air and so on, and won Oscars at Pixar for movies like *Toy Story*.

In my collection of the first decade of computer art, I said that there were four categories. The first one was mathematical equations and geometric images. This was my student, George Olszewski, who did four-dimensional drawings. He called this *Oscillating Wastebasket*. In my own work, the only real systematic work I did was the *Scale of Randomness*. If you start with a nine-by-nine randomly distributed square in the middle, and start going down to one side, you'll get more and more regular continuation until it all becomes one color. And if you start the other way, you end up with more and more regular alternation, actually similar to the one Frieder showed before. So, while I was looking for one scale of randomness, I ended up with two, which was rather interesting.

So here is another of the earlier random ones: squares within squares (see page 130).

But most of my work was with representational images. Around the same time as Charles Csuri in the US, I started working with them on the computer. This is a simple one of my Canadian National series: 1967 was our centennial year. So, there's the beaver in the middle, and you just change the x and y coordinates to stretch one way or compact the other. Thus you get the beaver scaled (see page 131).

In the *Girl's Face*, we used the SPARTA language, which was really a collection of FORTRAN subroutines, but it used terms that nonprogrammer artists could use. The pictures were generated with mathematical formulas which simply transformed each point [of the girl's face]. With SPARTA you could deal with points, lines, and whole pictures, and get some rather surprising results. They are forms of topology, actually.

In the other pictures [of the girl figure transformations], either the points or some of the lines are changed randomly (see page 131).

The next one is a story by itself. Pedro [Xisto] was a distinguished Brazilian poet, who came to us to the University of Toronto and he did this "Tower of Babel" — permutations on the word Babel. My nine (three by three) pictures were transformations of a Tower of a Babel based on Xisto's graphic poem. The interesting thing is that the University of Toronto Student Association made a huge-scale art environment out of this all over the campus. You had these huge figures of Babel all over and sounds "Babel, Babel," and so on. Interestingly, the person who approved the large expenditure was Bob Ray, now Canada's elder statesman (see page 131).

That is my *Bikini Shifted*, which ended up in the advertisement for Lawrence Durrell's now well-known book *Nunquam*. It was about a kind of electronic goddess.

I should say that I did most of my computer artwork basically in 1967, and then a little bit of the animation a couple of years after that. Then my students were working more in simulations of nature. I think had I remained at the university with computer graphcis, I probably would have gone into the area of simulation of processes of nature and elsewhere, and social data display. My interests were becoming more social and spiritual.

THEODORA VARDOULI: Leslie, thank you so much. This is all fascinating. I have a question for you, Frieder: Leslie painted this fascinating picture of the University of Toronto as a vibrant interdisciplinary place. What attracted you to Toronto? What made you go work with Leslie and move to Canada in the late 1960s? Then I had a few other questions, one on the "style" of the works themselves and how you navigated the eclectic space between figuration, irony, abstraction, precise systematic permutation; and another one probing you to reflect on the present status of digital art and its transformation with things like machine learning, where many of the conversations that you started in the 1960s are resurfacing in slightly different terms. I already overloaded this last question with too many questions, but you can address whichever one seems more useful.

FRIEDER NAKE: What attracted me to Toronto? Leslie. That's the answer. Nothing else. I had decided I did not want to work for a company but in academia. In Germany, a PhD is not enough to get a job as a teacher at the university, you have to do a second thing that they call "habilitation." The professors bring up their successors in their own style. I did not want to do this and decided to move away. Now, that would have meant going to the United States. However, they were in the war of Vietnam. So, the answer had to be: No! Canada was the only alternative. Britain was too boring. I had heard of and had read things by Leslie. I approached him and then he was friendly enough to say, "Okay, you're free to come."

The second question is much more complex, but I can answer it in this style also. In computer graphics, we can leave the making to the machine. The thinking is what we do and that will always remain with us. The machine then produces according to your program, you see the results, and you again, subjectively, select what you want to keep and what to throw away. I can say that even more clearly: think the image, don't make it.

Let me stress this: I don't say *think of* the image, I say *think the image*. Grammatically, it's the same as saying make the image. But I leave the making to the computer. When you *think the image*, you never think a single image, you immediately think in groups, sets, structures of images. Otherwise, it doesn't make any sense. You think it, and then have the computer produce it. That's the essence, I would say, of my approach up to this day. I was just commissioned by a collector to do an installation in the honor of artist Vera Molnár. I will write a program and I will sell it to the client, and it will run for at least 100,000 years before it will start to repeat. All the time, it will produce new images. It's not an animation. It's moving, it's dynamic. But what we see is new and different from second to second.

LESLIE MEZEI: Congratulations. That's great.

FRIEDER NAKE: Thank you. Thank you, Leslie.

LESLIE MEZEI: Your first question really set up what I wanted to say about our lab. Bill Buxton who was at the time a musician in Europe came to us. Now, he's well known as a designer and a senior researcher at Microsoft. This is what he said about our lab at the time of his honorary PhD: "Great innovations often come as the unexpected consequences of somebody just following their curiosity and their passion, with a good team, good resources and good encouragement. That is the lesson you take away from University of Toronto. The interaction I experienced turned out to have been hugely influential in shaping my career." He said to me, personally, that he appreciated most the opposite of what Frieder said was happening in Europe: We were all equal. Anybody, even the newest student, could make suggestions, try new things in those pioneering days, and everybody talked to everybody else and helped everybody else. It wasn't competitive. I attracted good people like Frieder and Ron Baecker and Bill Buxton, and many others. I was very happy about that. The lesson I want to leave to those interested in getting involved with computers and art, is to look back at what some of the early computer artists said they would like to do, because it's still not easy to do. The Dynamic Graphics Project actually took on HCI (Human-Computer Interaction), and it's still not easy in the visual field. So, it would be a good idea to look back at what some of these people tried to do, some of whom are here like George Stiny.

THEODORA VARDOULI: Thank you. I think that is a wonderful note to end our conversation and now engage the audience who must have a lot of questions for you both.

FRIEDER NAKE: In some sense, we are witnessing virtuality here and now. I believe I'm still an ordinary living human, but in some way, virtuality is here. Who enters in which way?

DANIEL CARDOSO LLACH: Thank you for an incredible journey through some of the key ideas and works in your careers. One thing that I felt was really interesting in your conversation is when, Frieder, you spoke of reduction. It felt like a very powerful idea, in terms of utilizing the computer as an expressive artistic medium. I am wondering if you could reflect a little more on the idea.

FRIEDER NAKE: In some way, Daniel, I believe, that nowadays, sixty years after the very beginnings of what then was called "computer art," if you take an arbitrary sample of images (it should be a large sample) you will find out that hardly any of those images has *not* in some way or other been influenced by digital equipment. In the 1960s, using a computer to make images may have been controversial. By the time, you might get a reaction like: "Are you crazy? Why do you show that in a gallery? That's stupid." But as the further development showed, there was some power inside. It was incredible. The computer really does not want to draw. The computer says: "Please, let me calculate, for that's my capability." But people forced the computer into drawing, and a little later, with better equipment available, even into painting.

Harold Cohen became the hero of this particular development. During the last three years of his life, I spent a few weeks each summer with him in his studio. He had been a famous British painter, before he came to San Diego, where he met the computer and started developing his software AARON, a work he never gave up again. He never really painted by hand again. This development started in the 1960s. Toronto was one center of it. It seems that in history there occasionally are moments when some develop a kind of sensitivity that makes them try out something new, with poor means and equipment only, but with deep and strong energy and will. It may lead to an explosion of the human mind.

Writing a program is a mental activity. Computers, however, cannot, and will never, "think." Never can there be "artificial intelligence" in the true sense of the word. It makes me sad when I hear intelligent people talk about "machine intelligence." For it is us ourselves who are projecting that "intelligence" onto the machine. This was the lesson I learned, once and forever, in those early days, when I was trying to do art by computer, very ignorantly and in a very modest way. Today we have great exhibitions, and people don't even think of whether we should call that "computer art." They do something that, indeed, contains digital and algorithmic components. That's it, and it's all, and it is okay and nothing to get excited about.

LESLIE MEZEI: I'll try to add to what Frieder was saying and then talk about Marshall McLuhan. So, back in 1967 when I founded the Computer Graphics Group, Kelly Gottlieb said to me, "Why don't you teach Artificial Intelligence?" I actually taught the first Artificial Intelligence course in Canada. What did I know about it? Nothing. However, the different computer labs were in touch with each other and we were able to find out what the other was doing. What I learned from that experience, and that's how I became a humanist, is what fantastic capacities we humans have, that computers cannot come near to. After Kelly wrote the book on computers and society, I got to teach the course one year, and thought about these things.

So, the fun part is Marshall McLuhan. Back in the interdisciplinary days at the New College [of University of Toronto], we had a club on future studies, and we had a meeting every Wednesday at noon. Marshall used to be there. One day, when he heard about my computer art, he asked me to come to his class. It was like an interview. We sat side by side and he asked me questions. Then I showed some of the artworks and it was very interesting. We didn't see him as the great master, perhaps it is the fate of the Prophet in his own home. But we did have contact with him.

FRIEDER NAKE: Leslie, let me add one short remark since you mention McLuhan. I call the images of the 1960s, '70s, '80s, that you still put up on the wall, "the McLuhan phase of algorithmic art." Why? Because then, the medium was, indeed, the message, as McLuhan's famous slogan claimed. "Hello, this is a drawing. You say, you don't like it? That's okay. But think of it — it was done by computer!" The medium was the message.

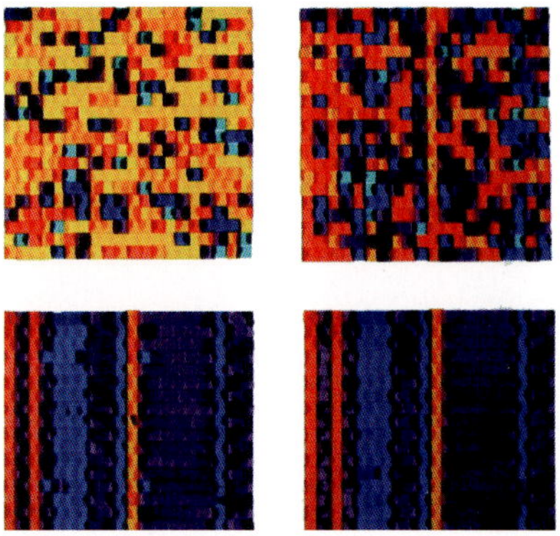

Matrix Multiplication Series 33, Friedeer Nake, 1967.

LESLIE MEZEI: Wonderful. So, I noticed in the chat line, Adam Lauder mentioned the name of Norman McLaren. That's an important name because he was *the* great animator at the Canadian National Film Board. And the story goes that he spent one weekend in with a computer. I forget which of our friends was working with him in Ottawa. He found it most frustrating. He came up with a little two-minute thing. It's a couple of little bird-like figures. But they moved in a way that was organic, it was dynamic. He managed to put so much into the figures.

——— THEODORA VARDOULI: There is a question in the chat by Paul Pangaro asking about reflections on the *Cybernetic Serendipity* exhibition in London. Frieder, you participated and Leslie, you consulted, right? There is also another question from Martin Orosz about *Gestalt* theory and influence from psychology when you were working around aesthetics and perception.

LESLIE MEZEI: I'll start. At that time, it felt as if anything we did was wonderful. In a way we were separate from the art world. My big regret — if there is a regret because you live your life as you do — is that I did not explore all these possibilities with computer art in any ongoing way. There was no other interest in computer art in our lab or in our department. It was considered something frivolous.

FRIEDER NAKE: When Harold Cohen appeared as the new bright light of computer art, he did not know anything of what had been done in Toronto. And I must mention Vera Molnár and Manfred Mohr, both of them trained artists who now, just before 1970, took to the computer. They became really great names in algorithmic art, individuals who stood for more than just representing new methods.

For example, read the four images of the figure as four states of an ongoing process. The upper left is state number one, the upper right is number two, then down to the lower left as state number three, and lower right is four. You probably agree that you see a certain development in this sequence. If you look at the first one (upper left), it is more or less chaotic: In the upper right, you already see close to the middle something like a column appearing, in yellow and red. In states three and four, this column is still there. That's the development that, in the lower two states, shows fewer and fewer disturbances. The color blue is taking over.

This kind of description applies to the visual surface. But what is behind this appearance? There is some mathematics, based on the mathematical structure of a "matrix." Think of it as a rectangle of small cells, each one of which containing a number. All these numbers are between 0 and 1, and for each of the rows, they add up to give 1.0. Such a matrix is called a stochastic matrix. If we multiply a stochastic matrix by itself, the result is a stochastic matrix again.

My decision now was to divide the interval of numbers between 0 and 1 into ten subintervals and let each of these be represented by a color. We thus translate the matrix of numbers into an arrangement of colored cells. As the matrix is, again and again, multiplied by itself, we get a sequence of stochastic matrices that get transformed into quadratic arrangements of colored grid images. In this way, a mathematical process becomes the source of a visual process.

LESLIE MEZEI: I would like to hear you, Frieder, in the remaining time answer the question about your 1971 statement that came under the title, *There Should be No Computer Art*, and then I'd like to make a comment about my 1975 one.

FRIEDER NAKE: Yes, fantastic. In the early 1970s, I had the feeling that I could now concentrate in my entire life doing such things [i.e. algorithmic art], because I had enough of a grip to come up with new schemata. But I also developed an uneasy, critical feeling that computers, in some sense yet to be described more clearly, were not really doing good for most of us. The war in Vietnam was my case. I told myself, "Look, those of us who use computers to produce something nice, something maybe even beautiful, and even art; but there always also is that other side, and therefore, we should not do all this." We create, I felt, a pretty little appearance that is not what computers are made and used for. The nice appearance is covering up for some hidden real purposes that we don't want to have. The conclusion was, that *there should be no computer art*. I gave up doing what I had done before. Only 14 years later, I gave up this negative position. During this time, no graphics, no beauty, no art.

LESLIE MEZEI: Interesting. I thought you were also against the capitalist world of art markets.

FRIEDER NAKE: Absolutely, yes, of course, thank you. I radically turned my back to anything you might connect art and computers. I was now engaging in something totally different, in far-left politics. I put all my energy and activities into the case of the workers and the people.

LESLIE MEZEI: Thank you. So, I'd like to also mention my radical statement, which was in 1975, which I think was full of hubris, in effect saying that the field has become stale, that there was no progress. We weren't going anywhere. I apologize for that. You are all here and are doing things. But I'd like to draw to what I did say in the last paragraph of that statement: "We need to find those things which uniquely suit this new media, which can be expressed only with their help, and does make the effort worthwhile." (To find those things that are particularly suitable to it, I meant). "To look for the fresh wind of ideas from the new wave of art students who will be literate in the Information Sciences" (I don't think that happened) "and conversant with interactive computers and new processes which they can help visually explicate." I shouldn't say it hasn't happened, because you are all doing it.

—— THEODORA VARDOULI: Thank you. I wish we could carry on our conversation for hours. We have more questions for you and maybe there will be a way of exchanging more thoughts. But for now, we wanted to thank you so much for your generosity and your stories.

FRIEDER NAKE: I want to thank you, Theodora and Daniel for the opportunity.

—— DANIEL CARDOSO LLACH: It was wonderful to have you both here. Thank you so much.

LESLIE MEZEI: I want to thank you too, and I hope to be at the opening of the exhibition.

Agencies

Materialities, Page 34 ↑

Visualities, Page 100 ↑

Archive

Works

Essays

Conversations

The ESL Console at the MIT Project MAC, Photographer unknown, MIT CAD Project, c. 1965, United States

Funded by a series of contracts with the United States Air Force between 1959 and 1967, the Computer-Aided Design Project brought together members from MIT's Servomechanisms Laboratory and Mechanical Engineering department to explore applications of computers into manufacturing and design. In 1963, the CAD Project was incorporated into Project MAC, a wide-ranging initiative at the institute whose acronym stood both for "machine augmented cognition" and "multiple-access computer." Some of the earliest experiments in computer graphics took place in time shared consoles, which allowed access to computing resources to researchers distributed across a large campus. The photograph shows a timesharing console connecting an MIT office with the IBM 7094 computer.

Courtesy of MIT Museum

Early CAD system in a PDP display with a light pen, Photographer unknown, c. 1970, United States

A user interacts with an early CAD system with a light pen on a PDP display.

Courtesy of Computer History Museum

A user of an early CAD system using the ESL console, Photographer unknown, MIT CAD Project, c. 1965, United States

At the Electronic Systems Laboratory, a timesharing console was equipped with peripherals such as an oscilloscope display and a light pen.

Courtesy of MIT Museum

KEE JOURNAL Sunday, May 12, 1968 Part 7

Architects, Computers Talk Out Designs

© New York Times News Service

New Haven, Conn. – Architects and computers are talking to each other.

At least some architects are. For those who have not learned what to say to a computer, Yale university held a conference last week on "Computer Graphics and Architecture."

Computer graphics have been coming fast. An early application was in the aircraft industry. At the Massachusetts Institute of Technology last year a building design conference saw how the computer could be used in all phases of planning.

Yet Stephen A. Coons, professor of mechanical engineering at MIT and at Harvard, who was introduced as "the father of computer graphics," predicted that architects had seen nothing yet.

"In a few years from now," he said, "you will be able to walk into a room and move your hand and have a plane or a surface appear before you in the light. You will be able to build a building in light so that you can walk around it and change it."

While waiting for Prof. Coons' ultimate marvel, the architects saw how they could plan and design with the help of a television monitor, light pencil and a memory bank.

Light Pencil Designing

Working from a preliminary building design, two MIT experts began to change things around. With a light pencil, resembling the markers children use, they touched its point on the television screen and gave the computer directions by pressing buttons on a small keyboard. The design, following instructions built into the computer's memory, changed rapidly.

At one point, the demonstrators, Leon Groisser and Ted Harano, told the computer to calculate the walk through distance from outside to inside. It was silent.

"We forgot to put in a door," Groisser said. "Let's put in a door."

So they put in a door and the computer, saved from a bump on the head by walking into a wall, measured the distance.

Computers were the focus of the conference. Yet to the layman, the highest value seemed to be put on "human imagination" and "human thought." Nicholas Negroponte, an instructor in computer aided design at MIT, said that the program he was working on, known as Urban 5, would have to be ditched because its restrictiveness and inflexibility were "too limiting to human thought."

Charles W. Moore, chairman of Yale's department of architecture, said that a computer could be "a very efficient money making dead end—the opposite of innovation."

Proper Use Described

"Yet for architects with souls," he said after the conference, "the proper use of these machines will be able to release our vision and free us from the constraint of the media we now use."

As the conference organizer, Luis Summers, assistant professor of architectural engineering and design at Yale, felt that Yale had done a good job in not pushing any one technique and had succeeded in showing the architects that "the computer is limited only by the limitations of the imagination."

Architects, Computers Talk Out Designs Milwaukee (WIS) Journal, 1968, United States

Under the influence of nascent ideas about artificial intelligence, early representations of computer-aided design technologies in both academic discourses and popular media exaggerated computers' capacities, often endowing them with human-like attributes such as judgment and thought.

Courtesy of MIT Libraries

'Fluent' Language Held Vital To Computer-Aided Design

DETROIT.—A "fluent natural language" will have to be developed to overcome the language barrier that now exists between man and computer if computer-aided design is to become a reality.

That is the belief of Douglas T. Ross, head, computer applications group, Electronic Systems Laboratory, Massachusetts Institute of Technology, who addressed the 1963 Spring Joint Computer Conference last week.

Mr. Ross and Jorge E. Rodriguez, co-author, won the 1963 SJCC paper award for outstanding contribution to the computer technology.

Their paper was one of five on various aspects of the MIT program on computer-aided design.

Mr. Ross said that presently the man-designer uses a combination of numerical, verbal and graphical languages to "talk" to the computer and elicit information. Not all of these are specially suited for "conversations" with computers, he said.

Mr. Ross suggested that these three languages will have to be integrated into a "fluent natural language" if man is to achieve real time communication with a computer in a problem-solving design system.

Freehand Sketches.

A computer-aided design system will allow a design engineer to make freehand sketches with a light pen on the face of an oscilloscope hooked to a computer. The computer would understand the drawings and the associated word statements and handle the vast and tedious details to arrive at a final and complete design.

The MIT papers, while discussing applications and use of a computer - aided design, were mainly devoted to fundamental theory of the many aspects and problems of such a system.

Messrs. Ross and Rodriguez, seeking a solution to the "language" problem, have evolved a theory of language based on algorithmic processes. They hope that the language will provide a common foundation for all types of language forms.

One of the main features of this language theory is that it passes statements in any language — graphic, arithmetic or verbal — into a tree form that represents the syntactic structure of the statement.

This tree form then generates a "precedence string" that represents the meaning structure of the statement, built up from "atomic units" of meaning.

This structure, Mr. Ross said, will eventually be able to carry over from language to design; with words being replaced by components, phrases by designed sub-assemblies and grammar rules by the rules of mechanics and electronics.

Two other papers in the MIT series dealt with actual applications of a computer-oscilloscope-light pen drawing system —dubbed Sketchpad.

In one instance, a bridge was drawn on the oscilloscope and the computer provided the various loading conditions and supports. As one of the elements of the bridge was modified, load conditions also changed.

Timothy E. Johnson described how a three-dimensional Sketchpad was used to design a lawn chair made from tubular material. The computer-aided design system enabled him to modify the chair's shape at will until all proportions were aesthetically pleasing when viewed from all angles.

The Sketchpad system enables the designer to turn the drawing around to view it from different angles, Mr. Johnson said.

Steven A. Coons, associate professor, Engineering Design division, MIT, also one of the speakers, in reviewing the design process as now practiced in industry, said that at the beginning a few engineers perform highly creative tasks. They are then followed by legions of draftsmen and technicians who perform "relatively uncreative tasks over a fairly long period of time," he added.

"Some of these tasks require high degree of intellectual effort, such as stress or aerodynamic analysis . . . but other tasks are purely mechanical in nature."

Outline Traced.

"For example, a detail draftsman merely traces the outline of a part from the layout drawing and adds the dimensions.

"These are mechanical and tedious operations," Mr. Coons asserted. Computer-aided design would free the designer for creative work and leave the mechanical to the computer, he added.

He suggested that a computer-aided design system would be able to reduce from years into days the lead time presently necessary to develop a new weapon. Much of the MIT work is under contract for the Air Force.

By turning a console knob, Mr. Coons said, the designer will be able to enlarge a small section of his sketch in order to draw in some small detail, or, by turning the knob in the opposite direction he can reduce the image on his scope so that he views the over-all design.

The magnification that can theoretically be achieved is such that the designer working on an oscilloscope "window" of less than 1 foot square will be able to work on a sheet of drawing paper that is one-third of a mile long, he said.

Light Pen.

The backbone of the MIT system is the display scope and the light pen. The light pen designed by MIT's Lincoln Laboratory is a hand-held cylinder—not unlike a pencil — with a photocell mounted inside at one end and a wire leading back to the computer on the other.

In addition to the photocell, a one-transistor amplifier is also housed inside the pen.

The photocell circuit is designed to respond only to the initial flash of the phosphor and is insensitive to the persistence observed by the human eye.

The photocell is ac coupled onto the dc voltage line back to the amplifier section, so that only a single coaxial wire is required to carry the power to the pen and the signal back to the computer.

The pen has a variable focus lens mounted in front of the photocell. This makes the pen more sensitive and yields a variable field of view depending on the focuses setting.

'Fluent' Language Held Vital to Computer-Aided Design, Unnamed author, c. 1963, United States

Members of the MIT CAD Project presented five papers at the 1963 Spring Joint conference in Detroit, Michigan. One concerned an algorithmic theory of language that its proponents — Douglas T. Ross and Jorge E. Rodriguez — believed crucial to overcome the "barrier that now exists between man and computer." This framing, which is echoed in this news article, was consistent with a contemporary interest in language processing and artificial intelligence, and guided the development of the AED (Automated Engineering Design) programming language.

Courtesy of MIT Libraries

Instant Design Latest Gadget By MIT Men

Those eggheads at MIT are scrambling up a gimmick that will take all the drudgery out of designing anything from an electrical circuit to a jet plane.

The high-domed researchers reported on the progress they're making with SKETCHPAD in a series of five papers they read in Detroit Thursday at the annual Spring Joint Computer Conference of the American Federation of Information Processing Societies.

Once SKETCHPAD is perfected, it will link a man to a light pen, an oscilloscope and a computer.

The man will make a freehand sketch with the pen on the oscilloscope and then let the computer do the rest. When it's through, the finished design will be on the drawing board.

The way SKETCHPAD is designed, it'll be another of man's "slaves." It'll draw absolutely vertical or horizontal lines on command, put circles through precise intersections, show stresses and distortions caused by weights, mesh separate parts, turn a geometrical figure completely around so it can be seen from the rear and solve complex equations as if they were kid stuff."

"On some far off day," said one MIT researcher in his paper, "it may even be possible to call up last year's auto on the oscilloscope, to wave the magic wand of the light pen, and, in a very short time, create the modified version from the old. This will be, in a sense, a mechanization of experience."

They keep on mechanizing experience — and they ain't gonna be much fun left in life.

Instant Design Latest Gadget by MIT Men, Record-American, 1963, United States

A news item reports on the presentations by MIT CAD Project members at the Spring Joint Conference, reinforcing a mythology of computer-aided design technologies as "another of man's slaves" and celebrating their male inventors.

Courtesy of MIT Museum

How We'll Design Products Tomorrow, Steel: The Metalworking Weekly, MIT CAD Project, 1964, United States

Members of the MIT CAD Project formulated and disseminated a view of design as a collaborative endeavor between humans and machines. In this article, which features an interview with CAD Project co-leader Steve Coons, design is described in these terms — as a conversation between a designer and a computer.

Courtesy of MIT Museum

How We'll Design Products Tomorrow

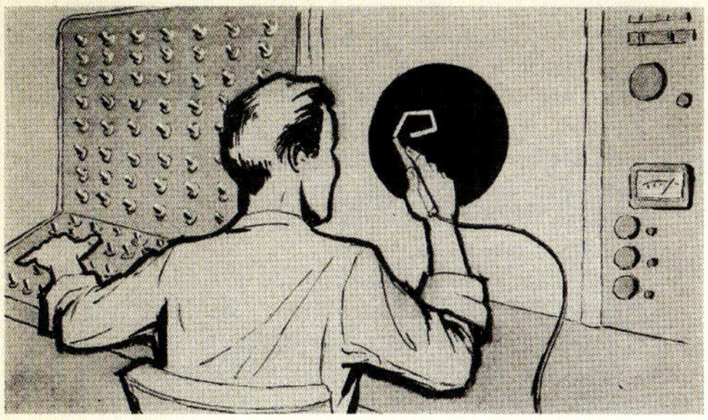

Draw six rough sides

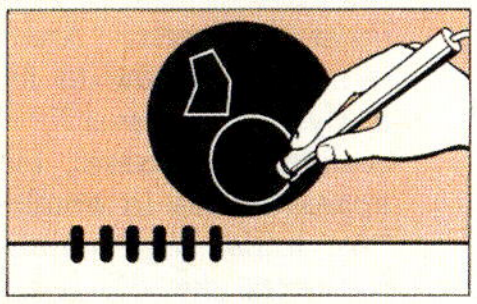

Draw rough circle

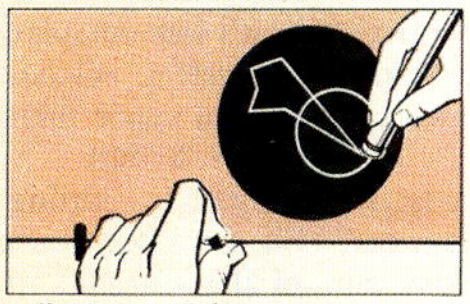

Pull corner of hexagon

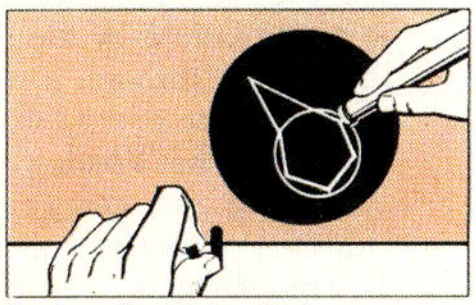

To inscribe it in circle

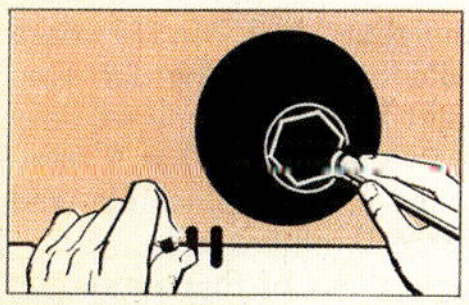

Make sides equal

Erase circle

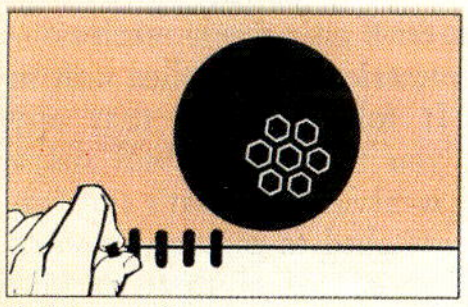

Call seven hexagons

Join corners

EVER CONSIDER exactly how many dollars are added to your product costs between the conceptual design and the production floor? How many costly manhours are spent hunting through handbooks and catalogs, making calculations, looking up standards, doing layout and detail drafting, building models—the horde of mechanical tasks required just to deliver the information inputs to the production department?

How much could you lower costs if you could bypass that design bureaucracy? And if designers could devote all their time creating, instead of spending so much of analyzing, calculating, and doing other mechanical tasks?

By 1970, you will be able to do just that, thanks to a project underway at Massachusetts Institute of Technology. Steven A. Coons, associate professor of mechanical engineering, Douglas T. Ross, an Electronics Systems Laboratory researcher, a cadre of their colleagues, and a platoon of graduate students are working under Air Force contract (No. AF-33(600)-42859).

Their goal: A man-machine system in which the computer is an active partner with the creative designer; two way communication is handled with ease; the computer accepts and analyzes the designer's rough sketches and performs all (or nearly all) the design calculations. Says Professor Coons: "The system does seem reasonable for the near future." He anticipates economic feasibility within ten years; technical feasibility is much closer.

The ultimate goal is automatic manufacture after the man-machine design team has established design features. You will be able to go directly from the designer's rough sketches to the tape controlled or computer controlled processing equipment. It means you will need the capability to communicate with the machine via words and graphics, have the machine fully comprehend your meaning, and have it translate your expressed wishes into models. Professor Coons says the system "will be as useful and flexible a tool as the lead pencil, easier to use than the pencil, and certain to find applications we've never even considered."

● **The Big Promise**—Consider this example of what the system will ultimately offer the manufacturer.

Thirty (or 40, or 20, or 1) designers will sit at oscilloscope screens, with light pens in hand. They're surrounded by toggle switches, a telephone, a few controlled knobs, and other simple electronic gear. Say one is designing a turbine shaft. Another—perhaps in a separate building—is designing the turbine blades. The designer drawing the shaft makes some rough strokes on the screen with his light pen, manipulates a few toggle switches, and a beautifully contoured shaft appears on the screen. Now he calls onto his screen the turbine blade assembly drawn by the other engineer and couples that assembly to his shaft. It's time to check out stress. He picks up the phone and dials a stress analyst. That man cranks into the computer all the inputs required to ana-

---

them? "Country doctor engineers. Diagnosticians. They'd analyze the problem and prescribe the remedy. Someone else would remove the appendix. Men who knew what all the new manufacturing techniques could accomplish, but didn't need any intimate knowledge of how the processes worked." Broad gage guys. Men who were entrepreneurs at heart. Who'd be more concerned with how to pay for a process than with the details of its operation.

What characteristics had Mr. Cyrol said such men should have? "Know the arithmetic of business. Have broad knowledge of manufacturing techniques. Know about the full range of durable goods manufacturing methods so they could adapt something from one in-

Views of the room housing the TX-2 computer at the MIT Lincoln Laboratory, Photographer unknown, MIT Lincoln Laboratory, c. 1964, United States

Sutherland programmed Sketchpad in the TX-2 computer, which occupied a large room in the basement of the MIT Lincoln Labs. Mainframe computers in the 1960s were colossal compared to modern personal computers, and occupied accordingly large spaces. The TX-2 was one of the world's first interactive computers. This enabled Sutherland and other researchers to develop some of the earliest interactive software applications. They often had to create their own new peripherals — such as the "light pen" — as needed for their projects. According to former CAD Project member Timothy E. Johnson, the TX-2 was "the glue that brought everything together physically." The photograph shows two women working at the TX-2 terminal. Sutherland — whose research was supported by the National Science Foundation — developed Sketchpad in the TX-2 computer at the MIT Lincoln Labs under the advice of Claude Shannon, Marvin Minsky, and CAD Project co-director Steve Coons. In addition, Sutherland credits CAD Project co-director Douglas Ross with contributing to technical aspects of the research.

Courtesy of MIT Museum

Ivan Sutherland using "Sketchpad," Photographer unknown, MIT Lincoln Laboratory, c. 1963, United States

This photograph shows Ivan Sutherland demonstrating Sketchpad, a system he developed as part of his PhD dissertation at MIT, an early example of interactive computer graphics which pioneered many of the features of modern CAD systems. Notable is the camera directed towards the computer's display, which was used to capture the user's on-screen interactions.

Courtesy of MIT Museum

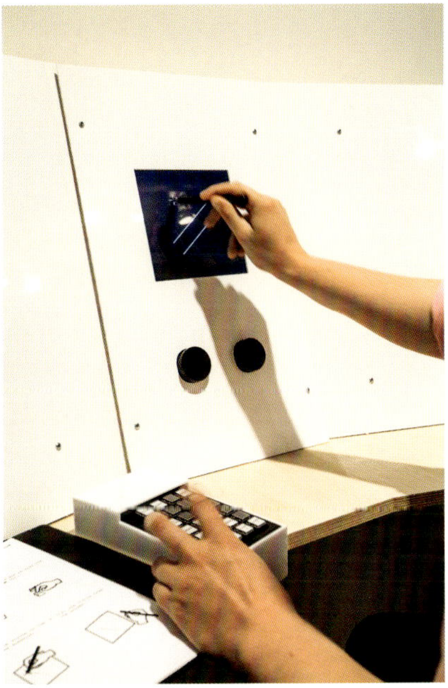

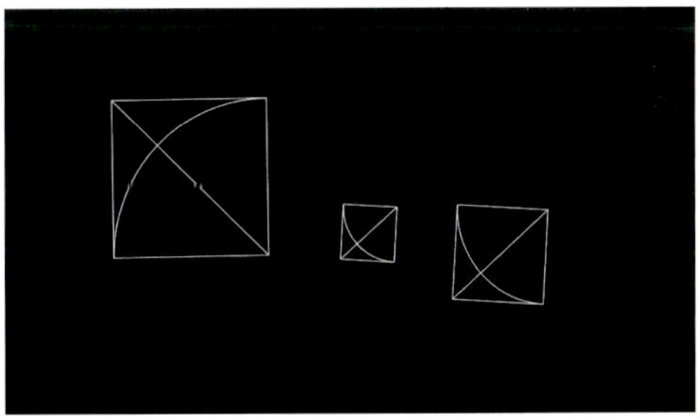

Sketchpad (Reconstruction), Ivan Sutherland, MIT Lincoln Laboratory, 1963, United States

Sketchpad allowed a user to draw with a "light pen" on a 9-inch wide cathode-ray tube monitor and, remarkably, included many of the features of modern CAD software systems such as constraint-based drawing, "rubber-banding," and drawing instantiation. This interactive software reconstruction developed at the Computational Design Laboratory at Carnegie Mellon University uses modern programming languages and hardware to evoke some of the visual, tactile, and ergonomic aspects of the experience of using Sketchpad in the TX-2 computer at Lincoln Labs.

Reconstruction by CMU Computational Design Laboratory, 2017 (updated 2021)

(*Sketchpad (Reconstruction)* pictured on following spread)

Nicholas Negroponte sketching on a touch sensitive display, Photographer unknown, The Architecture Machine, MIT, c. 1978, United States

Co-founded by Nicholas Negroponte and Leon Groissier at MIT in 1968, The Architecture Machine Group explored new applications of computers to building design and urban planning, and — later — interactive media more broadly. The group transformed into the MIT Media Lab in 1985. In this 1978 photograph, Negroponte tries "sketching" in a newly arrived touch sensitive display. One of Negroponte's mentors at MIT was CAD Project co-leader and CAD theorist Steven A. Coons.

Courtesy of Nicholas Negroponte

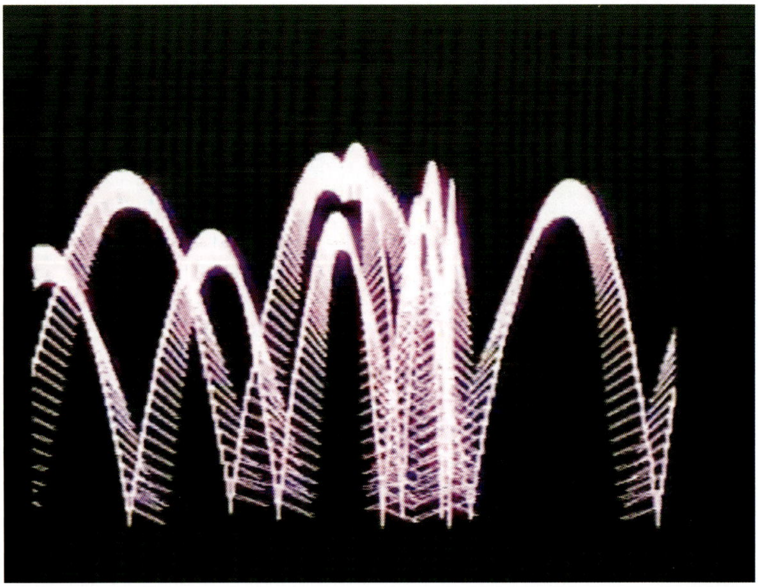

Stick Models, Paul Pangaro, The Architecture Machine, MIT, 1977, United States

The numerical structure of computer-generated images afforded artists and designers with new kinds of geometric and time-based plasticity. The two films featured here show early explorations into this new plasticity. In *Stick Models* Paul Pangaro animates a series of "sticks" which playfully occupy the screen following a programmed logic.

Courtesy of the artist

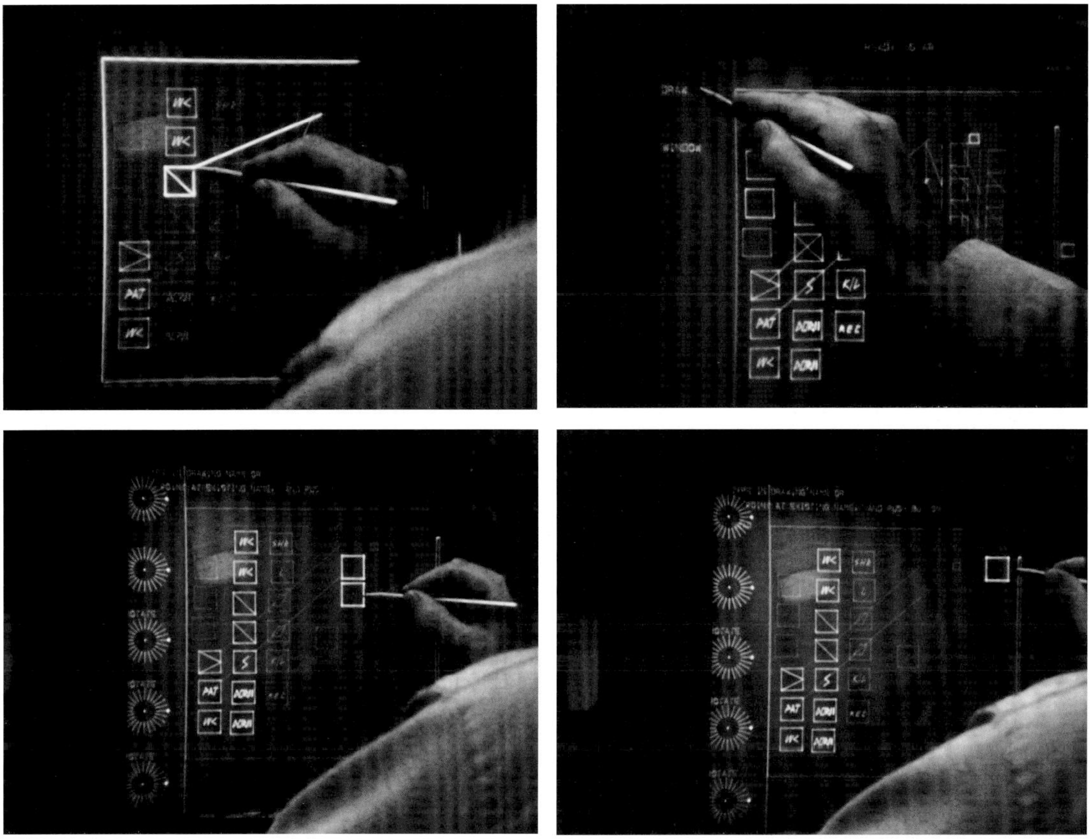

Space planning experiment, Timothy Johnson and Guy Weinzapfel, The Architecture Machine, MIT, c. 1972, United States

Some of the earliest research efforts in computational design sought to go beyond the use of computers to facilitate drawing tasks, exploring instead the potential of computers to assist in configurational aspects of design. This rare film demonstrates an early program for space planning developed at MIT by Timothy Johnson and Guy Weinzapfel, which generates building configurations given some user-defined constraints. The program is further documented in Weinzapfel's masters thesis, entitled IMAGE.

Courtesy of Timothy Johnson

Finger film, Rachel Strickland, The Architecture Machine, MIT, 1976, United States

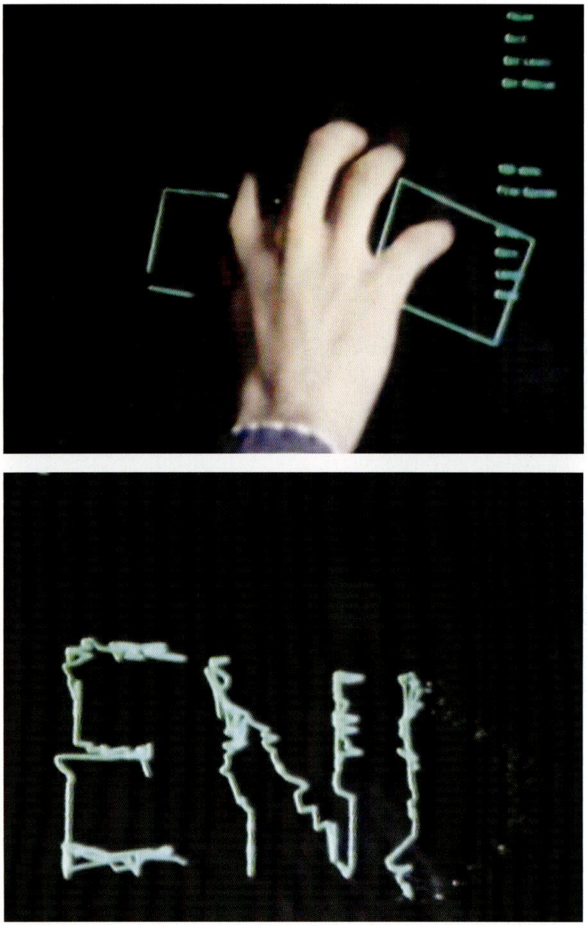

"Finger Film" is a cinéma vérité-style short film documenting early research on interactive displays at The Architecture Machine Group at MIT. The film's original approach to narrating these technological explorations — paying attention to their tactility, their materiality, and their unexpected failures — stands out among the pieces in this show and contrasts with conventional representations of technology as problem-free.

Courtesy of the artist

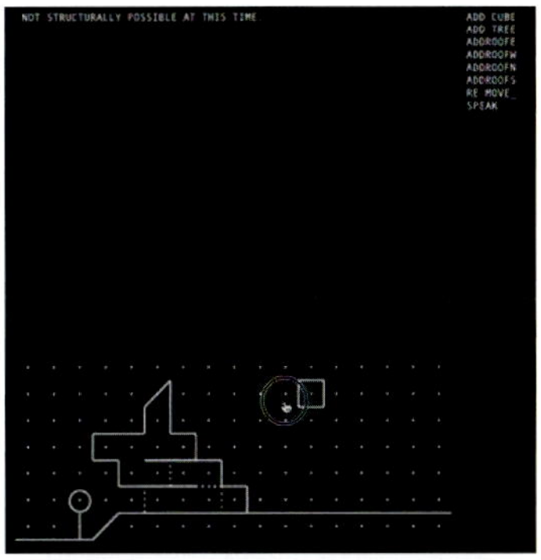

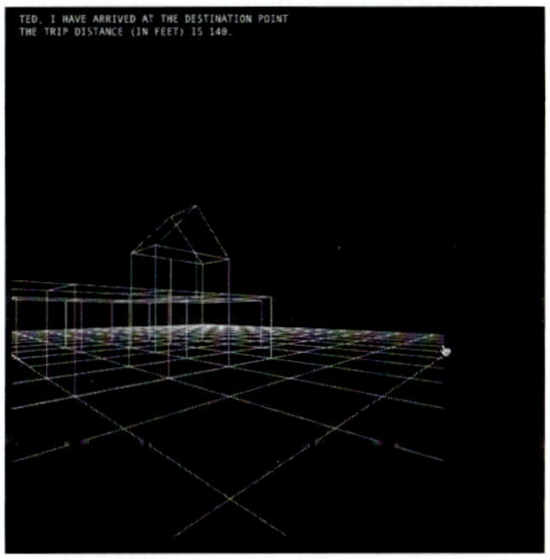

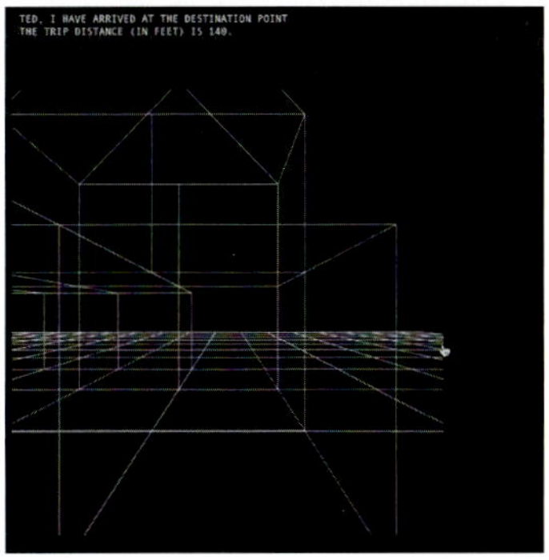

URBAN5 (Reconstruction), Nicholas Negroponte, The Architecture Machine, MIT, 1967, United States

URBAN5 is an experimental software for urban design developed by Nicholas Negroponte in 1967. Originally programmed in FORTRAN on an IBM2250 computer, URBAN5 sought to enact an intelligent assistant able to converse with users and thus help "democratize" design and planning. However, by its author's own admission, URBAN5 was never functional and "inexhaustibly printed garbage." Drawing from historical materials, this software reconstruction approximates some of this system's logic and functionality. This reconstruction, developed at Carnegie Mellon University's Computational Design Laboratory (CodeLab) in 2019, offers access to the author's ambition to bring contemporary ideas about language processing and artificial intelligence into the realm of architecture and urban design, and to the difficulties of its implementation.

Reconstruction by Computational Design Laboratory, CMU, 2019 (updated 2021)

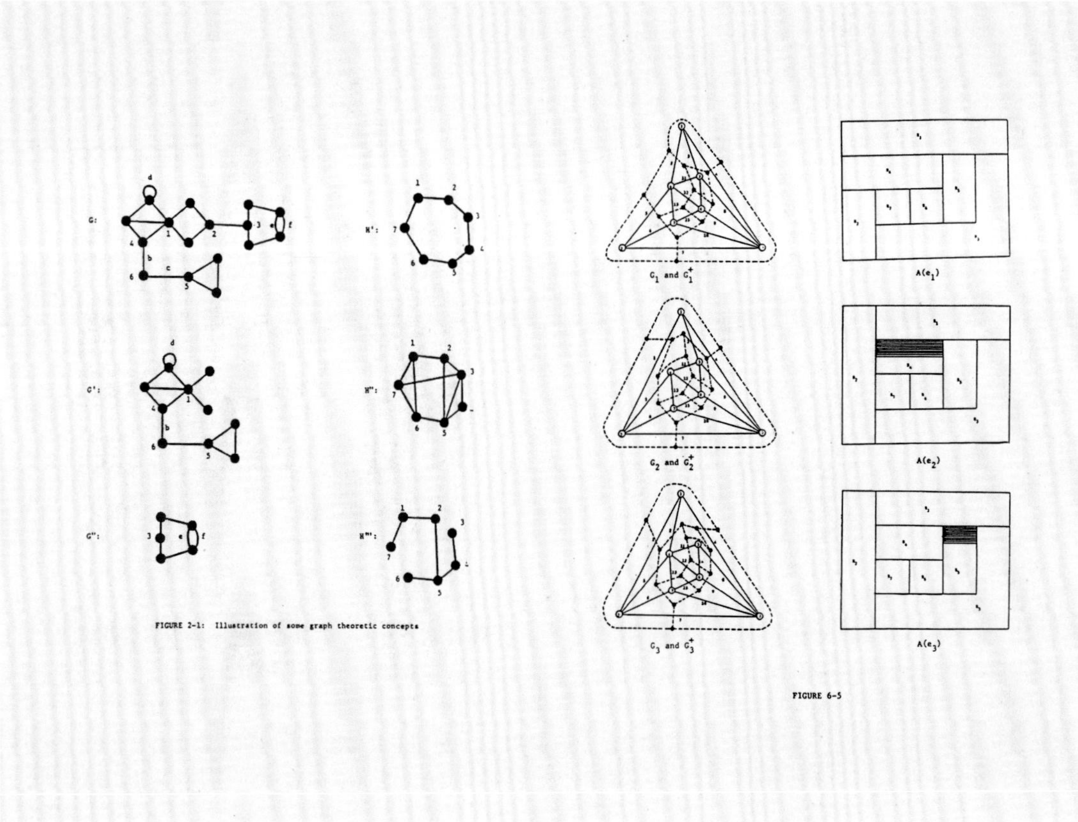

Illustrations of graph-theoretic concepts and architectural arrangements, Charles Eastman, Institute for Physical Planning, Carnegie Mellon University, 1980, United States

The creation in 1968 of Carnegie Mellon University from the fusion of the Carnegie Institute of Technology and the Mellon Institute of Research fostered new collaborations between architects, urban planners, social scientists, and computer experts. In this context, architect and computer scientist Charles M. Eastman led the development of a new interdisciplinary PhD program to develop "rigorous methods in architecture." Works on this section illustrate some of the concerns Eastman and his students addressed, often in collaboration with faculty and students from other departments. These include, from left to right, experiments in layout generation for automated space planning; graph-theoretical representations of architecture purporting to encode functional relationships — as opposed to formal features — of buildings; exhaustive enumeration of architectural arrangements; and research into data structures for managing building design. These evoke similar developments at centers at Cambridge, Waterloo, and MIT.

Courtesy of Carnegie Mellon Archives

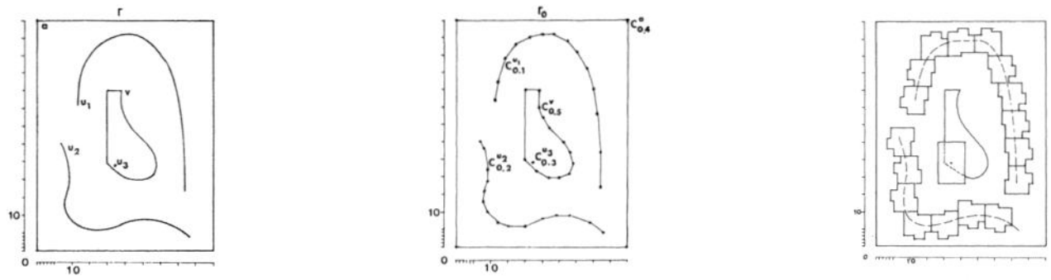

Pattern diagrams for space allocation, Christos I. Yessios, Institute for Physical Planning, Carnegie Mellon University, c. 1974, United States

A constant theme for these architects was the definition of a design space by establishing geometrical and functional constraints into account. Once a design space was defined, computational methods could be deployed to find satisfying solutions. These diagrams describe a space allocation algorithm taking such geometric and functional parameters into account to generate architectural layouts.

Courtesy of Carnegie Mellon Archives

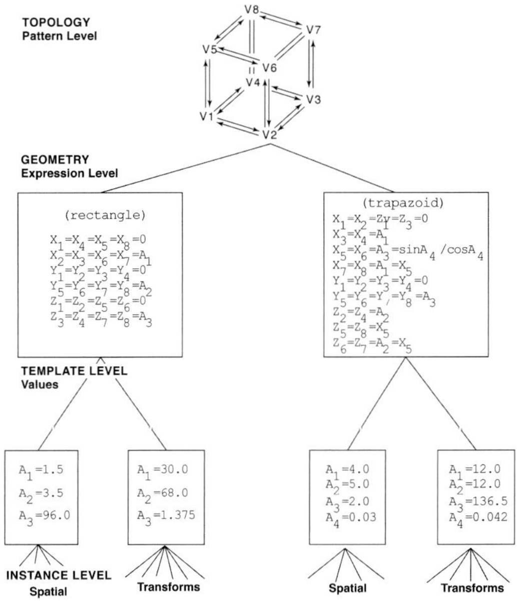

Building Description System (BDS) concept diagram, Charles Eastman, Institute for Physical Planning, Carnegie Mellon University, 1975, United States

As computers gained a foothold in research universities as vehicles of knowledge production, architectural researchers explored conceptual parallels between data and building structures. This diagram describes a "Building Description System" (BDS), aimed at replacing "drawings as the primary description for design and construction of buildings." BDS allowed users to define and manipulate assemblages of symbolic objects endowed with information attributes. A building is thus structured, architecturally, as data. Developed by Charles E. Eastman, a professor of architecture and computer science at Carnegie Mellon University, BDS foreshadows present-day developments in Building Information Modeling (BIM) — an increasingly dominant mode of design and construction management based on 3D modeling software and collaboration.

Courtesy of Carnegie Mellon Archives

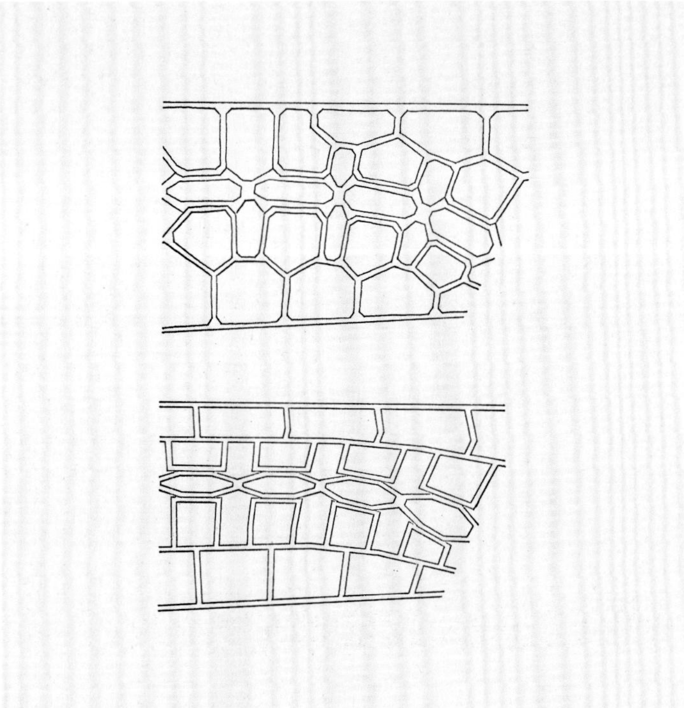

Parametric site planning patterns, Christos I. Yessios, Institute for Physical Planning, Carnegie Mellon University 1974, United States

Town design was a concern at the Institute for Physical Planning, which Eastman directed. This image illustrates research by one of the center's early members, Christos I. Yessios, into flexible languages to parametrically describe urban plans.

Courtesy of Carnegie Mellon Archives

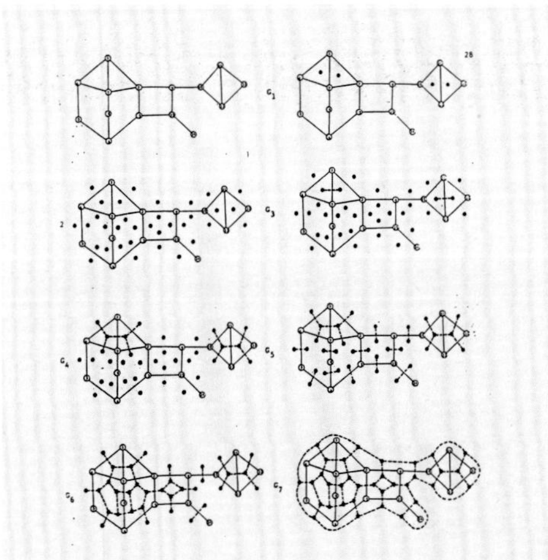

Obtaining the pseudo-geometric dual of the graph G, Charles Eastman, Institute for Physical Planning, Carnegie Mellon University, 1980, United States

Graphs offered mathematically-inclined architects a formalism to describe a building placing emphasis on its spatial structure, rather than on its shape or stylistic traits. The image illustrates graphs produced as part of a research project at the Institute for Physical Planning to exhaustively enumerate architectural layouts.

Courtesy of the Carnegie Mellon Archives

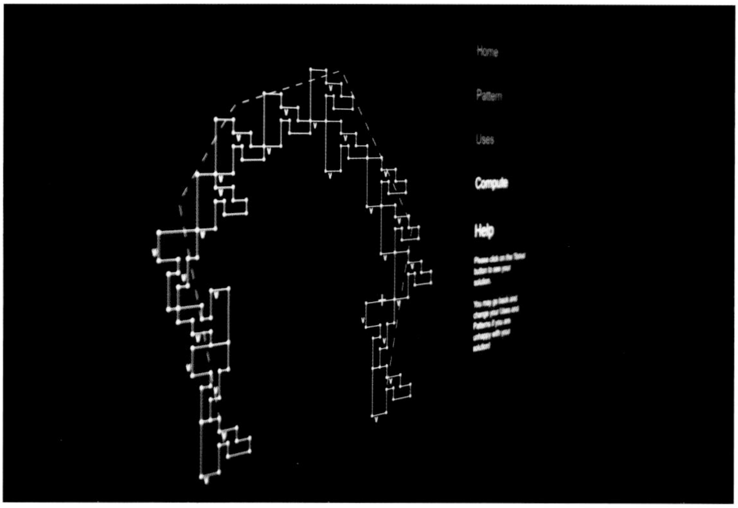

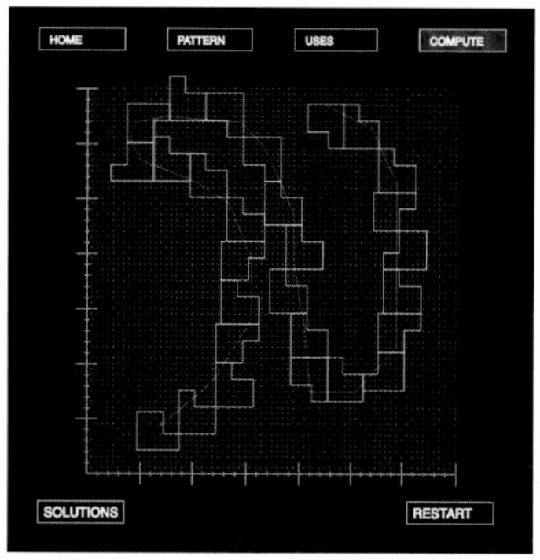

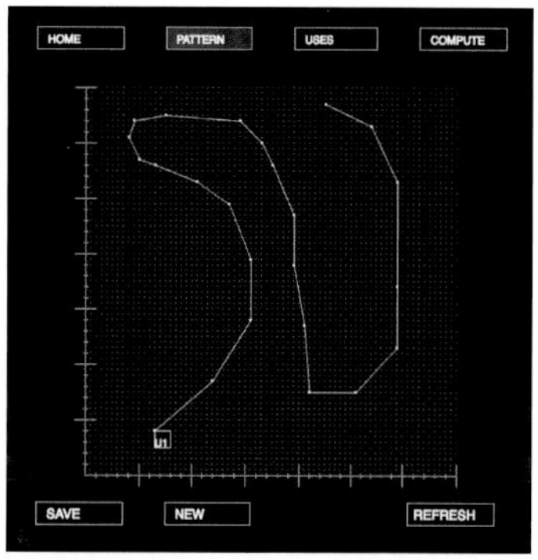

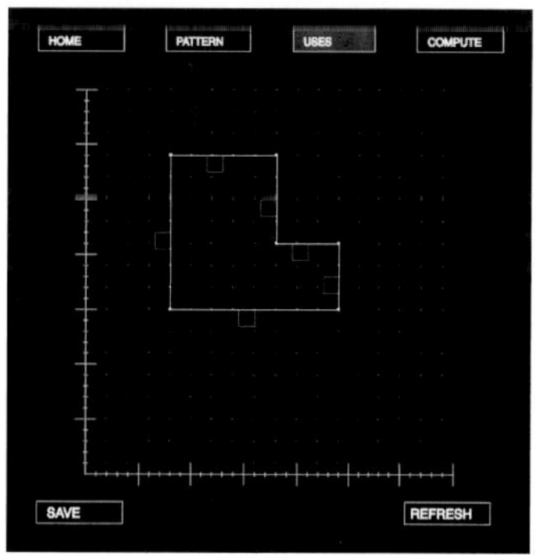

CISP: Computer Implemented Site Planning (Reconstruction), Christos I. Yessios, Institute for Physical Planning, Carnegie Mellon University, 1972, United States

Drawing from materials held by the Carnegie Mellon University Archives, and conversations with its original author, this interactive installation reconstructs CISP, a pioneering system for computer-aided urban design. Yessios, a PhD student at the time working with Charles E. Eastman and Allen Newell, premised CISP on a linguistic view of urban design. The system allowed users to specify a repertoire of units for site planning and establish constraints such as views or access points. Using a backtracking algorithm, CISP iterates through alternative placements until it finds a solution that satisfies those constraints. Combining ideas from computer science, urban planning, and architectural design, CISP illustrates the confluence of these disciplines in research universities around questions of design and the built environment.

Reconstruction by the Computational Design Laboratory, CMU, 2019 (updated 2021)

(*CISP (Reconstruction)* pictured on following spread)

Home
Pattern
Uses
Compute
Christos I. Yessios, Institute for Physical Planning, Carnegie Mellon University
Reconstruction du CISP (Conception urbaine assistée par ordinateur)
CISP

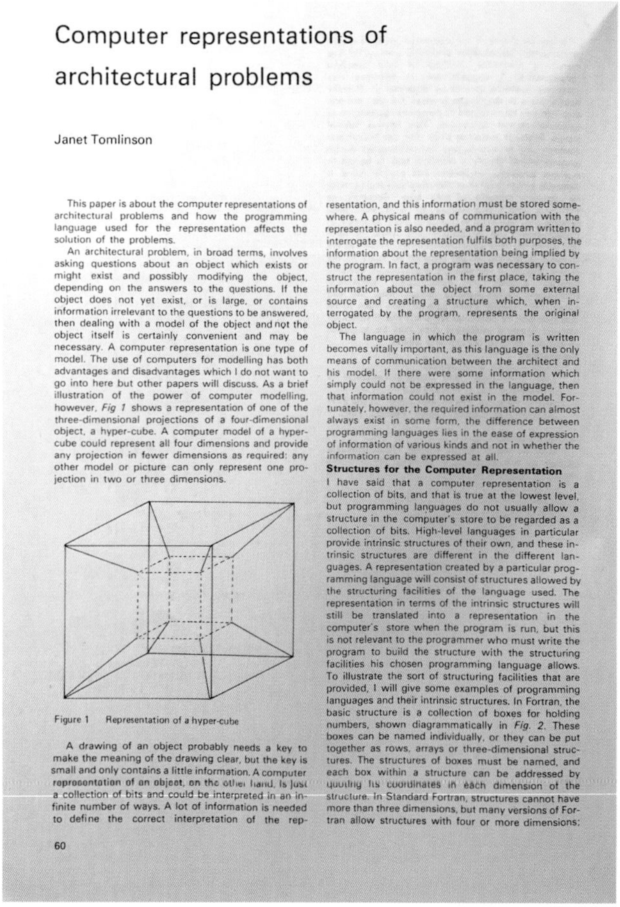

Computer representations of architectural problems

Janet Tomlinson

This paper is about the computer representations of architectural problems and how the programming language used for the representation affects the solution of the problems.

An architectural problem, in broad terms, involves asking questions about an object which exists or might exist and possibly modifying the object, depending on the answers to the questions. If the object does not yet exist, or is large, or contains information irrelevant to the questions to be answered, then dealing with a model of the object and not the object itself is certainly convenient and may be necessary. A computer representation is one type of model. The use of computers for modelling has both advantages and disadvantages which I do not want to go into here but other papers will discuss. As a brief illustration of the power of computer modelling, however, *Fig 1* shows a representation of one of the three-dimensional projections of a four-dimensional object, a hyper-cube. A computer model of a hyper-cube could represent all four dimensions and provide any projection in fewer dimensions as required: any other model or picture can only represent one projection in two or three dimensions.

Figure 1 Representation of a hyper-cube

A drawing of an object probably needs a key to make the meaning of the drawing clear, but the key is small and only contains a little information. A computer representation of an object, on the other hand, is just a collection of bits and could be interpreted in an infinite number of ways. A lot of information is needed to define the correct interpretation of the representation, and this information must be stored somewhere. A physical means of communication with the representation is also needed, and a program written to interrogate the representation fulfils both purposes, the information about the representation being implied by the program. In fact, a program was necessary to construct the representation in the first place, taking the information about the object from some external source and creating a structure which, when interrogated by the program, represents the original object.

The language in which the program is written becomes vitally important, as this language is the only means of communication between the architect and his model. If there were some information which simply could not be expressed in the language, then that information could not exist in the model. Fortunately, however, the required information can almost always exist in some form, the difference between programming languages lies in the ease of expression of information of various kinds and not in whether the information can be expressed at all.

Structures for the Computer Representation

I have said that a computer representation is a collection of bits, and that is true at the lowest level, but programming languages do not usually allow a structure in the computer's store to be regarded as a collection of bits. High-level languages in particular provide intrinsic structures of their own, and these intrinsic structures are different in the different languages. A representation created by a particular programming language will consist of structures allowed by the structuring facilities of the language used. The representation in terms of the intrinsic structures will still be translated into a representation in the computer's store when the program is run, but this is not relevant to the programmer who must write the program to build the structure with the structuring facilities his chosen programming language allows. To illustrate the sort of structuring facilities that are provided, I will give some examples of programming languages and their intrinsic structures. In Fortran, the basic structure is a collection of boxes for holding numbers, shown diagrammatically in *Fig. 2*. These boxes can be named individually, or they can be put together as rows, arrays or three-dimensional structures. The structures of boxes must be named, and each box within a structure can be addressed by quoting its coordinates in each dimension of the structure. In Standard Fortran, structures cannot have more than three dimensions, but many versions of Fortran allow structures with four or more dimensions;

60

Representation of a hyper-cube, Janet Tomlinson, Centre for Land Use and Built Form Studies, Cambridge University, 1975, United Kingdom

Computational representations offered architects new ways of conceptualizing problems. This image, a 3D representation of a 4D object — a hyper-cube — serves author Janet Tomlinson to illustrate her concerns about "the computer representations of architectural problems, and how the programming language used for the representation affects the solution of the problems."

Models and Systems in Architecture and Building: LUBFS Conference Proceedings Number 2, edited by Dean Hawkes. The Construction Press Ltd.

"Adjacency graph" for Frank Lloyd Wright's Devin House project, Lionel March and Philip Steadman, Centre for Land Use and Built Form Studies, Cambridge University, 1971, United Kingdom

This representation of a house designed by Frank Lloyd Wright describes the adjacencies between its different spaces. According to authors, architectural researchers Lionel March and Philip Steadman, "[a]djacencies on both floors are shown in a single graph, with the staircases denoted by zig zag lines. The graph is not planar."

Reconstruction from, Lionel March, and Philip Steadman. The Geometry of Environment: An Introduction to Spatial Organization in Design. *(London: Routledge, 2020) [1971]. https://doi.org/10.4324/9780429343346. P. 261.*

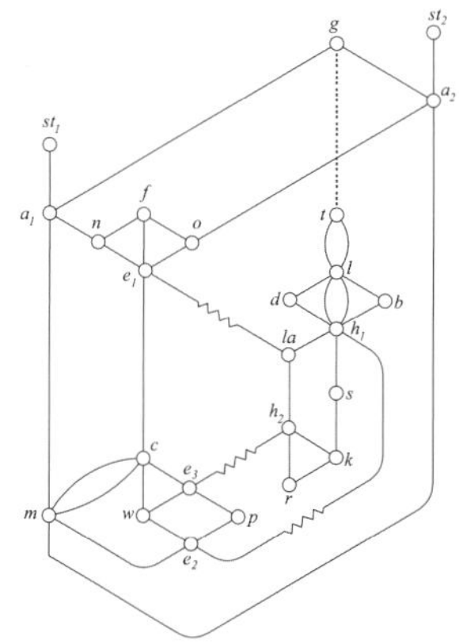

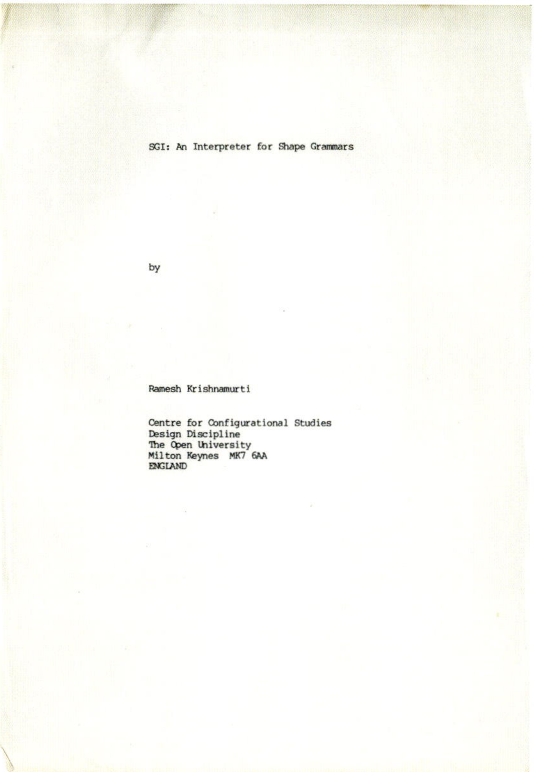

SGI: An Interpreter for Shape Grammars

by

Ramesh Krishnamurti

Centre for Configurational Studies
Design Discipline
The Open University
Milton Keynes MK7 6AA
ENGLAND

-5Ø-

Shapes generated using the R and A commands

Figure 9

Pages from *SGI: An Interpreter for Shape Grammars*, Ramesh Krishnamurti, Centre for Configurational Studies, Open University, 1982, United Kingdom

The Centre for Configurational Studies was established in 1971 by Lionel March at the Open University at Milton Keynes, UK, to investigate theoretical and applied aspects of combinatorial mathematics and enumerative methods in design and other fields. The new center extended the work March and collaborators had conducted at the Centre for Land Use and Built Form Studies at Cambridge (LUBFS), and included one of its former members, Philip Steadman, who became its director until 1998. Mathematician and design theorist George Stiny, whose work on Shape Grammars was of great interest to March, joined the center in the late 1970s. Ramesh Krishnamurti, who met March at the University of Waterloo, later joined the Open University as his PhD student, and developed the first computer implementation of Shape Grammars. On display here are pages from Krishnamurti's *SGI: An Interpreter for Shape Grammars*.

Courtesy of the author

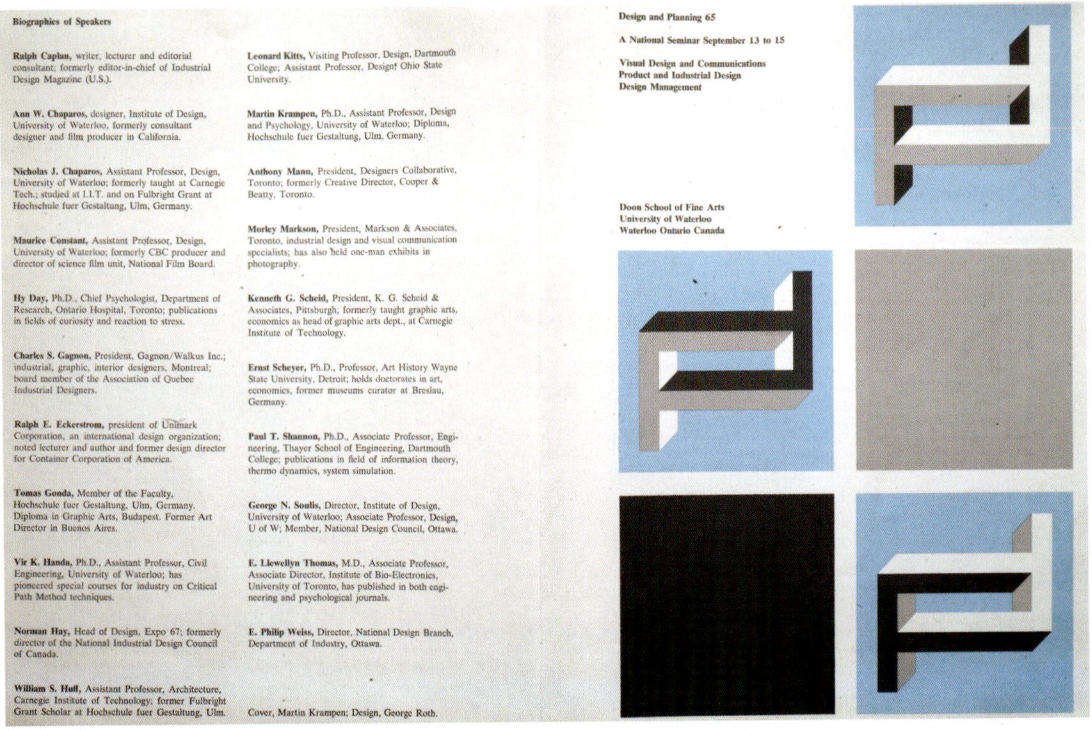

Biographies of Speakers

Ralph Caplan, writer, lecturer and editorial consultant; formerly editor-in-chief of Industrial Design Magazine (U.S.).

Ann W. Chaparos, designer, Institute of Design, University of Waterloo, formerly consultant designer and film producer in California.

Nicholas J. Chaparos, Assistant Professor, Design, University of Waterloo; formerly taught at Carnegie Tech.; studied at I.I.T. and on Fulbright Grant at Hochschule fuer Gestaltung, Ulm, Germany.

Maurice Constant, Assistant Professor, Design, University of Waterloo; formerly CBC producer and director of science film unit, National Film Board.

Hy Day, Ph.D., Chief Psychologist, Department of Research, Ontario Hospital, Toronto; publications in fields of curiosity and reaction to stress.

Charles S. Gagnon, President, Gagnon/Walkus Inc.; industrial, graphic, interior designers, Montreal; board member of the Association of Quebec Industrial Designers.

Ralph E. Eckerstrom, president of Unimark Corporation, an international design organization; noted lecturer and author and former design director for Container Corporation of America.

Tomas Gonda, Member of the Faculty, Hochschule fuer Gestaltung, Ulm, Germany. Diploma in Graphic Arts, Budapest. Former Art Director in Buenos Aires.

Vir K. Handa, Ph.D., Assistant Professor, Civil Engineering, University of Waterloo; has pioneered special courses for industry on Critical Path Method techniques.

Norman Hay, Head of Design, Expo 67; formerly director of the National Industrial Design Council of Canada.

William S. Huff, Assistant Professor, Architecture, Carnegie Institute of Technology; former Fulbright Grant Scholar at Hochschule fuer Gestaltung, Ulm.

Leonard Kitts, Visiting Professor, Design, Dartmouth College; Assistant Professor, Design; Ohio State University.

Martin Krampen, Ph.D., Assistant Professor, Design and Psychology, University of Waterloo; Diploma, Hochschule fuer Gestaltung, Ulm, Germany.

Anthony Mann, President, Designers Collaborative, Toronto; formerly Creative Director, Cooper & Beatty, Toronto.

Morley Markson, President, Markson & Associates, Toronto, industrial design and visual communication specialists; has also held one-man exhibits in photography.

Kenneth G. Scheid, President, K. G. Scheid & Associates, Pittsburgh; formerly taught graphic arts, economics as head of graphic arts dept., at Carnegie Institute of Technology.

Ernst Scheyer, Ph.D., Professor, Art History Wayne State University, Detroit; holds doctorates in art, economics, former museums curator at Breslau, Germany.

Paul T. Shannon, Ph.D., Associate Professor, Engineering, Thayer School of Engineering, Dartmouth College; publications in field of information theory, thermo dynamics, system simulation.

George N. Soulis, Director, Institute of Design, University of Waterloo; Associate Professor, Design, U of W; Member, National Design Council, Ottawa.

E. Llewellyn Thomas, M.D., Associate Professor, Associate Director, Institute of Bio-Electronics, University of Toronto, has published in both engineering and psychological journals.

E. Philip Weiss, Director, National Design Branch, Department of Industry, Ottawa.

Cover, Martin Krampen; Design, George Roth.

Design and Planning 65

A National Seminar September 13 to 15

Visual Design and Communications
Product and Industrial Design
Design Management

Doon School of Fine Arts
University of Waterloo
Waterloo Ontario Canada

Registration Brochure from the 1966 Design and Planning conference at the University of Waterloo, University of Waterloo, 1966, Canada

In 1966, the University of Waterloo hosted the International Conference on Design and Planning themed "Computers in Design and Communication." Conference organizer Martin Krampen, professor of Design and Psychology at Waterloo, described the event as "the first design conference in which the speakers were not mainly designers but computer specialists." Indeed, the presenters included MIT CAD Project leader Steven Coons and MIT AI Group leader Marvin Minsky among other eminent researchers in design and information technologies. The Conference also planted the seeds for the founding of the first American design methods organization in North America – the Design Methods Group.

Courtesy of the University of Waterloo Special Collections and Archives

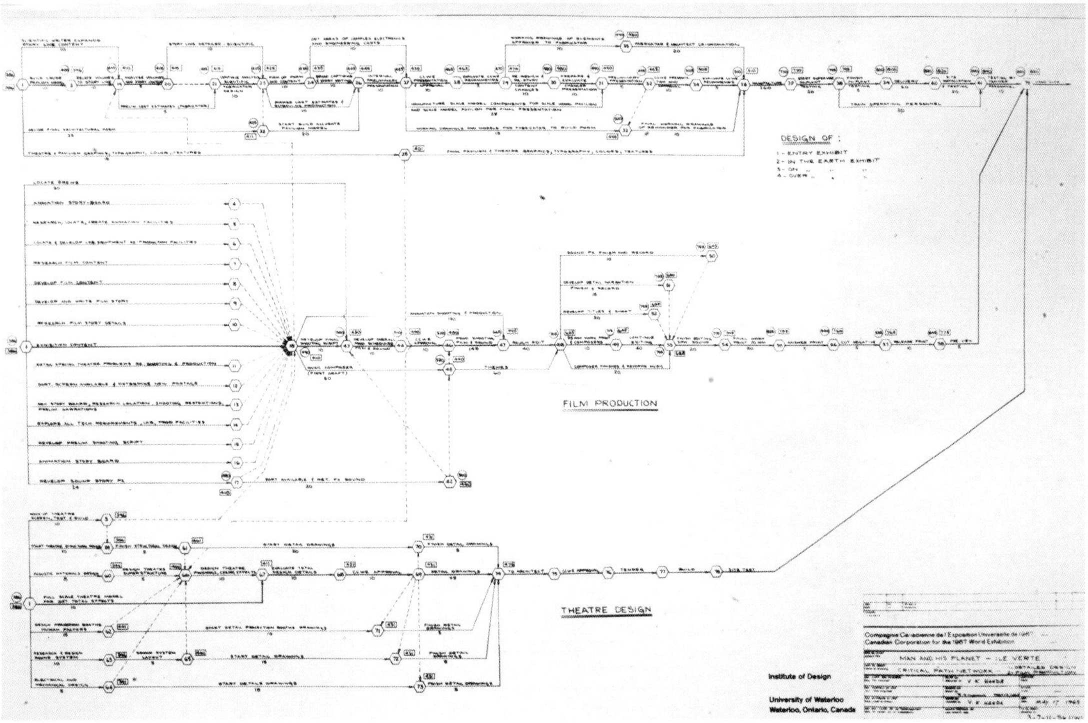

Diagram from the preliminary conceptual design of "Man and His Planet and Space" for Expo 67, George Soulis, Institute of Design, University of Waterloo, 1965, Canada

Waterloo's Department of Systems Design Engineering, which would become an international attractor of leading researchers in architectural computation and design methods, was founded in 1968 through funds that various engineering professors including Department co-founder George Soulis gained through their work for the Expo 67 in Montreal. This diagram comes from a series of documents developed for the conceptual design of one of the Expo 67's sub-themes ("Man and His Planet and Space") in response to the Canadian Corporation for the 1967 World Exhibition (CCWE) selection and presentation criteria. Within ten days of formal notification of the contract award, the exhibition designer ought to submit a detailed Critical Path Network (CPN) for approval (more on CPN on page 271). This rendered the CPM representation a key component of the design work and also of the contractual relationship between the designer and the commissioning organization.

Courtesy of the University of Waterloo Special Collections and Archives

Spatial predictions and residuals of Toronto's spatial form, Michael Batty and Lionel March, University of Waterloo, 1976, Canada

By the mid-1970s urban modeling was a well-established field drawing from disciplines that spanned mathematics, sociology, architecture, and urbanism. One of the key concerns in urban modeling was the explanation and prediction of the location of various activities. Researchers enlisted methods from information theory and statistics to answer the vexing question of the relationship between observed information and unobserved (predicted) data. During their time at the University of Waterloo in the mid-1970s, British researchers Lionel March and Michael Batty co-authored three papers on information minimizing based on the work of Waterloo mathematician János Aczel — a faculty member at the Department of Pure Mathematics along with eminent mathematician and Bletchley park code-breaker William (Bill) Tutte. Following these papers, March and Batty implemented American sociologist James S. Coleman's method of residues (a method excluding trivial information from the explanation of a phenomenon) to formulate a gravity model (an urban model showing relative locations of activities) for the Toronto region.

Reconstruction, Michael Batty and Lionel March. 1976. "The Method of Residues in Urban Modelling." Environment and Planning A: Economy and Space *8 (2): 189-214. https://doi.org/10.1068/a080189.*

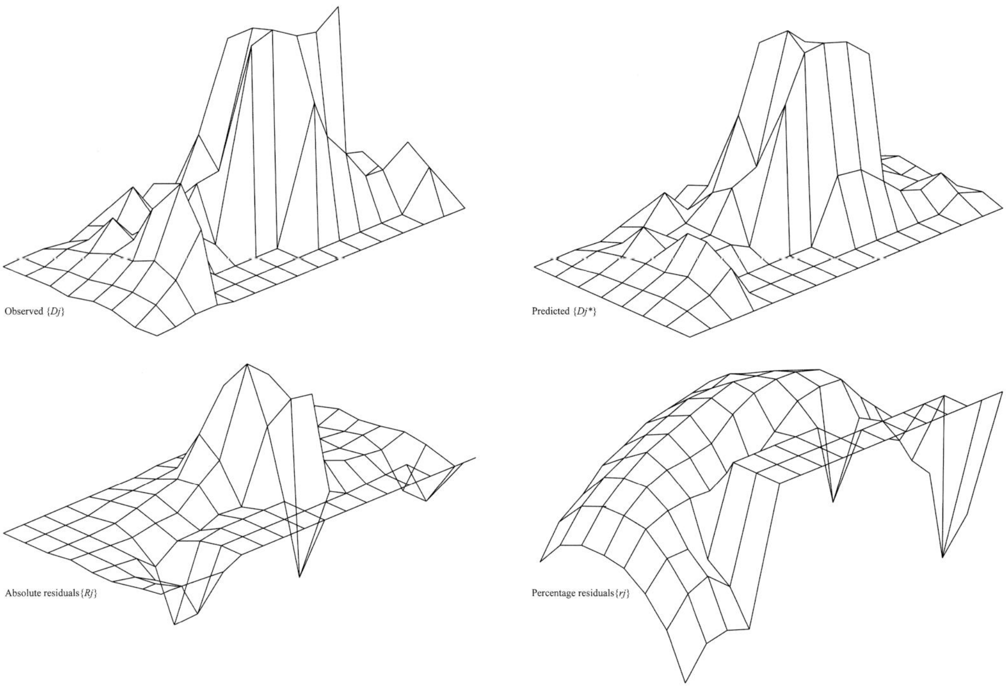

Proceedings of a conference organized by Michael Batty and Lionel March at the University of Waterloo in July 1975, Michael Batty and Lionel March, Department of Civil Engineering, University of Waterloo, 1975, Canada

Just about a decade after its foundation in 1957, the University of Waterloo had gained international reputation as a leading institution in mathematics, computing, and engineering. This prestige attracted various researchers from around the world, including the director of the Centre for Land Use and Built Form Studies Lionel March and Michael Batty, at the time a lecturer in Geography at the University of Reading. March and Batty shared their common plans to move to Waterloo during a conference on Land-Use Transport Models at Cambridge University in June 1974. Although they joined different departments — March was a professor in Systems Design and Batty was a visiting assistant professor in Civil Engineering — they collaborated closely and also interacted socially. A fruit of this collaboration was a two-day colloquium on socio-economic systems design co-organized by March and Batty in July 1975.

Courtesy of the University of Waterloo Special Collections and Archives

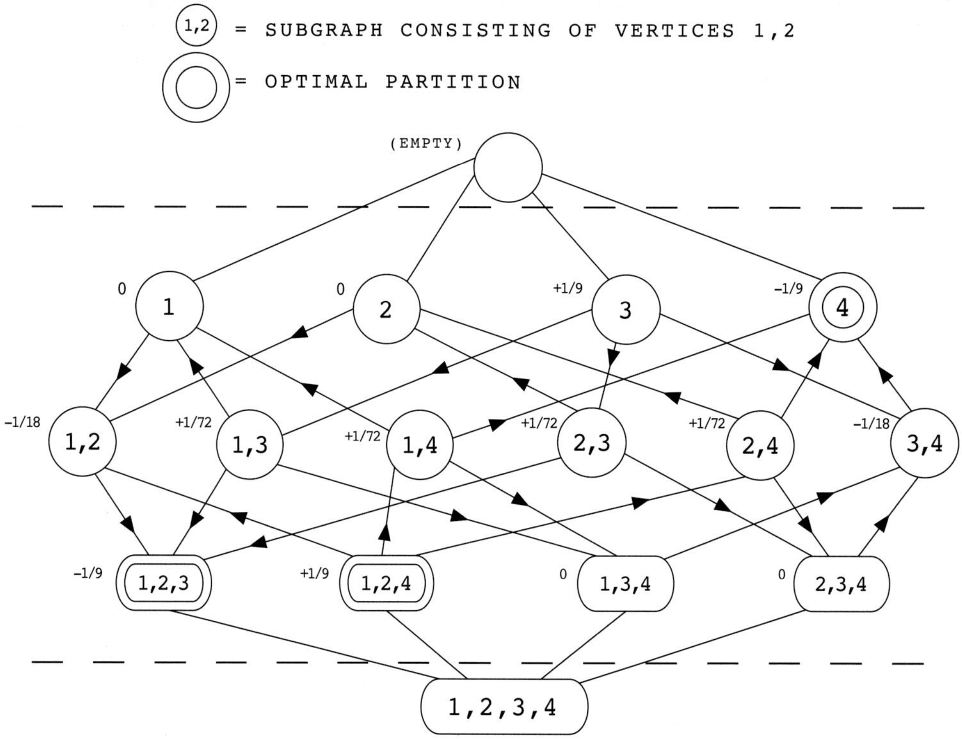

Printed output of HIDECS 2 and its representation as a hierarchical tree, Christopher Alexander and Marvin Manheim, Civil Engineering Systems Laboratory, MIT, 1962, United States (left)

Example of a graph and its lattice, Christopher Alexander and Marvin Manheim, Civil Engineering Systems Laboratory, MIT, 1962, United States (right)

Using the IBM 709 of the MIT Computation Center, under the control of the FORTRAN Monitor System, Christopher Alexander and civil engineer Marvin Manheim at the MIT Civil Engineering Systems Laboratory developed among the first programs for grappling with the growing "complexity" of design problems – their many and densely interlinked requirements. HIerarchical DEcomposition System 2 or HIDECS 2, as the program was called, took a complex network of design requirements that had specific interactions (relationships) with each other and used these relationships to order the requirements into a hierarchical tree that indicated the order and groups by which these requirements should be addressed. The designer then "solved" the tree by sketching out schematic, partial designs (the so called "diagrams") for each group of requirements and using the tree as a guide for how to then put them together to produce the full design. HIDECS 2 was not an interactive program: its algorithms processed data inputted in the form of punch cards and the output was a set of written statements about the grouping of requirements. The visual staple of the program and of Alexander's theories – the hierarchical tree – was produced manually by interpreting this written output.

Reconstruction, Christopher Alexander, and Marvin L Manheim. 1962. HIDECS 2: A Computer Program for the Hierarchical Decomposition of a Set Which Has an Associated Linear Graph. *Cambridge, MA: Civil Engineering Systems Laboratory Publication 160, MIT*

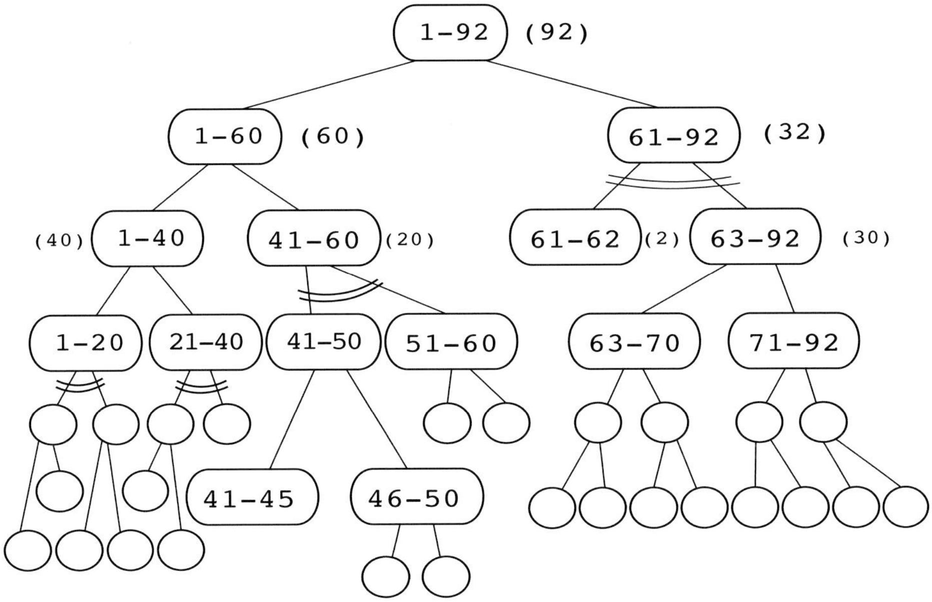

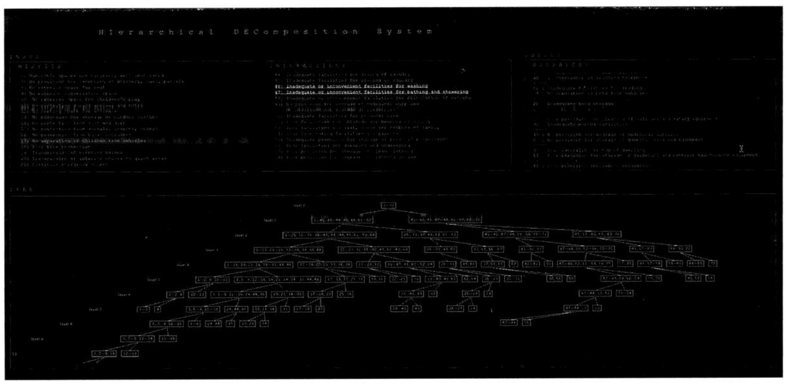

HIDECS 2 (Reconstruction), Christopher Alexander, Marvin Manheim, Civil Engineering Systems Laboratory, MIT, 1961, Canada

HIDECS 2 did not include a graphics display. The system's input was punch cards corresponding to relationships between various design requirements and output was a printed set of statements that the user ought to then manually translate into a tree. This reconstruction of HIDECS displays the key components of the system: the list of requirements, their relationships, and the tree resulting from the analysis of these relationships.

Reconstruction by CoDEx, McGill University, 2020

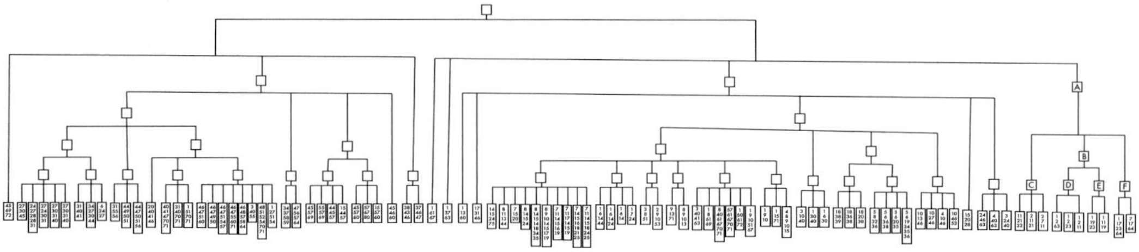

A 'program' for the design of a house, Allen Bernholtz and Edward Bierstone, University of Toronto, 1966, Canada

With funding from the National Research Council of Canada, Allen Bernholtz collaborated with Edward Bierstone, a faculty member at the Mathematics Department at the University of Toronto, to research applications of computers to housing. The paper resulting from that collaboration and titled "Computer-Augmented Design" was presented at the 1966 Design and Planning conference at the University of Waterloo and published in the 'Design and the Computer' Special Issue of *Design Quarterly*. The paper presented an application of a modified version of HIDECS for the design of a house using an IBM 7094 at the University of Toronto's Institute of Computer Science. The modifications that Bernholtz and Bierstone proposed concerned the recomposition of subsystems that the program produced.

Reconstruction, Allen Bernholtz and Edward Bierstone. 1966. "Computer-Augmented Design." Design Quarterly, Special Issue: Design and the Computer *66/67: 40–51*

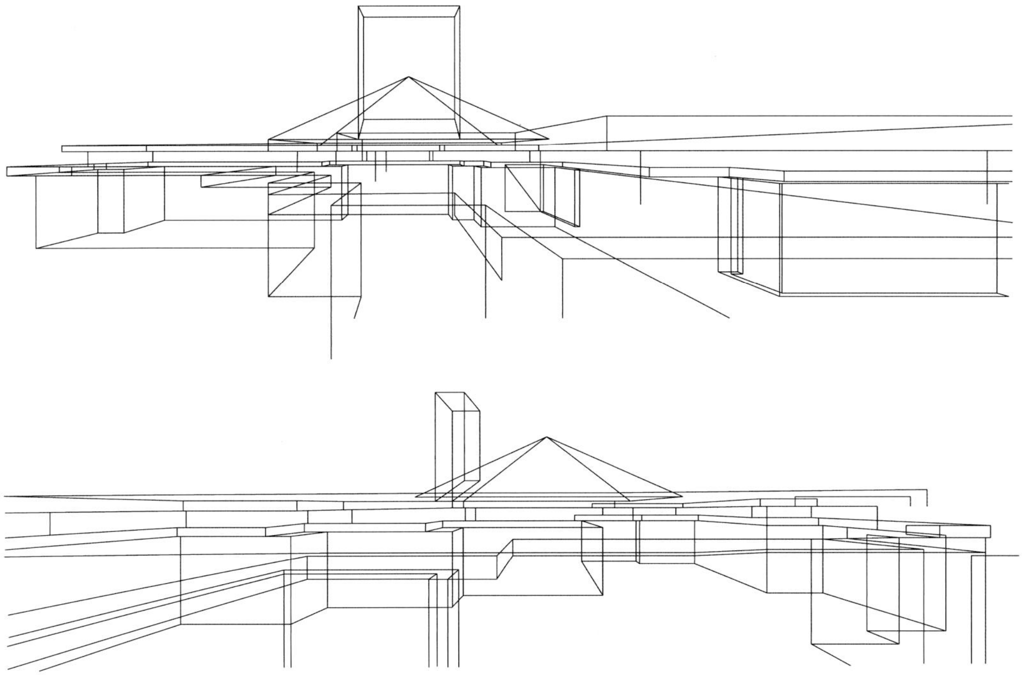

Computer perspective drawings of the first stages of the design of a house, Allen Bernholtz and Edward Bierstone, University of Toronto, 1966, Canada

Bernholtz and Bierstone combined the use of HIDECS for design analysis and problem solving with developments in computer graphics. Here two computer perspective drawings allowed users to visualize the first stages of house design so as to, as they wrote, "pre-test the design and to correct areas which would have caused detailing difficulties."

Reconstruction, Allen Bernholtz, and Edward Bierstone. 1966. "Computer-Augmented Design." Design Quarterly, Special Issue: Design and the Computer *66/67: 40–51*

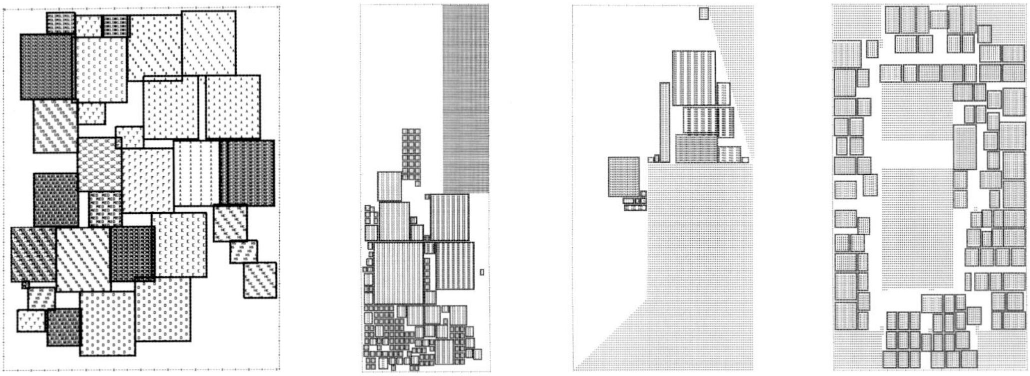

LOKAT output, including diagrams for a student union building, a car manufacturing plant, and an office building, Allen Bernholtz and Steve Fosburg, Harvard Laboratory for Computer Graphics and Spatial Analysis, Allen Bernholtz Consultants Inc., Bernholtz/Fosburg Computer Consultants, 1972, United States and Canada

After joining the Harvard Laboratory for Computer Graphics and Spatial Analysis, Allen Bernholtz – formerly faculty member at the University of Toronto – worked on four computer programs for automatic spatial synthesis (also referred to as "space allocation"). RUMOR, LOKAT, and ALOKAT (all written in FORTRAN) and DISTRB (written in PL-1) were all developed on an IBM 360/65 with the aim to automatically arrange spatial units based on various goals and constraints. RUMOR randomly generated a large number of room arrangements and then selected satisfactory ones based on input criteria (typically a matrix of spatial units and their relationships). Extending RUMOR, LOKAT, and its successor ALOKAT, allowed the consideration of zoning code and physical site features while also allowing its users to manipulate the size, type, shape and quantity of design units. Finally DISTRB allowed for the allocation of spatial units in multiple levels. The images shown here were produced by the LOKAT program using a chain printer, in which the type was placed in a horizontally moving chain. As rudimentary as it seems, this graphic output offered architects and other stakeholders an immediate intuitive understanding of spatial structure and was a key accompaniment to printed tables indicating the positions of various spatial units. ALOKAT allowed for more sophisticated graphic output replacing the chain printer with a plotter. Bernholtz commented on these advanced graphic capabilities as being mostly useful for marketing purposes: the chain printer, he wrote, captured everything one needed to know for research and learning purposes while being more time and cost efficient than the plotter.

Reconstruction, Allen Bernholtz and Steve Fosburg. 1972. "Spatial allocation in design and planning" DAC '72: Proceedings of the 9th Design Automation Workshop, *181–189.*

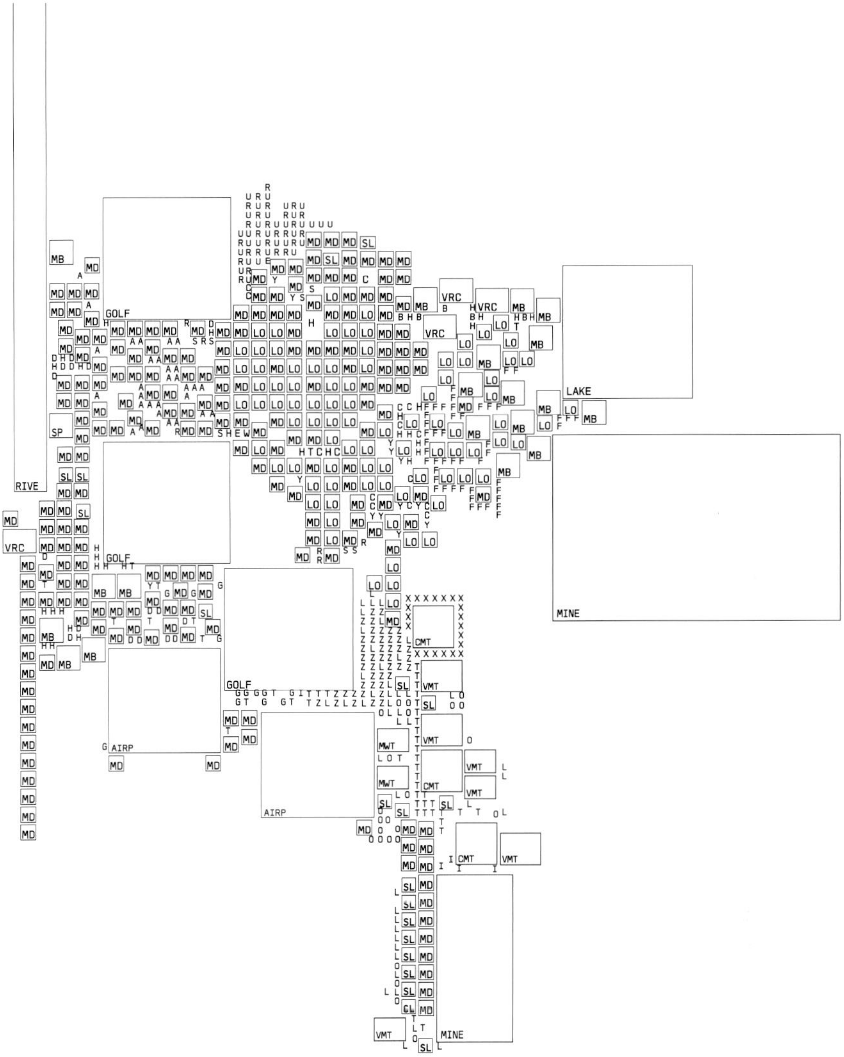

ALOKAT output for city of 25000 residents, Allen Bernholtz and Steve Fosburg, Harvard Laboratory for Computer Graphics and Spatial Analysis, Allen Bernholtz Consultants Inc., Bernholtz/Fosburg Computer Consultants, 1972, United States and Canada

This is a plotted output of ALOKAT, originally in color to indicate various land uses. The drawing represents a simulated city of 25,000 inhabitants based on 45 different land uses arranged in a 3-by-3-mile area that included two existing gold mines, a lake, and a river. In 6–9 minutes, an IBM 360/65 generated alternative urban arrangements based on models for the growth of the city by an economist and a management consultant. The graphic output was almost as important here as the computation: for the first time, as Bernholtz and Fosburg remarked, scientists could see what their abstract simulations meant in terms of houses and roads and sewers and parks and schools.

Reconstruction, Allen Bernholtz and Steve Fosburg. 1972. "Spatial allocation in design and planning" DAC '72: Proceedings of the 9th Design Automation Workshop, *181–189.*

The Cellule II workstation, Guy Desbarats and Leonard Warshaw, Université de Montréal, 1971, Canada

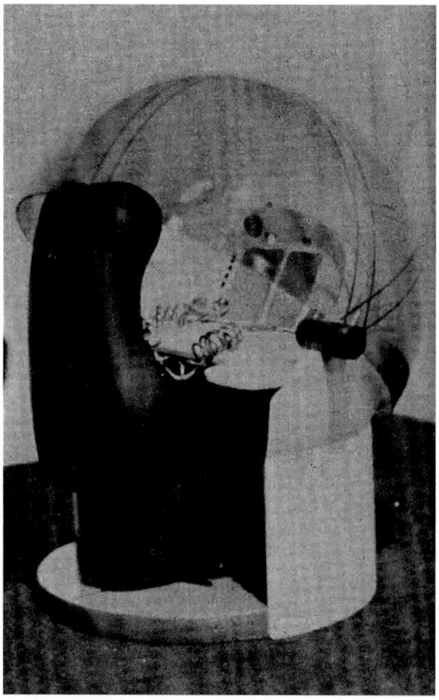

Canada Cellule II (Cellular Decision Making Module) was an environmentally controlled communication and information workstation for improving office work efficiency proposed by a team of researchers at Université de Montréal with support from the Department of Industry, Trade and Commerce, the National Design Council, and Bell Canada. Although the Cellule's bubble-like appearance is a telling metaphor for contemporary informational immersion, the report accompanying the work capsule also stands in stark contrast with the current realities of digital labor: the Cellule team purported that the maximum time for communicating with someone in another module or accumulating information from a computer ought to not exceed 30 minutes.

Courtesy of the RAIC Journal, *1971. "Cellule II - working towards a new environment for work,"* Architecture Canada (RAIC), *4–5*

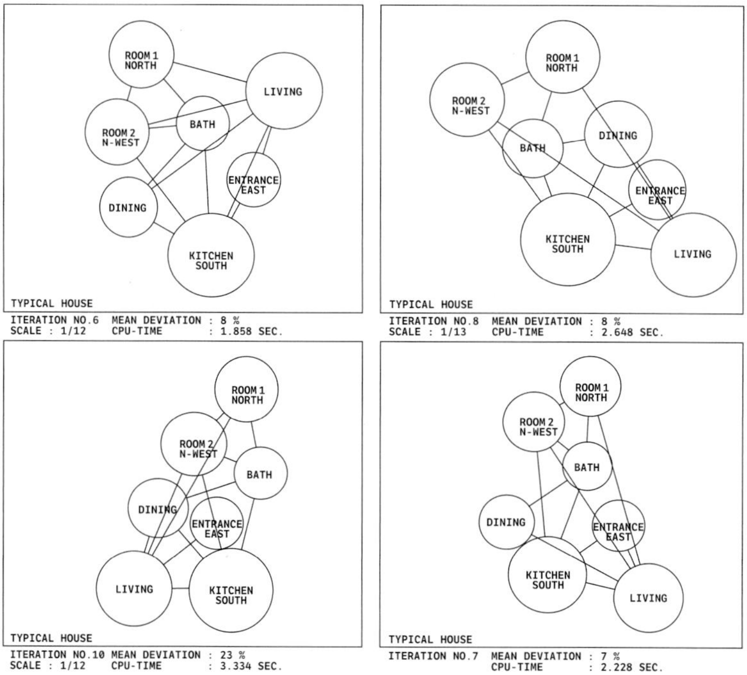

Use of BUBBLE to position a shopping center with respect to seven suburbs in the Quebec City area, Gilles Fortin, Université Laval, 1978, Canada

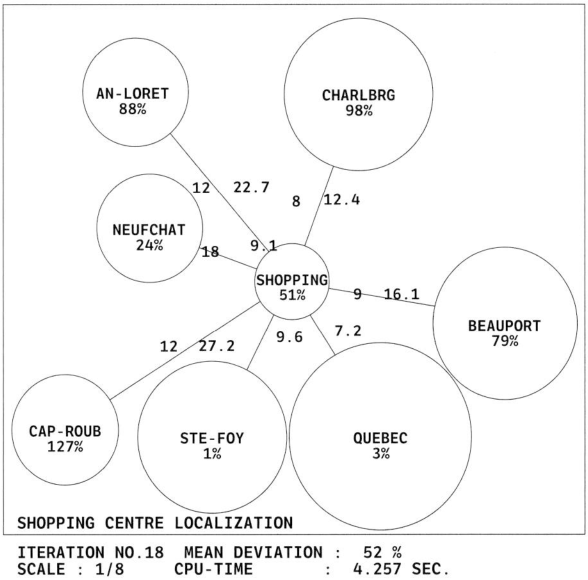

Graphs are not geometric; they are relational. Space allocation systems such as BUBBLE did not operate based on dimensions, instead they computed based on spatial relationships. This gave them the perceived advantage of being scale-free. Indeed, researchers would often demonstrate their systems by applying them concurrently to small-scale architectural and large-scale urban design scenarios: designing a house and locating a shopping center.

Reconstruction, Gilles Fortin. 1978. BUBBLE: Relationship diagrams using iterative vector approximation. In Proceedings of the 15th Design Automation Conference (DAC '78). *IEEE Press, 145–151.*

Diagrams of a house using the BUBBLE system, Gilles Fortin, Université Laval, 1978, Canada

Space allocation or automatic spatial synthesis was a burgeoning pursuit in the first decade of computer-aided design research, with more than one-fourth of computer applications for all aspects of architectural work dedicated to space allocation by 1973. The domin ant abstraction of the building undergirding such programs was the graph. The graph is a mathematical object whose points represent objects and lines represent their relationships, which in the case of space allocation algorithms correspond respectively to rooms and their adjacencies. One of the graph's appeals was its intuitiveness: representing a building with graphs was not unlike making a bubble diagram. Developed at Université Laval, BUBBLE performed space allocation operations using an iterative approximation algorithm, which placed all ele-ments together and then repositioned them until a satisfactory state was attained. This image shows the four standard "solutions" found by BUBBLE corresponding to a specific input of functions for a house.

Reconstruction, Gilles Fortin. 1978. BUBBLE: Relationship diagrams using iterative vector approximation. In Proceedings of the 15th Design Automation Conference (DAC '78). *IEEE Press, 145–151.*

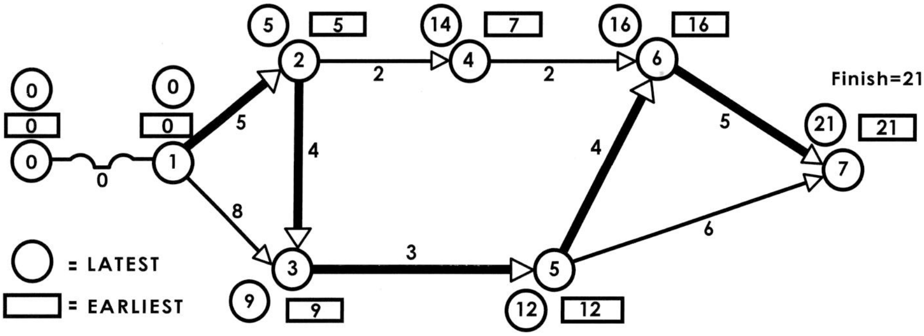

The Critical Path Method of scheduling, Ian McKenzie, 1964, Canada

The Critical Path Method (CPM) features prominently in the iconography of computational images as a graphic tool for making decisions about the sequence and duration of various activities in the context of a project. Developed by DuPont Engineering Services in the mid-1950s, the CPM represented a project as a directed graph, that is a set of points (events without duration) and arrows (activities with a given duration) arranged in logical sequence. Computers were often used in conjunction with CPM graphics to keep track of and update duration calculations. The CPM's implications extend beyond its logistical and managerial aspirations: CPM graphics recast processes which unfolded in time as structured, calculable, and amenable to rationalization.

Reconstruction, Ian McKenzie (Introduction by Dennis Peters). 1964. "The Critical Path Method of Scheduling" Journal of the Royal Architecture Institute of Canada *41(4): 63*

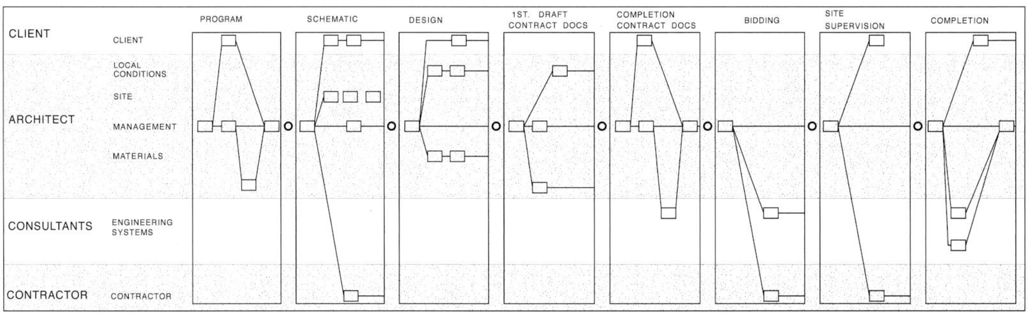

The Critical Path Method as a design tool, Randle Iredale, 1968, Canada

This diagram published in Architecture Canada shows an adaptation of the Critical Path Method (CPM) in the work of the large Vancouver-based architectural firm Rhone and Iredale. Instead of using the method for managing construction processes, firm co-founder Randle Iredale suggested its adaptation to processes of architectural design. Iredale suggested that CPM could become an introspective device by making visible the structure of the firm's design process.

Reconstruction, Randle Iredale. 1968. "CPM Graphics as a Design Tool," Architecture Canada (RAIC): *57.*

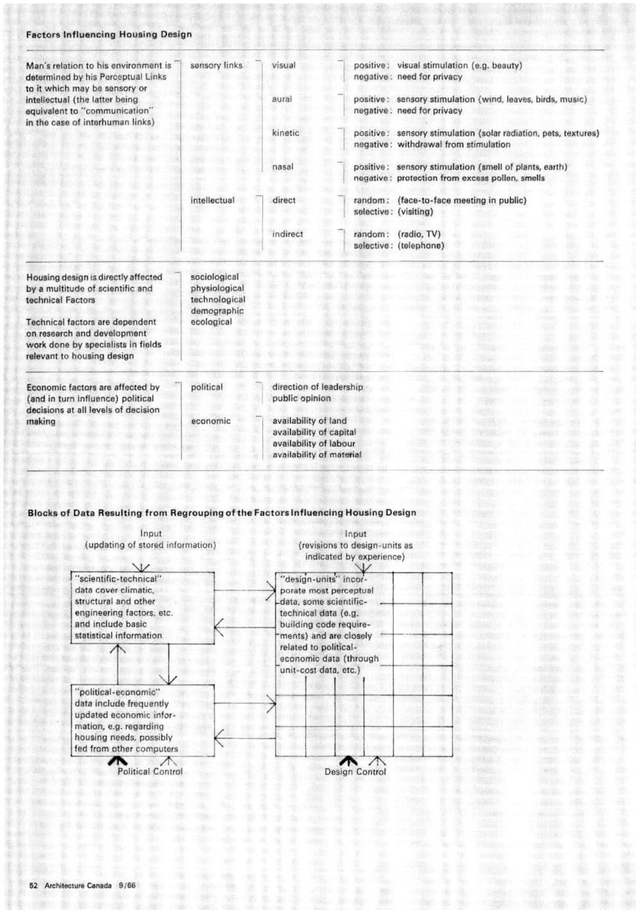

Factors Influencing Housing Design

Man's relation to his environment is determined by his Perceptual Links to it which may be sensory or intellectual (the latter being equivalent to "communication" in the case of interhuman links)	sensory links	visual	positive: visual stimulation (e.g. beauty) negative: need for privacy
		aural	positive: sensory stimulation (wind, leaves, birds, music) negative: need for privacy
		kinetic	positive: sensory stimulation (solar radiation, pets, textures) negative: withdrawal from stimulation
		nasal	positive: sensory stimulation (smell of plants, earth) negative: protection from excess pollen, smells
	intellectual	direct	random: (face-to-face meeting in public) selective: (visiting)
		indirect	random: (radio, TV) selective: (telephone)
Housing design is directly affected by a multitude of scientific and technical Factors Technical factors are dependent on research and development work done by specialists in fields relevant to housing design	sociological physiological technological demographic ecological		
Economic factors are affected by (and in turn influence) political decisions at all levels of decision making	political	direction of leadership public opinion	
	economic	availability of land availability of capital availability of labour availability of material	

Blocks of Data Resulting from Regrouping of the Factors Influencing Housing Design

Input
(updating of stored information)

Input
(revisions to design-units as indicated by experience)

"scientific-technical" data cover climatic, structural and other engineering factors, etc. and include basic statistical information

"design-units" incorporate most perceptual data, some scientific-technical data (e.g. building code requirements) and are closely related to political-economic data (through unit-cost data, etc.)

"political-economic" data include frequently updated economic information, e.g. regarding housing needs, possibly fed from other computers

Political Control

Design Control

52 Architecture Canada 9/66

Data Blocks for housing design, George Banz, 1966, Canada

The dissemination of computer-related imagery to architectural audiences in Canada relied significantly on avid reporters of technological change such as Toronto based architect George Banz, former student of Siegfried Giedion at the Swiss Federal Institute of Technology in Zurich. Banz was co-founder of the awarded architectural firm Brook and Banz and held teaching appointments at various universities in Ontario. Banz's data blocks for the design of multiple housing were an effort to conceive of modules for organizing housing-related information and of a process for assembling these modules into a sequence. The flowchart is a telling example of growing postwar efforts to consider data organization and process as interconnected problems, and as foundations not only for the use of computers but also for their prerequisite: a systematic understanding of design processes as information processes.

Courtesy of the RAIC Journal, *George Banz. 1966. "The Computer and the Design of Multiple Housing."* Architecture Canada *43: 48-54.*

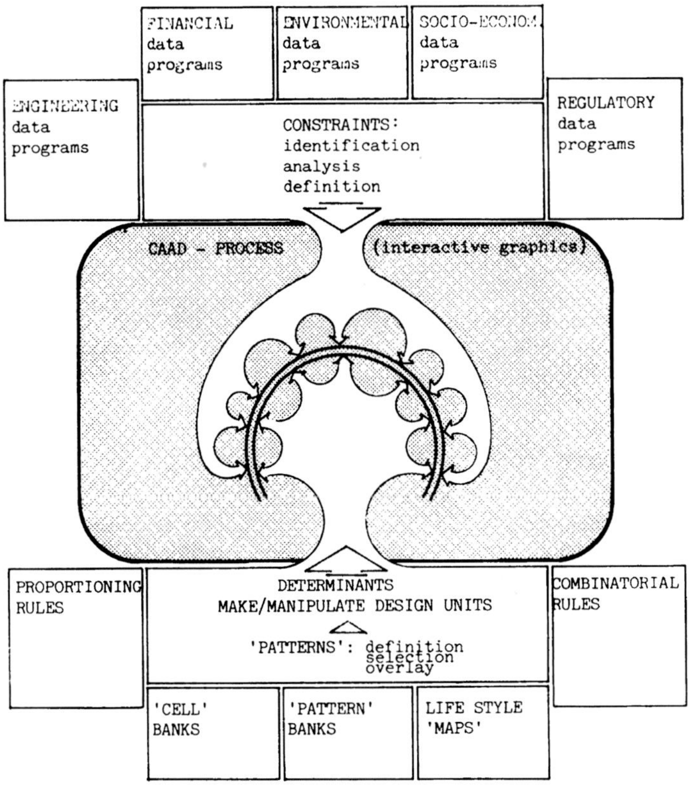

An iterative CAAD system, George Banz, 1985, Canada

Well into the 1980s and as computers were becoming increasingly associated with tasks such as the production of architectural drawings and mechanical calculations, Banz continued to argue that making full use of computers presupposed a methodological inquiry into the nature of architectural design processes. His diagram for an iterative CAAD system amalga-mated various landmark publications in the theory of architectural computation by research groups such as the Center for Environmental Structure at Berkeley and the Centre for Land Use Built Form Studies in Cambridge, UK. The diagram shows a CAAD process (method) and computer graphics techniques working together to process metric/numerical input and non-metric topological ideas.

Courtesy of the Journal of Architectural and Planning Research, *George Banz. 1985. "An iterative approach to Computer-Aided Architectural Design."* Journal of Architectural and Planning Research *2: 187–200.*

CONTEXTUAL REFERENCES: PATTERN 117 - SHELTERING ROOF
PATTERN 107 - WINGS OF LIGHT
PATTERN 116 - CASCADE OF ROOFS

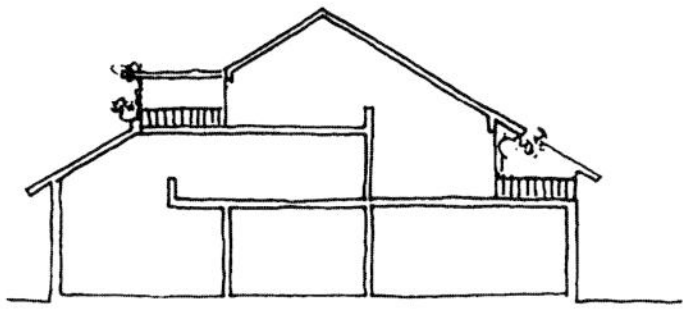

PATTERN 118 - ROOF GARDEN : Make parts of roofs usable as roof gardens at the same levels as lived-in rooms.

DIMENSIONAL ATTRIBUTES: none

POSITIONAL ATTRIBUTES: ROOF GARDENS ADJACENT TO LIVED-IN ROOMS
FLOOR LEVELS SAME AS ADJACENT ROOMS

TECHNICAL ATTRIBUTES: RELEVANT CODES AND STANDARDS
PAVING
MEMBRANE ROOFING
RAILINGS
METAL FLASHINGS
TILE FLOORING / WOOD DECKS
LIGHTING AND ELECTRICAL CONTROLS
DRAINAGE SYSTEMS

DETAIL REFERENCES: PATTERN 107 - WINGS OF LIGHT
PATTERN 140 - PRIVATE TERRACES ON THE STREET
PATTERN 166 - GALLERY SURROUND
PATTERN 167 - SIX-FOOT BALCONY
PATTERN 161 - SUNNY PLACE
PATTERN 244 - CANVAS ROOFS
PATTERN 163 - OUTDOOR ROOMS
PATTERN 177 - VEGETABLE GARDENS
PATTERN 245 - RAISED FLOWERS
PATTERN 246 - CLIMBING PLANTS

Display of a "pattern" on a computer terminal, George Banz, 1985, Canada

The theory of "pattern languages" developed since 1967 by Christopher Alexander and the Center for Environmental Structure at Berkeley and compiled in the well-known compendium *A Pattern Language: Towns, Buildings, Construction* (Oxford University Press, 1977) suggested that design could be developed based on building blocks ("patterns") indicating desirable relations between form and use and arranged at a specific sequence. Although Center for Environmental Structure researchers had briefly entertained the idea of a computer database of patterns, they opted for a Xerox-able book instead. This image is a prototype by George Banz on how a pattern, which he affirmed as a fruitful way of collecting non-geometric, diagrammatic knowledge about architecture, could be displayed on a computer terminal.

Courtesy of the Journal of Architectural and Planning Research, *Banz, George. 1985. "An iterative approach to Computer-Aided Architectural Design."* Journal of Architectural and Planning Research *2: 187–200.*

Reverb necklaces, Madeline Gannon, 2013, United States (also pictured on the previous spread)

To produce these three pieces, United States architect and computational designer Madeline Gannon created a custom 3D modeling environment combining computer vision and digital design and fabrication techniques, allowing her to translate hand gestures into intricate geometric patterns which she then 3D printed as wearable accessories. Gannon's work serves to illustrate how contemporary designers employ methods and concepts of computation to creatively reimagine both design and production processes.

3D prints
15 x 12 x 5 in (38.1 x 30.4 x 12.7 cm) each
Courtesy of the artist

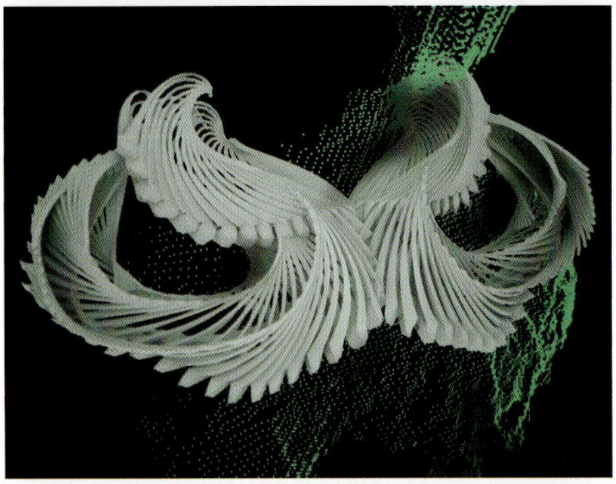

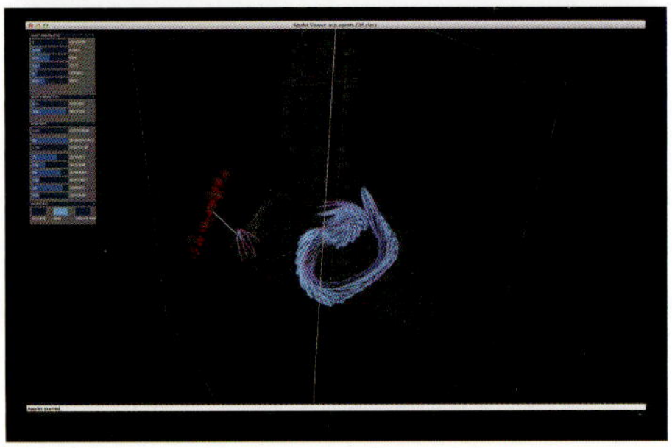

Blooms Day, George Stiny, 1969, United States

Mathematician and computational design theorist George Stiny created this painting in 1969 using visual rules. It comprises twelve triangular canvases which can be rearranged into different compositions. The painting foreshadows his later development of Shape Grammars, a theory of design as a kind of visual calculation he formulated with James Gips, where the design activity is conceptualized as an iterative cycle of visual perception and action. A conversation with George Stiny about this painting, and about Shape Grammars, is included at the end of the previous section.

Acrylic on canvas
Variable. Configuration on display at Miller ICA: 108 x 125 in (274.2 x 317.5 cm)
Courtesy of the artist

Patterning by heat, Felecia Davis and Delia Dumitrescu, 2012, United States and Sweden

Equipped with sensors, and crafted with specially modified yarns, these tubular structures respond to people's proximity by subtly changing their shape and creating different degrees of transparency. In this installation, US architect and computational designer Felecia Davis worked with Sweden-based textile designer and architect Delia Dumitrescu to investigate how computationally enhanced textiles might elicit new kinds of architectural responses to human presence.

100% low-melt polyester yarns using silver-coated conductive yarns weft knitted using an interlock structure
35 x 35 x 100 in (88.9 x 88.9 x 254 cm)
Courtesy of the artists

Indeterminate Set 003: Information, effect, interaction (Sentient object), Dana Cupkova with Daragh Byrne, 2017, United States

An electromechanically induced concrete cast responds to the proximity of a human body by changing colors. A "sentient object" that explores — and challenges — the division between humans and their environment, and suggests paths for architectural forms to respond to changing environmental conditions and human presence. Part of the Indeterminate Set series, the object's shape is a result of the same piece of code used to produce the lenticular print also on display. The design and production team also included Dan Cascaval, Josh Gy Kim, and Ammani Nair.

Concrete cast, electro-mechanical hardware, thermochromic paint
11.8 x 11.8 x 12 in (30 x 30 x 30.4 cm) closed
Courtesy of the artist

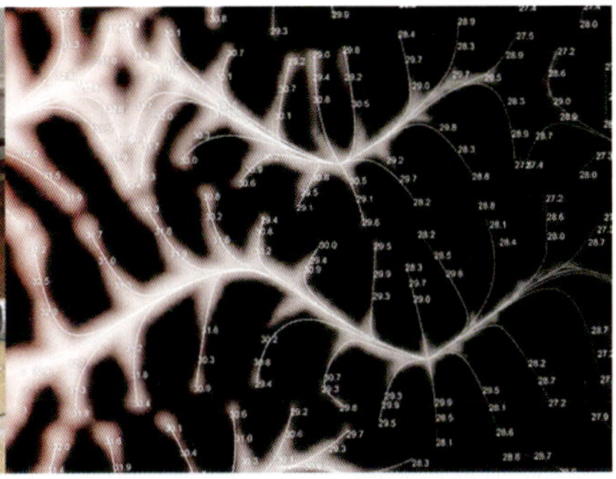

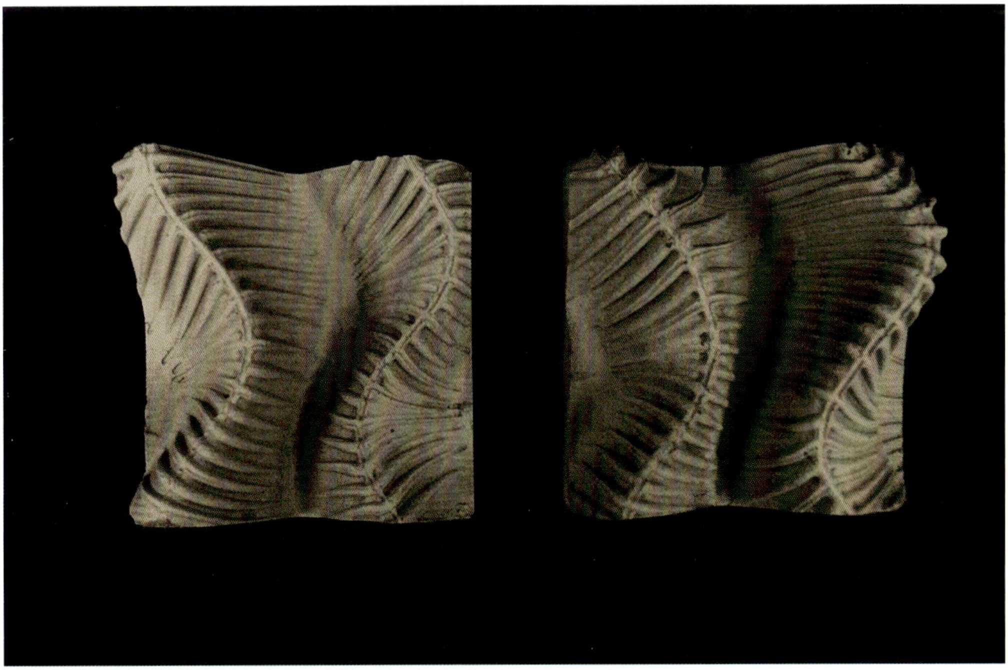

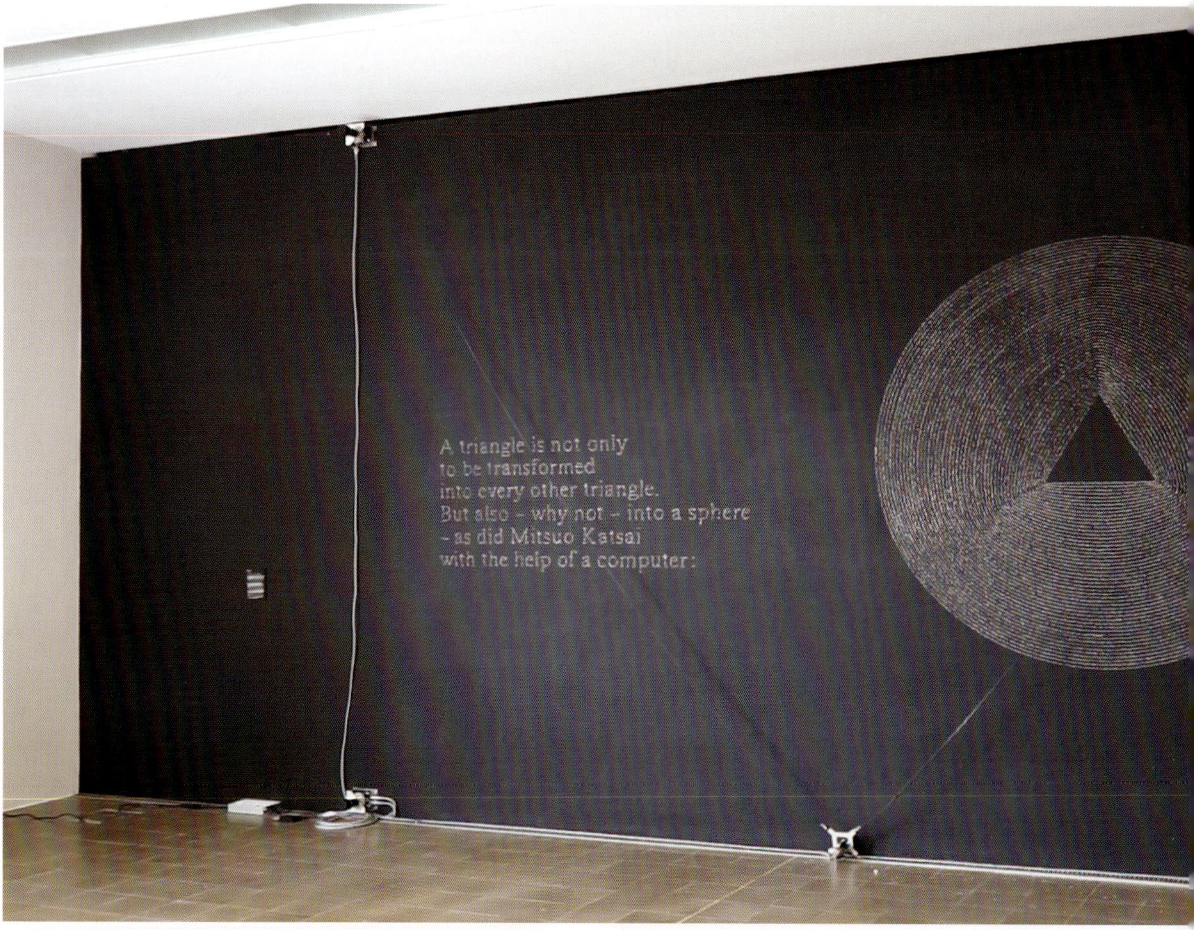
A triangle is not only
to be transformed
into every other triangle.
But also – why not – into a sphere
– as did Mitsuo Katsai
with the help of a computer:

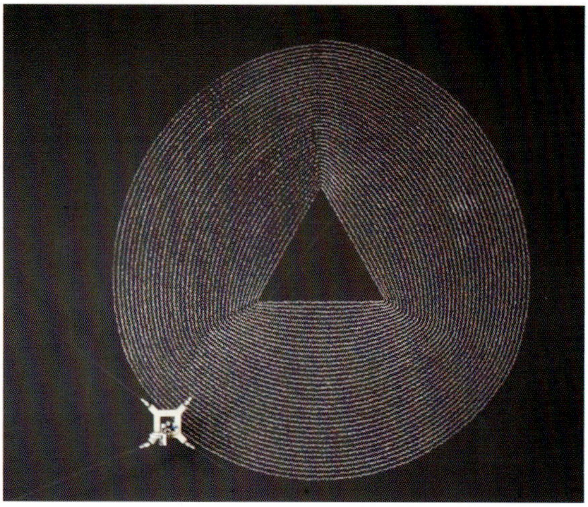

A triangle is not only

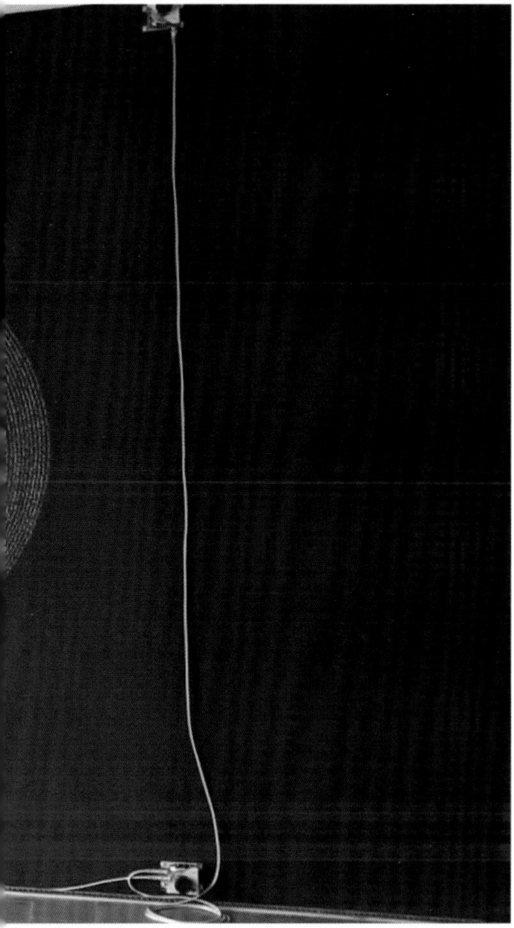

Otto, video documentation, Jürg Lehni, 2014, Switzerland

Otto is a refined version of Viktor — a scalable, robotic chalk-drawing machine for large surfaces of variable scale (up to 10 × 10 m). Both Otto and Viktor are used to reproduce choreographed drawings as performances, often taking the form of non-verbal lectures, with the sequenced drawings speaking anecdotally of a given topic through a series of images and text. As with their predecessor, Hektor, a spray-paint output device, the interest of all these machines is in their non-perfect, almost human expression and character through a tension between their high-tech components and precise software, their struggles with physical constraints, and the use of imperfect media. Their fragile physical constructions based on the principles of geometric triangulation, and the use of pulleys, leads to friction and inertia to which these devices owe their unique expression. The assumption is that any contraption and invention has a certain characteristic expression and poetic potential that can be leveraged by turning the process it offers into a medium through which topics can be communicated.

Video projection, 4 min. loop
Brushless DC motors, chalk tool head, sprung steel reels, cables, custom made controller, and software
Courtesy of the artist

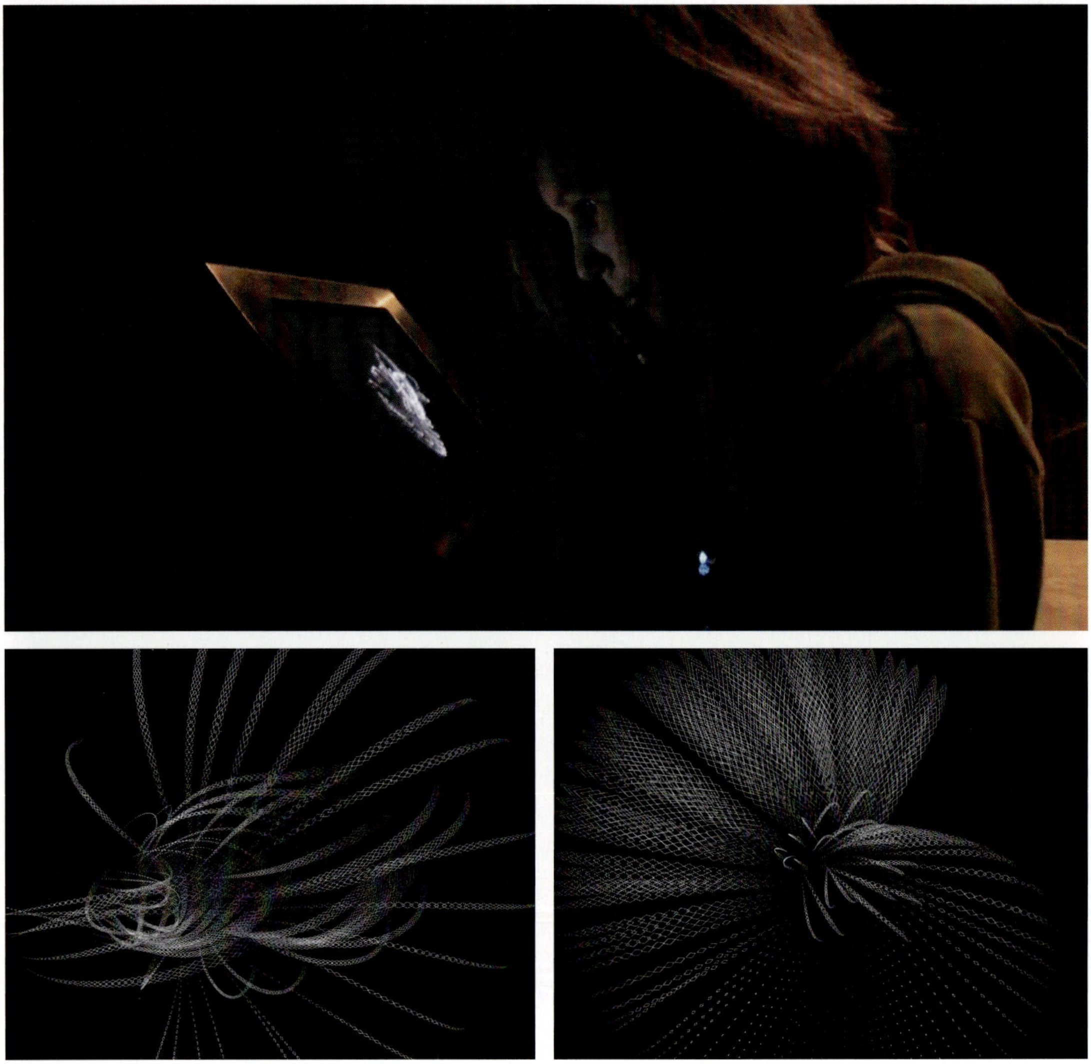

Meshy, Golan Levin, 1998 (revised 2017), United States

Meshy is an interactive drawing environment in which the user's strokes scaffold a gauzy mesh of animated elements. The mesh continually bridges the user's two most recent movements; by making new marks, users can tease and torque the mesh in real-time. One of Golan Levin's earliest documented works, *Meshy* was especially revised for this exhibition. Offering insight into Levin's trajectory as one of the United States' most prominent new media artists exploring computation whimsically and expressively.

Interactive Java applet, iPad
9.4 x 6.6 x ⅓ in (24 x 16.9 x 0.8 cm)
Courtesy of the artist

Digit Series, Elizabeth Vander Zaag, 1978–81, Canada

As discussed by feminist media scholar Gabriela Aceves-Sepúlveda in an essay included in this book, Digit was a female computer-generated character created by Elizabeth Vander Zaag and the protagonist of a program of short videos that appeared in the experimental television program *The Gina Show* broadcasted in Vancouver Cable 10 from 1978–1981. Every week and with limited access to computers, Vander Zaag improvised and took turns presenting Digit at *The Gina Show* as an animated character or as her artist persona as she performed in front of the camera. As a video technician at Simon Fraser University, Zaag had gained access to computing equipment, resources, and research including the work developed at the Sonic Research Studio, managed by Barry Truax, and the Kinesiology Lab directed by computer scientist Tom Calvert, where Jerry Barenholtz developed GRAX – a computer animation software that Vander Zaag used in the Digit Series. Vander Zaag's parallel involvement with artist-run-centers in Vancouver (including PUMPS Center for the Arts, the Western Front and the Video In, now VIVO Media Arts) gave her a unique position to question this scientific focus and creatively explore the potential of computer systems to simulate reality.

Color videotape, stereo
Digit Goes to Hawaii *2:36 min.,* Digit Does the Dishes *1:01 min,* Digit Reproduces *1:44 min on ½ " video tape*
Courtesy of the artist and Vtape

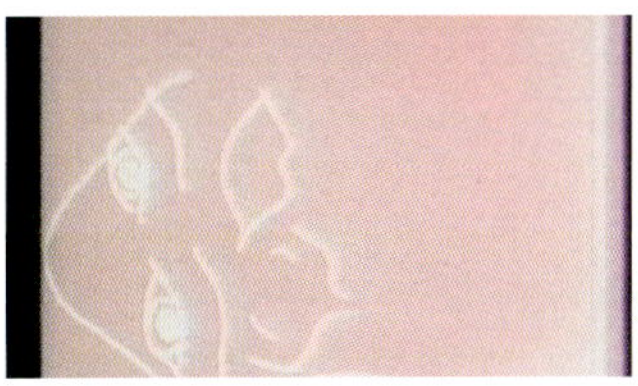

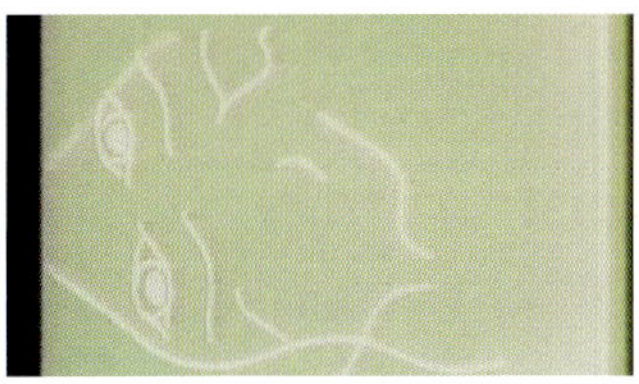

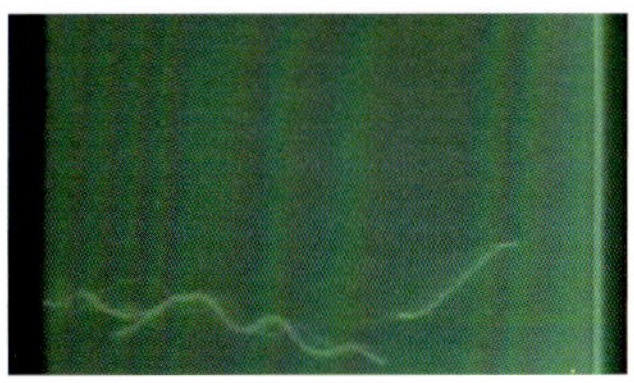

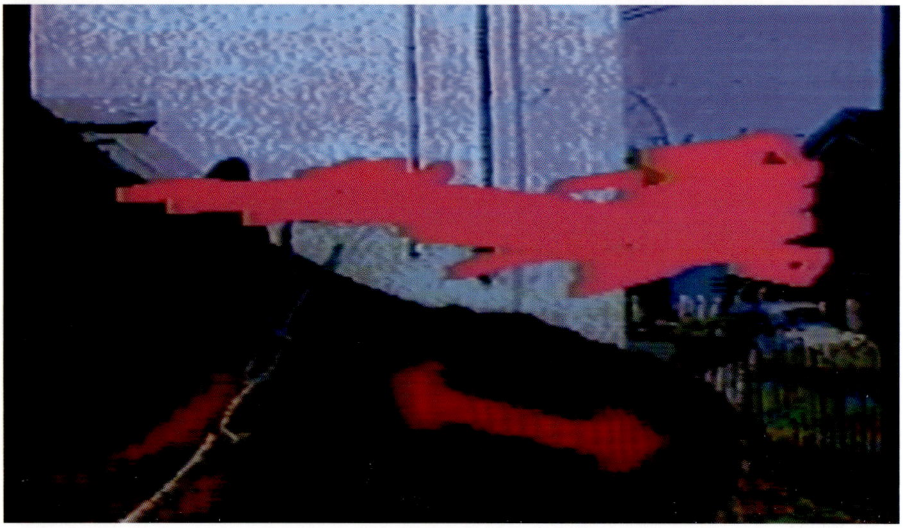

Baby Eyes, Elizabeth Vander Zaag, 1983, Canada (pictured on previous page)

Baby Eyes is a single-channel video produced by Vander Zaag after the end of *The Gina Show* to investigate, as Aceves-Sepúlveda writes (pages 170-175), the potential of technology in mediating mother and child relations and the capacity of the computer to describe human perception. Using Ko Nakajima's Aniputer to draw onto video images, Vander Zaag imagines how her baby daughter perceives the world. The composite visuals and the use of overlaid graphics, according to Aceves-Sepúlveda, point to Vander Zaag's interest in the reflexive capacities of video prevalent amongst video artists at the time.

Color videotape, stereo
2:57 min. on ¾" cassettes
Courtesy of the artist and Vtape

ALIGN, Daniel Iregui, Iregular, 2017, Canada

The Montreal-based new media art studio Iregular combines algorithmic methods, atmospheric effects, and communication protocols to produce multi-scale interactive and immersive works shaped by the engagement of their audience. *ALIGN* algorithmically fuses portraits of each onlooker to synthesize a new human. We might read the piece as oscillating between a positive vision of collective identity enabled by information technologies and contemporary anxieties tied to the ability of machine learning algorithms to synthesize deceptively realistic "fake faces" from large photographic datasets.

Interactive installation, video projection
Dimensions variable
Courtesy of the artist

Interaction
et intelligence
Interaction
and Intelligence

END

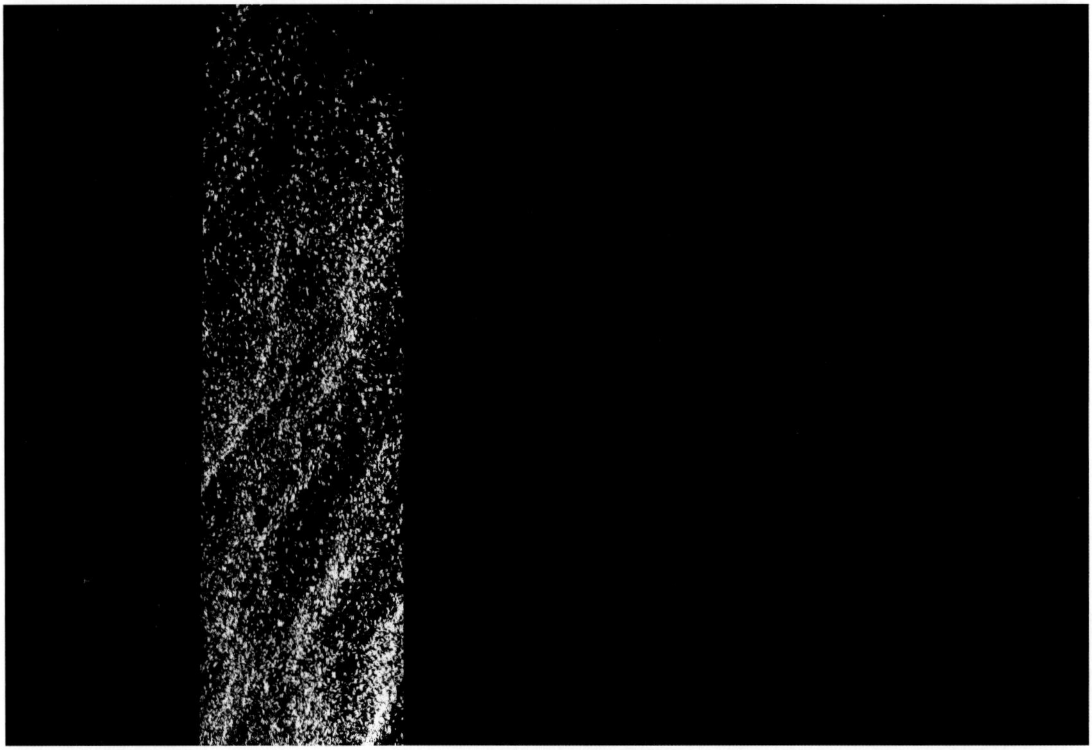

Double, Rafael Lozano-Hemmer, Antimodular, 2018, Canada

This piece by Mexican-Canadian artist Rafael Lozano-Hemmer animates the letters AGTC, representing DNA base pairs, as a turbulent stream of characters. At a given time, the piece shows the entire genetic code of the Haemophilus Influenzae bacterium, the first organism to have its genome sequenced, in 1995, with 1.8 million base pairs. Periodically, the display switches to show the artist's own entire genetic code, featuring 3.2 billion base pairs. The piece is at once a genetic self-portrait and a humbling comparison to a simple diminutive bacterium responsible for countless illnesses. The fact that at a glance the code looks very similar underscores the message of connectedness of the base pair instructions that give rise to complex living organisms.

Ultra-stretch display, computer, computer code for turbulence generation, 3.2 billion bases sequenced from the artist's DNA and 1.8 million bases sequenced from the Haemophilus Influenzae bacterium.
85 x 13.8 x 3.1 in. (216 x 35 x 8 cm)
Courtesy of the artist

Zones Franches, Jean Dubois, Université du Québec à Montréal, 1997, Canada

Zones Franches is an interactive piece that invites the viewer to explore a character by navigating photographic fragments of their body accompanied by sound clips. Letters etched on the skin and transformable by the touch gradually reveal the character's story. Oscillating between a caress and a digital signal, between the photograph and the surface of screen, touch here both installs and destabilizes intimacy.

Interactive installation with computer screen
40.9 x 16.1 x 18.1 in. (104 x 41 x 46 cm)
Courtesy of the artist

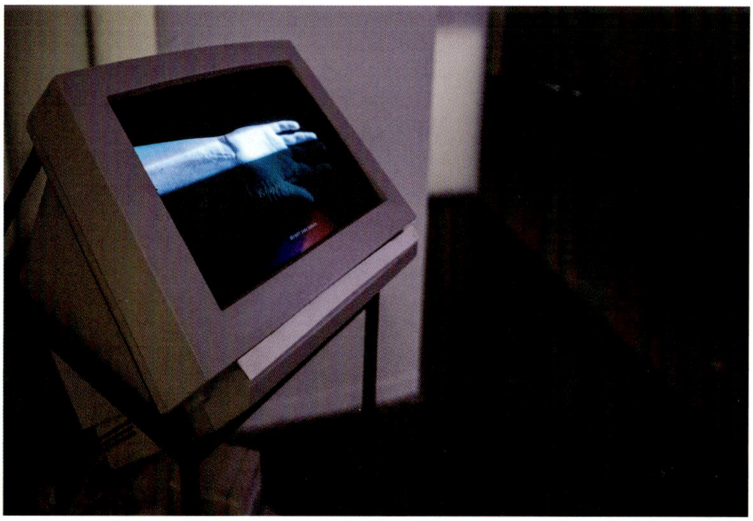

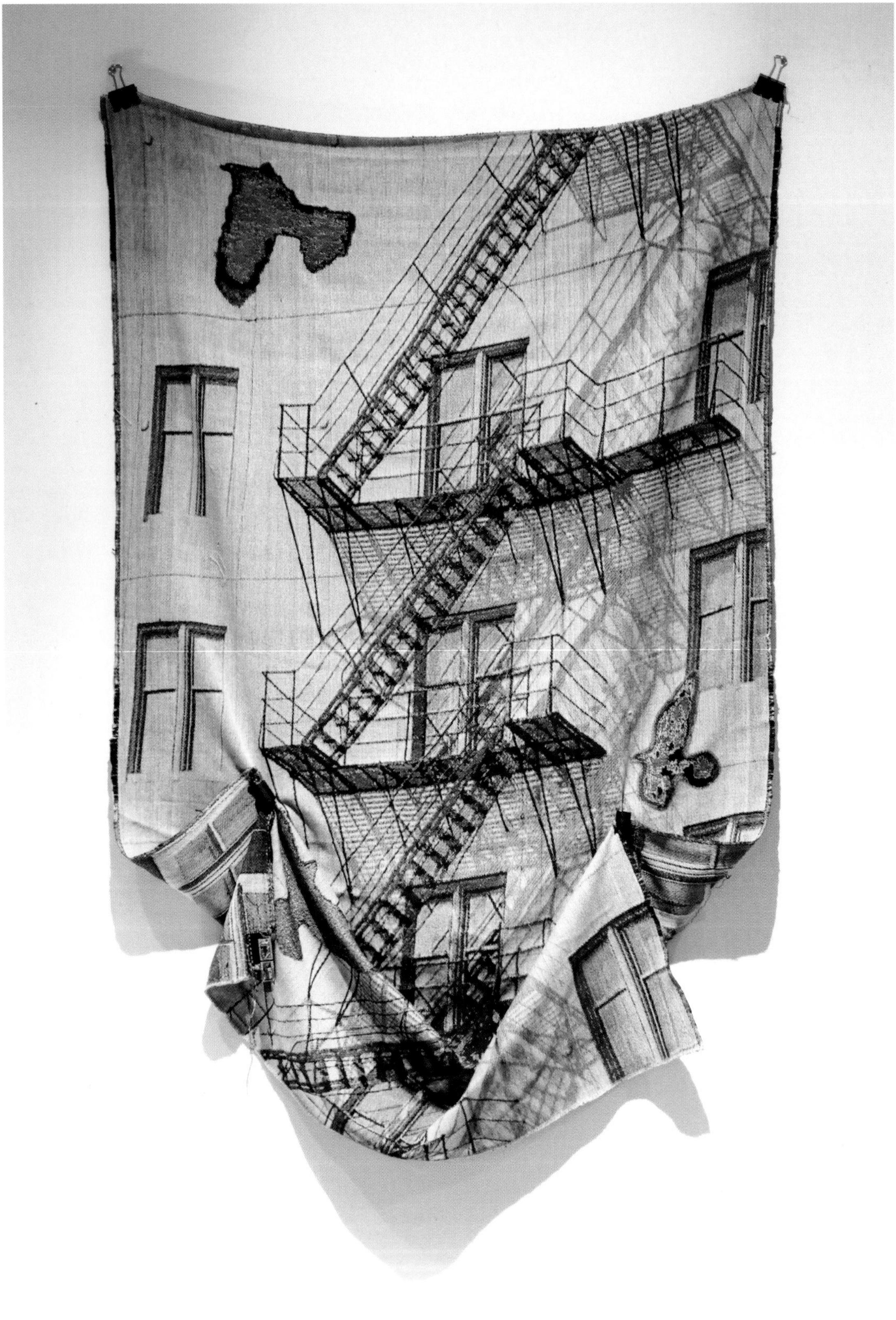

cidZiy, Joanna Berzowska, XS Labs, Concordia University, 2007, Canada

Montreal-based artist Joanna Berzowska focuses on electronic textiles that offer a soft and "squishy" computer-mediated interaction with bodies and environments. Shown here are two interactive textiles woven on a computer-controlled Jacquard loom. The physical and electronic characteristics of these textiles are effectively "programmed" using yarns and patterns of different electromechanical properties. *cidZiy* uses a brocade technique with conductive threads to create flexible electrodes on the surface of the fabric which are connected to capacitive sensors, allowing the piece to become an interface to any MIDI computer system. Moving with, against, and through the weaving triggers sound and media events in the environment. cidZiy was used in various performances around the world to create mediascapes responding to the bodies and movements of dancers and other performers.

Interactive textile
24 x 48 in (60.9 x 121.9 cm)
Courtesy of the artist

TangleForce, Joanna Berzowska, XS Labs, Concordia University, 2010, Canada

TangleForce is a stretchy interactive textile with elastic fibers in the weft as well as a pocket weave technique that houses custom electronic components such as piezo sensors. Physical interaction, including forceful actions such as punching, pulling, sitting, and otherwise distorting the stretchy substrate, are captured as data that can model bodily movements.

Interactive textile
36 x 72 in (91.4 x 182.9 cm)
Courtesy of the artist

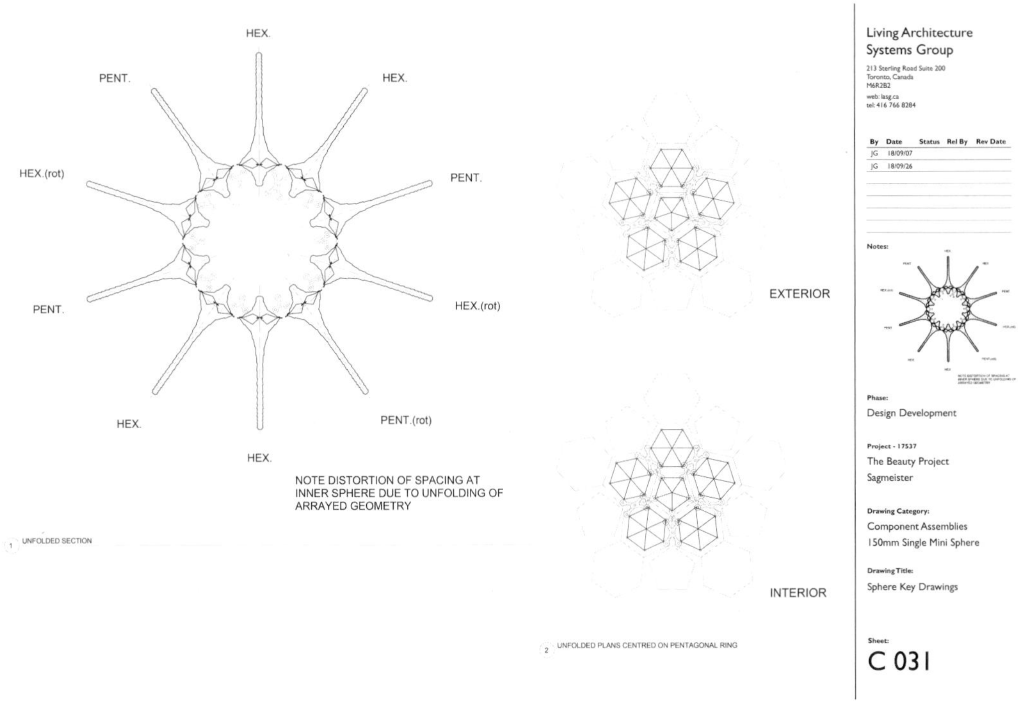

Sphere Cell, Philip Beesley, Living Architecture Systems Group, University of Waterloo, 2017, Canada (also pictured on following spread)

The Living Architecture Systems Group (LASG) is a multidisciplinary and multi-institutional partnership dedicated to developing environments that exhibit life-like qualities — movement, responsiveness, learning, metabolism, and even empathy. The LASG work integrates intelligent controls, machine learning, lightweight scaffolds, kinetic mechanisms, and self-renewing synthetic biology systems in prototypes that evoke new building practices, new aesthetic sensibilities, and new modes of living. The piece depicted in the drawing above is a component from the Nebula Prototype, an installation initiated for The Beauty Show at the MAK in Vienna in 2018 and traveling until 2022.

Drawings of the project
Acrylic scaffolds with aqueous copper sulfate-filled borosilicate glass
38.7 x 38.7 x 38.7 in
Courtesy of the artist and Living Architecture Systems Group

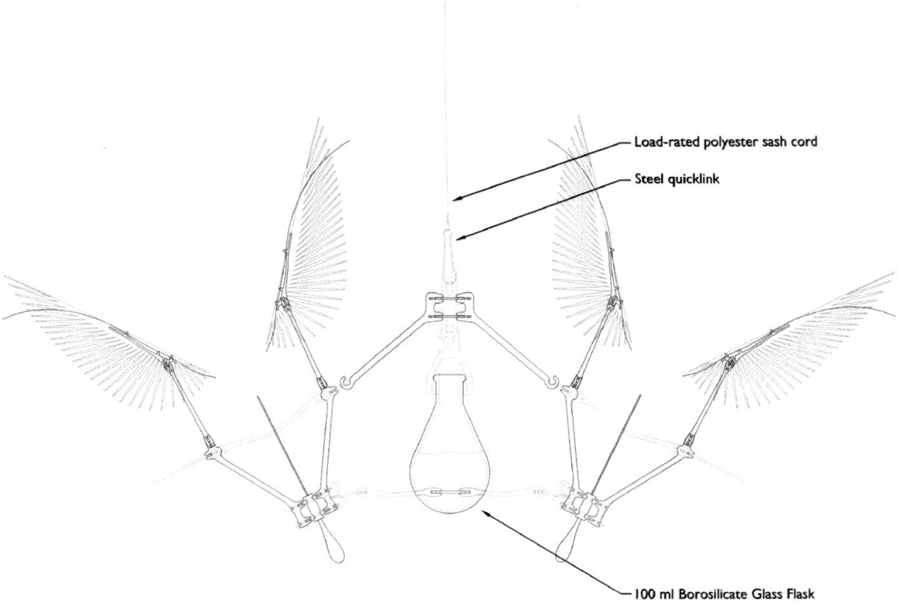

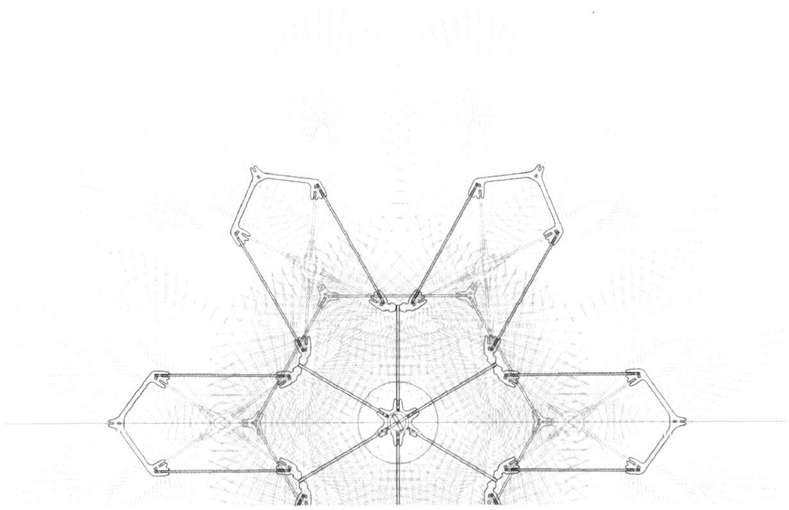

Ghost and Sargasso cloud, Philip Beesley, Living Architecture Systems Group, University of Waterloo, 2006, Canada (also pictured on following spread)

These prototypes for canopy structures have been developed for various installations since 2006. Through their physical presence and meticulously detailed representations the items on display usher a more light-weight, adaptable, and responsive architecture: custom hexagonal tiles are expanded into high-performing structural pyramidal struts and spiral forms connected by triangular junctions create an expandable canopy system whose feathered pores amplify functional air movement.

Drawings of the project
Acrylic, mylar, and silicone scaffolds with protocell-filled borosilicate glass
110.2 x 110.2 x 15.7 in
Courtesy of the artist and Living Architecture Systems Group

Data for Decision (film, 1967)

Moa Carlsson

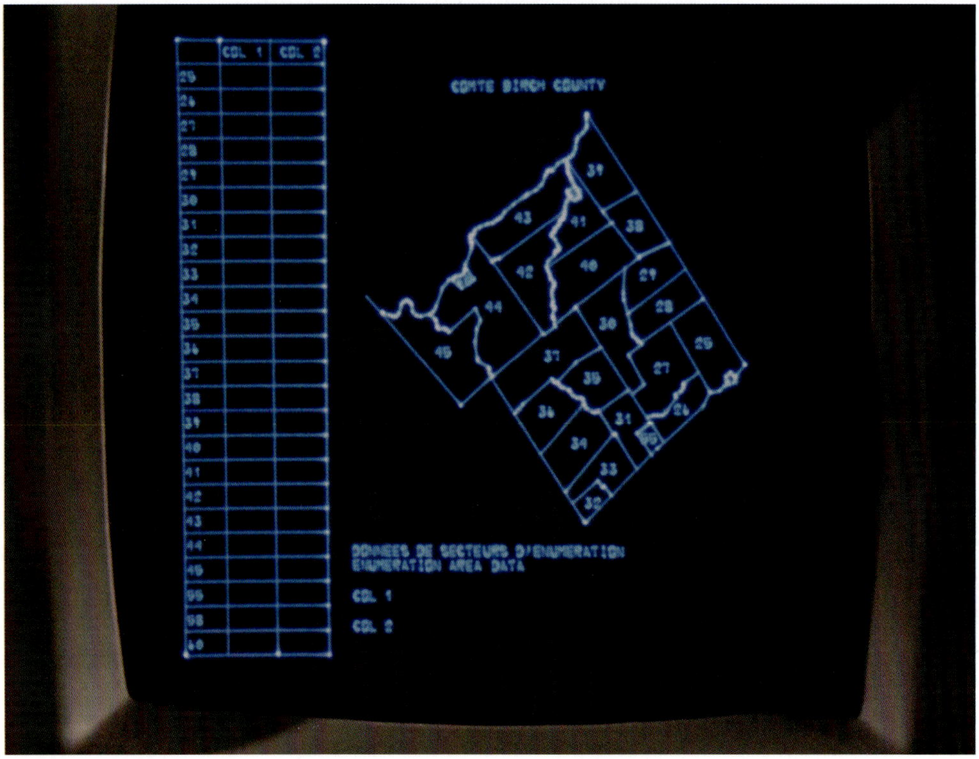

Stills from the film *Data for Decision*, David Millar, 1968 © National Film Board of Canada. Printed with permission.

1 David Millar, dir. *Data For Decision*. 1967; Canada: National Film Board of Canada, 1967. Film.

2 Roger Tomlinson and M. A. G. Toomey, "GIS and LIS in Canada." *In Mapping a Northern Land: The Survey of Canada 1947–1994*, edited by Gerald McGrath and Louis Sebert, 462–490. (Montreal and Kingston: McGill-Queen's University Press, 1999.)

3 McCormack, The Canada Land Inventory of ARDA, *Forestry Chronicle*. March (1966): 50.

The graphics on the display, flickering white lines on a black background, show a table of data and a map of the spatial boundaries to which the data corresponds. Entering keywords and instructions via the keyboard, a planner and computer technician collaborate in locating relevant data for a land use query. Tapping the display with a stylus, they zoom in and out, searching for the most appropriate scale at which to visualize the results of their query. In this image we see evidence of a new understanding of the territorial scale, enabled by numbers and machines, and by the people trained to orchestrate the process. In *Data For Decision* — the short promotional film from which the image is borrowed — we can see how, at this moment in time, information about land resources has irreversibly moved from paper maps to spools of magnetic tape, placing geographical data at the disposal of decision makers.[1] The tool being demonstrated is CGIS, the Canada Geographic Information System, now widely recognized as the world's first integrated geographical information system (GIS).

It was while working on an aerial photo interpretation contract in Kenya, for Canadian Spartan Air Services, that British geographer Roger Tomlinson recognized that automated computer technology and large-scale geographic analysis could be a match made in heaven.[2] If only geographical information was described in a language readable by machines, then new ways of querying vast territories would be possible. This would enable number-based spatial analyses, a process that Tomlinson envisioned would be both faster and more accurate than that carried out by humans at the time. In 1962, soon after Tomlinson's epiphany, a collaboration was established between Spartan and IBM Ottawa, which marked the beginning of the technology that we now know as GIS.

The Canada Land Inventory, a cooperative federal-provincial research project (a key component of the 1961 *Agricultural Rehabilitation and Development Act*), presented the perfect opportunity to demonstrate the potential of linking geospatial analysis and computers. The project was aimed at identifying unused areas suitable for agricultural uses and what farmed lands were underperforming and hence might be redesignated for alternative uses, and thereby contribute more effectively to the regional economy. It was a project of momentous scale with the ultimate goal of publishing mapped results on a national basis at the scale of 1:250,000. The Canada Land Inventory was, put simply, a comprehensive survey of Canada's national territory aimed at providing a logical base for understanding and deciding the use of land for which it is most suited.[3] This would be achieved, the federal and provincial governments envisioned, by providing provinces and municipalities with statistics on the quantities of land of various characteristics. Because manual production of such statistics from paper maps was extremely time-consuming and labor-intensive, the idea planted by Tomlinson was that computerizing the map analysis process would be both cost-effective and fast. He seized the monumental task of the Canadian Land Inventory as an opportunity to use computers to transform static paper maps into dynamic ones that allowed users to ask questions of spatially referenced data, and to produce and visualize information from such queries, the ultimate goal being to make better decisions about resource use.

This idea aligned well with a broader shift in planning discourse at the time. "Decision making" — a term from the lexicon of public administration and the academic disciplines of operations research and game theory — began to take the place of "resource allocation" and "policy making." While such deliberations could proceed continuously, "decision making" signified a goal-driven process and a decisive move from discussion to rational outcomes backed by data. Reflecting this change, *Data for Decision* is a 22-minute film created in 1967 to highlight the emerging computer mapping technology developed for the Canada Land Inventory project.[4] Produced for the federal government, which was funding the development, the video introduces a new paradigm of geospatial analysis and the computing technology that enables it. The film begins inside the vast map archive at the Department of Forestry and Rural Development, where administrators and librarians are busy searching for, retrieving, and returning maps in what appears to be endless rows and aisles of shelves and map drawers. This enormous repository contains the raw data and statistics, the "facts" that Tomlinson deems need be translated into machine-readable form. The information is fragmented and exists as separate survey documents, taking arduous work to catalogue, store, and summarize before the data can be used to make decisions. A clip narrated by Tomlinson, then director of CGIS, describes the enormous labor required: to compare only six basic factors for all of Canada would take 556 people, working 8 hours per day, 3 years to complete, and would cost 8,000,000 CAD. The need is pressing but the resources and funding for the manual work required are not available.

Offering a solution to this problem, the video cuts to a view of Tomlinson in front of an IBM S/360 model 50, with 512K bytes of storage. He explains how paper maps can be stored as numbers and how signals

4 The film was directed by David Millar and produced by the National Film Board of Canada in 1967.

can be stored on tape, how drum scanners convert maps into numbers, and how digitizers can be used to store geographic coordinates on punch cards. Accompanied by an electronic soundtrack of beeps, clicks, and rhythmic pulses — composed by renowned sound designers Sidney Pearson and George Croll — a hand-drawn animation (by Canadian animator Donald Stearn) explains that just as the human eye looks down through a stack of transparent overlay maps and sees patterns — a nudge to landscape architect and theorist Ian McHarg and others' simultaneous resource mapping methods — the computer can read and compare numerous factors faster than any human can, including soils, climate, topography, wildlife, farm and forest capability, and statistics on human resources, including census figures, average income, family size, age, and employment. The most innovative feature of CGIS was the layering of information, and Tomlinson explains how the computer can process these disparate figures, compare them, and output the analysis results as a map.

In the CGIS project, we can observe the role of the human worker shift, no longer shown at the drafting table but busy pressing buttons and turning knobs, feeding magnetic tapes and stacks of punch cards into the IBM machine. More than an advanced calculator or tabulator, the computer does not only carry out the until-then-human tasks, but also checks for errors introduced by the people involved in the process. In computer-supported decision making, demonstrated in CGIS, Tomlinson held that for the first time the vast and divergent sets of information about Canada's land, stored over the years, could be compared, queried, and used to make decisions. The electronic display, with its fleeting lines, was the interface between that vast repository of stored data and human planners, a link that helped achieve a certain rationality in resource management. In this image, we can see how Canada's land has been redescribed as a calculable resource, and how CGIS put the state in a position to manage and control it.

Seeing with a Machine: Notes on Early Spatial Computing

Ranjodh Singh Dhaliwal

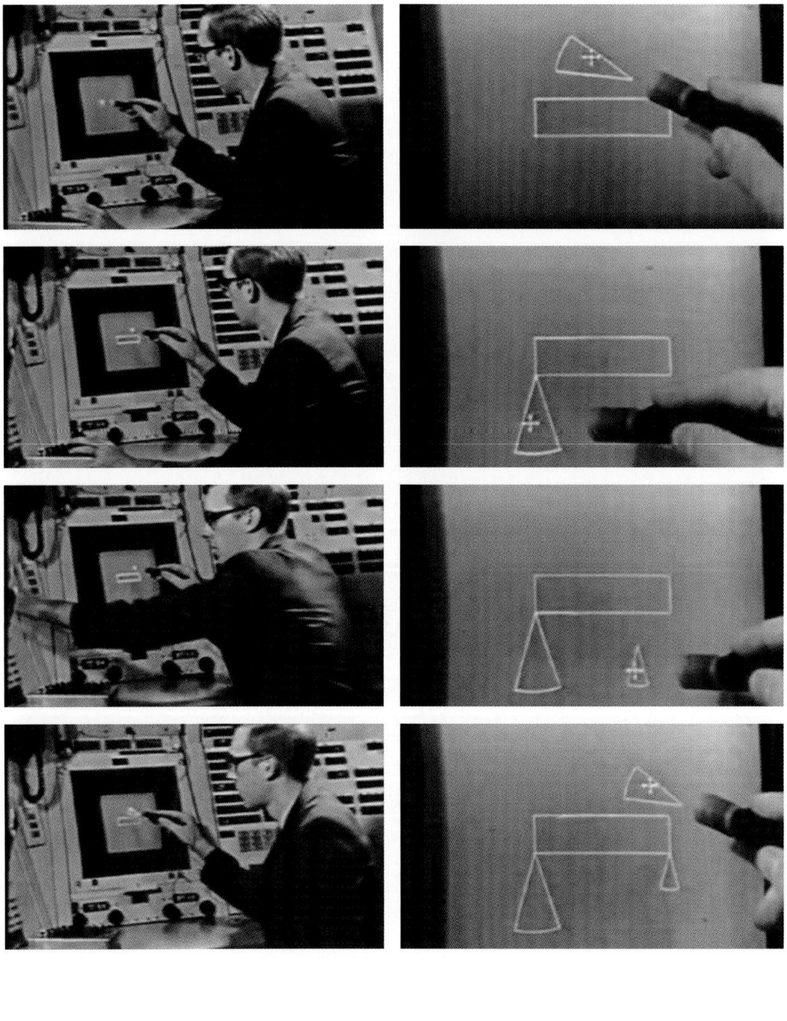

Stills from *MIT Science Reporter: Computer Sketchpad*, John Fitch, Dir. Russell Morash, WGBH-TV, Boston (21 mins), 1964.

In 1963, the MIT Science reporter, John Fitch, interviewed several people in the MIT Lincoln Lab for a television segment on Sketchpad, one of the first ever computational graphical user interfaces. One of his interviewees, Timothy E. Johnson, asked him to *imagine* a fixed, two-mile long sheet of paper behind the window in order to understand the device. His left hand extended and fiddling with switches and knobs as he operated a light pen with his right, Johnson drew shapes on this imagined paper for the demonstration. As he zoomed in and out, making drawn objects disappear at a scale and leading Fitch to chuckle in surprise, Johnson concurringly called it a "real nightmare material." The nightmare was not just a zoom function; it stemmed from the fact that the visual interface, at this point in history, was not yet a screen but a spatializing scope that pulled representation into the realm of speculation.[1] Referring to the oscilloscope, the term "scope" here brings to fore precisely the experimental spatial engagement with the machine that was at display in 1960s computational apparatuses.

As both the object of inquiry and as a medium for one, this scope relied on coding the "window" as a movable device for investigating another object, namely the imagined paper behind it. This paper speculatively functioned as the prototypical inscriptive surface that would be already familiar to anyone in the 1960s. And one might, thus, conclude that the computational scope tells the story of a paper transforming into a screen. After all, amidst conversations of drafting implements like rulers and compasses, Sketchpad, one of the first ever computer-aided design tools, was indeed a redimensionalization of inscriptional representation, from 2D paper/screen to 3D architectural models. But a closer look at the machine instructively reveals a far more conflicting intellectual genealogy, with art historical "perspectives," photographic optics, cinematic screens, militarized resolutions, architectural windows, and science fictional fantasies of cold war all exerting their influence as predecessors of the contemporary screen-world along with the aforementioned techniques of inscription.[2]

In the words of Ivan Sutherland, the creator of the Sketchpad, his apparatus was a far more dynamic, adaptive, imaginative, and physical operationalization of interaction than the simple representational conception of a screen would have us believe.

> *Since to the user the scope is physically there, and no sense of body motion goes with motion of the window, the knobs turn so that the operator thinks of moving the drawing behind his window: rotation to the right results in picture motion to the right or up... No such convenient manner of thought for*

1 All quotations here, unless otherwise specified, are taken from *MIT Science Reporter: Computer Sketchpad*, John Fitch, Dir. Russell Morash, WGBH-TV, Boston (21 mins), 1964. The still images are also taken from the aforementioned video.

2 N. Katherine Hayles, *Writing Machines*, (Cambridge, MA: MIT Press, 2002); Matthew G. Kirschenbaum, *Mechanisms: New Media and the Forensic Imagination*, (Cambridge, MA: MIT Press, 2012); Bernard Geoghegan, "An Ecology of Operations: Vigilance, Radar, and the Birth of the Computer Screen," *Representations 147*, no. 1 (2019): 59-95; Lev Manovich, *The Language of New Media*, (Cambridge, MA: MIT Press, 2002).

> *the scale knob has been found. Users get used to either sense of change about equally poorly; the major user so far (the author) still must try the knob before being sure of which way it should be turned.*[3]

This insistence on "trying" until you are sure about what is wrought by your interaction with the machine is indicative of how the scope-window metaphor functioned spatially: the (macro)scope operationalized the window to make it examinable and usable, and the moving window itself let one imagine the varying scales of the dynamically shifting space behind the window, with a grammar of bodily practices ("turn the knob") serving as the experimental *cogs in medias res.*

This imagined space behind the window, which then became critical for the subsequent development of computational media, followed Brunelleschi's perspective and Alberti's grid in making 2D representations of a 3D world.[4] But more importantly, it relied on the *imagination* of a space that need not be representational *per se*, an imagination that became a physical, literal component of the cultural trajectory of media in the late twentieth century, lying hidden in plain sight over the next six decades of computational evolution. Navigating between the phenomenal and the dimensional, even today, we speculate spatially — what lies behind, beyond, or through the screen (a *desktop*, a *cyberspace*, a *webpage*?) — and then align it with input devices, shaking our knobby mice and caressing our haptic trackpads. As windows, scopes and knobs have proliferated over the years,[5] the role of imagining other spaces has become critical in human-computer interaction. Much like how the first wave of cybernetic thought relied on a steering/navigating (*or kyber*) metaphor, human-computer interaction in its early days was all about creating an experimental space, one where the imagination of a space beyond the window was as much a mental experiment as a physical one.

But this project of interactivity was not unique to Sketchpad. T-Square — one of the first architectural drafting programs written by Peter Samson, Alan Kotok, and Robert Saunders at MIT — and *Spacewar!* — another historically co-terminus, collaborative MIT creation that is frequently (mis)attributed with the tag of being one of the first videogames ever — both shared not just their developers — Kotok and Saunders worked on both the projects — but also a mode of communication that did not rely on pre-figuring the projects. And thus emerged a sense of experimentation that depended on the computer for its experimental dynamism and not just its calculation. Consider the fact that the world's first joystick, created for alleviating bodily discomfort from the time spent playing *Spacewar!*, was seamlessly ported to be the controller for T-Square. *Spacewar!* — which featured

3 Ivan Sutherland, "Sketchpad: A Man-Machine Graphical Communication System" (Technical Report 574, University of Cambridge Computer Laboratory, 2003), 110. https://doi.org/10.48456/tr-574.

4 Anne Friedberg, *The virtual window: from Alberti to Microsoft*, (Cambridge, MA: MIT Press, 2009); Erwin Panofsky, *Perspective as symbolic form*, Trans. Christopher S. Wood, (New York: Zone Books, 1997).

5 Rachel Plotnick, Power Button: *A History of Pleasure, Panic, and the Politics of Pushing*, (Cambridge, MA: MIT Press, 2018). For more on the combination of visualization and control, see Shannon Mattern, "Mission Control: A History of the Urban Dashboard," *Places Journal* (2015).

the science fictional, expansionist dreams from popular colonial, cold-war space operas, instantiated in play by early "hackers"[6] — and computational architectural design[7] — with its functional displacement of vision and labor towards computational tools — partook, at this moment, in the same interactional paradigm as Sketchpad. Instead of writing out "all of the steps of the ritual on a typewriter or [punch] card," this paradigm tried to choregraph an speculative dance between the human body and the machinic peripherals.[8] The command of the algorithm had been subsumed by the partnership of the interface; the tool was now a medium.[9]

This human-computer partnership opened by the "real-time" interactivity harbored a technoscientific, experimental version of the operational aesthetic, one where the imagined space is equal parts suspending the disbelief and relying on it.[10] In other words, this was literally a new way of seeing, not just through or into, but *with* a machine. *Spacewar!*'s apparatus for spatial navigation — literally the trajectories of spaceships and buttons for shooting in "outer space" — became one point of origin for a specific kind of human-computer interaction that forged a relationship between the human-user and this horizon that lay on the "other" side, be it beyond, behind, or through the window. These scopic apparatuses, hovering between design and play, introduced a profound disturbance in extant spatialities. And they brought with them an aesthetic throughline that demanded that we imagine and inhabit experimental and interactive spaces.

This brief glimpse into early 1960s treatment of computing shows that spatial contiguity and concerns around visual analogies were important sites where development of computational media made its historical pitstops. Such a convergence of technical and rhetorical practices introducing spatial-visual elements in early graphical computing systems calls for a visio-historical critique of computing technologies to help us better understand how the computer as a medium can manipulate social, material and conceptual spaces. Looking at how spaces get configured not just in, on, and through but also around computers (from computer rooms in high schools of 1990s to VR cafes today) lets us interrogate and seek alternatives to the ways in which computing infrastructures influence our contemporary moment: socially, perceptually, environmentally, epistemically, and politico-economically. Technics of vision are never neutral; what we see is always a social "struggle over *how* to see?"[11] So, if an imagined space behind the surface is so important for the very functioning of the computational paradigm, what speculations are the speculative media today enabling and disabling? What emerges from speculating on the spaces of our speculative media?

6 Colin Milburn, *Respawn: Gamers, Hackers, and Technogenic Life*, (Durham, NC: Duke University Press, 2018).

7 Daniel Cardoso Llach, *Builders of the Vision: Software and the Imagination of Design*, (London: Routledge, 2015).

8 Steven Coons, then an associate professor at MIT, interviewed by John Fitch, *MIT Science Reporter*.

9 Jacob Gaboury, *Image Objects* (Cambridge, MA: MIT Press, 2021).

10 Neil Harris, "The Operational Aesthetic" In *Popular Fiction: Technology, Ideology, Production, Reading*, Ed. Tony Bennett, (London: Routledge, 1990). See also, Jussi Parikka, *Operational Images: From the Visual to the Invisual*, (Minneapolis, MN: University of Minnesota Press, 2023).

11 Donna Haraway, "Situated knowledges: The science question in feminism and the privilege of partial perspective," *Feminist studies* 14, no. 3 (1988): 575-599. See also, Jonathan Crary, *Suspensions of perception: Attention, spectacle, and modern culture*, (Cambridge, MA: MIT Press, 2001).

Alternative Land-Use Map of a Simulated City

Matthew Allen

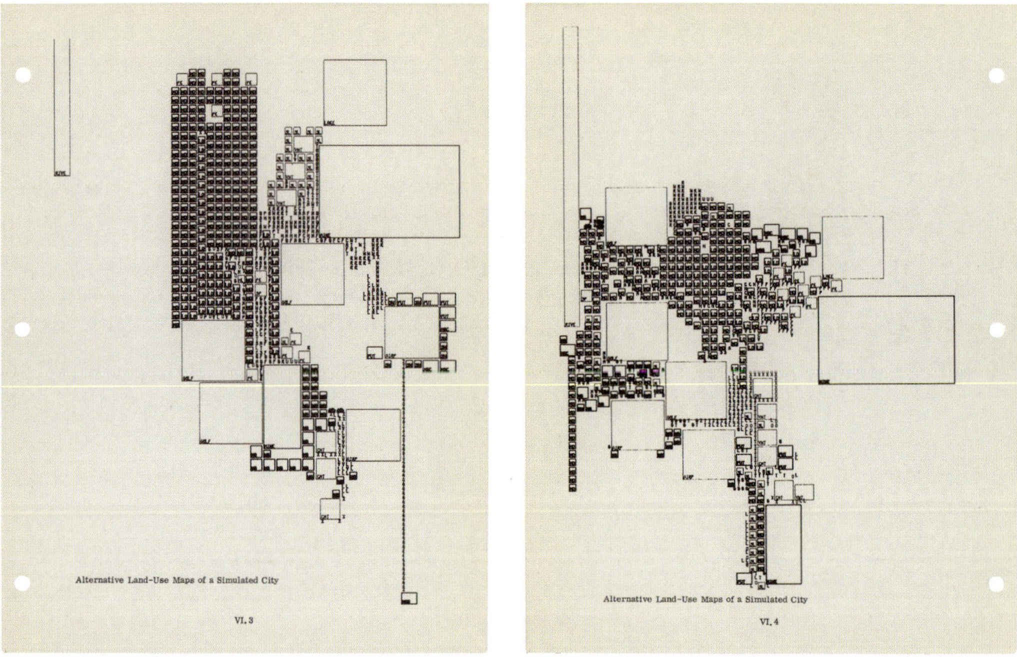

Pages VI.3 and VI.4 from the "Selected Projects" of the Laboratory for Computer Graphics and Spatial Analysis (Persistent link: https://nrs.harvard.edu/urn-3:GSD.loeb:14397644

These illustrations represent two possible plans for a city of 2,500 inhabitants produced using "location-allocation" software. They were created by the architect and programmer Allen Bernholtz for a new government ministry in Canada that was tasked with finding innovative solutions to a perceived urban crisis. Housing, stores, schools, warehouses, cemeteries, and forty other land uses — all represented by differently sized squares organized in plan — were placed and jostled around by the software to satisfy adjacency criteria among themselves as well as existing mines and bodies of water. The computation took around 8 minutes per plan on an IBM 360/65; the result was output by a digital pen plotter, originally in color.

The simulated city was the culmination of nearly a decade of software and design research that many thought would transform the field of architecture. Bernholtz and his partner Steve Fosburg foretold the emergence of a new persona for the architect. The "programmatic engineer," they mused, will combine "some mix of architect, engineer, [and] computer-psychologist type."[1] In the years following the introduction of the first interactive computers (that is, in the late 1960s), it was common for forward-looking design theorists to see computers as "partners."[2] The main theoretical innovation of Bernholtz, was to explain that the job of operating computers and acting as their spokesperson would fall to the programmatic engineer. The simulated city was a demonstration of how this would work in the context of urban design.[3] Bernholtz and Fosburg described how experts would gather around a table, decide upon starting conditions and generative rules to be followed, play out the architectural implications with the aid of the software, examine the resulting plans, and revise and rerun the process as necessary.[4] The printouts thus became the key working document at the focal point of a search for interdisciplinary consensus.

Bernholtz believed that gaming and role-playing would offer crucial models for design practice in a world that was growing ever more complex.[5] The notion that design could be carried out as a "game" has a history that originates in military strategy and the consulting industry, culminating in Cold War era "think tanks."[6] The best-known application of this approach was Buckminster Fuller's World Game, which he conducted mainly at universities in the 1960s.[7] Bernholtz proposed his own elaborate game to be run in an architecture studio at Harvard's Graduate School of Design in 1967.

For Bernholtz, the value of computers lay ultimately in how they could augment human minds.[8] With computational "brains" for comparison, psychologists in the post-WWII era charted the limits of human

1 Allen Bernholtz and Steve Fosburg, "Spatial Allocation in Design and Planning," in *Proceedings of the 9th Design Automation Workshop* (New York: ACM, 1972), 185.

2 Daniel Cardoso Llach, *Builders of the Vision: Software and the Imagination of Design* (London: Routledge, 2015). See also Steven Coons, "Computer Aided Design," in *Architecture and the Computer: Proceedings: First Boston Architectural Center Conference, December 5, 1964, Boston, Massachusetts* (Boston: Boston Architectural Center, 1964), 26–28.

3 For a detailed outline of this complex process using similar software in the context of architectural design, see Allen Bernholtz and Edward Bierstone, "Computer-Augmented Design: A Case History in Architecture," *Design Quarterly* 66/67 (1966): 40–51.

4 Bernholtz and Fosburg, "Spatial Allocation in Design and Planning."

5 Allen Bernholtz, "Some Thoughts on Computer Role Playing and Design," *Ekistics* 26, no. 157 (December 1968): 522–24.

6 Jennifer S. Light, *From Warfare to Welfare: Defense Intellectuals and Urban Problems in Cold War America* (Baltimore: Johns Hopkins University Press, 2005); Paul N. Edwards, *The Closed World: Computers and the Politics of Discourse in Cold War America* (Cambridge, MA: MIT Press, 1996).

7 Josh Pang, "World Game: An MS Thesis on Engineering Buckminster Fuller's Unfinished Computer Game" (University of California, Santa Cruz, 2017).

cognition. A widely read paper by George A. Miller on the "magical number seven" sketched the implications of limited short term memory capacity.[9] Computers presented their own enigma: they were almost miraculously logical, precise, and quick, but they required painfully specific programming and data — they could not "think outside the box" (a phrase popularized in 1969). The Sixties was an era of techno-scientific optimism, and many believed that interfacing with computers would fundamentally alter the way people think. A famous early colleague of Bernholtz at the University of Toronto, Marshall McLuhan, explained how the printing press inculcated linear thinking and visuality, and that the "electronic age" would generate its own mentality and social organization.[10] Bernholtz followed McLuhan in thinking that computation would usher humanity itself into a new epoch.[11]

The earliest method used by Bernholtz was originally formulated by the architect and programmer Christopher Alexander. Alexander outlined his method of design in *Notes on the Synthesis of Form* (1964), inspiring a generation of theorists to believe that a rigorous, mathematical, computational approach to design was within grasp. Along with Marvin Manheim at MIT, Alexander codified his method in some of the first architectural software, called HIDECS (c. 1962), which was used to turn a list of architectural requirements (a "program") into an initial planimetric layout.[12] While working at Harvard's Laboratory for Computer Graphics and Spatial Analysis, Bernholtz ported this software to Harvard's computers. In the following years he wrote his own software to accomplish similar tasks using his own logical procedures. The first was RUMOR (1968), then came LOKAT and LOKAT II and ALOKAT (1968–72). This software made Bernholtz a player in the burgeoning field of "spatial location-allocation planning," and they formed the basis of his consultancy practice with Fosburg.[13] Like Alexander, Bernholtz recognized that human decision-making would still be essential; his software would not design buildings automatically, but it would help designers to be rigorous.

At least as important as Bernholtz's technical acumen was his entrepreneurial vision. Computers were becoming affordable and useful in many fields; they would need operators and software. Enter the computer consultant. As large government-funded computation projects wound down, highly trained programmers dispersed across North America, bringing their expertise to the corporate world and sometimes starting their own computer services firms.[14] Bernholtz started consulting firms in Boston and Toronto, and he consulted on projects for Perkins & Will, CambridgeSeven, and others.

8 Bernholtz drew on the research of contemporary design theorists at MIT, particularly Douglas Ross and L.C.R. Licklider. Douglas T. Ross, "Computer-Aided Design: A Statement of Objectives / 8436-TM-4" (Cambridge, MA, 1960); L. C. R. Licklider, "Man-Computer Symbiosis," *IRE Transactions on Human Factors in Electronics* HFE-1, no. 1 (1960): 4–11.

9 George Miller, "The Magical Number Seven plus or Minus Two: Some Limits on Our Capacity for Processing Information," *Psychological Review* 101, no. 2 (1955): 343–52.

10 Marshall McLuhan, *The Gutenberg Galaxy: The Making of Typographic Man* (Toronto: University of Toronto Press, 1962).

11 See, e.g., Allen Bernholtz, "Architecture and Communication" (University of British Columbia, 1963).

12 Molly Wright Steenson, *Architectural Intelligence: How Designers and Architects Created the Digital Landscape* (Cambridge, MA: MIT Press, 2017).

13 Erich Bunselmeier, *Computerized Location-Allocation: Exchange Bibliography No. 414* (Monticello, IL: Council of Planning Librarians, 1973).

Following the peak of the software boom, Bernholtz became a sort of in-house consultant at a new government agency in Canada, the Ministry of State for Urban affairs.[15] It was here that he applied his skills to the design of gold mining towns, among other projects.

Aspects of Bernholtz's vision for computation in architecture can be seen in the illustrations of a simulated city. It is not a finished product, but a work-in-progress printout meant to spur a conversation among experts. It employs placeholder boxes instead of neatly designed floor plans, making clever use of graphical limitations to present the design in an open-ended manner. Rather than a coherent ordering system applied by the hand of an author, it is a product of a complex set of interactions that cannot be easily traced back to a single source. It appears to be an outcome of organic growth; it is expedient and authorless. Bernholtz hoped to shift the center of gravity of architecture away from beautiful drawings and buildings and towards the thought process that gave rise to them. Through his printouts we can imagine the "computer-psychologist type" as a key figure in architectural practice.

14 In other words, the late 1960s were the years of the "software boom." Martin Campbell-Kelly, *From Airline Reservations to Sonic the Hedgehog: A History of the Software Industry* (Cambridge, MA: MIT Press, 2003). Nathan Ensmenger, *The Computer Boys Take Over: Computers, Programmers, and the Politics of Technical Expertise* (Cambridge, MA: MIT Press, 2010).

15 For a more detailed account of the life and times of Allen Bernholtz, see Matthew Allen, *Architecture becomes Programming: Modernism and the Computer, 1960–1990* (forthcoming).

@home

Mario Carpo

Perhaps the time has not yet come to bid farewell to those vertiginously vainglorious corporate monuments that have defined the great downtowns of the twentieth century. But they no longer seem so inevitable. Given a choice, many of us may prefer working with a net.

At Home / @Home

The domestic living room is emerging as a major site at which digitally displaced activities are recombining and regrounding themselves in the physical world. It's not just in the homes of electroyuppies, digirati, and chiphead hobbyists. In many places now, news and entertainment, education, work, shopping and banking, and lots of general social interaction are starting to flow in and out through small, housebroken, electronic boxes. We are,

William J. Mitchell, *City of Bits: Space, Place, and the Infobahn*, (Cambridge, MA: MIT Press, 1995), 98.

Around the mid-1990s many started to claim that digital technologies were about to change the world — for the better. Architects and designers were enthralled by the creative potentials of the new digital tools for design and fabrication; at the same time, sociologists and town planners were trying to make sense of a new information technology with the potential to upend all known patterns of use of urban space, and of cities in general: the Internet was still a relatively new concept (many still called it "the information superhighway" or the "infobahn"), yet some started to point out that, with the rise of the Internet, many human activities were inevitably poised to migrate from physical space to what was then called "cyberspace" (i.e., again, the Internet): Amazon sold its first book in the spring of 1995.

In the years that followed every company with a dot and a "com" in its name, as per its URL, seemed destined for the brightest future. So was the Internet in general, and with it, many then thought, the world economy. As the late William Mitchell pointed out in his seminal *City of Bits* (1996), many things we used to do in physical space can now be more easily and more efficiently done electronically: think of e-commerce, e-learning, e-working (or remote working, or telecommuting), etc. As one proverb frequently cited at the time went: for every megabyte of memory you install on your hard disk, one square foot of retail space downtown will disappear.

Strange as it may seem today, everyone at the time thought that was a splendid idea. The valuation of all dot-com companies (companies doing business on the Internet, or just saying they would do so at some point) soared. Between January 1995 and March 2000 the NASDAQ composite index, where many of these young companies were quoted, rose by almost 600 percent. As the then chairman of the Federal Reserve of the US, Alan Greenspan, famously said, that extraordinary surge was not due to "irrational exuberance": valuations were rising because the Internet made our work in general more productive, and many things easier to find, buy, or sell, hence cheaper. Thanks to the Internet, we were told, we were all doing more with less: more work, more reading, more teaching, more learning, more researching, more interacting, more dating — you name it. The electronic transmission of data costs so much less than mechanical transportation of persons and goods: think of the advantage of reading a scholarly article from your office — or from your couch! — without having to travel to a faraway library. What's more, the elimination of the mechanical transportation of persons and goods could be environmentally friendly (or, as we would say today, would reduce our "carbon footprint").

The NASDAQ peaked on March 10, 2000. It lost 80 percent of its value in the 18 months that followed. That was the dot-com crash, aka the burst of the Internet bubble. Many tech companies disappeared; Amazon barely survived, after losing 88 percent of its market capitalization. The NASDAQ itself took fifteen years to crawl back to its peak valuation of March 2000. In the contrite climate of those post-crash years (which were also the post 9/11 years) few still saw the Internet as a benevolent, or even a promising, technology. The anti-Internet backlash was swift, and predictable. As many had warned from the start, technology should not replace human contact; there can be no community without physical proximity. Ideologues and philosophers from various quarters soon chimed in, fueling the anti-technological spirit of the time. Christian phenomenologists, for example, had long held that the elision of human dialogue started with the invention of alphabetic writing: if we write, we use a technology to transmit our voice in the absence of our body. For those sharing this worldview, disembodiment is the original sin of all media technologies: after that first and ancestral lapse into the abyss of mediated communication, things could only get from bad to worse; the Internet is just more of the same.

All the above was said and resaid, again and again, between 1995 and, say, 2002. Then, early in the new millennium, the heated discussions on the future of "despatialization" (the migration of information and functions from physical space to cyberspace) prompted, among others, by Mitchell's book subsided, somehow — as everyone agreed, with different nuances, that *that would never happen*. We all love human contact — commuting two hours a day to go to work, or to the library, or to the shopping mall, is a small price to pay for the pleasures of gregariousness. History repeats itself, but in this instance Karl Marx's famous proverb is reversed: first came the farce. The tragedy is happening now.

Digital Pantheisms: A Conversation about Computational Agencies across Art and Design

Madeline Gannon
Andrew Heumann
Dana Cupkova
Golan Levin

Moderated by
Felecia Davis

FELECIA DAVIS: Thank you very much for your presentations. They were absolutely wonderful and enriching. I would also like to thank Daniel for putting this together.[1] It's been a really wonderful weekend and I'm sure we're all enriched for it and have learned a lot. I would like to loop back on the question that I started with this morning. Some of you have answered this question in your presentations in some ways, but just to get our conversation started I'd like to ask what kinds of interactions bring about what kinds of intelligence, and who or what is given agency by these interactions.

GOLAN LEVIN: I recently had the grueling experience of traveling up to Boston to give a presentation about artificial intelligence to people at Google. And I, amidst all these experts who are thinking about artificial intelligence, particularly with social data and the arts, had the challenge of telling Google something original and interesting about their own field of expertise. And after dwelling on the topic for a long time, the thing which really occurred to me is that intelligence is in the mind of the observer. These systems that we make are increasingly able to speak to our perceptual apparatus in ways that are seemingly

1 Panel discussion at the Computational Design: Practices, Histories, Infrastructures Symposium (Edited for length and clarity), Carnegie Mellon University, October 2017.

familiar to us. You know, we can make machines that can *sort of* hallucinate, or accurately detect things that we recognize — such as faces and speech — and that's great, but when we project onto them, and think that, for example, Siri is a person, that's happening inside of us. And everything, then, is kind of the animators' art of creating the illusion of life. That's all I have to say on the matter. I think that we fool people and we are willing fools. We have a perceptual apparatus that wants to see life in things, you know? Think about the phenomenon of pareidolia, where we see faces in things. If I were to put three push pins in the board there, in the shape of two eyes and a nose, you would see a face. So, we are preconditioned, we're genetically wired and biologically, you know, *ready*, to see life where it isn't happening — and to see intelligence where it isn't happening. I think deep down, deep inside of us, we are sort of pantheistic. And if we make something that acts in the least bit in a way that conforms to our expectations of what a living thing would do, then we ascribe intelligence to it.

MADELINE GANNON: That's certainly something that I looked to as an interaction design technique, and I think of it as a material palette that I can manipulate and wield. The hope, at least for me, when I try to implement these systems is to provide some transparency and legibility into what's happening under the hood. So, when I try to exploit our lizard brain — the primeval side of our mind that sees life in inanimate objects — I try to be as honest as possible with it. There's a trend in robotics to make little cute things that are secretly recording you, and you have no idea what's inside these black boxes. The work that I do is obviously [based on] a machine — a threatening machine — and I am not trying to sugarcoat that. I rather embrace it and use it as a low level way of broadcasting high level information. I think it is a valuable tool to have, to think about machines that are intelligent, autonomous, and coexisting with us in our space and our built environment.

ANDREW HEUMANN: And I think there's something interesting about the way that interfaces predispose or lay out a space of possibility — a way for us to understand what is or isn't possible as we interact with them. So, for example, with Golan's piece in the exhibition at the Miller Gallery you don't really know quite what to do with it. But you start interacting with it, and you sort of figure it out. In Madeline's work there is a reliance on animal-like behaviors, and then you start to build a mental model of what's possible. And in a lot of my professional work I'm building really boring dashboards with a bunch of buttons, sliders, and text fields to lay out what is or isn't possible. But one of the things that I noticed with my designs is that they don't rely on those mechanisms — they are more open-ended. For example, the Twitter Bot opens up this space of all kinds of different interactions. Instead of tweeting the set of operations that I encoded in the bot, people use lines from Shakespeare, or say rude things to the bot, or whatever. Not that there's any interpretive power on the part of the bot, but that sort of changes the way that people want to engage with it, ascribing intelligence to it.

Meshy, Golan Levin, 1998 (revised 2017), United States.

DANA CUPKOVA: Built space is ultimately incredibly dumb, and the overlap of architectural design and computation has been, over the past twenty years, in a kind of a crisis. Primarily because we rely on our ability to govern intelligence through interpretations — such as virtual reality, artificial intelligence, and robotics — where virtuality and physicality don't necessarily align. The space between the physical and the virtual is really very ambiguous and open to interpretation. I'm the only architect on the panel dealing with the physicality of building spaces. The notion of a scientific inquiry within the building sciences is really tricky, and can be very deterministic about the role simulations play in a building design process, or about the truthfulness of the performance metrics we use to understand the built environment. The problem of imposing computing on those is that we reduce the pools of variables we are dealing with. So, we can simulate one thing really well but that excludes other possible variables. For me, a more interesting questions is: How to think of embedded systems, of our own physicality, and rethink the role of computation in bringing architecture out of the realm of mechanization — perhaps closer to the realm of biological systems? How to build an intelligence through an incremental understanding of material and architectural behaviors? I don't think we have intelligence in that sense at all. But I think that some of the work currently being done offers glimpses of it. Building a tool of unconsciousness, that we can have a certain control over. I'm feeling incredibly sort of excited and confused, at the same time.

MOLLY WRIGHT STEENSON: I like that notion of excitement and confusion. I thought it was interesting that Golan and Madeline answered two parts of the same coin: the mind of the observer, versus the mind of the creator. And it's always the notion of us modeling intelligence, and the paradigms we have at hand. So, it's hardware in the 1940s and '50s and '60s; it's software in the '60s and '70s; it's algorithms that we understand less of the black box today. And one thing I find myself thinking about is the history of boredom. You touched on it just for a second, Madeline, with your work Mimus, but it's so important. It's something that actually plays out in a piece in [the landmark 1968 exhibition curated by Jasia Reihardt] *Cybernetic Serendipity*: Gordon Pask's Musical Machine. The point here is that these are machines that can get bored with you, and spur other interactions. This was something that Cedric Price also played with in his Generator project. If you didn't come up with enough new layouts, it would get bored and come up with layouts for itself, and then reorganize itself. Too scary when you've got a big crane moving cubes around! But I find myself wondering if there's a question about architecture, or about intelligence, in the uncanny. Playing with the uncanny might be one of the things that intelligence does best. I keep thinking of Janell Shane's recent work using neural nets to come up with other things, like color names — my favorite one is "burble simp," or "stummy brown," or "stoner blue." She also comes up with guinea pig names, death metal band names, pokemon names, action figure names, and sometimes she puts them all together, for the best guinea pig names ever. But the point is that maybe there's something about intelligence, when you actually play the uncanny valley right. And when you're playing it at the scale of architecture which I love that Dana points out that built spaces are inherently dumb, then you get some really freaking uncanny going on. I think that there's something there in everybody's presentations today about that question.

2 See *Indeterminate Set 003: Information, effect, interaction (Sentient object)* on page 267.

DANA CUPKOVA: The last project I showed in my presentation is currently in the gallery as part of the exhibition, and it's not working — so, it's even dumber than it was supposed to be! The idea of that project is that it reads your brainwaves, and senses your mood, or your way of understanding where things are.[2] The idea of architecture as a "mood ring" wherein we are inherently connected to the physicality or materiality of a space, and have a way for the space to read us — and for us to read the space. A lot of it is both gestural and emotive, related to how we perceive microclimates, temperatures, and humidity levels, factors which are computable and understandable through current tools of numerical analysis, but these are translated into a sensorial framework. It tries to look at specifics, rather than averages. If you look at the history of building science or engineering, the idea of building our physical spaces has to do with the notion of an average, or worst case scenario. Andrew's work is interesting in that the value of judgment is taken out — there is no average, there's just a choice — but what if you don't know how to choose, or what to choose for? This brings to mind an idea of a bias, that you need some bias to start creating these interactions with the uncanny. The lenticular print [*Indeterminate set*] was a subtle experiment on this. Can I move people in a space in a way that they start understanding the space in a different way? Can the dumb drawing make you move through space differently?

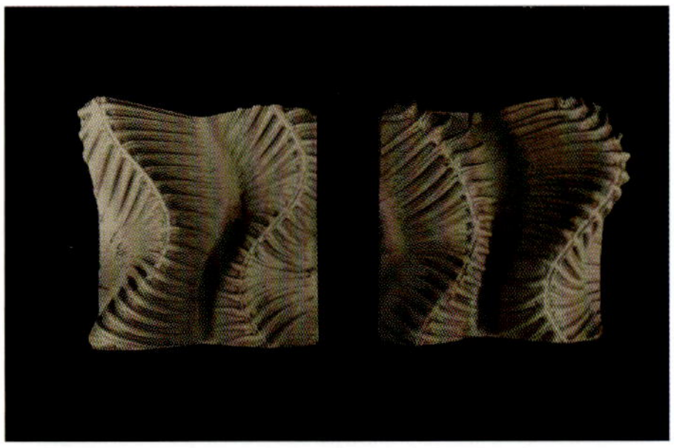

Indeterminate Set 003: Information, effect, interaction (Sentient object), Dana Cupkova with Daragh Byrne, 2017, United States.

FELECIA DAVIS: Many of the projects have focused on images on screens. People dealing with screens, people clicking buttons to make things happen on screens. I think that those foster a certain idea of intelligence, and I'd like us to talk about that. For example, in the exhibition there is a reconstruction of Ivan Sutherland's Sketchpad, where you have to sit in front of it, lift your arm up, hold it there, and click in and get the system to draw for you. When you are moving your body, interfacing with a system in this way, it really changes how you think about making a circle or a square. Madeline, your work engages with images in a whole different way. How does the screen change what we receive back in our "intelligence" about drawing? And I think it was shown in several different ways in the projects that we just saw, for example in Molly's historical account of Asymptote's NYSE project.

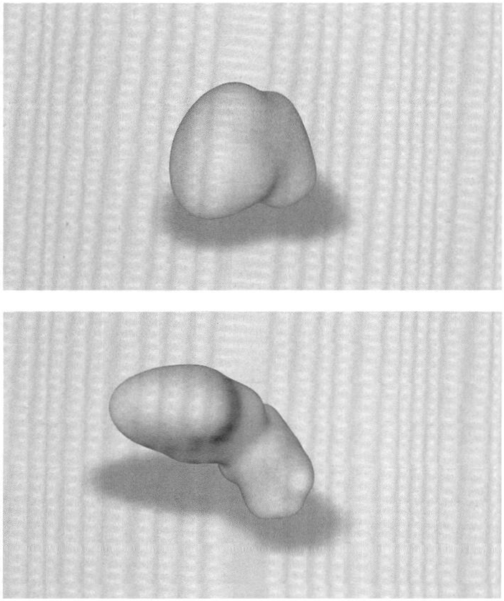

Merce's isosurface, Golan Levin, 2009, United States.

GOLAN LEVIN: We have 30,000 years of looking at flat images. And we have long histories of visual vocabularies, and writing and graphic systems. I think we're really lucky now to have these lightweight flat screens that we can carry around, that are also time-based. I don't mean to take away from the value of producing physical forms, and pavilions, and 3D printed objects, and *blobjects*... These are all important things to do, and I also do them — not pavilions, but 3D printed things. And I think that we look at things and we also move around in the world and we hold things and they are right there: images, buildings, and objects. Those are all part of the built environment that we have made for ourselves. Each of these has its own logic, and they also intersect nowadays in really complex and interesting ways.

DANA CUPKOVA: My three pieces in the exhibition are completely different, yet kind of connected by an aesthetics of the code, more than by the code itself. I tried to actually remove the screen from the experience of them — especially with the lenticular print, which is generated through an incredible amount of data. If you haven't seen it physically in a gallery, you cannot really understand how it operates, because an image on a screen does not allow you to read each layer singularly depending on your position. You have to walk around it to understand. But there is no "right" way of looking at it, and you can never actually read the entirety of the information it offers. It stays somewhat unrevealed. I was interested in this little interplay, which deals with how architecture and design workflows are overwhelmed by information. How do we do things right? We had this conversation yesterday. What is the "best"? How do you define what is most desirable? How do you define, access, and reason through large quantitative and qualitative data sets to define these? I think different approaches to these questions are evident through the history of computational design. The curation of the historical part of the show seems quite brilliant, as we start looking at the removal of the effect itself; the embracing of gestures, experience, and physical form, through numerical encodings; Chuck Eastman's early formulation of BIM models; the emphasis on production logics; and how we use computation to create something uncanny.

MADELINE GANNON: The only thing I could add is that in my practice, my engagement with screens really comes in the debugging stages. That's where the abstract geometry that communicates to my machines are. And if I do my job right, I'm able to take my training as an architect — my hypersensitivity to how people interact in space — and translate that into a machine, so hopefully the boundary between the digital and physical goes away, and you see that this abstract geometry actually occupies our built environment with us.

ANDREW HEUMANN: With respect to the screen, I've always been somewhat ambivalent. On the one hand, I can't think without a screen. A screen has been attached to my person for as long as I've been doing any sort of creative work — it is the native medium of what I do. But I also can't deny the difference with the physical artifact. The thing that escapes from the a screen-based image — even if it's pretending to be a painting — is this implicit effort, or energy, which is the product of the physical materials, but also of the time, involved in having something printed. Even if all I do is go online, upload my file, and then receive it a couple weeks later as a canvas print. I love the dif-

3D visualization of the Virtual Trading Floor for the New York Stock Exchange (NYSE), Asymptote Architecture, Virtual New York Stock Exchange (3DTF), 2000. Image Courtesy of Hani Rashid and Lise Anne Couture.

ference between that canvas print in the image that generated it.

MOLLY WRIGHT STEENSON: For some reason that makes me think of the Bruno Latour and Steve Woolgar's account of what scientists really do — and what they really do in the end is to write papers. If you were a space alien watching what was going on, maybe that's the conclusion you would draw. And you know, maybe at the end of it, it's that these screens were really the important thing — and not the robots, and not anything else. So, the work that I've presented by Asymptote has been funny because people have begged me not to take it seriously.[3] I've been told to go look at something else. I've been told Rashid was a blowhard anyway — and, you know, you should actually look at other people who are in the Paperless Studio at that point in time. But I am in love with that weird image with the ribbons, and the strange perspective. I really want to look hard at what it was. And I like this idea of the space between the quantitative and qualitative. Whether that's an architectural question, or whether that's a design question where people get all heated up over the distance and similarities between those two.

Madeline mentioned human-centered design in her talk and over in the School of Design, where I reside, that is so central to what we think of ourselves as doing, and how we produce people. Our notions of research are so bound up in that, that if we leave out the human centeredness we got nothing for what we do in my building over there. And it's a little problematic, because there is a lot to say about the space between the quantitative and qualitative. There's a lot to say about the missing history of human-centered design and architecture that fell out around 1989. But it was absolutely there at the beginning of robotics, and in Design Methods in the late '60s. The emergence of the environmental design movement in schools like Berkeley and Yale with programs like the Master of Environmental

3 Molly Wright Steenson's presentation focused on an image of the design of the virtual floor for the NYSE developed by the New York architectural firm Asymptote (Pictured above). See "Virtually Material: Architecture, Media, and the New Economy, 1997–2003," *Perspecta 51: Media*, Yale School of Architecture Journal (2018).

Design. But that started out as being sociology, and technology, and architecture. So there is a lot to say about the screens. And I think there is a lot to say about the world where people in the School of Design creep over into the School of Architecture, or the School of Planning. I think that it's difficult and important in architecture, at least to consider the status of that screen and what it is and what it's doing and what it's done at different points in time.

FELECIA DAVIS: I'd like to open the panel up to questions from the floor, are there any questions from the floor?

JAVIER ARGOTA SÁNCHEZ-VAQUERIZO: You have been covering the uncanny aspects of coding. Emergence is unexpected. Do you think "emergence" can be coded? Or does it just depend on the observer?

MADELINE GANNON: I can tap into this idea of emergent behavior. I think Dana and I use simulation in very different ways. In Dana's work it's about understanding materials to make a better material world, and for me it's really an interaction design technique. I make simple rules for my virtual, or physical-mechanical creatures, so that they exhibit something like intelligent behavior — as Golan was pointing out. My role as the author of that system is to thread a balance between defining enough stuff that's interesting, and leaving enough things open-ended so I can engage with the system beyond my initial imagination of what I thought it could be.

DANA CUPKOVA: If you think of emergence as a moment where you discover novelty within a process or workflow, I think it is highly rooted within the cognitive framework of the one who is producing it. It typically relates to how constraints are set up — to a certain ideology, or parameter-space. For example, I'm doing a lot of studies using genetic algorithms for surface generation, which deal with very specific kinds of passive thermal behavior in buildings. There are a lot of patterns coming up in that process which I haven't thought of because the process is generative — and yet, it's highly constrained. So, I control the parameters, and within that field, you can come up with something which is probably surprising. This is very similar to Andrew's combinatorial design process producing infinite variations within a constraint field. I suppose this relates to scientific discovery, and to how fields are organized within a university — going back to Molly's comments. That's what we write papers on. This one thing which emerges, where you realize that certain things work differently than your presumptions. And I think that's where the similarity lies across our different kinds of work. Even though we use a similar framework, the constraint-sets are radically different, and our interests are different.

GOLAN LEVIN: In computation arts, it certainly seems that there's no question at all that emergence can be coded. We have fifty years of generative art, and in the last twenty or thirty we've seen a heavy use of simulation: systems that are surprising to us. I mean, just to take two quick examples, one is like a reaction diffusion situation where very small changes to parameters can produce very radically different kinds of patterns. Fish stripes, zebra patterns, leopard spots, and so forth, all emerging in different ways and with a great deal of variability. Another example is the sort of flocking algorithms Craig Reynolds has developed, where we are certainly able to create systems that appear to exhibit emergent behavior. Something I find interesting now is a kind of system that sits on top of these things, that is able to detect novelty. I'm thinking of a specific project I really liked by Mario Klingemann — he's an artist who uses neural networks and he's made this novelty detection machine. He feeds it images, and I mean millions of images — the entire British Library and all of Flickr and things like this — and the order that he feeds them in I guess ultimately preconditions it to understand what is sort of typical. As time goes on the neural network essentially gets more and more jaded. All right, it's like "Oh I've seen that," "seen that," "seen that"...

MADELINE GANNON: It's so human!

GOLAN LEVIN: It's a Twitter Bot. He's got this computer running all the time, feeding it more and more images, and when it sees an image that's different enough from what it's seen before, it tweets it. And it tweets some pretty weird images. They look like "whoa that's, that's... I haven't seen that before." And it's because it basically finds atypical things in these huge datasets. To me that's interesting. We have this kind of emergence already. After we've made these generative systems that produce infinite variations, how can we find the things that are atypical and unique, and sort of special to talk about? Maybe shitty, but still worth talking about.

ANDREW HEUMANN: There was a quote on Twitter on the relationship between emergence and generativity, and I am going to bastardize it. I don't remember who said it, but the point was something like: "Just the fact that you don't understand what your algorithm is doing doesn't make it generative." I actually think it's the opposite. Not understanding what your algorithm is doing is precisely what makes it generative. The extent to which you know you can build a mental model of a thing, or understand the space of what it's going to generate, is what makes it unsurprising to you. The capacity for novelty arises from introducing situations that you couldn't forecast or predict. That's why generative algorithms or reaction diffusion algorithms are used in generative design processes in the pursuit of novelty. I don't know about you, but I can't build a reaction diffusion model. I'm just building fairly procedural, step-based code that makes certain decisions at certain points, and introduces a degree of randomness. And I'm always trying to expand the extent to which a given algorithm will produce as many emergent, or novel effects as possible. But I measure that in terms of how many frames it takes to produce something that I want to see? When do I get bored with the output of one of these generative processes?

Abstraction II (Unsmooth), Andrew Heumann, 2011, United States.

MOLLY WRIGHT STEENSON: There's a letter that John Frazer wrote to Cedric Price — it's actually a handwritten note on the typed correspondence. I don't have it in front of me right now, but more or less it says, "you seem to imply that one thing that you would expect from any half decent plan is that you get at least one thing that you didn't expect." The nature of intelligence plays out in that lack of expectation. That's why Cedric Price hired these two computer programmers, John and Julia Frazer, to work on his Generator project. To come up with a lens that people didn't expect. Because he couldn't do it on his own.

GOLAN LEVIN: When I think about intelligence, I certainly have no way to tell anyone what it is. But I know what it isn't: the automation of routine tasks. In many ways I think that the job of artificial intelligence is to create surprise for us and to me this goes right back to the very title of the [1968] exhibition Cybernetic Serendipity. It's about using these kinds of machines to produce serendipitous things. Things that surprise us.

AUDIENCE MEMBER: I have a kind of unfair or annoying question, framed in terms of a metaphor, and would like to ask you to step into it. I wanted to see computation through the lens of nature, and particularly through a problematic understanding of nature in opposition to humans. How most attitudes towards nature have been about harnessing it — to domesticate animals, make pets, create artificial landscapes, and so on — and how this translates to technological comfort pets and technological landscapes. Or to encoding fractals or physics to do interesting things like form finding. I am wondering how you approach it, and what other metaphors you see, or what other parts of the landscape of nature do you see that don't seem to be yet accessed by computation and automation.

GOLAN LEVIN: I'll give a brief stab. I think an alternative is to sidestep the reproduction of nature altogether. There's a huge strain in the arts of creating the illusion of life — whether it's in an animation, a romantic landscape painting, or a Greek statue. All of these things are producing some copy of the great master right? Nature herself or itself. And there's an entirely different realm — of symbols, and dreams. And I think to sidestep into that place is to not be interested in reproducing nature at all. It's the difference between doing documentation and imagination — so, to not feel like one needs to create a verisimilitude but rather to explore symbols which are I think uniquely ours.

MADELINE GANNON: From my point of view technology, like nature, is often in our service. In the work that I do, I am trying to explore how we flip that on its head. If you guys have been around Pittsburgh before, or maybe on your wanderings these past couple days, perhaps you have seen some of the driverless cars on the street. Those are large machines that could crush you; we have no legibility into what is behind their mind. But they are already out of the lab and in the wild, living with us. We have no way of negotiating that relationship. We have no agency in that. In the work that I do, sometimes I describe the robots as having a puppy-like excitement. But they can also be very intimidating. They can seem like bears when they loom over your head. And that flight or fight mechanism can be a useful thing if this machine is about to do something dangerous. These machines are entering into a world with their own agenda. In a way I hope for these machines to sort of coexist with us, rather than necessarily having to collaborate with us, or being our servants. And that's just how I try to think about it.

DANA CUPKOVA: The definition of nature has shifted quite radically in the last twenty years, from both cognitive and scientific standpoints, with the emergence, or acceptance, of the anthropocene. Especially, if you're dealing with the built environment, you have to recognize those natural processes. There is an ideological position about how these processes should be utilized within a design process. What I do in my design studios is to give my students an overview of environmental-ethical positions and philosophies, and ask them what the architecture would look like through a deep ecology model versus a Marxist materialist model, and explore this range materially and computationally. And the answers are radically different.

MOLLY WRIGHT STEENSON: I think this question allows us to ask something about subjects in architecture — and this goes back to a conversation I was having at dinner last night with Kristy Balliet. If you look at the turn toward technology, or the turn toward visualization, in architecture, you see how object's positions, and not so much the subjects', are privileged. Subjects are difficult because we have to talk about people, and gender, and race, and class, and haves, and have nots, and oppression. When we start dealing with subjects and — I wonder — with metaphors about different kinds of intelligence, we actually have an opportunity to confront those issues. We have an opportunity to confront lines of subjectivity. What is subjective intelligence? A subjective objectivity? What do we believe the object to possess?

ANDREW HEUMANN: That raises something really interesting for me. I think that working algorithmically predisposes you to operate on objects, because the entire field of programming is dominated by the object oriented programming paradigm. Perhaps someone else has said this before, but what would a "subject-oriented programming" look like? Maybe that's one of these domains or territories in the ecology or nature that is programming, that is under-explored or under-investigated.

FELECIA DAVIS: I love what you just said. I want to see that happen. So, maybe on that note I would like to close the conversation and thank the presenters.

Feminist Embodiments of Interactivity: A Conversation with Elizabeth Vander Zaag

Moderated by
Gabriela Aceves-Sepúlveda

GABRIELA ACEVES-SEPÚLVEDA: Thank you, Daniel and Theodora, for inviting me.[1] It's such an interesting conversation. Before I introduce Elizabeth Vander Zaag, I want to acknowledge that I'm connecting from the unceded territories of the Coast Salish peoples, the Musqueam, the Squamish and Tsleil-Waututh nations, what is known as Vancouver, British Columbia. I am very honored to be part of this conversation and it is my pleasure to introduce to you Elizabeth Vander Zaag. I am going to read a little of her bio, but her work is so extensive that I am not going to be able to cover everything that she has done. She has been working in video and computer arts since the 1970s. Her practice combines video, computer graphics, and performance to construct an aesthetic language that describes women's lives through technology. She received a BA in English and Film from the University of Western Ontario, and briefly studied creative electronics at Fanshawe College in London, Ontario and Computer Arts at Simon Fraser University. She has been based in Vancouver since the mid-'70s and has an extensive exhibition history internationally. She founded and coordinated the Western Front multimedia school from 1993 to 1999, where she trained other artists in the uses of video technology.

1 Panel discussion at the Computational Design: Practices, Histories, Infrastructures Symposium (Edited for length and clarity), Carnegie Mellon University, October 2017.

She has lectured and given many workshops across Canada and the United States since the 1980s. Her research on the visual sense of language to explore subjective and cultural sensibilities through interactive systems is published in her book *Mother Tongue: A Study of Participant Affect in an Interactive Installation*, which was published by Verlag in 2011. We are going to be a bit casual with this presentation.Elizabeth is going to be showing us a lot of her work. I am just going to prompt her with some initial questions, and we will see how the conversation goes from there.

I would like to start by asking you, Elizabeth, about the relationship between the content and the technique of your work. And more specifically, on how you began to develop your own software and your own systems in your work starting in the 1980s. I am thinking, for example, of the custom software that you developed for *Whispering Pines* interactive videos.

ELIZABETH VANDER ZAAG: I was working at the Western Front, and there were two fellows called Spencer Cavey and Kai Goodwin, who were actually the ones that were developing the software. I was there cheering them along and participating in every step of the way without really offering anything in the realm of coding. This was before you could do menu-driven computer things: you had to do everything with batch files in DOS. In order to create a sequence of images, you would just change one or two values, because otherwise you had to do so many repetitive sentences. So I think that kind of programming environment made it so that we didn't do drastic changes, we just watched for very subtle changes over a sequence of 100 frames or something similar; just tiny little variations. I did a piece called *Whispering Pines*, after having done a lot of time with these batch files, embossing the lines of images.What I was looking at was aging. In the tree, for instance, the rings show its age. And of course, with a woman, her skin also reflects time. I found this kind of commonality, this point of transformation between the tree and the human. So I created these MS-DOS sequences. That is the intro-

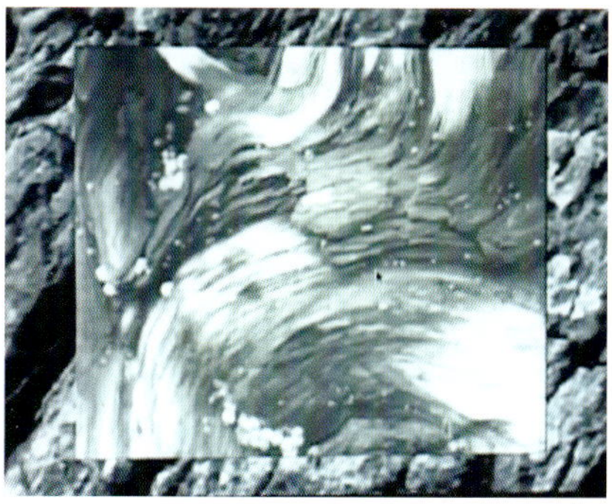

Screenshot from *Whispering Pines* (1993) shown by the artist at *Digital.Visual.Material.*

duction to the first nonlinear work I did in 1995. The music is played by a wonderful musician called George Lewis. It is a Johnny Horton song called *Whispering Pines*, which, of course, he found very amusing to play. The nonlinear narrative was an important part of this project. Initially, I think, most of the early computer games, like *Myst*, were really about geography, about going to different places and moving through walls and changing where you are going. That was one of the first metaphors for nonlinear narratives that I can remember and that's what inspired me to work *Whispering Pines* that way.

GABRIELA ACEVES-SEPÚLVEDA: You were part of a group of people who were developing, testing, experimenting with new technologies and you were also thinking about aging and how the MS-DOS filter reflected the life of a woman in her 40s. How did your work influence or impact those conversations as those developers were working on software? There must have been very interesting dialogues and sharing of ideas. I don't know if you want to speak to that?

ELIZABETH VANDER ZAAG: I would say that it was really exciting, because it wasn't just me that was doing this work. They kept tweaking and changing the software because I was always using it. And then other people came along and wanted to do a completely different type of project. And then we could use the software for that. There was constant experimentation, because the Western Front was a center for all kinds of artists. So, yes, it was very collaborative, and everybody had a different way of using it [the software].

GABRIELA ACEVES-SEPÚLVEDA: Let's turn to how your work deals with the question of materiality, which we already started thinking about through the question of aging. I want to talk about materiality in a very broad way, related to both how your life seeps into your work, and also the access to the technology that you had at that particular time. How do you translate those lived experiences into your work and how does the digital, the computer, mediate such relationships? I am thinking here, for example, of your other works, that had to do with the female voice, and particularly *Talking Back* and *Talk Nice*, for which you also participated in the development of a custom software. Right?

Screenshot from *Talking Back* (1996) shown by the artist at *Digital.Visual.Material.*

ELIZABETH VANDER ZAAG: This was still at Western multimedia training. We had funding from the government that allowed us to buy technological equipment. So, we had access to things, plus we had all these really interesting people that would come from the industry and from the arts to give workshops and show us how to do different things. I remember in the '90s, we didn't think the Internet was going to be as big as it was. We thought it was just going to be interactivity that was the key thing. The Internet sort of came along, slipped up on us so to speak. Remember there was a software called *Dragon* for text to speech and speech to text? You would have to speak in a certain way so that the computer could understand you. Well, that apparently causes carpal tunnel syndrome of the throat, believe it or not, because naturally our voices are used to going in very large dynamic ranges. They are built for that. I felt that we were doing the wrong thing. We were thinking about the computer as a prosthetic device, like an extension substituting for part of ourselves. I thought let's look at the computer as a filter, a way to look in more detail at our humanity, our voice, the different functions of our bodies. So, I looked at the tone, the prosody, of the voice. Part of that, of course, happens being a mother and becoming aware of the tone of your voice when you are interacting with your child. So, I did this project [*Talking Back*]. It wasn't simple, actually, because we had to get a sound into a sound analysis tool, which was then a program that we used to create interactive projects called *Director*. The main thing that it was looking at was amplitude. That's pretty easy to pull out of a speech signal. We divided amplitude into five different segments. Under each one of those levels of amplitude, there were about ten different responses by the user. These are video clips that were then pulled up by the *Director* program, when the user had a voice that was within those parameters of volume. I used it to get a kid to do the dishes, which is always a challenge. The loop between the interactive experience using the computer to help you look at yourself was a really interesting way to experience interactivity as a way to put a lens on ourselves, instead of creating an external prosthetic and external device — as a way of externalizing ourselves.

One of the things that I have discovered with the flow that happens when you're in an interactive situation, is the reflective ability of the system to feed back into your reality. This is something that we don't really consider that much, but I think it is an important part of what I discovered from this work. When you're making these projects, you're just trying to make them work. And then we suddenly have this embedded tool within our systems that helps us observe and analyze human behaviors. Whether that is something that we want to do or not, it is fairly powerful that these tools allow people to explore what the affect of the user is. It's exciting to have this feedback about your presence, about what your state of mind is. We are also at a place where we could be severely manipulated by having that awareness be out there for other systems to analyze.

This idea put me into another project around sound and socialization of young women called *Talk Nice*. This involved a more complex piece of software. I was able to develop it so robustly because Sarah Diamond had a fabulous project at the Banff Centre for the Arts, which I was successful in gaining access to. *Talk Nice* was facilitated by some of the software people at the Banff Centre for the Arts, and also by programmers that I brought from Vancouver. I was able to take the voice analysis to another level. At this point, we are dealing with the detection of the end of phrase, and then backing up just a fraction, to see if there's a change in pitch going up. It was fairly complicated but as soon as we got the end-of-phrase, it wasn't too hard to quickly backtrack and see whether or not the pitch was going up. So, not only pitch detection but end of phrase.

Talk Nice was shown in quite a few different countries in the world, such as South Korea and São Paulo, Brazil, because the Banff Center has such a big reach. I was really interested in the very different ways the piece was perceived in different places and the kinds of interactions that took place. I realized that language and culture had a lot to do with speech. This is probably what brought me to the next piece, *Mother Tongues*. So, the show that *Talk Nice* was part of in São Paulo was called *Emoción Artificial* and it was about the place of affect in computer interaction. This had to be brought to attention, it had to be like "let's talk about emotion in computer interaction." For some reason, affect — that kind of emotional human component — has to be constantly emphasized in discussions on how we design our computer interactions. I think that's really difficult even now, because we're limiting ourselves all the time, every time we come up with a new technology. Emoticons are like this. In the future, when we look back at emoticons, we'll say, "those poor people that couldn't even express happiness or anything, they had to do a smiley face." I just feel like our bandwidth of affect has really been narrowed down through our technology. Of course, technology has helped us because we've been able to interact right now, for instance, in a cold, non-geographic coexistence. But at the same time, I think we're missing a lot of the gestures and a lot of the affect that we could have if we were in the same room with each other. And then, one of the things that this project [*Talk Nice*] led to, for me, was an idea about the embodiment of language: that it's performed physically by your body and that your body and your emotions are linked. Neuroscientists like Antonio Damasio have really established those connections but we've never really looked at it in terms of the production of language. There are many theories around language embodiment. But one of the things that I took away from further research into this area was that once you start looking at the materiality of sound, you can really start to look at the different ways that sounds are made. For instance, I took apart the Frisian language, which is my mother's and grandmother's language, so it would be my mother tongue but I don't even know how to speak it. I analyzed it in a speech lab and I examined

Screenshot from Talk Nice (2000) shown by the artist at *Digital.Visual.Material.*

the vowels by externalizing them into a picture, into a spectrograph. I could see that Frisian uses more variations between two, three, or four vowels in a row, whereas our languages tend to have a constant pattern of consonant-vowel-consonant-vowel, or two vowels, or something like that. So, I talked about a lot of different things in this piece [*Mother Tongues*]. And I talked to many people with many different languages. We did spectrographic displays on that. People were able to perform different languages by trying to copy the spectrographic display of the sound samples of different languages. And people did experience that they had *flow*, what [Nicole] Lazzaro calls "the flow" in the gaming environment. But at same time, they also said they had a different feeling — a different affect — during the experience of these different languages. I just wanted to play one tiny little clip of Sally Lee talking about what speaking your mother tongue and speaking English was for her as an experience.

[VIDEO OF SALLY LEE] *Even though English is something that I use on a daily basis, it's quite secondhand [inaudible]. Still, it's way more logical when I am speaking another language other than my mother tongue. But at the same time, when I'm expressing something, when I'm talking in Cantonese, sometimes it can be too overwhelming for me that I find that it will be easier to use another language to express something that might be too personal.*

ELIZABETH VANDER ZAAG: I think that may be true for many people. I just like the way she said that, but I also wanted to show you the spectrograph and how her words become so material. I think, shifting towards materiality is something that we can do by parsing out the realities that are around us all the time. Being able to parse those out and tease out those things that are invisible, we can have a greater understanding and sympathize with what we are in our world, how we exist here. I do like that part about the digital and the material: the digital can tease out material that we don't necessarily see or hear. But with the digital manifestation of it, by recalculating or syntactically repurposing it into something that we can acknowledge to our other senses, I think we

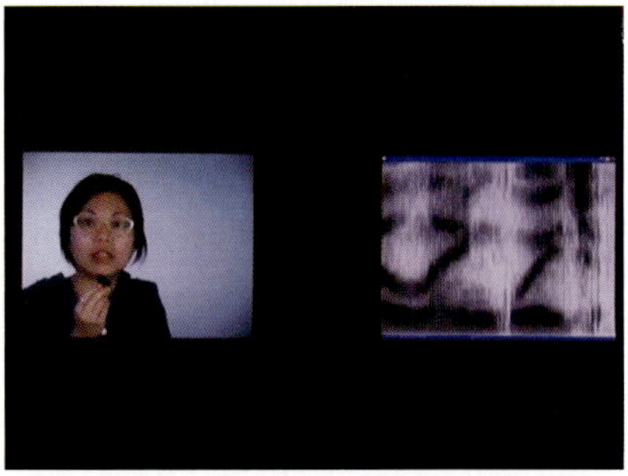

Screenshot from video of Sally Lee shown by the artist at *Digital.Visual.Material.*

are getting a wider awareness of ourselves. I enjoyed that piece for doing that. There are other artists that do these things, too. I really like the idea that there are ephemeral things around us that we don't know, but artists can pull those out. It really speaks to me when those ephemeral things take a piece of imagery. For instance, there is something out there, such as the information that's going through our air right now, on our Internet. Some artists have visualized that in different ways, and it's just so interesting to see that. So, that's sort of the digital-material transformational idea that I like.

GABRIELA ACEVES-SEPÚLVEDA: I want to ask you more about sound. I find it fascinating how you're thinking about affect and emotions and how, in your work, sound has played a very important role since the beginning. I know that you have been working on new projects that have to do with sound and the translation of sound into material and I would like to prompt you to talk about those.

Elizabeth Vander Zaag weaving at the textile art society in Vancouver.

ELIZABETH VANDER ZAAG: Well, I don't know how many people here are digital artists, because it is one of the most frustrating mediums to work with. The work that I have done that will be at the [*Vers un imaginaire numérique*] show are two videos [*Digit and Baby Eyes*]. The videos I made, thanks to great nonprofit societies that work with me and distributors. They have moved it to beta, and backed it up and moved it over to an archive, and updated the archive every ten years. Those media have to be updated and then archived again. However, *Whispering Pines* is sitting here on a mini-Mac. And suddenly, you need to have a USB mouse and a USB keyboard and some sort of monitor as well, but I don't have those things. So, *Whispering Pines* is sitting on a mini-Mac, but I don't have a way to put it out. I could do it if I needed to. For example, I showed it at a gallery in 2014 and the person there managed to get it off the CD-ROM that it was on, put it through emulator software for gaming, and put it on an operating system that no longer exists. So, the whole problem with digital art is that the operating systems, the archiving systems, the connectors, everything goes away, and you lose it, it's gone! *Talking Back* and *Talk Nice* just exist in that tiny little document that you see. The thing that frustrates me is the materiality of the actual artwork. One of the first thoughts I had when Daniel and Theodora invited me to participate here was that the materiality of the digital artwork is such a problem. However, this challenge is being tackled — later on I'd like to talk a little bit about NFTs [non-fungible tokens] and how artwork exists completely in the digital realm.

But one of the things I did as a result of that, and also because I really liked the idea of doing this, was a project with the Jacquard loom. There was a textile art society in Vancouver that had [a Jacquard loom], and I would have access to workshops on how to use it. I'm going to just share some pictures of this. I wanted to talk a little bit about the material of weaving that is a manifestation of what's still a material signal — a spectrograph.

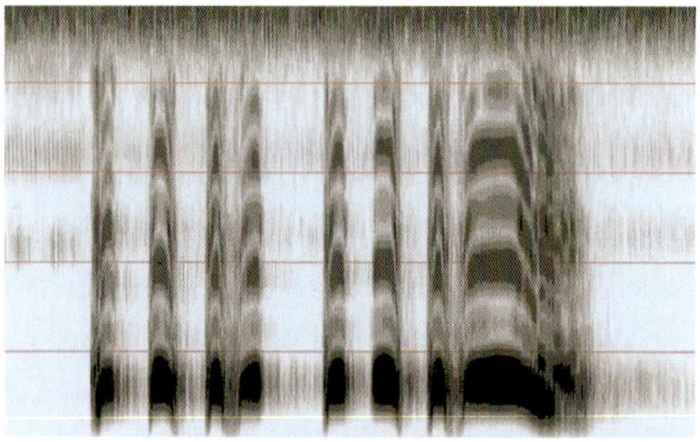

Spectrograph used by the artist to produce a weaving pattern.

These are sound signals, this is just a test. The complexity of the digital signal source provides a great texture, image rhythms and content. This is a Jacquard loom, which has a computer running the spectrographic image that I've processed through software, and then it's on the computer which is on the left of there. And then it tells the little threads, which ones have to come down. So, all I have to do is the shuttle, the bar and the shuttle that I'm holding in my left hand there. This is a way to sort of preserve your digital moment. And I find this to be really interesting. I really love the low-resolution factor of this, each line takes a little while to do. I like the way that it turns into a tangible thing, the most tangible work I've ever made. And there's Ruth [working in the Art society] dyeing the thread so that we can have the blue instead of black because it's the black and white, generally black and white.

I've been working with bird song. This is the sound of an eagle and this is its spectrograph when I've reduced it to ten points. Then you have to put it in Photoshop and attach weave patterns to it. And this is the eagle sound, which is the little jiggly part in the back there. I've also got one here of an owl, which is coming up in a second here. And then the crickets are at the top there, those crickets that you hear. And then you have your process that again, reducing it.

This is so different from the high-resolution initiatives that are being done in technology. This is so low-res that it's unbelievable. But it doesn't photograph well, I have to say. Because it's material, it doesn't translate photographically back into the digital screen very well, in my opinion. So, that's the project I've been working on for the last little while. I also really like the fact that it comes out of the Jacquard loom. The Jacquard loom was really the very first iteration of the punch card. And what was it used for? For making fabric, for doing the weaving to supplant labor, but also to create repetitive patterns — you have the Jacquard pattern, which is this kind of repetitive pattern. I'm still looking for the actual link between the concept of the loom to create a piece that would reflect that. Right now, I'm taking content from somewhere else, which is the birdsong, and a concern about environment, and applying that to the loom. I'm trying hard to find what would be the lovely synthesis between the concept of the Jacquard loom and the weaving that would do it. I'm really looking forward to seeing Jer Thorpe's weaving in the exhibition you're having this fall, because he said he was using data sets to generate the imagery. Also, I was really interested in Joanna Berzowska's work at Concordia University with the tactile fabrics. I wasn't going to put this into the talk, but then after I saw that, I think there's a theme here. I think we're starting to go back to more organic materials and ways to work with technology, because we don't necessarily want to always work with this high-res environment.

GABRIELA ACEVES-SEPÚLVEDA: It's fascinating to think about your work in retrospect, how you started by being interested to make images with the electronic signal that had no apparent materiality and now you are going back all the way to actually making things that are real, material, and thinking about the issues that we have with archiving and preserving digital art, and how the actual thing that stays with us longer, when thinking about archives, is the paper rather than the digital file. Fascinating. I don't know if there's anyone in the audience that wants to make a comment on the recent pieces on textiles and the Jacquard loom and the translation between the audio and the textile? Oh, there's a question from the audience about how games influence your work; following your reference to the game *Myst* and the term "flow" as it is used in game design.

ELIZABETH VANDER ZAAG: I found that the only way to describe interactive experiences from an academic point of view was by going back to games. I think the people that are talking about flow, in terms of when people get involved with playing games, have a better understanding of what's going on. One of those people was [Nicole] Lazzaro and she was employed in the gaming industry to talk about flow. The game *Myst* was when we were doing the Western Front multimedia training in the 1990s. So, of course, we had really early pieces. And this was one of the really important games for our students to look at because it had this sort of navigational branching that was quite sophisticated at the time. But other than that, I haven't done too much computer gaming. I'd like to, I'd love to find a new game to play. Right now, I think it's called gambling, or you know, those kinds of things that people do online with numbers.

GABRIELA ACEVES-SEPÚLVEDA: I know that you have been doing a lot of research on NFTs, bitcoins, and blockchains. Earlier in the symposium, we talked about the possible futures that artists can show us. On the one hand, you're going back to the material of the textile when computers just began, and on the other side, you're thinking about NFTs and blockchain. Perhaps you could talk about that.

ELIZABETH VANDER ZAAG: I think technology is always inventing itself and that's why it's so interesting. I always like to be involved in something when it's coming about. I think no one had any idea in the '70s that digital technology would be what it is. When I was doing the digital stuff in the '70s people were like, "why would you do that?" I worked at CBC [Canadian Broadcasting Corporation], I was the first digital video operator because nobody wanted to do it, because it was just punching up and pulling stuff out of addresses. It wasn't analog enough. I think this next stage that we're seeing here with the blockchain is really going to change the way the web functions — they call it Web 3. And I've read some places like Africa are going to adopt blockchain before they get all the other types of systems. And I think in terms of materiality, honestly, we want to change what we're seeing right now. I'm just gonna spend a few minutes just reading some stuff, if that's okay. So I'm saying here: "We are limited by our senses as to what we perceive to be material. So, there's lots of layers of material that we can't perceive. So, the energy and tangible math has to be made into something for us to perceive. However, now we're getting this whole other kind of tangible math, which has a value associated to it, which is called cryptocurrency. And another question is whether the online world of value and the analog world of fiat [currency] will remain distinct routes. That hasn't been through the Internet. Broadly, the distinction between meatspace and cyberspace has broken down very nearly completely, except in extreme cases, online life is just life. That said, most people spend most of their time on platforms like YouTube, Facebook, newspapers, Zoom, and that presents a unified structure, a top of the chaos of the worldwide web." And I really find the interesting thing about the fact that now it's almost completely gone away from any kind of physical fiat [currency]. We're seeing an emergence of these NFTs, which is kind of revolutionizing the art world a little bit because it reflects the financialization of art, which is really what's been going on in the last while, at least since the 1970s and '80s. And so, it's really just saying "Oh, yes, it's just about money." But they're not actually things. I don't really understand the medium yet. I'm really working on it everyday researching, and there's tons of material out there.

I've just wanted to bring an artist to your attention, who I think is fabulous. Her name is Sarah Meyohas and she's only thirty years old. And she's got a project called *BitchCoin*, which she started in 2014. Now remember, Bitcoin only was invented in 2010, or something. And so, she was like before *Ethereum*, which is the second biggest crypto out there. So, she was early. There was a friend of hers who had a gallery in Brooklyn, which was just a shipping container, she painted it bright pink, and then she filled it with computers and generated her own *BitchCoin*. Just the agency of that for a young woman, I love it. And right now she's in an auction with these *BitchCoins*, because this is called making money with art. And she did a piece in 2017 called *Cloud of Petals*. That piece was a project at the Bell Labs that she took over, and they photographed 100,000 rose petals, and then she has approximately 3,000 petals in storage in a vault someplace where each person had to pick out one petal from each flower. So, the *BitchCoin* that you're going to buy at an auction right now, which is running for the next three days, will be reflecting a token for one of those actual real material, rose petals, which are in storage, and you don't actually get them. It is uniquely establishing the symbiotic value of token and backing. The backing part is the part that is material at this point, but how much longer will it be material, how much longer will we have NFTs, cryptocurrency, anything that has a relationship with anything material? I think that in ten years, we will not have a material reference to the things that we consider to be an asset, or intrinsic value. I think that's really a shift from the kind of weavings and the kind of projects that we've done. Of course, I don't know anything about this at this point in time. I'm just learning. But I'm telling you, I think there is a great deal of confusion with what it is really and what is mathematics. I think we've seen this complete rise of this and it has got to be the most mathematical thing there is. And of course, it takes a great deal of energy. So, one of the weirdest NFT projects would be an NFT project that said, "Oh, it's so bad to have climate change, you've got to do something about energy" and then put it as an NFT. That would be an oxymoron. I think these are issues that are being resolved. And we've become very aware of our energy usage. These things are bringing it to light, but I don't think we're going to go to fiat currency. Or can I think art is going to change to be tokens that point at something, maybe an experience, maybe a performance. It won't necessarily be an artifact. I don't know where I'm going to fit into this space. I haven't figured that out.

GABRIELA ACEVES-SEPÚLVEDA: It's a very interesting space and very rapidly moving, so it's hard to keep up with what's happening. But it also made me think about the common perception of digital technology not being material. And I know that there are several people in the audience thinking about how the digital is linked to the material. And it has always been like that. But our capitalist economy is built on abstractions currency being one example; we're extracting resources from the earth to be able to fund those abstractions. So, I am wondering what would happen if we unplugged the servers and you know, we cut out the service so that cryptocurrency and NFTs don't exist anymore. Then we would have to go back to our embodied experiences. I see a recurrence here, wanting us to think that the digital is completely abstract, that it's creating different things that there's no material backing, but there's always the material back-end, it's just always being obscured from us.

ELIZABETH VANDER ZAAG: **Except if you heat your house with all the computers that are churning out the numbers. [Laughs] I would be very interested to see if there's more artists working in this space [cryptocurrency], I would really like to find out more about it. I'll do more research on that area. I think it's really something new. So far, it's turning everybody into artists, by the sounds of things.**

DANIEL CARDOSO LLACH: I have a question, Liz. First of all, thank you so much, it was so wonderful to hear you talk about your work. You talked about the digital as extending or tracing part of our lives and interactions and, in that process, allowing us to learn something about ourselves. I found that very compelling and very powerful. My question has to do with the changing conditions of technological interactions today. In these wonderful pieces, you use sound processing, or image processing, to stage interactive moments that are so incredibly full of life, and unexpected, and beautiful. Do you see new potentials emerging for interaction in an artistic context connected to things like facial recognition, or machine learning algorithms, and other data intensive processes?

ELIZABETH VANDER ZAAG: That's a really good point. It was in 2000 that I was looking at these things. But now I actually feel that if I change my face in some way, the computer will see it, and it will feed me some advertising. I have become very nervous about the openness I had in the 1990s and 2000s to the computer giving us information about ourselves so that we could expand our understanding of our relationships and our interactions with other people and various aspects of our being. I am afraid that the next period of time will be one of hiding. When the Internet started, it was sort of a response to mainstream media, which broadcast one central voice. It was about decentralization and many voices. My feeling right now is that anytime someone comes up with a technology that can parse a little bit about ourselves, it will be picked up so quickly by a technology company that wants to exploit it.

DANIEL CARDOSO LLACH: I think I am with you. I grapple with how to engage creatively with technologies that so often seem to support surveillance or advertisements; with infrastructures that are geared toward governing rather than liberating.

ELIZABETH VANDER ZAAG: Maybe I will engage with these technologies in my work again but in a hiding kind of a way.

GABRIELA ACEVES-SEPÚLVEDA: Interesting. Maybe your turn to textiles is a way of hiding.

ELIZABETH VANDER ZAAG: That's why I'm really curious to see what artists are doing in the digital realm right now. I think blockchain is going to become a hiding place.

THEODORA VARDOULI: Liz, thank you so much, it's all so incredibly thought provoking. I had one particular curiosity about children when seeing the videos of them interacting with your work. There's always this sense of wonder and play. As a mother of young children, I keep thinking, is there space for that kind of interaction today in a world that's so saturated with digital media?

ELIZABETH VANDER ZAAG: I think because of the tiny little telephone, you go anywhere and you see people are sitting like this on their little tiny telephone. I think our tiny little viewpoints are very tight right now. I think kids are dying to explode out of their bodies and have more dimensionality. So, I don't know why the gestural interfaces haven't taken off. I remember, in HCI back in the '90s, the gestural stuff was so big. For example, the *Wii*, that's all physical. If the physical interaction comes back, kids are going to love it, I think.

GABRIELA ACEVES-SEPÚLVEDA: One would wonder if the exploration of interactivity through technology is turning now toward a more pessimistic tone. I'm thinking of the work of Kate Crawford and other artists, as well as students. I think that there's a more sobering discourse coming out from artists that is more critical in comparison to the '90s when it was more about exploring playfulness.

ELIZABETH VANDER ZAAG: I also think that the narratives change. When we first had interactive media, we were really experimenting with what the narrative could be. I don't think people are quite so interested in exploring that anymore. We are pretty happy with just going "click-click," because it's a functional thing in our lives. If I went to read the news, I would want the most direct link. What's going to happen is what Leslie [Mezei] was talking about yesterday: it will go right into our brain.

GABRIELA ACEVES-SEPÚLVEDA: I wonder if Leslie wants to say something.

LESLIE MEZEI: I'm an optimist who's having a hard time. Fifty years ago, I wrote about how we should make all major institutions, especially public institutions like universities, democratize access to technology like computers, especially to artists. And then we were talking about how to bring the "Two cultures" of C.P. Snow together. Now, it seems to be not just two cultures, but we've got more silos that we want to bring together. There's a huge number of organizations, some very small, some large, that are trying to make this a better world. I still hope that the artists can help.

GABRIELA ACEVES-SEPÚLVEDA: Oh, that's interesting that you have hope for artists, that's good. Artists and engineers together, that's the way it should be. And designers.

LESLIE MEZEI: A new renaissance!

ELIZABETH VANDER ZAAG: And educators. Educators have a big role in this because they are a little bit neutral from the commercial interests that are prevailing in technology at this point. A little bit neutral, not 100 percent.

I just want to make one last little point if that's okay. I think that the interactive social nature of digital media, our whole way of interacting the way we're doing currently, how much of our lives are spent interacting digitally, has changed the materiality of digital media. I think before it was more outside of us, an external thing, as you see in the early works I did. But now I think it's really changed the materiality. And my question is how to touch or sense the fabric of our social lives and the impact of digital technology on that? This is a question to myself or to anybody. That's a thought I'm having these days about what is the materiality, what is the sense of our social lives in this new mediated environment? I think there are many aspects of that that are hard to parse out, but I'm looking at it. That's one of the things I'm interested in right now. Which is why this symposium was good timing. This discussion has been pertinent to the times that we're in.

GABRIELA ACEVES-SEPÚLVEDA: I am also thinking about how we're all situated in different places, and all those different places have different regulations. It's interesting to think that when we think about digital mediation, not everyone has that same reality. There's so much in your work, Elizabeth, that needs to be addressed. There are so many layers and through your work one can trace a path of development of the technology, but also a very committed interest in thinking about our relation to it and how it manifests in our everyday lives.

Machine Misbehavior and Ethical Interfaces: A Conversation with Rachel Strickland and Paul Pangaro

Moderated by
Daniel Cardoso Llach

DANIEL CARDOSO LLACH: We are delighted to have Rachel Strickland and Paul Pangaro for today's final session.[1] Rachel Strickland works as an independent filmmaker, documentary videographer, interaction designer, inventor, and media artist. Since making documentary films with *cinéma vérité* pioneers Richard Leacock and Ed Pincus in the 1970s, her research and art have focused on cinematic dimensions of the sense of place, the animate and ephemeral dimensions of architectural space, and new paradigms for narrative construction in digital media, pursuing of a vision of "spontaneous cinema."[2] Paul Pangaro has been studying conversation and design, both human-human and human-machine, for over thirty years. His design practice, lectures, and writing have centered on designing for conversation and seeing design as conversation. His career spans roles as interaction designer, entrepreneur, researcher, performer, and professor — and I'm pleased that he's now a colleague of mine at Carnegie Mellon University, where he is Professor of the Practice in the Human-Computer Interaction Institute. We will start our conversation by seeing one piece from each of them showcased in the exhibition. The two pieces were both created in 1976, when Rachel and Paul were at MIT, in the orbit

1 *Digital.Visual.Material* Symposium, Virtual event, May 2021.

2 See https://spontaneouscinema.com/

3 The Architecture Machine Group was a research laboratory co-founded by Nicholas Negroponte and Leon Groisser at MIT in 1968. Initially focused on applications of computer technologies in architectural and urban design contexts, in the mid-1970s the group's research shifted towards broader questions concerning media, interactivity, and space. In 1985, the group transitioned into the MIT MediaLab.

of the Architecture Machine Group.[3] Rachel's is *Finger Film*, a 10-minute film she produced to document ArcMac's research on touch-sensitive displays. Paul's is the film *Stick Models*, which explored the expressive possibilities of computer graphics, also in 1976. These two films connect themes across our different sessions: they offer a glimpse of the postwar convergence of computer research and artistic exploration in research-funded laboratories at institutions like MIT — a subject other speakers have also hinted at. They also offer us an opportunity to think about issues of tactility and performance in early computer research, and about the work of staging and representing technological visions — evoking points made earlier about how computer art can be mobilized to radically different ends.

Let's start with the *Finger Film*. Rachel, one thing that I love about it is that it doesn't shy away from showing technologies' glitches and imperfections. You are looking at the development of some of the earliest touch sensitive displays, but instead of just documenting it, you also make an argument about tactility. Could you tell us a little more about the context of the film, how it was produced, and what you had in mind at the time?

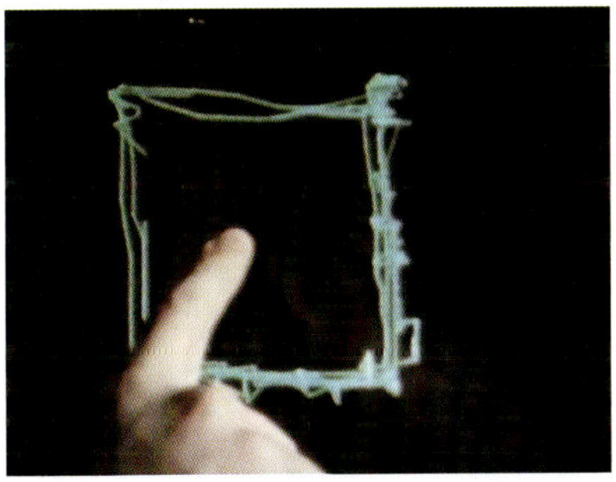

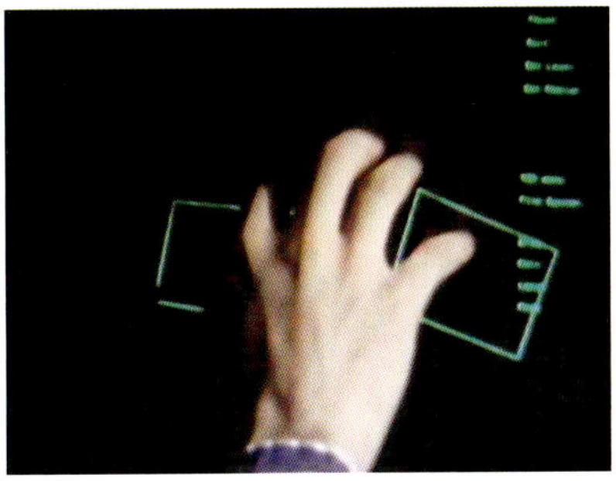

Stills from *Finger Film*, Rachel Strickland, 1976

RACHEL STRICKLAND: In the Annals of the Architecture Machine Group, there was something named SDMS (Spatial Data Management Systems) that Nicholas Negroponte regarded as key to making computers accessible to four-star generals and six-year-old children. The idea underlying SDMS was that we find things with our bodies in space, rather than filing them by names and keywords. Touch sensitive displays were one piece of this research agenda. Another grander and flashier one was something they called the "Media Room," which was a kind of military cockpit, outfitted with a large projection screen and instrumented with an Eames lounge chair. This room needed video programs that could be displayed when the generals and the corporate sponsors came to visit. For that purpose I was commissioned to make a short Super-8 film that would get viewers thinking about the potentials of haptic user interfaces. I'm not sure why Daniel has taken an interest in the *Finger Film*. It certainly got me into trouble at the time with the lab director, Nicholas Negroponte. I initially conceived it as a taxonomy of gesture, manipulation, and touch. It shouldn't have surprised me that Nicholas would, at some point in the process, decide that the movie should also showcase their prototype touchscreen technology. The trouble was that the prototype was unreliable and subject to crashing, and its primitive graphics looked like a mistake to any discerning observer. As an observational filmmaker focused on people's architectural transactions with machines and space, what intrigued me most was watching the researchers engage with this flaky prototype. It was when it misbehaved that it actually came to life: they started to talk to it, and bang on it, and coax it as if there were a sentient creature inside the box. This was exactly what Nicholas didn't want to see or share with the generals. What I was delivering seemed like reality TV, when the audience might have preferred something more along the lines of science fiction. So it's been sitting in the dark for a long time.

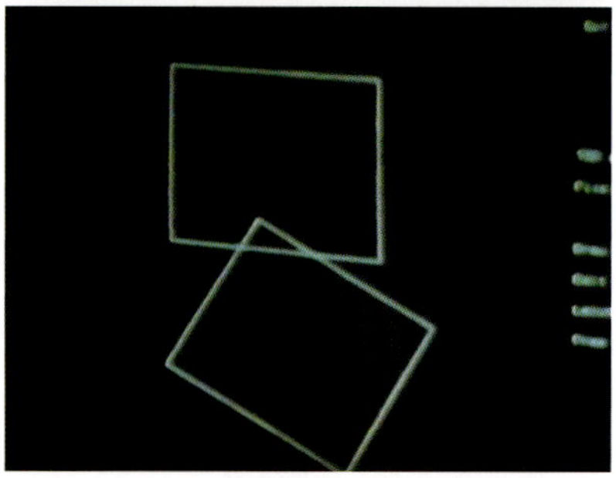

Stills from *Finger Film*, Rachel Strickland, 1976

DANIEL CARDOSO LLACH: That's perhaps one reason I've been so keen on including the *Finger Film* in the exhibitions: for me it has a critical sensibility that is rare in representations of technology coming from places like MIT and ArcMac — it's truly unique. Paul, you actually appear in the film. We hear your voice and see your hands, and I think we also see your reflection on the screen a few times. Could you also help us understand more of the project's context, and reflect on your participation?

PAUL PANGARO: Needless to say, it was a fascinating time. This device was one of the very earliest, if not the first prototype of something that you could touch, and register the points that you touched as XY coordinates. But — as Rachel was beautifully describing — it wasn't working very well: for example, the data rates were low and caused a lag between the user's touch and the display's response, among other things. It was imperfect. The idea was to experiment and to try to see what would happen with such a device. The nature of ArcMac, different from other labs making things for other people, was that we were the users. I think Nicholas would say that this was the main idea behind the Media Lab, although that may be an oversimplification too. The idea was to mount the display on pressure sensitive sensors — so-called "strain gauges." The harder you pushed, the greater the pressure it would register. We take it for granted today, but at the time it was completely from outer space! But it was an experiment and it didn't always work. We came in in the mornings and we tried to see what it would do. And then we kept going and tried to incrementally improve it. At the time, we thought of it more as sci-fi, even though in fact it was far from that, as Rachel pointed out.

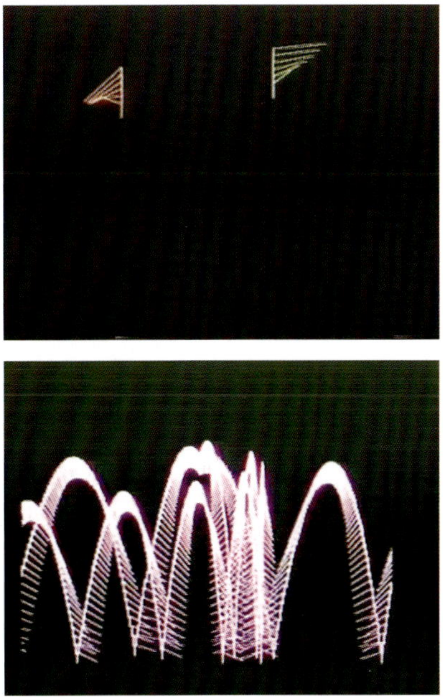

Stills from *Stick Models*, Paul Pangaro, 1976.

DANIEL CARDOSO LLACH: Maybe this is a good moment to think about your film *Stick Models*, which I think stands out in a number of ways. The film shows these sticks dancing gracefully, following a programmatic logic. It conveys a sense of playfulness with and discovery of the possibilities of computer graphics as an expressive medium which seems integral to our visual culture today. At the time other labs and researchers — including some we've been talking with today, were also exploring those possibilities. But at first glance the film seems to be a little different from other ArcMac products. Could you help us understand how this film fits within the group's trajectory?

PAUL PANGARO: At the time, I had been a computer animator, which meant that for eight years or so before joining the Architecture Machine I had been programming vector scopes that drew lines — and lines were all they could draw. I was hired by Nicholas Negroponte because I walked in with these movies that were made with an animation camera in 16 millimeters, and produced mathematics films. But he had just made a raster scan machine. This is a cover of MIT's *Technology Review* that says, "Painting by computer, new realms for animation."[4] This was the beginning of what we're now looking at every day — so-called raster scan machines, or full-color displays with rows and rows of pixels. So, here I am: I have a history working with vector scopes, I come into this amazing world where there is this amazing machine, and I am on research staff to help program it. And yet, you couldn't do animation on it because it was so slow. So, I started building an animation system based on simulation. It's all Newtonian mechanics, gravity and mass, and there are springs and all kinds of other things. Real-world simulation, you might say. Much as the iPhone display springs back when you get to the bottom of a list of things, and so on. I wanted to build an animation system, I wanted to use this magic screen with all its new capabilities. Yet, because the animation was so slow, I just began by building these very simple figures and simulations. The sequence of the movie is the simplest possible program move step-by-step to incrementally more complex programs. And maybe that's the metaphor: you start somewhere, it's very early days for all these technologies, and you incrementally see where it goes. You're finding your way as you're exploring. They would use the word "tinkering" — they still do I think — rather than planning, designing, and *then* making. The making is the starting point, and the rest is in the center of the loop. Besides, of course, I was losing the technology that I had made a name in: vector machines. So, I wanted to do something that was subterfuge; I wanted to be sarcastic about an era that was clearly going to full-color, flat, raster — more pixels than you can imagine. I wanted to do something that also had that quality of teasing and sarcasm. It was all of those things together. By the way, the animation you saw could not be shown frame by frame at thirty frames a second, it had to be written to a video disk, and then played back and recorded in real-time on VHS tape.

4 At this moment, Paul Pangaro showed the audience a copy of the October/November 1977 issue of the *MIT Technology Review*. (pictured below)

DANIEL CARDOSO LLACH: You've talked about that experience as a kind of performance. And I'm wondering if you could tell us what inspired that. Was it the programming logic perhaps? Could you tell us more about the making of the piece — what languages and what hardware was involved?

PAUL PANGARO: I come from theater, more so than from computer science. I was doing both at MIT. Part of the charm of the *Stick Models* system was that you could start it and then see what happened. Only the initial conditions of every single one of those segments is set. All the rest is performance in the sense of a calculation based on initial conditions. It happened to be written in PL/1. It was not very fast, as I said. The programming environment itself was what we would now call a data flow programming language. You would have the names of the routines and the values of variables would flow from top to bottom. The most fun about it was that you could place something up here, and that's where it started. Or, if you moved it and you started it again, it would move from there. In an era of purely text-based programming capabilities this was a visual programming language, and that was also part of the experiment.

DANIEL CARDOSO LLACH: We can now think a little bit about the context of this research, the Architecture Machine Group and MIT. I would love it if you both could tell us a little more about how you encountered MIT and this group. What factors led you there? And how did you two meet?

RACHEL STRICKLAND: My architecture professor at MIT, Maurice Smith from New Zealand, observed that over-determinacy ruled architecture for the most part because most designers want to control too much. Instead, he was training us to prefer what he called "consistent incompletion" — a kind of open-ended approach, like the logic of Spanish hilltowns, or barns he had photographed in Switzerland, or a scatter of leaves, or the arrangement of pebbles on the shoreline. Architecture is not the object that you see and bump into — the building, the mass, the solid. It's rather the space that's defined, and the process — what Maurice termed "open field composition" or "projective construction." I was his protégé, and simultaneously got carried away with the possibilities of motion pictures and computer based-media for exploring and expressing the dynamic and ephemeral dimensions of architectural space. I borrowed a Bolex 16-millimeter camera that was in the equipment closet of the Architecture Machine Group, and with that I made my first movie. I took a friend who was a dancer out into the lawn in front of MIT's Student Center to do somersaults and cartwheels, and then I took the camera to downtown Boston and had the buildings perform somersaults, and cartwheels. I was completely hooked. And Nicholas said I should take a film course. Keep in mind that this was 1976. "Storytelling" had yet to become a buzzword. "Design" was not widely appropriated by software developers until around 1990. And the Computer Science and Engineering students at the Architecture Machine Group didn't think of themselves as designers — they were more eager to affiliate with artists. At that time, there was very little conversation between the architecture faculty at MIT and the Architecture Machine Group. The architecture faculty were skeptical of computer-aided design and anything that smacked of new media. They belonged to a profession which had operated successfully slowly for centuries with pencil and paper, and you know, what could an architect need any of this newfangled stuff for?

——— DANIEL CARDOSO LLACH: What about you, Paul?

PAUL PANGARO: I already gave a little bit of this away. I had been making movies and finally managed to graduate from undergrad at MIT. Because I was spending so much time doing theater, I had to keep dropping and taking classes over and over again. One day I looked in the *Tech Talk* MIT newspaper, and there was a job description that looked like it was written for me, which was shocking. I went in with my 16 millimeter cans of film and showed the movies to Nicholas and whoever else was in the room, and he hired me right away because the

5 See Stewart Brand. *The Media Lab: Inventing The Future At MIT.* First edition. New York City, NY: Viking Press, 1988.

6 At this moment, Paul Pangaro shows his copy of Nicholas Negroponte's book *The Architecture Machine.* See Nicholas Negroponte, *The Architecture Machine: Toward a More Human Environment,* (Cambridge, MA: MIT Press, 1972).

expertise of making animated movies with computers at the time was minimal. I guess I had whatever other requisite skills were necessary. When I started working, I remember clearly I was making $17,500, which today is about $82,000 — not bad for a first full-time job right out of school. That's how I was immersed into it. But my interest was firmly in the humanities. Although I had done a lot of coding by then, I was not so much interested in the tech as in the human and in its analog qualities — that's what I'm trying to do in *Stick Models*: a simulation of how the real world moves, because I think it's interesting, and intrinsically more human. So, that's the basis of that story. For me, the important thing was the idea of the Architecture Machine: interactions with machines in many sensory modes. That's how Steward Brand characterized the Media Lab. You have touch, you have speech, vision, sound, et cetera.[5] But for me, it was Gordon Pask's idea of having a conversation with a machine — not in a trivial but in a sophisticated way. He had a whole way of talking about that, and a formalism for talking about that. When he walked into the lab one day, I was smitten with his ideas, and with his extraordinary character, and his genius. That was the pivot for me to want to continue on a path of seeking the kind of conversation that we have here, and yet somehow mediated by machines or even with machines. And I might disagree a little bit with what Frieder [Nake] was saying earlier. I agree with him regarding AI. But I do think there are structural ways in which you can have a conversation [with the machine] about why you want to do something, how you're going to do it. And that interaction can be very rich. That was the idea of the Architecture Machine. That was this book.[6] It was not about playing with devices for the sake of whatever. It was playing with devices in order to do design through conversation with machines. I was happy when I was there.

DANIEL CARDOSO LLACH: Can tell us a little more about the interplay of your experience and work in theater, and your work with technologists and artists in ArcMac?

PAUL PANGARO: Well, it was improvisation, iteration, trial and error, waiting to fail so that you can learn from the failure, and keep going. Also, it was building up: not saying I'm going to make X and deciding on how you're going to get to X, but seeing where it goes. The *Stick Models* film is itself, as I said earlier, an exploration of how very simple, minimal, Newtonian rules can generate more complex arrangements. It's simple, in a way. As Frieder was saying earlier, "programming is trivial." I would add: it's the ideas that are hard and maybe he would agree with me. To answer another question that you asked, I think Rachel and I — and a few other people — wanted to have a kind of interaction that was not about the bits and the bytes or the digital aspects of it, but the desire to explore our sensibilities in various media; in her case in movies, in my case in interactivity.

DANIEL CARDOSO LLACH: Rachel, you mentioned that you were an architecture student at the time and I wonder if you could tell us a little more about what that meant at the time in the 1970s at MIT, what was the atmosphere politically and intellectually there, and how that related with the technological or artistic work that was taking place in the group?

RACHEL STRICKLAND: I am just going to follow up on Paul. "Beginners and machines follow rules," Gordon [Pask] might have said. "Experts know that rules are made to be broken." So, improvisation, spontaneity... When I came to MIT in 1970, the Architecture Department, and all of MIT, was on strike because of the war in Cambodia. Architecture students were coordinating the graphic design and the protests for the entire Northeast. There was this rupture going on in society that was very much felt by students and faculty and made its way from the environment to the curriculum. At the MIT Architecture School, which was founded in the Beaux-Arts tradition, everybody was trying to break the rules and break the boundaries.

DANIEL CARDOSO LLACH: One way to look at the Architecture Machine Group is as a place where computers started to be imagined as more human, more conversational, and more tactile

— or at least that was the ambition. Also, as a place where some early ideas about democratic participation through computers developed. How did that political climate intersect with those ambitions? You just mentioned that architectural students were revolting against traditional forms of representation. In past conversations, you've mentioned that descriptive geometry, for example, was the target of revolts from architecture students. I wonder if you could talk a little more about how the work of the lab was perceived in that context.

PAUL PANGARO: My comment on that, Rachel, if you don't mind me jumping in, is that I think there was the idea that we were democratizing technology in a very naive way: democratizing it for us, white guys, mostly...

RACHEL STRICKLAND: White guys and six-year-olds.

PAUL PANGARO: That's right! Four-star generals and six-year-olds. Nicholas really was making that comparison quite a lot. The idea, though, was, "Shouldn't it be us, the users, making the machines and developing them, rather than the engineers over there and giving them to users?" In a sense, we got back to that in design much later, when we shifted to designing *with* [users]. We're not quite at designing *by* [users] — but we were transitioning out of designing *for* someone else. We were a little bit on that path, despite the fact that we were not diverse in any sense. Of course, it wasn't until 1984 that the idea of democratization of the personal computer became widespread, thanks to Steve Jobs. This stuff was so expensive and so outrageously new and so weak in its operation — and yet, so promising — that I don't feel like there was a lot of awareness, certainly not in my mind, about the political implications. We're just trying to get the thing to work.

DANIEL CARDOSO LLACH: Before moving to Q&A, I would like to talk a little bit about your career arcs as artists, researchers, technologists, and entrepreneurs. For example, Paul, after ArcMac you went on to pursue a PhD with Gordon Pask on cybernetics and conversation theory, and crafted a career across industry and academia drawing together the subjects of conversation and design. I understand that you did not pursue work on computer graphics any further. Are there traces of *Stick Models* in your later and current work?

PAUL PANGARO: I've been pursuing this path of conversations — designing for conversations. That is for me the ultimate ethical machine interface: to enable others to have conversation, but also construing design as a conversation. My wonderful long-term collaboration with Hugh Dubberly got me into the idea of the design process. So, "design for conversation" has been my career from Pask, whom I met at ArcMac, because that was where some of the stuff was all beginning. Maybe I'm not a visual artist, but an interactive artist of a kind — I don't know that I like that phrase and haven't used it before. But the idea of engendering better interactions, for myself and for others, has perhaps been the arc of my career. Pask gave me a formalism, and I built systems large and small. My PhD thesis with him was essentially an adaptive training system of some complexity built in an AI workstation that was worth $100,000 at the time. Since then, even recently in a 2015 start-up of my own devising, I've wanted conversations with content, and built browser-based interactive systems where you could say to the machine, "Hi, I don't want to go read that article. Can you give me the paragraph from that article that you would tell me if you were the author, and you knew me?" It's a kind of a conversation. You're asking us questions, and we respond. There's a context, there's a set of presumptions about what's been going on before. We know who the people are a little bit here and there. So, we answer a question with that intelligence. Let's get machines to do that. That's what I've always done since meeting Pask — who gave me a way of writing code to do it. And so that's where my arc really began.

DANIEL CARDOSO LLACH: A quick follow up question related to Pask: one of your recent projects was to reconstruct Gordon Pask's 1968 installation *Colloquy Mobiles* and I am hoping you

7 The original *Colloquy of Mobiles* was an interactive installation by Gordon Pask which was part of the landmark exhibition *Cybernetic Serendipity,* curated by Jasia Reichardt at the London ICA in 1968. Paul Pangaro and T. J. McLeish's reconstruction was showcased in the Centre Pompidou in 2020. (pictured above)

can tell us about the significance of that piece.[7] What led you to reconstruct it in such precise detail?

PAUL PANGARO: Hugh Dubberly said to me one day: "Paul, why don't you reproduce it?" The first idea was to do a Kickstarter where for $5,000, you get a little scale-model kit and you can put it together. And then one day he said to me: "Wait a minute, isn't 2018 its fiftieth anniversary? You should make it for that!" And I said: "Okay, who can help me do it? Because I'm not a fabricator." He knew TJ McLeish, and TJ and I got together to build it. *Colloquy* is important because it's all the things that digital technology is not. It's organic. It's conversational in a true sense. It's analog — and sometimes things happen, and sometimes they don't. There's cooperation and competition. It was a metaphor of male and female — essentially of love-making between robots. The female forms were designed by a very prominent ballet production designer for the time, Yolanda Sonnabend, who had this amazing collaboration with Gordon Pask. And it was part of *Cybernetic Serendipity*, Jasia Reichardt's fever dream: not making a distinction between art and engineering, and between artists and engineers. That was the profound origin of her idea. We are not going to say who's who, we're just going to put it all in there, in the same exhibit hall. The idea that you could rebuild Colloquy fifty years later and have it work as we imagined it did — there are some movies, there's some contradiction, there's the way Gordon used to exaggerate what it did, and all that stuff, you had to take all this into account — and having people move through it was an extraordinary experience. Imagining what that was like fifty years ago was one thing, but then saying, "Wait a minute, we don't have much of this today. Why don't we have it today? How can we get more of it today?"

DANIEL CARDOSO LLACH: Wonderful. Rachel, I'd like to ask you the same question. After your work at ArcMac you taught at a number of places, including at MIT; you worked with visual producers for technology companies — I already mentioned Atari, Apple, and Interval Research Corporation — and also have crafted, throughout your career, the vision of "spontaneous cinema." How did *Finger Film*, and more generally your work from that time, shape those next steps — if at all?

RACHEL STRICKLAND: **I might mention that I've never written a film script. My filmmaking was rooted from the beginning in *cinéma vérité* — a method of documentary filmmaking that emerged in the 1960s, which favored spontaneous observation of everyday life over the reenactment of events. From the perspective of the audience, *cinéma vérité* was striving to be a kind of motion picture that would be self-revealing, and permit discovery on the part of viewers. And because I was interested in using cinematic media to communicate about places, I've spent many years pursuing a way of making movies that would be more like architecture than like narrative.**

DANIEL CARDOSO LLACH: I recently learned about this beautiful project of yours, *The Social Lives of Urban Trees*, where you install solar powered cameras on a tree in the Columbia University campus. You register its motion, pace, and temporality.[8] Could you tell us a little more about this part of your artistic practice, and about the kind of observation that you cultivate with your projects? How were the technologies you used in these projects put in the service of that artistic vision linked to spontaneity? How does it relate to your *Finger Film*?

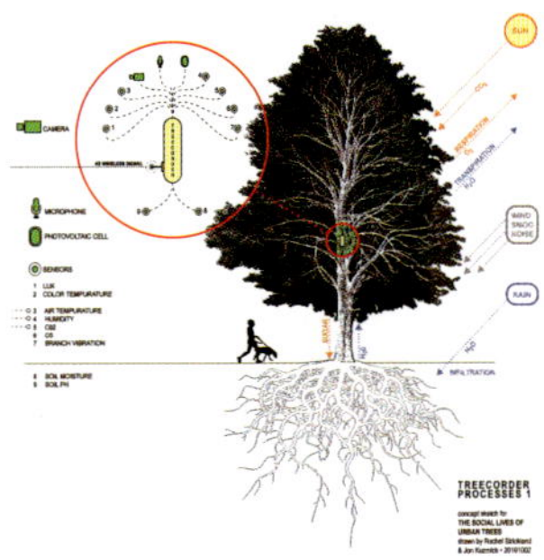

Images (above and on the following page) from *The Social Lives of Urban Trees*, shown by Rachel Strickland at Computational Design: Practices, Histories, Infrastructures

RACHEL STRICKLAND: **It's all connected. A tree growing in the sidewalk is an architectural organism. Through its body language it gives definition to the urban milieu, and to a public space. It also happens to be a living creature and a habitat, and it's very hard for most people to appreciate that the tree is alive because its time frame is so much slower than ours. What are the experiences and coping mechanisms associated with being large, stationary, and long-lived? *The Social Lives of***

8 For an in-depth description of this project, see Rachel Strickland, and Jeremiah Moore. "Embodied Cinema and the Body Language of Trees." *Adjacent*, no. 7 (Spring 2020). https://itp.nyu.edu/adjacent/issue-7/embodied-cinema-and-the-body-language-of-trees/.

Urban Trees is an experiment that merges new environmental sensing technology with traditional observational cinema. I am trying to invent a *cinéma vérité* approach whose revelations emerge from ongoing data capture with these solar-powered cameras, microphones, and sensory instrumentation installed in the tree canopies allowing the trees to trigger recording and, in a way, produce their own self-portraits.

DANIEL CARDOSO LLACH: Wonderful. I think this is a nice moment to open up the conversation.

MOLLY WRIGHT STEENSON: I'll preface this by saying I wrote the wrong book about the Architecture Machine Group, because that book relies on Nicholas Negroponte's master narrative.[9] What other stories might we tell about this period of time? Rachel and Paul, you present some of these stories. Storytelling is a term that comes up. Simulation is vital. Daniel raised a question about democracies, and, Rachel, you were talking about Cambodia. And this so utterly did not figure into Nicholas's lockdown master narrative of what ArcMac was. He was oblivious by his own admission — or statement— to that protest. All of this, as you can tell, makes me a little bit uneasy these days. I'm wondering what stories we need to be telling. What should we be digging into so that we can break up some of these master narratives, and tell something a little more spiky around the edges?

9 See Molly Wright Steenson. *Architectural Intelligence: How Designers and Architects Created the Digital Landscape.* (Cambridge, MA: MIT Press, 2017.)

RACHEL STRICKLAND: I feel like I am finding out in retrospect what it was like to be associated with the MIT School of Architecture and ArcMac in those days. As Marshall McLuhan would say, whoever discovered water was not a fish. We were indeed the fish. The environment that we were swimming around in wasn't necessarily logical, or rational, or perceivable to us at the time. We were making it up.

PAUL PANGARO: I would say two things. First, follow the money. Where did the money come from? The trouble is that today, the designers that we educate are still following the money. They would love nothing less than to work at Facebook, or Google, or YouTube, or Twitter, or name your nefarious AI-purveying scourge — maybe that's a little strong. Secondly, follow the intentions. And I think the intentions were, as you said about Nicholas a minute ago and I would say so for myself also, not political. I love the idea of thinking again about those histories from these other perspectives. My suggestion would be to follow the money, and follow the intentions.

MATTHEW ALLEN: Do you mind if I ask a follow up question? What was the place of countercultures in this? This idea of "following the money" came up in a fifty-year conference on the Harvard mapping laboratory which famously spawned ESRI. They asked whether ESRI is a nefarious company or not. There was a lot of soul-searching among audience members who claimed their mapping software was used for bombing campaigns in Vietnam. Their funding didn't come from the government. A lot of it came initially from the Ford Foundation. The fact that it was cheap, easy to use, and had correspondence courses suggests that they intended to make the software available to everybody. The counterculture could use the same mapping software to produce sort of alternative maps or make an argument against bombing in Vietnam. This was the discussion in the audience. I have to believe some of that was true, right? There was a kind of countercultural discussion going on that drove [the technology] to a certain extent.

PAUL PANGARO: I would say yes, to a certain extent. It was an era where in the SDMS room you might, you know, smoke a joint. And you might walk across Mass Ave, and be encountered with tear gas because of what was going on by way of protests — this was my experience in 1973. Having said that, again, I was a fish, and maybe not that aware. So, I can't really say, from a historical point of view, what those relationships were, or answer a question regarding how it affected us. As Nicholas has said, this didn't really come into our discussion at the time. That's fundamentally true. I would vouch for the idea that we wanted these machines to work for people, where "people" meant what we thought of as people then — more than just the elite at the university, and more than just us. "Personal computer for everyone" — the Apple slogan before its time.

DANIEL CARDOSO LLACH: There's an element here of hiding the military associations of these technologies in order to "humanize" the computer, or civilianize it, and craft a different narrative about it. This was not exclusive to ArcMac. Other groups were part of that, and if you look at their history, which includes some of Negroponte's mentors at MIT, it's a project that starts earlier — in the 1950s.[10]

10 See Daniel Cardoso Llach. *Builders of the Vision: Software and the Imagination of Design.* (London, New York: Routledge, 2015.)

MOLLY WRIGHT STEENSON: I'm thinking about this common element in Paul and Rachel's work. Daniel, it was certainly part of your exhibition and the book project — the movement through film. That's something that we've really been talking about: what it is to move between media. If you each had a thought to give us here today about that movement, what would you tell us about what is gained in that "interspace" between media?

RACHEL STRICKLAND: I'd start with quoting [Welsh film director] Peter Greenaway, who commented that "cinema is far too rich and capable a medium to be merely left to the storytellers." The essence of cinema is actually not storytelling, it's not narrative. This was a method, a mode of filmmaking that was imposed by Hollywood very early in the trajectory of the technology and the development of the form. I think that the real fundamental thing about cinematic language is the collection and juxtaposition of multiple points of view. This is what montage is about. This is about connecting things in time and in multiple threads. Computers, combined with cinematic media, provide this space of interactivity and polylinear construction. These are areas with great potential that continue to get overlooked and neglected because of the emphasis on storytelling.

PAUL PANGARO: My response to that might seem bleak. We like to think that it's the technology that's new. I think ArcMac had more of a concept, or a *parti*: it had this "conversation" idea, but kind of lost its way, if I can be blunt about it. What do you do? What is your organizing principle? Conversation might be part of it, but more important for me is this concept that Humberto Maturana talks about, which asks, "Why are we so fascinated by what's new? Let's wait a minute and say, before we act to make something new, what do we want to conserve? What do we want to keep? What is it in our values, or our humaneness, or in our way of living together that we don't want to let go of? Let's understand that to a degree that we can." What that does, in his words, is it creates a space in which change can take place. That's one way forward as far as I'm concerned.

DANIEL CARDOSO LLACH: There was a wonderful comment from Leslie Mezei in the chat, pointing out that he received some American students in Toronto during those years. Leslie, would you like to speak to that? Because I think it helps understand the larger contexts of these conversations in that.

LESLIE MEZEI: I think I would merely say that we were pretty naive. On the one hand, we felt we were part of the counterculture. This was the 1960s, these were utopian times. We thought we were going to solve all the problems of the world. And yet, here were these young Americans who needed help to get across the border. We offered them jobs, and some of them actually worked in our lab. At the same time, we never thought twice about being part of ARPANET. I had a terminal in my home. This is in the early '70s. We didn't think of the fact that this was set up by the same US Army that was bombing Vietnam. We were of two minds. These were very interesting times, when everything was possible. But then the last discussion, the question of selecting which technologies we would apply, has been lost a long, long time ago. There have been many books about how technology is going to take over — back since the nineteenth century, I believe.

Paul Pangaro shows his copy of Norbert Wiener's book *The Human Use of Human Beings*. See Norbert Wiener. *The Human Use of Human Beings; Cybernetics and Society*. (Boston: Houghton Mifflin, 1950.)

As I said earlier, how are we going to apply AI? We rush into these things without being clear on whether we're doing the right thing.

PAUL PANGARO: I simply want to respond to Leslie's wonderful comment by showing a book from 1949 or '50 where Norbert Wiener wrote about exactly what you're talking about. And I want to point out something which is often lost. Do you see how the first "human" is typeset?

——— LESLIE MEZEI: Yes.

PAUL PANGARO: It's italicized. The *human* use of human beings. That's usually lost.

LESLIE MEZEI: Yes, and in artificial intelligence research there is not enough consideration of what the truly human abilities are, or how we can get to the heart of the matter in nanoseconds. The whole matter of context, and values, and bodies, and so on.

——— VERNELLE NOEL: I just want to say this conversation is so stimulating. Paul's beautiful comment about who was in the lab's radar at that time: white men and six-year-olds. My question is about that naivety, which can be seen as "convenient" — possible for some, but not for others. Today, in addition to this convenient naivety, we have almost forced naivety preventing us from understanding this politics. And we have technological developments that, as you said, Paul, follow the money. What's being invested in and exacerbating these issues of *who* and *what* is visible and what is invisible? My question for all is about the direction that we seem to be going. When it comes to education and practice, where are we now, and what thoughts might you have for us moving forward?

PAUL PANGARO: Leslie Mezei says "humanism" in the chat. Great... We have no excuse now. We can't be naive anymore. Once you look at your own *looking*, and realize that you weren't seeing what you should have seen, you must see what you can see now. Maybe that's a part of the humanistic education Leslie's referring to. It needs to be everywhere. Sometimes we have the discussion in education: "Well, let's see, we've got all these courses, they're great, and over there we'll have a course on ethics." The counter to that is: "No, wait a minute. In all of these courses, we have to be talking about ethics." But it's not clear that all professors want to fit that in because that takes time from other things. When you Google something, Google doesn't tell you why it's telling you what it's telling you. If you went to visit a friend of yours, and you said, "Would you recommend a place to eat?" And they recommended pizza from across the street, and then you asked them why, imagine how you would feel if they said, "Screw you, I'm not going to tell you!" Well, that's Google. It tells you what it recommends, but it doesn't tell you why. We don't accept that from human beings. Why do we accept it from our machines? This was the beginning of a path toward ethical interfaces. Transparent, honest, and responsive in a conversational sense. I can get that far, and I can tell students about that — and then, of course, they go work for Google. My hope is to create patterns, and kits, and design ideas that can be perhaps part of their thinking, and maybe ultimately part of what they carry into the world.

RACHEL STRICKLAND: I wish I had something profound to say, I just got back last night from two weeks practicing silence in the Oregon coast and the Sitka spruce forests and my head is empty.

DANIEL CARDOSO LLACH: I think this is a nice way to end the session in an open-ended note. Thank you so much, Paul and Rachel, for participating in this conversation, and for sharing with us these journeys you have done across technology, industry, and education. They've connected to so many of our symposium sessions — and I am sure we will continue to think about them for a while. Thank you also, Molly, Vernelle, Matthew, Leslie, and everyone who participated in the conversation. It's so great to be among a community of people whose questions are complementary and mutually enriching.

THEODORA VARDOULI: I just wanted to thank Paul and Rachel for these extremely thought-provoking stories. As Molly was saying, these are stories that — even those of us who have studied the group — don't often hear. It's wonderful to start thinking about the intentions, contexts and multiple existences of the Architecture Machine through its members and their work.

PAUL PANGARO: Thanks, everyone. Daniel, you're brilliant at the moderation and the preparation and all of it. Thank you for keeping us together in the way you have, much appreciated.

RACHEL STRICKLAND: Thank you for inviting us. It's been a pleasure.

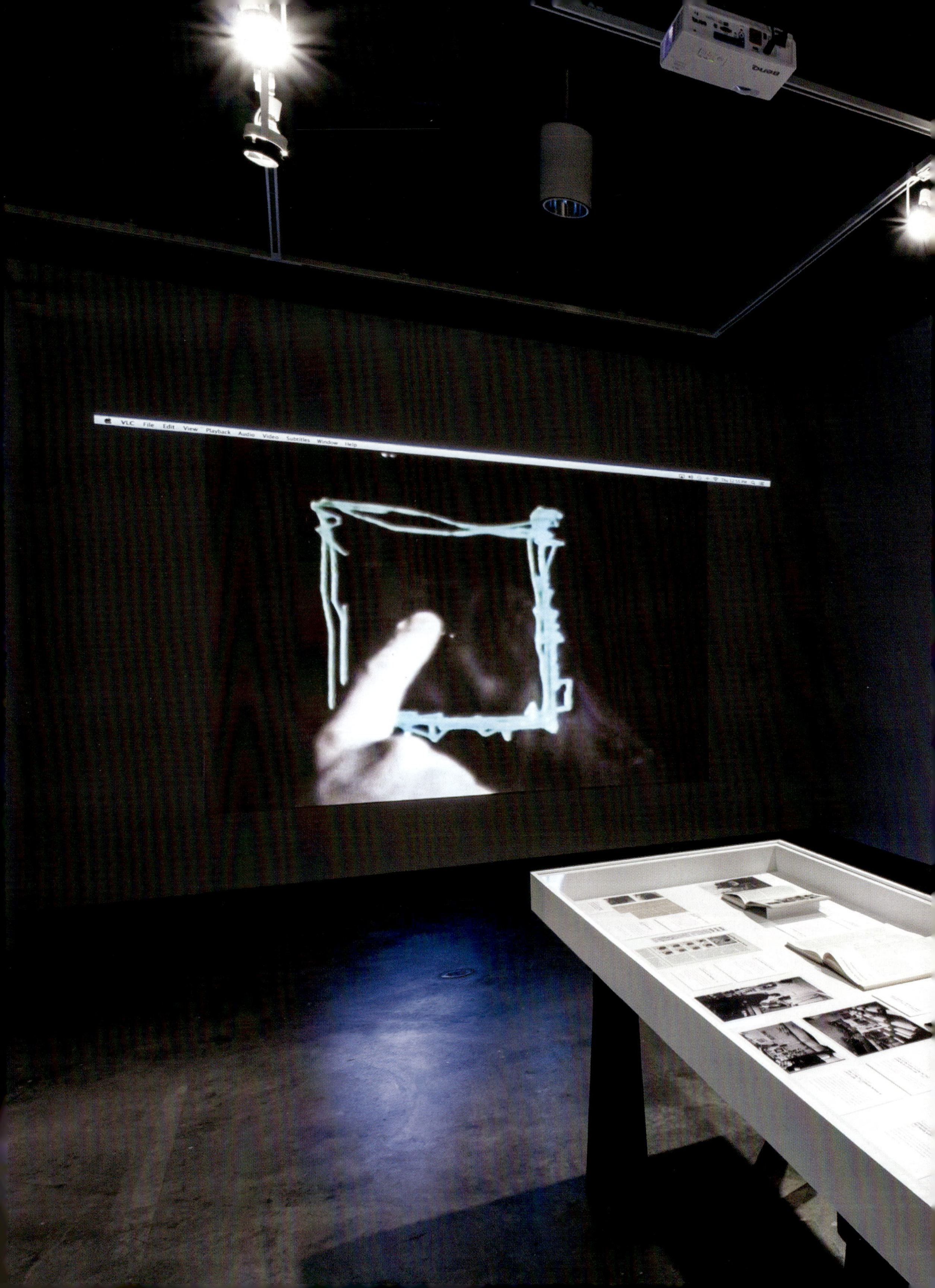
VLC File Edit View Playback Audio Video Subtitles Window Help

Biographies

01 Gabriela Aceves Sepúlveda, *Essay.* Gabriela Aceves Sepúlveda is associate professor and director of cMAS at the School of Interactive Arts and Technology at Simon Fraser University. She is the author of the award-winning book *Women Made Visible: Feminist Art and Media in post-1968 Mexico* (University of Nebraska Press, 2019). Her research and artistic practice centers on the histories of women, art, and technology; feminisms; and networks of artistic exchange.

02 Christopher Alexander, *Archive.* Christopher Alexander (1936–2022) was an architect and mathematician trained at the University of Cambridge and at Harvard University, who taught at the University of California, Berkeley for over forty years. He is renowned for instigating mathematical and rational approaches to design (through the book *Notes on the Synthesis of Form*, Harvard University Press, 1964) but also fiercely critiquing their pitfalls (for example through the article "A City is Not a Tree," *Architectural Forum*, 1965).

03 Matthew Allen, *Essay.* Matthew Allen is an architectural historian, visiting assistant professor at Washington University in St. Louis, and theorist of the design of large socio-technical systems. He is the author of the forthcoming book *Architecture becomes Programming: Modernism and the Computer, 1960–1990*, as well as essays in venues such as *Log*, *e-flux*, *Domus*, and the *Journal of the Society of Architectural Historians.*

04 Ron Baecker, *Archive.* Ron Baecker is emeritus professor of Computer Science and emeritus Bell Chair in Human-Computer Interaction at the University of Toronto, where he also co-founded the Dynamic Graphics Project in 1974. Baecker completed a PhD in Computer Science at MIT in 1969 where, working at Lincoln Lab, he developed a pathbreaking conceptual framework for computer animation and implemented one of the earliest interactive computer animation systems, GENESYS.

05 Kelly Bair, *Works.* Kelly Bair is partner at BairBalliet and associate professor at the University of Illinois at Chicago. Bair has published articles and exhibited work nationally and internationally including the Chicago Architecture Biennial and the Venice Biennale. Bair is co-founder of *Possible Mediums* (Actar, 2018), a published book and collaborative project interested in shaking up the context and format in which architecture is engaged.

06 Kristy Balliet, *Works.* Kristy Balliet is partner at BairBalliet and design faculty at SCI-Arc. BairBalliet is a design venture invested in architecture in the form of both speculative and built projects. Balliet has published articles on topics related to volume and co-edited several books; *Massive Attack: Selected Friends and Enemies* (Birkhauser, 2015), *Visual Catalog: Greg Lynn's Studio* (Springer, 2010), and *Possible Mediums* (Actar, 2018).

07 George Banz, *Archive.* George Banz was a Swiss-born architect who co-founded the Toronto-based architectural firm Brook and Banz and subsequently Urbanprobe Associates. He held teaching appointments at various universities, including the University of Toronto, the Ontario College of Art, and the University of Waterloo. Banz was prolific in publishing articles about the state and prospects of computer-aided design in Canadian architectural magazines such *Canadian Architect* and the *RAIC Journal.*

08 Michael Batty, *Archive.* Michael Batty is a pioneer of computer modeling for cities, currently Bartlett Professor of Planning at University College London and Chair of the Centre for Advanced Spatial Analysis (CASA). His prolific publication record includes sevral books and hundreds of articles. He is the Editor of *Environment and Planning B: City Science and Urban Analytics.*

09 Philip Beesley, *Works.* Philip Beesley is a practicing visual artist, architect, and professor in Architecture at the University of Waterloo and professor of Digital Design and Architecture & Urbanism at the European Graduate School. Beesley's work is widely cited in contemporary art and architecture, focused in the rapidly expanding technology and culture of responsive and interactive systems.

10 Allen Bernholtz, *Archive.* Allen Bernholtz taught as an assistant professor of Architecture at the University of Toronto before joining the Graduate School of Design, Harvard University to teach and research architecture and computer technology. His work at the Harvard Laboratory for Computer Graphics and Spatial Analysis yielded several computer applications for automatic spatial synthesis that he, among other things, employed as a consultant for the Ministry of State for Urban Affairs in Canada.

11 Joanna Berzowska, *Works.* Joanna Berzowska develops methods and materials for innovative electronic textiles and reactive garments. Her art and design work has been exhibited internationally at the V&A in London, the Cooper-Hewitt in New York City, the Australian Museum in Sydney, and Ars Electronica Center in Linz, among others. She consults for industry, most recently for OMsignal to produce the Ralph Lauren PoloTech biometric garments. She is associate professor of Design and Computation Arts at Concordia University.

12 Nathalie Bredella, *Conversations.* Nathalie Bredella is a Visiting Professor at the Berlin University of the Arts (UDK), where she teaches architectural history with a focus on media and gender studies. There she led the research project "Architecture and New Media," identifying and tracing emergent design approaches during the 1990s, and their contemporary effects. Her latest book is *The Architectural Imagination at the Digital Turn* (Routledge, 2022).

13 Andrés Burbano Valdés, *Essay.* Andres Burbano is a media artist and scholar with a PhD in Media Arts and Technology from the University of California Santa Barbara. He has developed an academic career at Universidad de los Andes in Bogota, Colombia, and is currently a professor at the Open University of Catalonia in Barcelona, Spain. In addition, Burbano is the ACM SIGGRAPH 2024 chair.

14 Daragh Byrne, *Works.* Daragh Byrne is an associate teaching professor in the School of Architecture and the Integrated Innovation Institute at Carnegie Mellon University, where he explores the design of experiential media systems through process-oriented methods and human-centered exploration of emerging technologies. His teaching and research explore and reflect this interest with a current focus on the Internet of Things and tangible interaction design.

15 Daniel Cardoso Llach, *Author.* Daniel Cardoso Llach is the author of publications, exhibitions, and artifacts exploring the nexus of design and computation through historical and socio-technical lenses, including the book *Builders of the Vision: Software and the Imagination of Design* (Routledge, 2015). He is associate professor of Architecture at Carnegie Mellon University, United States, where he chairs the Master of Science in Computational Design and co-directs CodeLab.

16 Moa Carlsson, *Essay.* Moa Carlsson is an architect, historian, and lecturer at the Edinburgh School of Architecture and Landscape Architecture (ESALA), UK. Focusing on histories of landscape, planning and computing, her research and teaching explore past and present relationships between lived environments and their abstractions, with a specific focus on Great Britain after 1945. Moa was awarded her PhD (2019) and Master of Science (2013) in Design and Computation from MIT, and her Master of Architecture (2008) from Lund University, Sweden.

17 Mario Carpo, *Essay.* Mario Carpo, Reyner Banham professor of Architectural History and Theory, the Bartlett, University College London; professor of Architectural Theory, Die Angewandte (University of Applied Arts), Vienna. Carpo's research and publications focus on the relationship among architectural theory, cultural history, and the history of media and information technology. He is the author of *Architecture in the Age of Printing* (MIT Press, 2001), *The Second Digital Turn: Design Beyond Intelligence* (MIT Press, 2017), and other books.

18 Joseph Choma, *Works.* Joseph Choma is the director of the School of Architecture at Florida Atlantic University and director of the Design Topology Lab. Recently, he has also taught at the Massachusetts Institute of Technology, The Cooper Union, and Clemson University. He completed graduate studies in design and computation at MIT and completed his PhD in Architecture at the University of Cambridge, UK.

19 Steven A. Coons, *Archive.* Steven A. Coons (1912–1979) was a self-taught mathematician, designer, and a computer graphics and interactive design pioneer from the United States. As an associate professor of Mechanical Engineering at MIT he co-led the US Air Force-sponsored Computer-Aided Design Project, innovatively theorized design as a collaborative human-machine assemblage, and advised students including Ivan Sutherland, Lawrence Roberts, and Nicholas Negroponte. After MIT, he became a Professor at the University of Syracuse.

20 Dana Cupkova, *Works.* Dana Cupkova holds an Associate Professorship at Carnegie Mellon School of Architecture and directs EPIPHYTE Lab, a design and research collaborative that was recognized in 2018 as the "Next Progressives" design practice by *ARCHITECT* Magazine. Engaging environmental ethics, Dana's design work is situated at the intersection of built environment and ecology, focused on materiality, embodied energy, and advanced manufacturing frameworks.

21 Felecia Davis, *Works.* Felecia Davis's work in computational textiles questions how we live and she reimagines how we might use textiles in our daily lives and in architecture. Dr. Davis is an associate professor at the Stuckeman Center for Design Computing in the School of Architecture at Pennsylvania State University and is the director of SOFTLAB@PSU.

22 Guy Desbarats, *Archive.* Guy Desbarats (1925–2003) was an award-winning Canadian architect and academic. An alumnus of McGill University, Desbarats was appointed as director of the architecture school at the Université de Montréal Architecture School in 1964 and subsequently, in 1968, dean of the newly established Université de Montréal Faculté de l'aménagement. For the decade 1975–85, Desbarats also served as an assistant deputy minister for design and then design and construction for Public Works Canada.

23 Jean Dubois, *Works.* Jean Dubois's artistic practice and research cross digital technologies, random structures, intersubjective reflections, textual imagery and site specific approaches. He teaches at the Université du Québec à Montréal's École des arts visuels et médiatiques. He is also a founding member of the research-creation network Hexagram. His work and his communications have been presented at a number of international events and renowned institutions in Canada and abroad.

24 Delia Dumitrescu, *Works.* Delia Dumitrescu is professor in textile design and head of the Smart Textile Design Lab at the Swedish School of Textiles, University of Borås, Sweden. Her research focuses on developing textiles aesthetics and design methods using practice-based research methodology. A central aspect of Delia's research is how smart textile design knowledge can be expanded in architectural design to develop cross-disciplinary material practices.

25 Charles Eastman, *Archive.* Charles E. Eastman (1940–2020) was a United States architect and academic, and one of the earliest and most articulate advocates of computational methods for building design. His research sought to reorganize architectural and building design practices around 3D models enriched with data about materials, structures, and logistics — foreshadowing the now-dominant paradigm of "Building Information Modeling." He taught at the University of Wisconsin, UCLA, Carnegie Mellon, and Georgia Tech.

26 Emek Erdolu, *Essay.* Emek Erdolu is a PhD Candidate in Computational Design at the Computational Design Laboratory (CodeLab) at Carnegie Mellon University's School of Architecture. By using qualitative and computational methods, Emek investigates the connections between the development of on-site robotic systems and how these systems reconfigure building construction work.

27 Gilles Fortin, *Archive.* Gilles Fortin was a faculty member at the School of Architecture, Université Laval, where he conducted research on computer-aided design as it related to problems of space allocation and floor plan layout.

28 Steve Fosburg, *Archive.* Steve Fosburg worked as a researcher in the Harvard Laboratory for Computer Graphics and Spatial Analysis where he developed computer programs for space allocation with Allen Bernholtz. He was principal of the Bernholtz/Fosburg Computer Consultancy in Cambridge, Massachusetts.

29 Jacob Gaboury, *Essay.* Jacob Gaboury is an associate professor of Film & Media at the University of California at Berkeley, specializing in the seventy-year history of digital image technologies and their impact on contemporary visual culture. He is the author of *Image Objects: An Archaeology of Computer Graphics* (MIT Press, 2021).

30 Madeline Gannon, *Works.* Dr. Madeline Gannon is a multidisciplinary designer inventing better ways to communicate with machines. Her creative practice blends techniques in art, design, computation, and robotics to forge new futures for human-robot relations.

31 Benedikt Groß, *Works.* Benedikt Groß is a speculative and computational designer who works antidisciplinarily. His work deals with the fascination of relationships between people, their data, technology and environments. Benedikt is co-author of *Generative Gestaltung* (Schmidt Hermann Verlag, 2009) which is one of the standard books for computational design. He is professor of Strategic and Interaction Design at the HfG Schwäbisch Gmünd.

32 Andrew Heumann, *Works.* Andrew Heumann is an architectural designer, generative artist, software developer, and educator whose work interrogates the technical and creative possibilities of design computation and architectural automation. He is an adjunct assistant professor at Columbia GSAPP, and currently works as an engineer at Hypar building the next generation of software tools for architects.

33 Randle Iredale, *Archive.* Randle Iredale (1929-2000) was a Canadian architect known for his emphasis in design methods and for his participation in many well-known projects including the Sedgewick Undergraduate Library at the University of British Columbia, the Park Site 19 Project in Vancouver, and the Systems Control Center at Simon Fraser University. Iredale co-founded the architectural firm Rhone & Iredale Architects and in the 1980s became a managing partner of The Iredale Partnership.

34 Daniel Iregui, *Works.* Daniel Iregui is a new media artist who creates interactive sculptures, spaces, and architectural interventions using technology and aesthetics as tools. His works combine geometry, typography, light and sound with software, mathematics, and algorithms resulting in systems with infinite possibilities. Iregui founded Iregular in Montreal in 2010. Working at the intersection of art and technology, the studio approaches design using a code-driven and real-time mindset.

35 Timothy E. Johnson, *Archive.* Timothy E. Johnson joined the MIT Computer-Aided Design Project as a Research Assistant in 1961. In 1963, he demonstrated Sketchpad III, an interactive program for drawing in three dimensions he developed at the Lincoln Laboratory's TX-2 computer. He later became a principal investigator at MIT Architecture Department's Computer-Aided Design Group, leading a research team developing interactive computer programs for synthesizing architectural space/activity plans using graphically applied architectural constraints.

36 Sean Keller, *Essay.* Sean Keller is an award-winning architectural historian and critic. He is the author of *Automatic Architecture* (University of Chicago Press, 2017). He is associate professor and associate dean at the IIT College of Architecture; and has previously taught at Harvard, Yale, and the University of Chicago. He is a trustee of the Graham Foundation.

37 Ken Knowlton, *Archive.* Ken Knowlton (1931–2022) was a United States scientist and computer graphics and arts pioneer. With degrees in physics (Cornell, 1955), and a PhD in electrical engineering (MIT, 1962), Knowlton joined the experimental Bell Telephone Laboratories where he collaborated with artists including among others Lillian Schwartz, Leon Harmon, and Laurie Spiegel, and developed graphics programming languages such as BEFLIX, producing ten U.S. patents along with dozens of research papers.

38 Ramesh Krishnamurti, *Archive.* Ramesh Krishnamurti is emeritus professor of Computational Design in the School of Architecture at Carnegie Mellon University. His research is primarily on the formal, semantic, and algorithmic aspects of generative composition, and development of design as computation via intricately coupled parallel explorations of form and description, best known for shape grammar implementation. He received the CAADRIA Sasada Award for 2022.

39 Jürg Lehni, *Works.* Jürg Lehni works collaboratively across disciplines, dealing with the nuances of technology, tools, and the human condition. His works take the form of scenarios for production and expression, such as computer controlled drawing and mark-making machines, as well as software-based works. Lehni has shown work internationally at the MoMA New York, Walker Art Center, Centre Pompidou, among others.

40 Golan Levin, *Works.* Golan Levin is an artist, engineer, researcher, and educator interested in new intersections of machine code, visual culture, and critical making. At Carnegie Mellon, he teaches studio courses in computer science on themes like interactive art and generative form; with Tega Brain, Levin is co-author of *Code as Creative Medium* (MIT Press, 2021), an essential guide to creative coding for software arts educators.

41 Zach Lieberman, *Works.* Zachary Lieberman is an artist, researcher, and educator exploring generative and interactive design. He creates artwork through writing software and is a co-creator of openFrameworks, an open source C++ toolkit for creative coding and helped co-found the School for

Poetic Computation, a school examining the lyrical possibilities of code. He is a professor at MIT Media Lab, where he leads the Future Sketches group.

42 Carl Lostritto, ***Works.*** Carl Lostritto is a professor and the director of the School of Architecture at the University of Tennessee, Knoxville. His research, practice and scholarship focus on design computation with respect to drawing and rendering. His latest book is *Impossible and Hyper-Real Elements of Architecture* (forthcoming with AR+D, 2023). Previously, Lostritto taught at RISD where he led the Master of Architecture program.

43 Rafael Lozano-Hemmer, ***Works.*** Rafael Lozano-Hemmer is a Mexican-Canadian electronic artist who works with ideas from architecture, technological theater, and performance. He holds a Bachelor of Science in physical chemistry from Concordia University in Montreal. Currently, Lozano-Hemmer lives and works in Montreal and Madrid.

44 Lionel March, ***Archive.*** Lionel March (1934–2018) was an architect, mathematician, and artist originally trained at the University of Cambridge. Throughout his impactful career across institutions including the University of Cambridge, The Royal College of Art, the University of Waterloo, The Open University, and UCLA, March explored the nexus of modern mathematics, architectural history and practice, and artistic creativity.

45 Jonah Marrs, ***Works.*** Jonah Marrs is a research engineer at Université Paris Saclay where he teaches design, digital fabrication, introductory computer science and hands-on electronics. Marrs has worked as an intern architect in Berlin, an intern electro-mechanical prototyper at the Brooklyn Navy Yard, a guest digital archival researcher at Montreal's Canadian Center for Architecture, and an Artist in Residence at Autodesk's Pier 9 in San Francisco.

46 Anna-Maria Meister, ***Essay.*** Anna-Maria Meister is an architect, historian, and writer, and professor of architecture theory and science at Technical University of Darmstadt. In her work she focused on interdependencies between the bureaucratization of design and the design of bureaucracies. Meister holds a PhD from Princeton University and architecture degrees from Columbia University and the TU Munich, and is a co-editor of the collaborative international research project "Radical Pedagogies."

47 Leslie Mezei, ***Archive.*** Leslie Mezei started with computers in 1954; in 1965 became associate professor of Computer Science, University of Toronto. In 1967, he established the Computer Graphics Group, which became the highly successful Dynamic Graphics Project. He wrote much on early Computer Art, now archived at the Art Gallery of Toronto, including an unpublished book, and his own computer art. He left in 1978, concentrating on social and spiritual matters.

48 Frieder Nake, ***Archive.*** Frieder Nake is a mathematician, computer scientist, and pioneer of computer art. He is best known internationally for his contributions to the earliest manifestations of computer art, a field of computing that made its first public appearances with three small exhibitions in 1965.

49 Nicholas Negroponte, ***Archive.*** Nicholas Negroponte is best known as chairman emeritus of the MIT Media Lab, and as chairman of the One Laptop Per Child (OLPC) foundation. But his career as an academic, technological entrepreneur, and futurist is rooted in his architectural studies at MIT, where he was mentored by, among others, Steven A. Coons. In 1967, he co-founded with Leon Groissier The Architecture Machine Group, where he formulated experimental computer-aided design systems and human-machine interactions.

50 Vernelle Noel, ***Works.*** Vernelle A. A. Noel, PhD is a design scholar, architect, artist, and director of the Situated Computation + Design Lab. She investigates traditional and digital practices, interdisciplinary creativity, and their intersections with society. She builds new frameworks, methodologies, expressions, and tools to explore social, cultural, and political aspects of craft and computation for new reconfigurations of practice, pedagogy, and publics.

51 Paul Pangaro, ***Archive.*** Paul Pangaro is a performer, coder, entrepreneur, and teacher. Since working with Gordon Pask his goal has been to bring rich agency to human collaboration, with and without technology, by "design for conversation." He is president of the American Society for Cybernetics and teaches at Carnegie Mellon University. Pangaro and TJ McLeish reconstructed Pask's Colloquy of Mobiles, now at ZKM.

52 Nicolas Reeves, ***Archive.*** Nicolas Reeves studied at the University of Montreal and at MIT. In 1995, he founded the NXI GESTATIO laboratory, dedicated to research and creation in arts, architecture, design and computer science. He headed the Artificial Life and Robotic Arts research axis at the Hexagram Institute for Research and Creation in Media Arts and Technologies before becoming scientific director of the same institute (2001–2008).

53 Douglas T. Ross, ***Archive.*** Douglas T. Ross (1929–2007) was a mathematician and software engineering pioneer from the United States. At MIT he headed the Computer Applications Group, worked with the Whirlwind computer, and spearheaded some of the earliest technologies for numerical control at the Servomechanisms Laboratory. Funded by the US Air Force he co-led, with Steven A. Coons, the first computer-aided design research effort between 1959 and 1967.

54 Lillian Schwartz, ***Archive.*** Lillian Schwartz is a United States artist and computer arts pioneer who developed groundbreaking techniques for the use of computers in film and animation. In 1968, she took a position as an artist in residence at Bell Telephone Laboratories — a position without salary or a dedicated space — where she collaborated with Ken Knowlton and other personnel in the development of films innovatively exploring the visual and aesthetic possibilities of randomness and other computer techniques.

55 Kyuha Shim, ***Works.*** Kyuha Shim is a designer, researcher, and educator. He is a Professor of Convergence Design at Korea National University of Arts and a fellow of the Royal Society of Arts. He has served as a National Steering Committee Member for the Design Educators Community (DEC) of the American Institute of Graphic Arts (AIGA). He holds an MFA from the Rhode Island School of Design and conducted doctoral research at the Royal College of Art.

56 Ranjodh Singh Dhaliwal, *Essay.* Ranjodh Singh Dhaliwal is Ruth and Paul Idzik College Chair in Digital Scholarship and assistant professor of English and Film, Television, and Theatre at the University of Notre Dame. His work spans media theory, science, and technology studies, and literary criticism. His current book project, *Rendering: A Political Diagrammatology of Computation*, shows how our cultural, politico-economic, and epistemic formulations crystallize into hardware and software architectures.

57 Akshita Sivakumar, *Essay.* Akshita Sivakumar is a PhD Candidate in Communication and Science Studies at the University of California-San Diego. Her research broadly addresses the politics of representation and knowledge production in the built environment. Her current project examines the use of technical tools to mediate environmental justice and environmental governance and why state and non-state agents inadvertently reproduce toxicity in the process.

58 Ben Snell, *Works.* Ben Snell is an artist who listens to and amplifies the inner dialogues of machines. Using contemporary techniques and traditional motifs, he navigates the space between creation and automation, suggesting a humanist approach to technology. Exploring what it means to be born from code, he creates drawings, images and sculptures embodied with the voice and vitality of machines.

59 Philip Steadman, *Archive.* Philip Steadman is emeritus professor of Urban and Built Form Studies at University College London. He was charter member of the Centre for Land Use and Built Form Studies at the University of Cambridge and director of the Centre for Configurational Studies at the Open University for over twenty years. His landmark work on architectural morphology and the enumeration of building floor plans paved the path for mathematical understandings of architectural possibility.

60 John Stehura, *Archive.* John Stehura is a filmmaker and computer graphics experimentalist from the United States. According to United States media theorist and historian Gene Youngblood's *Expanded Cinema*, Stehura began studying computer programming in UCLA in 1961, started producing images that informed his film Cybernetik 5.3 (included in this book) in 1965, and devoted significant effort to the development of a special programming language for computer graphics and music.

61 George Stiny, *Archive.* George Stiny is professor of Design and Computation at MIT. He is the author of *Pictorial and Formal Aspects of Shape and Shape Grammars* (Springer, 1976); *Algorithmic Aesthetics: Computer Models for Criticism and Design in the Arts* (University of California Press, 1978) with James Gips; *Shape: Talking about Seeing and Doing* (MIT Press, 2006); and *Shapes of Imagination: Calculating in Coleridge's Magical Realm* (MIT Press, 2022).

62 Rachel Strickland, *Archive.* Rachel Strickland works as an independent filmmaker, documentary videographer, interaction designer/inventor, and media artist. Educated in architecture with a concentration in *cinéma vérité* filmmaking, her research and art have focused on cinematic dimensions of the sense of place, the animate and ephemeral dimensions of architectural space, and new paradigms for narrative construction in digital media. spontaneouscinema.com

63 Ivan Sutherland, *Archive.* Ivan Sutherland is a United States computer scientist and computer graphics pioneer who developed one of the earliest interactive graphics programs, *Sketchpad*, as part of his PhD research at MIT in 1963, developed under the advice of Claude Shannon and Marvin Minsky, and with input from Steven A. Coons and Douglas T. Ross. *Sketchpad* is widely regarded as a groundbreaking development in computer graphics, computer-aided design, and human-computer interaction.

64 David Theodore, *Essay.* David Theodore is the Canada Research Chair in Architecture, Health, and Computation and Director at the Peter Guo-hua Fu School of Architecture, McGill University. He has contributed to *gta papers, e-flux, Log, Harvard Design Magazine,* and *arq*, and serves on the editorial board of the Journal of Architectural Education.

65 Jer Thorp, *Works.* Jer Thorp is a Canadian data artist from Vancouver, British Columbia. Before becoming a data artist, he was originally trained as a geneticist. He holds an adjunct faculty position at New York University's Tisch School of the Arts in the Interactive Telecommunications Program. He is the author of *Living in Data* (MCD, 2021).

66 Janet Tomlinson, *Archive.* Janet Tomlinson was a member of the Centre for Land Use and Built Form Studies at the University of Cambridge. In collaboration with fellow LUBFS members including Phil Steadman and Nicholas Bullock, Tomlinson researched urban activities and was the lead author of "A Model of Students' Daily Activity Patterns," which explored ways to computationally model human activity and to use these models in urban planning and design.

67 Olga Touloumi, *Essay.* Olga Touloumi is assistant professor of Architectural History at Bard College. Her forthcoming book *The Global Interior* examines the architectural formulation and media techniques of liberal internationalism in the United Nations. Touloumi has co-edited *Sound Modernities: Architecture, Media, and Design* and *Computer Architectures: Constructing the Common Ground* (1945-1980). She is co-founder of the intersectional group Feminist Art and Architecture Collective.

68 Elizabeth Vander Zaag, *Works.* Elizabeth Vander Zaag is a Vancouver media artist since 1974. She has exhibited in numerous video and new media exhibitions around the world. Her early experiments in digital/video technologies contributed to the dialogue in digital arts. Currently she is working with more traditional media such as textiles and yellow cedar to replicate sound spectrographs.

69 Theodora Vardouli, *Author.* Theodora Vardouli is an assistant professor at the Peter Guo-hua Fu School of Architecture, McGill University where she founded and directs the Computational Design Exploratory (CoDEx) research group. She is author of the forthcoming book *Graph Vision: Digital Architecture's Skeletons* (MIT Press, 2024) and co-editor of *Computer Architectures: Designing the Common Ground* (with Olga Touloumi, Routledge, 2020).

70 Alan Warburton, *Works.* Alan Warburton is a multidisciplinary artist exploring the use of software in contemporary culture. His hybrid practice feeds insight from commercial work in post-production studios into experimental arts practice, where he explores themes including digital labour, gender and representation, often using computer-generated images (CGI).

71 Christos I. Yessios, *Archive.* Christos I. Yessios arrived in the United States from Greece in 1968 to pursue graduate studies in City Planning. After one year at the University of Pittsburgh, he moved to Carnegie Mellon University, where he developed pioneering experiments on computational urban design under the advice of Charles E. Eastman and Allen Newell. In 1990, he co-founded AutoDesSys, which developed FormZ, a 3-D modeling software widely used in architecture and product design.

72 Shaheer Zazai, *Works.* Shaheer Zazai is an Afghan-Canadian artist with a current studio practice both in painting and digital media. Zazai received a BFA from OCAD University in 2011. Zazai's practice focuses on exploring and attempting to investigate the development of cultural identity in the present geopolitical climate and diaspora.

Acknowledgments

Professor Cardoso Llach is indebted to to Margaret Cox and Kara Skylling for expert coordination and development at the Miller Institute for Contemporary Art, and to Louise Pelletier, Nicolas Reeves, and the entire team at the Centre de design de l'UQAM for welcoming and brilliantly supporting the exhibition in Montréal. Special thanks to colleagues Harrison Apple, Wendy Arons, Mary-Lou Arscott, Elizabeth Chodos, Darlene Covington-Davis, Dina El-Zanfaly, Linda Hager, Thomas Hughes, Omar Khan, David Koltas, Steve Lee, Golan Levin, Camila Afanador Llach, Andrew McGee, Diana Martin, Mary-Ellen Poole, Sarah Rafson, Nida Rehman, Nica Ross, Franco Sciannameo, Dan Taeyoung, Charlie White, and Spike Wolff for their various contributions to this project, and to Molly Wright Steenson for steadfast intellectual allyship and support. Students in the graduate program in Computational Design at Carnegie Mellon University's School of Architecture, especially Scott Donaldson, Emek Erdolu, Harshavardan Kedia, Jinmo Rhee, and Erik Ulberg made essential technical contributions to the development of the software reconstructions on display; Cecilia Ferrando, Atefeh Mahdavi, Liale Nijem, and Chitika Vasudeva supported curatorial and logistical aspects of the Miller ICA exhibition and symposium. *eikones*, the Center for the Theory and History of the Image at the University of Basel, Switzerland, provided an intellectual atmosphere that helped foster the project's early stages; special thanks to Sabine Ammon, Nathalie Bredella, Remei Capdevila-Werning, and Inge Hinterwaldner. The University of Cambridge Department of Architecture hosted a scholarly visit that facilitated access to key archival and human sources; special thanks to Francois Penz, Alan Blackwell, and Robin Forrest. Finally, the expertise and generosity of archivists who helped navigate the historical collections, including Katherine Barbera, Emily Davis, Jana Dambroglio, Sydney Gulbronson, Norah Murphy, and Massimo Petrozzi, are warmly and gratefully acknowledged.

Professor Vardouli gratefully acknowledges Martin Bressani, David Theodore, and Ipek Türeli for their unfaltering encouragement, intellectual stimulation, and facilitating vital material support. Warm thanks go to the student research assistants, Arlene (Jiaqi) Chen, George-Étienne Adam, Eliza Pertigkiozoglou, and Maxime Leblanc, who contributed to the *Vers un imaginaire numérique* exhibition through archival research, reconstructions of images and software, and historic research network databases. Bernard Geogeghan, Jacob Gaboury, and Till Heilman, were essential interlocutors in the rich and expansive topic of histories of digital visual culture in the context of an eponymous panel in the 2021 Meeting of the Special Interest Group on Computing, Information and Society (SIGCIS 2021). A hearty thank you goes to Louise Pelletier, director of the Centre de Design de l'UQAM, for the trust, work, and resources she mobilized in support of the exhibition, as well as to former Centre de Design directors Börkur Bergmann and Patrick Evans for sowing the seeds of the collaboration with the UQAM. Nicolas Reeves is warmly acknowledged for his expertise, feedback, and collegiality. Gratitude finally extends to Marnee Gamble, David Greene, Nick Richbell, and Radoslav Zuk for providing essential access to rare archives and collections that were key to the historical materials from Canada featured at the Centre de design exhibition.

Exhibition credits

	2017	*2021*
Curation	Daniel Cardoso Llach	Daniel Cardoso Llach and Theodora Vardouli
At	Miller Institute for Contemporary Art, at Carnegie Mellon University, Pittsburgh, United States	Centre de design de l'Université du Québec à Montréal (UQÀM), Canada
	Elizabeth Chodos, director Margaret Cox, assistant director	Louise Pelletier, director
Dates open	September 23 – November 12, 2017	September 15 – November 7, 2021
Coordination and development	Margaret Cox, Kara Skylling	Victor Bernaudon Cointe, Éric Daoust, Vincent Thibault-Mezina
Graphic design	Margaret Cox	Operative Space
Graphic integration		Magalie Rouleau
Administration	Linda Hager, David Koltas, Thomas Hughes	Michèle Hébert
Research assistants	Cecilia Ferrando, Scott Donaldson, Atefeh Mahdavi, Liale Nijem, Chitika Vasudeva	CMU CodeLab Scott Donaldson, Emek Erdolu, Harshvardhan Kedia, Jinmo Rhee, Erik Ulberg, Jamaal Mali Tribune, Maria Vlachostergiou CodEx McGill George-Étienne Adam, Jiaqi (Arlene) Chen, Rachel Law, Maxime Leblanc, Eliza Pertigkiozoglou
Advisory	Mary-Lou Arscott, Golan Levin, Nida Rehman	Gabriela Aceves-Sepúlveda, Nicolas Reeves
Sponsors	Graham Foundation for Advanced Studies in the Fine Arts; Miller Institute of Contemporary Art; Frank-Ratchye STUDIO for Creative Inquiry, Carnegie Mellon University; School of Architecture, Carnegie Mellon University; College of Fine Arts, Carnegie Mellon University	Social Sciences and Humanities Research Council of Canada; Centre de design de l'UQAM; Peter Guo-hua Fu School of Architecture, McGill University; Research Group on Democracy, Space, and Technology at the Yan P. Lin Centre, McGill University; Frank-Ratchye STUDIO for Creative Inquiry, Carnegie Mellon University; School of Architecture, Carnegie Mellon University; College of Fine Arts, Carnegie Mellon University

Photo Credits

Michel Brunelle
pages 14, 104, 290, 292

Hugh 'Smokey' Dyar
pages 86, 98, 236

Maxime Leblanc
page 61, 130, 131, 136, 161 (top), 204, 296

Tom Little
pages 8, 57 (top right), 62, 247, 281

Mélanie Olmstead
pages 32, 54, 66, 68, 248, 253 (top right), 258, 282, 293, 298, 380

Chitika Vasudeva
pages 188, 317

Loans

Kelly Bair and Kristy Balliet, Ron Baecker, Philip Beesley, Joanna Berzowska, Carnegie Mellon University Archives, CMU Computational Design Laboratory, Computer History Museum, Joseph Choma, Dana Cupkova, Felecia Davis, Jean Dubois, Delia Dumitrescu, Charles E. Eastman, Robin Forrest, Madeline Gannon, Benedikt Groß, Montreal Gazette - a division of Postmedia Network Inc., Hagley Museum and Library, Andrew Heumann, Ingenium, Daniel Iregui, Timothy E. Johnson, Ramesh Krishnamurti, Jürg Lehni, Golan Levin, Zach Lieberman, Carl Lostritto, Rafael Lozano-Hemmer, Jonah Marrs, Leslie Mezei, MIT Museum, MIT Libraries, McGill Library Rare Books and Special Collections, Frieder Nake, Nicholas Negroponte, Vernelle Noel, Paul Pangaro, Nicolas Reeves, Ben Snell, George Stiny, Rachel Strickland, Jer Thorp, Elizabeth Vander Zaag, Alan Warburton, University of Waterloo Special Collections and Archives, University of Toronto Archives, Christos Yessios, Shaheer Zazai, Radoslav Zuk.